D1364288

Protecting All Animals:

A Fifty-Year History of The Humane Society of the United States

By **Bernard Unti**

Humane Society

An affiliate of

THE HUMANE SOCIETY OF THE UNITED STATES.

D1509709

Bernard Unti received his doctorate in history
from American University in 2002.

First edition
ISBN 0-9658942-8-2

Library of Congress Cataloging-in-Publication Data

Unti, Bernard Oreste.
  Protecting all animals: a fifty-year history of the Humane Society
of the United States / by Bernard Unti. -- 1st ed.
       p. cm.
Includes bibliographical references and index.
  ISBN 0-9748400-0-9 (hbk.) — ISBN 0-9658942-8-2 (pbk.)
1. Humane Society of the United States–History. I. Title.
  HV4763.H8524 U58 2004
  179' .3'06073--dc22

                                        2003021699
Printed in the United States of America

Humane Society Press
An affiliate of The Humane Society of the United States
2100 L Street, NW
Washington, DC 20037

CONTENTS

Acknowledgments

During the course of the work on this history, it has often occurred to me that one day, in a better world, the people and the events described in these pages (some ten of whom have died since I began my research) will be more commonly known. The individuals I acknowledge here, and many others who work with or for The HSUS, are doing their part to hasten that day. Because of them, writing a history of The HSUS has been a satisfying and encouraging experience, and I thank them.

Paul G. Irwin, president of The HSUS, evinced strong support for this project, recognizing that an organization's heritage is a precious asset, worthy of recording and sharing with the broader public. Dr. Andrew Rowan, chief of staff, first suggested the idea of a full-length work, and we quickly concurred that there were important questions and issues to explore. Our subsequent conversations on the historical contributions of The HSUS, and more broadly on what history has to say to the present, have been rewarding. Deborah Salem, director and editor in chief of Humane Society Press, kept this work on track, making timely professional interventions, providing crucial observations, sharing her own historical perceptions, and generally keeping faith with its frequently beleaguered author. Patrick Parkes, retired executive vice president and himself a keen and able historian of The HSUS's work, generously shared his recollections, answered dozens of questions, and took me beyond the trail of documents in search of deeper insights about the organization's activities. Paula Jaworski of The HSUS's publications section put her full staff to work in the identification and selection of photographs that bring to life the richness and complexity of the organization's history in a way that no text alone could ever do.

The assistance and cooperation of numerous staff members, past and present, and the children of Fred Myers, have further enriched this work. I am grateful to those who assisted me with practical matters, answered questions, and shared their ideas and memories concerning The HSUS. They include Eve Anderson, Michael Appleby, Martha Armstrong, Marianne Myers Atkinson, Jonathan Balcombe, Arnold Baer, Carol Baker, Kathy Bauch, Kay Benedict, Laura Bevan, Michael Blankenship, Jennifer Boyer, Tim Carman, Ann Church, Vince Connelly, Frantz Dantzler, Bill DeRosa, Barbara DeMambro, Julie Falconer, Richard Farinato, Larry Field, Tammi Myers Field, Debra Firmani, Laura Folden, Patricia Forkan, Janet Frake, Pat Gatons, Sharon Geiger, John Grandy, Emmett Graves, Susan Hagood, Geoff Handy, Ben Hayes, Charles F. Herrmann, III, Dale Hylton, Kim Intino, Ulric Johnson, Lesley King, John Kullberg, Randy Lockwood, Dina McDaniel, Elizabeth McNulty, Ed Myers, Donna Mochi, Belton Mouras, Tanya Mulford, Wayne Pacelle, Dave Pauli, Donna Pease, Kate Pullen, Linda Reynolds-Hinds, Naomi Rose, Melissa Seide Rubin, Eric Sakach, Kathy Savesky, Stephanie Shain, Chad Sisneros, Brian Sodergren, Janet Snyder, John Snyder, Martin Stephens, Rick Swain, Neil Trent, Ellen Truong, Tom Waite, Susan Washington, and Dorothy Weller.

1955

1957

1971

1978

1992

THE HUMANE SOCIETY
OF THE UNITED STATES.

1999

FOREWORD

he HSUS formed fifty years ago with a straightforward but challenging agenda: to eliminate and prevent the abuse and suffering of animals through advocacy, education, legislation, research, investigation, field service, and legal initiative. Since 1954 we have continued to operate on the basis of three premises our founder Fred Myers articulated, "that kindness can be effectively taught or encouraged, that cruelty can be substantially prevented, [and] that suffering can be significantly decreased." For half a century, we have advanced these convictions in every arena where animals suffer. At the same time, we have stood firm behind the principle that the promotion of concern for nonhuman animals carries with it numerous social benefits for humankind and for our entire planet.[1]

We of The HSUS have not spent a lot of time during these past fifty years crowing about our accomplishments. But we are proud of them, and we thought our golden anniversary year was the right occasion for a comprehensive account of the work that has made The HSUS the most successful organization of its kind. There are literally hundreds of animal cruelty issues at loose in the world, and there are few against which The HSUS has failed to mount campaigns of opposition and reform.

In the years since its founding, The HSUS has grown into the world's largest animal protection organization, currently drawing on the support of over eight million supporters and constituents. The HSUS has expanded to include ten regional offices, four affiliates, an international arm, and almost 300 staff members—including veterinarians, wildlife biologists, lawyers, animal behaviorists, and other professionals. We do not just piously deplore cruelty, we also fight hard against it from the conviction that the vision, energy, and effort of the humane movement are badly needed in this world. At the same time, we have striven to honor standards of honesty, integrity, rationality, and concern for human dignity in our work. The promotion of compassionate regard for nonhuman animals demands no less.

It is especially satisfying to me that this study does justice to the many good and decent individuals who have made The HSUS's history such a proud one. This book is testament to the fact that many hands have been set to the oars during fifty years of determined effort, and that HSUS staff members have crisscrossed this globe—from Alaska to Zimbabwe—to extend the principles and practices of humane treatment of animals.

I am moved to recall, too, that through all of these years, and in so many places, and on so many occasions, HSUS supporters have been there, because their energy, their moral influence, and their financial contributions have made these accomplishments possible. The HSUS is not a solo act. Organized animal protection has not in the past been able to rely on the support of great foundations or corporate largesse, and, to a very great degree, the work we have accomplished has depended on the might of individuals. The active involvement and support of our constituents count, and we are the better for it.

To the several thousand people who have worked as employees of The HSUS during these fifty years and to the millions of supporters who have made that work possible, we say, "Thank you"—not simply for the privilege of serving you, but also for the extraordinary opportunity you have extended to us—the chance to make this world a better one for all of its inhabitants.

Paul G. Irwin
President and CEO
The Humane Society of the United States

CHAPTER 1

Every Field of Humane Work—EVERYWHERE

n simple terms the founding of The Humane Society of the United States (HSUS) in 1954 was the incorporation of a new group by a breakaway faction dissatisfied with the activity, direction, and political weakness of the American Humane Association (AHA), the then-dominant organization in the field of animal protection. Over the years, however, the decision to create a new kind of animal protection organization, established in the nation's capital, determined to recruit a national membership base, and focused on confronting national cruelties beyond the scope of local societies and state federations, proved to be far more significant. Within several decades of its modest beginnings, The HSUS would eclipse the organization from which it sprang, and many others as well. Five decades later The HSUS was the largest and most influential animal protection organization in the world.

Animal Protection before 1954

Organized animal protection in America dates from the 1860s, when like-minded citizens launched societies for the prevention of cruelty to animals (SPCAs) in one city after another and pursued their goals of kind treatment on a range of fronts. After a period of considerable vitality, however, the movement lost ground after World War I and its concerns dropped from public view. Several generations of leaders failed to match the vision, energy, or executive abilities of the humane movement's founding figures. Moreover, the period between World War I and World War II proved to be an infertile social context for the consideration of animal issues, and the American humane movement became quiescent and ineffectual. This decline in movement strength coincided with an expansion of animal use in such major segments of the twentieth-century economy as agriculture, biomedical research, and product testing. The magnitude of institutional use of animals overwhelmed a movement whose greatest success had been in stigmatizing and policing individual acts of cruelty. Humane advocates were unable to effect reforms of practices that were increasingly hidden from view and often exempted from extant anticruelty statutes and regulations. By 1950 animal protection, once a vibrant reform, stood mired in a phase of insularity, lack of vision, and irrelevance.

The decision to take on the challenge of municipal animal control did not help matters. During the first decades of the century, the anticruelty societies shifted their energy and resources away from the promotion of a coherent humane ideology and a broad-based approach to the prevention of cruelty. Instead, they focused their attention on the management of animal overpopulation and educational activities tied to pet keeping. The assumption of urban animal control duties by humane societies throughout the country made it difficult to sustain broader educational campaigns about the cruel treatment of animals in other contexts. This was largely thankless work, undersubsidized by municipal governments, which completely engrossed the staff and financial resources of local SPCAs. AHA, the movement's umbrella association, catered mainly to the interests of its constituent societies, all of which were absorbed with urban animal control issues.

As it turned out, the same activists who parted ways with AHA over its pound release policy (see page 64) found other reasons to chart a new course for the work of animal protection. They were determined to focus on areas of animal use that their predecessors had either failed to address or had neglected for some time. Although they were in sympathy with the problems and challenges that local SPCAs faced and wanted to enhance the quality of management, services, and impact of community-level animal care and control organizations, they also set their sights on cruelties they felt could only be addressed from a national perspective. They directed much of their energy toward the objectives of federal legislation, regulatory reform, and the amelioration of cruel practices through humane innovation and policy evolution. Among other accomplishments they revived and revitalized early twentieth-century campaigns devoted to humane slaughter, the regulation of laboratory animal use, and the abolition of the steel-jawed leghold trap. They developed in-depth critiques and proposals for reform of animals' treatment and handling in these contexts. Cruelty investigations at both the national and local levels played an important role in advancing this work and helped to place humane issues on the public agenda.

The founder of the American humane movement, Henry Bergh, had hoped to follow the model of the Royal Society for the Prevention of Cruelty to Animals (RSPCA), establishing branches all around the United States that would work in support of common goals. However, he could not secure a national charter, and, while his own American Society for the Prevention of Cruelty to Animals (ASPCA) provided inspiration for the formation of numerous societies elsewhere, it had very little actual reach outside of New York City.

AHA, formed in 1877 but not fully incorporated and properly staffed until 1904, could do no more than coordinate a loose federation of autonomous societies following a variety of purposes and policies, often at odds with one another, and ranging from excellent to horrible in their standards of work. The HSUS's first president, Robert Chenoweth, compared the state of the movement in the mid-twentieth century to that of the original thirteen states operating under the Articles of Confederation.[1]

The most limiting effect of this arrangement was the movement's pronounced inability to develop truly national campaigns against certain obvious cruelties. By 1950 many felt that the broad-gauge approach to the work that AHA and its constituent societies had pursued at the turn of the century had narrowed. Very little was being done about the horrific cruelties of the slaughterhouse, the trapping of animals for fur, the use of animals in laboratories, and the mistreatment of animals in zoos, rodeos, and other entertainment venues. HSUS organizers were convinced that the American humane movement had to develop the capacity to attack national and regional cruelties, which often were beyond the scope of any local humane society or even any state federation of organizations.[2]

The Formation of The HSUS

A specific grievance rooted in principle and policy—the surrender of animals from municipally run animal shelters and pounds, known as pound seizure—precipitated the transformation and revitalization of organized animal protection in the early 1950s. By that time both AHA and the wealthier local and regional humane societies had largely narrowed their focus to companion animal issues. The general opinion among those who formed The HSUS was that key management decisions within AHA had come under the control of the salaried staff executives of larger member societies, who were more interested in perpetuating their own positions than in expanding the organization's work and unwilling to risk action that might make them appear to be a controversial force in their own communities.[3]

The postwar boom in expenditures on biomedical research greatly increased demand for animals, and in the mid-1940s, scientific institutions began to devote great energy to the passage of animal procurement laws. The National Society for Medical Research (NSMR) led efforts to gain access to animals from municipally operated pounds and shelters, and these laws generally passed without much difficulty. However, they were a great provocation to local humane society officials in many communities, who felt strongly that forcing such institu-

The American Humane Association staff, pictured before AHA's headquarters was moved from Albany, New York, to Denver. Fred Myers is seated at the far left; Mel Morse is standing, third from left; Larry Andrews is standing, second from right.

tions to provide research animals to laboratories compromised their mission and integrity.

In 1954 a determined attempt by reform-minded members to elect a slate of candidates to the AHA board appeared to set the stage for its revitalization. The crucial moment came at the organization's annual convention in Atlanta. A majority of the members present endorsed the goals of the insurgent candidates, and elected all three—J.M. Perry, Raymond Naramore, and Roland Smith—to the board. However, the reform candidates could not alter the policies of AHA in the face of the majority's resistance. Furthermore, this campaign drew determined opposition from the old board and resulted in the voluntary or forced resignation of four staff members.[4]

The central figure of the breakaway faction was Fred Myers (1904–1963), hired for his journalism skills in 1952 by AHA president Robert Sellar. In the years before he joined AHA, Myers had worked as a reporter, editor of the publication of a newspaper employees' union, and executive director of the American Society for Russian Relief (a World War II charity) and in public relations and administration for the New York Central Railroad and the New School for Social Research. In 1953, when AHA relocated from Albany, New York, to Denver, Myers and his family made the move, too. In the wake of Sellar's death, as the pound seizure issue heated up, Myers, editor of AHA's *National Humane Review*, attacked the NSMR with so much vigor that AHA management began to censor his writing. After the dispute over Myers's journalism and the clash at the 1954 annual meeting, he and three other staff members—Helen Jones, Larry Andrews, and Marcia Glaser—left the organization.[5]

The four dissidents decided to form their own organization and to compete directly with AHA for national leadership. Together they founded the National Humane Society, incorporated on November 22, 1954, in Washington, D.C. They borrowed money against their life insurance policies to get the organization started and for some months took no salaries. By 1956 The HSUS's guiding policy was in place, encapsulated in a statement its membership approved virtually unanimously by referendum: "The Humane Society of the United States opposes and seeks to prevent all use or exploitation of animals that causes pain, suffering, or fear." While determined to be aggressive in the struggle against cruelty, those who formed The HSUS were equally resolute in their conviction that the organization must pursue a practical, effective course that accepted the path of incremental improvements. They committed themselves to "action that will actually help animals and achieve practical humane education." [6]

While AHA had moved to Denver as part of an effort to extend humane influence to the west, The HSUS's founders took another tack altogether. They deliberately set up their new organization in Washington, D.C. In the nation's capital, they believed, they could better serve a national movement and develop sustained efforts to spur action by the federal government.

In its early years, The HSUS benefited from the support and guidance of dedicated board directors, a few of whom had bolted from AHA along with Myers, Jones, Glaser, and Andrews. Some of these directors, like Robert Chenoweth (1954–1976), Oliver Evans (1954–1975), and D. Collis Wager (1955–1974), served for close to two decades each. Other directors, like Edith Goode, Delos Culver, and Frederick "Doc" Thomsen, pursued their reform interests independently or through organizations separate from The HSUS, moving in and out of direct service over the years.

The HSUS's formation was strongly influenced by the founders' moral indignation at the stockpiling of funds by a handful of major humane societies, as well as by AHA. Although these groups accumulated substantial endowments, Myers and his colleagues judged, they had not been willing to spend their money to effect change in important arenas of animal use. Article IX of The HSUS's bylaws specified that "all available funds of the Society shall be used for the immediate relief of suffering and the vigorous prosecution of humane education." While providing liberal exceptions for the establishment and maintenance of prudent reserves or for meeting the terms of law or a donor's mandate, Article IX embodied the conviction of The HSUS's founding generation that action, not accumulation, should characterize the organization's program and agenda. The *HSUS News* regularly carried editorials critical of local and regional humane societies that had accrued large sums and failed to search for ways to spend money on animal protection work.[7]

Those who founded The HSUS also resolved to build an organization of individual supporters rather than one that functioned as a confederation of organizations. AHA had relied primarily on local humane societies for its support, benefiting from institutional memberships and some individual recruitment done through those organizations. The HSUS appealed directly to individuals for its support, not through local organizations. Most agreed that this was a crucial distinction and an important factor in its success.[8]

The rift between The HSUS and AHA created considerable ill will and even sparked rumors linking Fred Myers to the Communist Party. In March 1956, in the heat of the battle over humane slaughter legislation, Myers appeared before the Senate Internal Security Committee to refute the accusation that he had been a member of the Communist Party while active in a newspaper writers' union during the 1930s. The charge followed Myers, as antagonists both within and outside the movement resurrected it to tarnish both his reputation and that of The HSUS.[9]

In May 1956 AHA filed suit in federal court in the District of Columbia, asking that the National Humane Society be compelled to change its name on the grounds it was too similar to that of the American Humane Association and its publication, the *National Humane Review*. The suit alleged that potential donors might not be able to distinguish between the two organizations and that they might give money intended for the use of AHA to the NHS instead. In December 1956 AHA secured a temporary injunction barring the use of the name, "National Humane Society," despite the NHS's claim that the titles only had one word—"humane"—in common and that the word appeared in the corporate names of numerous organizations. Rather than litigate the issue in a costly and protracted battle, however, the NHS renamed itself The Humane Society of the United States.[10]

Backbiting between AHA and The HSUS continued for many years afterward, as the two organizations worked at cross-purposes in a number of instances. The HSUS was especially critical of the AHA positions on pound seizure and laboratory animal welfare and of its supervision of rodeos, which The HSUS thought highly inappropriate. It also questioned the ability of AHA's Hollywood watchdog office to prevent the mistreatment of animals used on television and film sets. In time, the two organizations would also square off over the humaneness of the Euthanaire decompression chamber for the destruction of unwanted animals (see chapter 3).[11]

Within five years of leading the break from AHA, two of The HSUS's founders, Larry Andrews and Helen Jones, went their own way. As The HSUS's field director, Andrews had maintained a demanding schedule of travel, throughout the United States, covering 350,000 miles in two years. Working on the road, he helped local organizations to identify and address their needs, sought to support the formation of new societies, and oversaw early efforts

The HSUS booth at the Episcopal Quadrennial convention held in Detroit in 1961.

to launch a branch system for The HSUS. In 1956 Andrews left to become the executive secretary of the Arizona Humane Society, although he sat on the HSUS board until April 1958. Some years later he founded the National Humanitarian League, later renamed United Humanitarians, which promoted the spaying and neutering of animals as its principal goal.[12]

Before joining AHA, Jones had worked as a hotel publicity director in New York City, while maintaining a significant commitment to the animal shelter in her hometown in Pennsylvania. She had been working at AHA less than a year when the break occurred. Dividing her time between Washington and a New York office, Jones served as The HSUS's director of educational activities, working on the surplus animal problem and humane slaughter legislation.[13]

Jones and Fred Myers frequently talked about the deficit of religious support for the humane movement. In the late 1950s, The HSUS staffed a booth at a ten-day convention of the Episcopal Church involving thousands of its officials, and Myers wrote to the Pope and other religious leaders to ask about their positions on the treatment of animals. One of those who replied, Joseph Fielding Smith, president of the Council of Twelve of the Church of Jesus Christ of the Latter Day Saints, commended The HSUS's efforts to "bring about universal love not only between man and his fellow-creatures but between man and all other living creatures."[14]

In 1959, wanting to do something more toward establishing greater rapport with the religious community, Jones founded the National Catholic Society for Animal Welfare (NCSAW), with The HSUS's blessing and a start-up grant of $5,000. At first she continued in her position at The HSUS, working on NCSAW business in the evenings and on weekends. After some years, however, Jones shifted her efforts from promoting concern for animals within the Roman Catholic Church to pursue a full range of issues under a new organizational name, the Society for Animal Rights.[15]

Although Andrews and Jones had labored long and hard for The HSUS in its first years, their departures had little effect. As the principal leader of the 1954 break, Fred Myers was a more influential figure from the start, and it was his vision and spirit that shaped the organization's early agenda. Myers was a charismatic man who inspired great confidence, energy, and determination in co-workers, board members, crucial donors, and the individuals and organizations that comprised the broader humane movement. Whatever significance the fledgling organization enjoyed by 1960 was largely a credit to his leadership. He personified the balance of idealism and pragmatism that would become characteristic of The HSUS in the years to come.

It was Fred Myers's vision and spirit that shaped The HSUS's early agenda.

Program and Policy in the Early Years

The principal activities of The HSUS during the 1950s consisted of aggressive efforts against breeding of surplus animals, the pursuit of national legislation for humane slaughter, focused investigations of specific cruelties, support for local societies and individuals trying to form them, and the conscription of local organizations into broader national campaigns to benefit animals. While determined to raise the quality and extent of humane work at the local level, The HSUS also sought to instill a broader vision of the importance of nationally organized initiatives and to lead local organizations in setting their sights on the achievement of larger strategic objectives.

Because one of the urgent points of tension in the AHA schism concerned the pre-slaughter handling and slaughter of animals used for food, the first national campaign that emerged in the post-1954 era focused on that question. Fred Myers, Edith Goode, and others affiliated with The HSUS were leading figures in the campaign for a national Humane Slaughter Act. During 1955 and 1956, The HSUS diverted every available dollar from its budget into the drive for slaughterhouse reform and generated intense publicity concerning the issue. Myers and Goode lined up significant sources of public support for the legislation, and Myers testified on behalf of the Humane Slaughter Act in 1958, the year it finally passed.[16]

Myers took great encouragement from the fact that, between 1954 and 1958, the movement had really united, for the first time ever, to achieve enactment of a federal humane slaughter law that would spare approximately 100 million animals a year from pain and suffering. The law's passage was also a vindication of the proposition that had driven the formation of The HSUS, the idea "that hundreds of local societies could lift their eyes from local problems to a great national cruelty."[17]

Even before the closing of the Humane Slaughter Act campaign, The HSUS had begun to turn its attention to the suffering of animals in research, testing, and education. This, too, had been an arena of conspicuous failure for the humane movement in the twentieth century. The HSUS set the acquisition of information about the problem as its first priority. By 1958, after identifying and training suitable investigative personnel, The HSUS had launched its first undercover investigations of laboratory use of animals. In 1961 The HSUS hired an investigator to focus special attention on the laboratory animal trade. Subsequently Myers commissioned a statistical study of biomedical experiments that attempted to identify the potential for rapid reduction of animals used. These actions prepared the way for national legislation on laboratory animal issues.

The HSUS hoped to forge closer ties with local humane societies through its affiliates program.

While its founders intentionally launched their efforts in the nation's capital, The HSUS did not focus exclusively on the Washington scene. Even as The HSUS zeroed in on national solutions to national cruelties, it strove to enhance and extend the work of local societies. All of The HSUS's founding figures were in sympathy with the problems and challenges that local SPCAs faced. They pursued local and hands-on work for animals as individuals or through other organizations. Andrews had been helping local societies address their needs as AHA's director of field services before the formation of The HSUS. Jones and Glaser were deeply involved with cat rescue work. Myers served as a humane agent for the Maryland Animal Welfare Association, a federation of humane societies, and carried a euthanasia kit in his car in case he encountered animals beyond the point of saving.[18]

Newcomers to The HSUS also got "hands-on" immersion. Patrick Parkes, who became assistant director of services in 1961, recalled that when he came to the office for his interview, Myers gave him "a stack of material on the decompression chamber" and asked him to write a report recommending for or against its use. As Parkes later learned, this happened at a time when The HSUS was still working out its position about the humaneness of decompression as a euthanasia technology. After hiring Parkes Myers sent him out for training at a small shelter in Lucerne County, Pennsylvania, that The HSUS had helped to establish. There Parkes euthanized animals, cleaned kennels, and studied the typical methods in the field at that time.[19]

There was a strong programmatic rationale for such training and commitment. The original bylaws of The HSUS provided for its ownership and operation of shelter facilities through established branches conceived as integral units of the parent organization. Such ownership proved to be impractical on several grounds, but it did not prevent The HSUS from becoming deeply involved with local animal shelters and their problems. Ultimately, it did so by establishing an affiliates program to forge closer ties to local societies for the prevention of cruelty to animals.[20]

The regional offices that were such an integral part of The HSUS's work in 2004 had their origins in a branch and affiliate system envisioned by Myers and other founders. This system dated from 1957, when staff and board members resolved to organize a self-sustaining branch in every state. Myers and others considered the branches essential to membership recruitment for the national office. The first branch, incorporated in Illinois, emerged from the politics of pound seizure in Champaign County. Branches incorporated in New Jersey, Maryland, and California during 1958. In 1960 the organization's bylaws were amended to allow local societies to affiliate with The HSUS. Eventually this led to the incorporation of branches in five states (California, Connecticut, Minnesota, New Jersey, and Utah) and affiliated societies in eleven.[21]

The HSUS California branch of 1959. Clockwise beginning at front: Dale Deatherage, Mrs. Edward Newman, Amy Spano, Alfred B. Lawson, Carol Jenks, Norton Cowden, Henry Burmester, Mary Davidge, Russell Pray, Lois Banfield, and Stewart Rogers, incorporators and directors.

According to Parkes, who oversaw the transition from branches and affiliates to the system of regional offices in place today, the branch and affiliate system was the cornerstone of The HSUS's early program for development. "They wanted the new organization to be the chief instrument of unification in a movement which, at that time, was so badly fractured," Parkes recalled. The state seemed a natural geographical unit around which to base a program, since state legislatures were responsible for most of the anticruelty laws in place. Other groups, like the American Red Cross and the American Legion, operated through a similar system.[22]

The branches were not part of a scheme of "empire-building," Parkes emphasized, but rather a system of "strong, organically related, and unified" entities, self-supporting, each with an independent board of directors. Each branch "had to maintain minimum standards of program and policy, that, in turn, [it] would spread through the local societies nationwide." Local societies "were considered an essential adjunct to branches," and, hence, "provision was made for an affiliate connection."[23]

Through this structure, Parkes continued, early administrators believed they could "establish an interlocking structure between the national HSUS and its branches, and, through them, the local humane groups—all in a tighter unity than had ever existed before." A nationwide constituency and an unprecedented unity of purpose and approach could then be harnessed toward the relief of animal suffering, abuse, and exploitation, through the pursuit of legislation, regulation, and education at all levels.[24]

The branches were expected to help to organize and strengthen local humane societies wherever and whenever feasible. If such societies desired affiliation with The HSUS, they were expected to "operate on sound business principles, have realistic goals with practical approaches, maintain high HSUS operational standards, and pass an on-site inspection by a HSUS field representative." They were also expected to support national work to the best of their ability.[25]

From 1955 to 1961, The HSUS combined its annual corporate meeting with a two-day National Leadership Conference, ordinarily held in a large city. In 1962 the organization opted to stage the conferences in smaller hotels in attractive resort locations, to encourage greater personal contact with HSUS officials. Fred Myers wanted the event to be a place where new entrants into the field could meet and learn from experienced hands and where movement leaders could come together in a free exchange of ideas and approaches. "What I want

Annual Reports
of the President
and the Treasurer

*The Humane Society
of the United States*
1958

The diminutive (4" x 5 1/2") HSUS annual reports of 1958.

most—and think most important—is to attract more and more participation in these meetings by those who think. These conferences should be... conferences on our biggest national problems, with our best brains looking for solutions. For practical reasons we must also do some teaching—how to kill an animal humanely, how to keep financial records, etc.—but I think that we will be most useful if we think of our national leadership conference as a university, not a high school."[26]

While The HSUS was a staff-driven organization, its vitality did not depend solely upon employees. Board directors played crucial roles in the organization's early years, carrying out tasks that would have properly been assigned to staff members in a better-funded operation.

The HSUS board of directors, 1972. Front row, left to right: Amy Freeman Lee, Grace Korsan, Thelma Shawley, Hal Gardiner, Amanda Blake, Joyce Gilmore. Middle row, left to right: Murdaugh Stuart Madden, William Kerber, D. Collis Wager, Roger Caras, Robert Chenoweth, Raul H. Castro. Top row, left to right, Robert Welborn, Everett Smith, Jr., Jacques Sichel, Coleman Burke, and John A. Hoyt (president).

THE PHOTOMAKER

The HSUS's early board of directors was a "working" board whose members participated in numerous aspects of planning, development, and execution. Some, like Oliver Evans and Robert Chenoweth, were chairpersons of local humane societies in their own communities. Others brought special concerns, preoccupations, talents, or celebrity that made them ideal contributors for a fledgling organization. Alice Wagner (1906–1977), editor of *Popular Dogs* magazine, was honored with The HSUS's Humanitarian of the Year award in 1961 and later served as a board member for a number of years. William Kerber (d. 1990), a businessman and onetime official at the War Production Board and the Office of Price Stabilization, was on the board for almost a quarter-century, serving as treasurer during most of the 1960s and 1970s.

Cleveland Amory (1917–1998), author and social critic, served on the board between 1962 and 1970. Journalist and nature author Roger Caras (1929–2001) joined the board in 1970. Amanda Blake (d. 1989) did public service announcements for The HSUS and served as a board member in the 1970s. From the nation's political ranks, senators Richard Neuberger (1912–1960) and Gaylord Nelson, Representative Gilbert Gude, and future governor of Arizona Raul H. Castro served as board members.[27]

There were other, less celebrated board members who distinguished themselves through selfless and substantial service. Jacques Sichel (1909–1981), of Union, New Jersey, served on the board from 1961 to 1981, led the New Jersey Branch from 1960 onward, and was an early member of The HSUS's Program and Policy Committee and the board's

Alice Wagner accepted The HSUS's Humanitarian of the Year award in 1961.

executive committee. He was the author of *History and Handbook of the Humane Movement*, which served as an HSUS operations manual for many years. In 1961 Sichel organized a conference on humane education at Newark State College that helped to chart a course for the organization's subsequent efforts in this field. A supporter of state-level efforts to secure supplementary legislation after enactment of the 1958 Humane Slaughter Act, he also worked for the development of a humane restraining device for the ritual slaughter of animals.[28]

Another longtime collaborator, Frederick L. Thomsen, Ph.D. (1898–1978), who served as a board member from 1963 to 1966, offered early scientific and technical advice to The HSUS in an era when it had no one on staff equipped to provide such in-put. In 1965 "Doc" Thomsen launched his own organization, Humane Information Services, but he remained close to The HSUS. Thomsen was known for his meticulous research and his refusal to rely on hearsay. His lengthy analyses of humane problems provided sensible explanations of available options and strategies that were widely heeded by HSUS staff and board members.[29]

HSUS director Edith Goode speaks during the HSUS national leadership conference, Waterford, Virginia, 1964.

A third early board member, Edith Goode (1881–1970), was responsible for some of The HSUS's earliest and most important international and educational initiatives. Goode, a Springfield, Missouri, native and a graduate of Smith College, had devoted her entire life to public service and to campaigns for women's rights, peace, and birth control. She was a founder of the National Woman's Party and a member of the Women's International League for Peace and Freedom who worked actively for the passage of the Twentieth Amendment. A charter member of The HSUS and a generous supporter during its earliest years, Goode spent nine years on the board of directors and donated the land for The HSUS's National Humane Education Center in Waterford, Virginia. She and lifelong friend Alice Morgan Wright (1881–1975) took steps to perpetuate their commitment to concern for animals through the creation of an endowed trust. Since their deaths The Alice Morgan Wright-Edith Goode Fund has supported The HSUS and affiliated organizations in a broad range of activities aimed at the reduction and elimination of animal suffering.[30]

By 1960 The HSUS was a stable organization whose survival staff and board members had guaranteed through their hard work. Fred Myers's strategy of "action and fund-raising," which assumed that if the organization did a "vigorous, effective job," it would be able to "confidently count on a steadily increasing flow of gifts," had been amply vindicated. That year, officials estimated, the organization issued two million pieces of printed material, received 11,000 pieces of first class mail, and sent out 50,000 items through the U.S. Postal Service.[31]

HSUS supporter Alice Morgan Wright and board chairman Robert Chenoweth at the HSUS national leadership conference, Waterford, Virginia, 1964.

By then, too, Marcia Glaser (1930–2000) and Moneta "Dixie" Morgan were well established in their essential administrative support roles within The HSUS. Both women had a strong regard for animals and, twenty years later, were known to smile knowingly whenever overconfident newcomers would suggest that the organization ought to try this or that approach or that it should not have undertaken this or that campaign in the past. Glaser and Morgan were also legendary in their determination to keep office expenditures down through diligence, thrift, and control over expenses. Morgan, a meticulous ex-Marine, was responsible for accounts and financial reports on the organization's condition. HSUS investigator Frank McMahon once sent Patrick Parkes an expense account with an unusually large item on it, along with a note that said he was "scared to submit it direct to Dixie." Parkes returned the form to McMahon with his own handwritten note that said, "So am I!"[32]

The year 1960 also brought compelling evidence of The HSUS's legitimacy, in the form of a substantial bequest—$300,000—from Anna Belle Morris of Colorado. The handling of the bequest proved complex, for Morris had imposed certain restrictions on the funds. Two-thirds of the bequest was an outright gift, but both principal and income had to be used for "development of the Rocky Mountain Region." The other one-third of the principal was earmarked for the support of the Boulder County Humane Society, which would receive the interest income.[33]

Myers came up with the plan that the HSUS board would adopt for the Morris bequest, designed to honor the intention of the testator while maximizing the benefits that would accrue to The HSUS. Using an AHA definition of the Rocky Mountain region, and a formula based upon its geographic and demographic size relative to the rest of the United States, Myers assigned a fair proportion of the expected annual draw from the bequest to cover headquarters and general field expenses. At the same time, he proposed that The HSUS open an office in Denver, to serve as a "Livestock Department." Its director would do virtually all of his physical work in the Rocky Mountain region, Myers proposed, but would be detailed for occasional activity outside the region and outside the field of his specialty. Only so many animal shelters could be organized in a sparsely populated region like the Rocky Mountain States, and an effective staff member seeking to promote the humane ethic among livestock producers, educational institutions, 4-H clubs, county agents, and other agricultural interests would do as much to fulfill Morris's hopes for the spreading of animal protection values. The board of directors adopted Myers's proposal, and the man he subsequently hired, Belton P. Mouras, began work in January 1961, launching an investigation of livestock transportation in the United States, helping to advance the campaign for state-level humane slaughter laws, and carrying out important field work in other areas of interest.[34]

In 1961 The HSUS also hired its first full-time investigator, Frank McMahon, setting the stage for its crucial contributions to the laboratory animal campaigns of the coming decade. Apart from his essential role in the investigations that undergirded the passage of the Laboratory Animal Welfare Act in 1966 (see chapter 3), McMahon provided evidence for legislation and reform initiatives concerning rodeos, slaughterhouses, animal fighting, and the clubbing of seals. McMahon also established many of the precedents and procedures that would guide The HSUS's investigative work during and after his tenure.[35]

The HSUS's program agenda as it entered the 1960s included extension of humane slaughter legislation at the state level, the pursuit of federal legislation to regulate laboratory animal use, an end to pound seizure, the improvement of pound and shelter work, and the promotion of humane education. In addition to these goals, the organization worked opportunistically on investigations of rodeos, "soring" of Tennessee Walking Horses, and other issues brought to its attention. While lack of funds and staff precluded the full realization of such a vision, The HSUS sought to address as many cruelty issues as it could, a goal encompassed by the statement printed on every membership card issued during those years: "Every field of humane work—EVERYWHERE."

An HSUS membership card from 1960.

In some respects, as HSUS president Robert Chenoweth noted in 1959, the American humane movement had not been especially successful in the twentieth century. In a nation of more than 3,000 counties and 50,000 villages, there were nearly 500 independent societies focusing on a variety of issues, about 350 of which were active humane societies, almost all of them purely local in character. Of these societies, Fred Myers further observed, fewer than twenty-five published regular bulletins or newsletters. "Small wonder," he suggested, "that the general public is unaware of the staggering amount of cruelty and animal suffering that can be found in every one of the thousands of communities in our country."[36]

There was no doubt in the minds of anyone associated with The HSUS during its first decade, however, that the organization had made a crucial difference in the fortunes of the humane movement. By 1963 Myers was proud to note that, since the formation of The HSUS only nine years earlier, more than 100 new societies had been organized in the United States and 60 new shelters constructed. At that time, The HSUS was focused on six program concerns: the surplus population of dogs and cats, laboratory animal welfare, cruelty to agricultural livestock and wild animals, humane society operating procedures, humane education of children, and financing of both national and local humane work.[37] The HSUS's main challenge, he thought, was to strike the right balance between serving those local organizations and developing a big-picture approach with strategic thinking.[38]

Years of Transition

By summer 1962 Fred Myers was ready for a change. Eight years of hard work had worn him down, and he publicly fretted that he had not been effective as executive director. Expressing a desire to work more directly on the promotion of humane education, he proposed to let someone else assume his position while he shifted his attention to educational outreach.

Oliver Evans became president of The HSUS in 1963.

Myers's health also motivated his proposal. He had suffered two heart attacks, and a long hospital stay led him to push for changes in The HSUS's organizational structure.[39]

In 1963 the board responded to his concerns by endorsing a by-law change, which HSUS members approved in a nationwide referendum, to make the position of president, until then a voluntary position, a full-time office. The president would thus be the principal executive, and the position of executive director was abolished. Myers acquired the title of vice president and took over a newly created department of education. Oliver Evans, who had long been an official of the Animal Protective Association of Missouri, which maintained a shelter and other facilities in suburban St. Louis, became president. Evans relocated from Clayton, Missouri, to Washington with his wife and assumed direction of the HSUS office. Robert Chenoweth, who had led The HSUS as president since 1954, continued to do so under the title of chairman.[40]

On December 1, 1963, just six months after the new arrangements were approved, Fred Myers died of a heart attack at age fifty-nine. The death of the man who had led The HSUS through its first decade of existence was a catastrophic blow. Fortunately, however, Myers had foreseen the necessity of assuring the continuation of strong leadership. Not only had he inspired the restructuring of The HSUS, but he also had recruited Oliver Evans to the presidency and Chenoweth to the chairmanship.

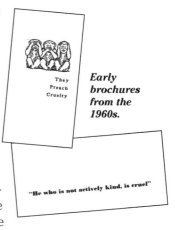

They Preach Cruelty

Early brochures from the 1960s.

"He who is not actively kind, is cruel"

As time would demonstrate, Myers had chosen well. Evans and Chenoweth exemplified the exceptional dedication of board members who labored to strengthen and sustain The HSUS in its early years. Chenoweth, president of the Wayside Waifs shelter in Kansas City, Missouri, had also served on the AHA board. Both men, and several other individuals who joined the HSUS board, had made the move with the AHA dissidents in 1954. Thus, they helped to perpetuate the steady determination of The HSUS to differentiate itself from AHA.[41]

FABIAN BACHRACH

Evans carried on in the presidency until 1967, running The HSUS without taking any compensation. In fact, staff members recall that on occasion Evans would write personal checks to cover financial shortfalls in The HSUS's accounts.

HSUS Chairman Robert Chenoweth.

He testified on behalf of the legislation that became the Laboratory Animal Welfare Act and supported the organization's strong efforts to investigate the dog trade that supplied laboratory animals. In another important initiative, Evans commissioned a survey on the feasibility of introducing humane education into the classroom. The survey, carried out at George Washington University, marked The HSUS's first serious move into the field of humane education. Evans's other priority was the completion of the National Humane Education Center at Waterford, Virginia, a training facility that had emerged from discussions among Fred Myers, Edith Goode, and other members of the HSUS family (see chapters 4 and 6).[42]

Within just a few days of Myers's death, Evans hired Dale Hylton, who worked with Frank McMahon, Declan Hogan, and others on investigations of the laboratory animal trade and traveled on behalf of The HSUS as a field representative in a range of contexts. Hylton was also charged with responsibility for overseeing the construction of an animal shelter and educational facility at Waterford. Numerous challenges were associated with the project—limited water supply, improper practices by contractors, historically appropriate design for a pumphouse located near an eighteenth-century farmhouse, and the construction of a euthanasia chamber by local talent—most of which fell to Hylton to resolve. It was also Hylton who recommended that Evans hire Phyllis Wright (1927–1992), who had just retired from the Washington Animal Rescue League and—already on a first-name basis with the companion animals of most congressmen and senators in the capital—was then planning to become a partner in an exclusive boarding kennel. Instead, Wright, who had supervised Hylton's own training when he first joined The HSUS, began to work part-time at Waterford, helping to train staff and conduct workshops with Hylton and other HSUS personnel.[43]

As it happened, Hylton shared Oliver Evans's deep enthusiasm for the humane education component of the Waterford project, and as Wright gradually worked her way into The HSUS

Phyllis Wright and HSUS President Oliver Evans, Waterford, Virginia.

as manager of the Waterford shelter and training programs, Hylton shifted his energies into the development of The HSUS's first humane education initiatives. The two worked there side by side for a number of years, and despite the pace, seriousness, and emotional burdens of the work, there was always time to savor the ironies it sometimes generated—like the time Hylton and Wright received a garbled Western Union telegram from a local society, asking them to forward all of the information they had on "youth in Asia."[44]

Building upon the organization's early commitment to field work and investigations, The HSUS employed several individuals during this era as field representatives. These staff members provided advice and assistance to humane societies on their work, investigated cases of animal abuse with national implications, and attended and/or provided testimony at legislative hearings on animal-related issues. Field representatives also traveled to provide direct assistance to local societies, helping to evaluate procedures and recommending program improvements.

In 1966 Evans steered The HSUS through a significant set of bylaw changes, brought on by membership petition. With the endorsement of the board of directors, The HSUS adopted the most important of the proposed changes. Among other things, a referendum of the national membership led to a system by which directors were elected by mail ballot instead of by the members assembled at an annual meeting.[45]

Despite his sincere dedication and sacrifice, Evans was not able to make a full-time commitment to The HSUS. He came to the office several days of the week to plot strategy, participate in meetings, sign correspondence and documents, and handle other responsibilities. On a day-to-day basis, key staff members like Glaser, Hylton, McMahon, Morgan, and Parkes operated with considerable autonomy, if not with full authority, in discharging their duties. It was not a perfect situation, but board and staff members tried to make it work until 1967, when family and business affairs made it impossible for Evans to continue serving as president.

Former HSUS president Mel Morse (left) met with John A. Hoyt in 1977, when Morse received a special Joseph Wood Krutch Medal.

At that point, Vice President Patrick Parkes, a longtime employee with a management background, took the reins. Parkes and Marcia Glaser had been writing and editing *HSUS News* since Myers's death, and Parkes had cultivated extensive contacts on behalf of The HSUS during his years of service. As director of Field Services, he had broad experience in dealing with HSUS chapters and in the provision of services to local humane societies.

In 1968 the HSUS board persuaded Mel Morse (d. 1988) to become president. Morse had begun his career in animal protection in the 1930s, as a kennel man, driver, and humane officer for the Los Angeles SPCA. He served as executive director of both the Humane Society of Marin County and AHA. In the early 1960s, Morse and Fred Myers had repaired their relationship, despite Morse's role in the political conflict between AHA and The HSUS in the mid-1950s, and the two men corresponded about Morse's taking a position with The HSUS. Eventually he did, working intermittently for the organization in a variety of capacities until 1974.[46]

His family's ambivalence about residing on the East Coast weakened Morse's tenure as HSUS president, and he did much of his work over the telephone from his home in California. By every account, Morse gave it his best, but no one involved thought this the best arrangement, and members of the office staff felt badly overworked under the circumstances. Eventually Morse decided to relinquish his office and return to the West Coast. The board of directors again faced the challenge of identifying a suitable leader for the day-to-day operations of The HSUS.

John Hoyt Joins The HSUS

In the early 1960s, board member Jacques Sichel recalled that, while discussing the search for a New Jersey chapter head, Fred Myers once had suggested that a clergyman was the right sort of candidate. "'To our members,' Myers explained, 'a humane society is akin to a church, dedicated to the improvement of personal attitudes with nothing to sell but a code of ethics and morality.'" The same logic, it seemed, guided those who selected John A. Hoyt to serve as president of The HSUS. When he was hired, Hoyt was serving as senior minister of the First Presbyterian Church in Fort Wayne, Indiana. He was on a successful track as a clergyman, but evolving theological concerns and the administrative burdens of his office—which distanced him from some of the responsibilities he loved most about the pastorate—led him to conclude that a career change was in order.[47]

Coleman Burke, a New York attorney, was instrumental in bringing Hoyt to The HSUS. Burke had joined the organization's board in 1967, at about the time that his firm had been asked to administer a trust, one of whose major beneficiaries was The HSUS. The Jeffery Trust accounted for $100,000 a year, almost 25 percent of The HSUS's annual budget at the time. An official of the American Bible Society (ABS), Burke strongly believed that a minister was the appropriate candidate for the HSUS presidency and focused the search on candidates brought to his attention through the ABS network. On April 1, 1970, John A. Hoyt became president of The HSUS. Mel Morse was appointed vice president in charge of West Coast Operations and allowed to pursue special assignments.[48]

Hoyt was a total newcomer and brought no knowledge of the animal welfare movement to the job, although he did read Morse's *Ordeal of the Animals* in preparation for his candidacy. Although Hoyt could not have known this, Morse's work was largely a collaborative effort involving Marcia Glaser, Patrick Parkes, Frank McMahon, and other HSUS employees. In reading the book, Hoyt was in fact becoming familiar with some of the staff members and program concerns he would inherit.[49]

Ultimately, Hoyt believed, it was his record as an accomplished institution-builder within the Presbyterian Church that won him the position. Once hired, moreover, he concluded that his clerical background had provided excellent preparation for the job. For one thing, he observed that, while many participants in the field were unchurched, they brought a quasi-religious dedication to their work. While cognizant of the moral energy that drove the organization's founders, Hoyt nevertheless believed that The HSUS had subordinated its efforts to promote ethical reflection on the status of animals to a program of practical reform. "Coming out of the church," he recalled, "gave me an opportunity to infuse some of the moral, ethical concerns I felt were appropriate to an animal organization." [50]

Hoyt was also strongly motivated by the conviction that animal protection had to be consistent in approaching the reconciliation and advancement of human and animal interests with a "both/and" rather than an "either/or" attitude. Rightly or wrongly, the charge of misanthropy had haunted the humane movement for years, and it was one that Hoyt consistently sought to counter in his public statements and writings. He returned to the subject again and again during his years of service. [51]

Hoyt's first five years at The HSUS were a time of mapping out strategies for building a national organization. A vital step in this process was the establishment in 1970 of a committee to chart a long-range course for The HSUS. The Program and Policy Review Committee consisted of board and staff members who met to develop and refine program objectives for the near and longer term. [52]

At about the same time, The HSUS commenced its practice of periodic and ongoing issue assessment. "Doc" Thomsen had promulgated a scale of measure for evaluating priorities as early as 1968. However, Robert Welborn, Esq., a Denver, Colorado, attorney who served on the board, actively championed the idea within The HSUS after 1970. The goal was to inventory and weight every animal issue as an organizational priority. It was one of the humane movement's earliest and best efforts to assess cruelty by answering such questions as: how many animals were used in different arenas? In what ways? What was the nature and intensity of that suffering? Where were animals most severely harmed? What were the possibilities of changing that suffering? What were other organizations doing? The assessment conditioned the organization's reaction to the issues, by providing context for its decisions about how to invest its time, effort, and resources. [53]

Krutch Medal ceremonies at the 1971 HSUS annual meeting included (from left) new HSUS president John A. Hoyt, Mark Van Doren, Mrs. Joseph Wood Krutch, honoree Joy Adamson, and HSUS board chairman Coleman Burke, Esq.

One of Hoyt's priorities was the abolition of the organization's five state branches. Under long-standing arrangements, The HSUS designated 60 percent of all funds raised from members within the branch states for use by the chapters, with the national organization taking the rest. The state chapters were essentially independent entities using the same name and determining their own program and were in effect friendly competitors with the national organization. Hoyt strongly believed that The HSUS had to be just one entity. [54]

Others besides Hoyt had expressed their frustration with the chapter system. While Fred Myers considered it crucial to the expansion of The HSUS, he fretted over the friction that sometimes developed between regional boards of directors and staff members in the branch offices—friction about which he and the central quarters could do very little. When California chapter director Belton Mouras broke from The HSUS in 1968 to found the Animal Protection Institute, he did so partly out of frustration with the cumbersome decision-making processes of an organization with both regional and national boards of directors. Under the circumstances, Hoyt had little trouble persuading The HSUS's national board members to support the branches' abolition.[55]

Most of the staff members of the branches supported their consolidation into a system of regional offices. However, branch board members, who were being asked in most cases to disenfranchise themselves, were less enthusiastic. The branches did not all go willingly, and their particular circumstances shaped their response. The Minnesota branch was virtually defunct, so the matter was moot. The Connecticut branch was in debt after building an education center and welcomed the national office's commitment to absorb its indebtedness as part of consolidation. The Utah branch sought independent identity, as the Utah Humane Society, as did the California branch, which reincorporated as the Golden State Humane Society. New Jersey proved to be the longest holdout, but as the prospect of complete dissociation with the national office loomed, its principal figures came around; in the late 1970s, it would reinvent itself as one of The HSUS's most successful regional operations.

The HSUS's townhouse headquarters at 1604 K Street, N.W., Washington, D.C.

What Hoyt liked about the branch chapters was the degree to which they gave The HSUS a regional grassroots identity. Hoyt sought to replicate and extend this advantage by establishing five regional offices—Great Lakes (Fort Wayne, Indiana), covering Ohio, Indiana, and Illinois; Southern area (Pinehurst, North Carolina), serving North Carolina, South Carolina, Florida, and Georgia; Rocky Mountain area (Salt Lake City, Utah), covering Utah, Wyoming, Colorado, and Idaho; Gulf States area (Corpus Christi, Texas), serving Texas, Louisiana, and Arkansas; and New England (East Haddam, Connecticut), covering Connecticut, New Hampshire, Vermont, Massachusetts, Rhode Island, and Maine. These offices were in place by late 1972.[56]

Regional office staff visited humane shelters and public pounds; conducted investigations; reached out to the public through newspaper, radio, and television work; handled inquiries by letter or telephone; and addressed civic and other groups. In time staff members in these offices began to make central contributions to the program, campaign, and development goals of The HSUS. Not only did they provide a regional grassroots presence for advancing the general goals of the organization, however; they also perpetuated the legacy of the state branches by continuing to emphasize regional priorities and opportunities that deserved The HSUS's attention.

Another benchmark of Hoyt's tenure was the purchase of permanent headquarters, a step made possible by substantial bequests. For its first seventeen years, The HSUS had operated from rented suites, the last of which was in the Associations Building at 1145 19th Street, N.W., Washington, D.C. In 1971 the organization purchased a townhouse at 1604 K Street, N.W., from which to operate. In 1975 The HSUS purchased a building at 2100 L Street, N.W., for use as its permanent headquarters.[57]

In 1978 The HSUS board also modified the organization's policy about using every dollar taken in during a given year. When Hoyt accepted the presidency, the budget was approximately $450,000 per year, and The HSUS used 100 percent of every bequest, with no reserve or mechanism for reserve funds. Under the new policy, the organization tried to place a significant percentage of each new bequest in an escrow account, to be spent over the next five years. By that mechanism, The HSUS could develop a budget and make a reasonable guess at its likely income for any given year. At the same time, none of these monies became part of any permanent reserve.[58]

Hoyt inherited one problem that had marked The HSUS's history since its first day of operation. To a great extent, when people thought beyond their local organization, it was still to

The HSUS's headquarters at 2100 L Street, N.W., Washington, D.C.

AHA—not to The HSUS or any other national groups—that they looked. Although this had begun to change by the early 1970s, The HSUS's leadership continued to face this issue, making determined efforts to underscore the contrasts between its policies and those of AHA. HSUS representatives did so by stressing the policy differences that divided the two organizations on such issues as trapping, rodeos, animal experimentation, and shelter and euthanasia practices. Hard feelings and old conflicts dating back to the 1950s continued to be influential several decades later.[59]

Cruelty, Values, and The HSUS

The values that informed the organization of The HSUS in 1954 were values its founders inherited from an extant American humane movement whose formal origins lay in the 1860s. The idea of kindness to animals made significant inroads in American culture in the years following the organization of the first societies for the prevention of cruelty to animals. The development of sympathy for the perceived pain of animals, the acknowledged satisfaction that attended the keeping of animals, and concerns over the reflexive impact of cruelty upon the character of its perpetrators all strengthened the movement's hold on the popular imagination.

Humane advocates also believed that "a universal acceptance of kindness to other forms of life would help develop a better society for all." True humanitarianism, Jacques V. Sichel contended in an early organizational manual, "believes that kindness is indivisible; it should include all species of animals and birds and man. It may embrace those who love a single species like dogs or cats, but in its purest form it is love and concern for every living thing."[60]

This broader legacy notwithstanding, the most immediate philosophical influence on 1950s advocates, including early supporters of The HSUS, was Albert Schweitzer's concept of reverence for life. Recognizing the "will-to-live" of every living being, Schweitzer concluded that a theory of right conduct must consist of giving "to every will-to-live the same reverence for life that he gives to his own." Schweitzer's notion had emerged from years of reflection on the most valid basis for ethics.[61]

For humanitarians, it was significant that Schweitzer included a notion of regard for non-human life in his cosmology. In his 1952 Nobel Peace Prize speech, Schweitzer noted, "compassion, in which ethics takes root, does not assume its true proportions until it embraces not only man but every living being."[62] Such words buoyed humane advocates laboring to give their concerns a higher profile. Eventually, Schweitzer's expressions of support went beyond words. He approved the Animal Welfare Institute's establishment of an annual award in his name, served as honorary president of Aida Flemming's International Kindness Club (later incorporated into The HSUS), and even sent a letter expressing his support for legislation to regulate animal use in American laboratories in 1963.[63]

The humane movement did not find similar inspiration in philosophers of conservation like Aldo Leopold, just as animal protection groups did not have much affinity with the major environmental organizations of the pre-1970 era. As Fred Myers put it, "I know of no national conservation organization—including Audubon—that is officially interested in the suffering of animals or in humanitarianism. They are interested only in ecology, conservation of species, etc. In terms of philosophy, most of the conservation organizations are dedicated to 'management' of animals for man's benefit. That doesn't run very close to our own philosophy."[64]

Myers and his colleagues found a highly suitable exemplar of their values in Joseph Wood Krutch (1893–1970), who became one of America's leading thinkers and literary critics with *The Modern Temper* (1927). Krutch's intellectual explorations of Thoreau and his physical experiences in the Arizona desert in the late 1940s and early 1950s sparked a new level of appreciation for wilderness and for nonhuman life. From that time onward, Krutch sought to articulate a philosophy that acknowledged and celebrated the importance of the natural world and all of its inhabitants.[65]

With *The Great Chain of Life* (1957), Krutch established himself as a philosopher of humaneness. Krutch was particularly disturbed by the devaluation and demise of traditional natural history education, which, he felt, had alienated many human beings from the natural environment and nonhuman nature. "The grand question remains whether most people actually want hearts to be tenderer or harder. Do we want a civilization that will move toward some more intimate relation with the natural world," Krutch asked, "or do we want one that will continue to detach and isolate itself from both a dependence upon and a sympathy with that community of which we were originally a part?" In May 1957 a review of Krutch's seminal work in the *HSUS News*, almost certainly the product of Myers's pen, noted with approval, "Krutch believes that if men can be made to feel their relationship with the other living creatures of earth, something akin to Schweitzer's 'reverence for life' will follow."[66]

Krutch took a pragmatic role in helping the cause. His blanket condemnation of sport hunting was reprinted regularly in the pages of the *HSUS News*. In March 1965, as the controversy over animal use in laboratories grew, he wrote a piece for the *Saturday Review*, criticizing various cruelties perpetrated against animals and making an implicit case for proposed legislation that would eventually be approved as the Laboratory Animal Welfare Act. In 1968 Krutch contributed a foreword to Mel Morse's *Ordeal of the Animals* and received The HSUS's Humanitarian of the Year award, its highest accolade. In 1970 the award was renamed in his honor.[67]

The growing environmental movement of the early 1970s also influenced the ethical and practical development of The HSUS. The era's environmentalism had inspired a "new awakening," John Hoyt believed, in relation to which the humane movement needed to position itself. As theologian John B. Cobb, Jr., put it, "The environmental crisis is making us aware that we should change our behavior toward other living things. The need for change follows from our traditional concern for human welfare, but it also raises the question of whether our traditional anthropocentric ethics and religion are adequate or justified."[68]

As part of its general efforts to impress upon the public both the implications and the value of a philosophy of humaneness toward all life, The HSUS sponsored a 1976 conference, "On the Fifth Day," bringing together philosophers, anthropologists, biologists, and other scholars. The conference represented the

The Krutch Medal

culmination of a long-held vision—shared by Oliver Evans and other board members—to bring together scholarly perspectives on the proper relationship of humans to nonhuman animals. A book based upon the proceedings was published in 1977.[69]

By that time, of course, the treatment of animals had become a topic of serious debate within moral philosophy. That debate spilled over into public consciousness with the 1975 publication of Peter Singer's *Animal Liberation*. Singer's book decried the mistreatment of animals as "speciesism" and sought to recast concern for animals as a justice-based cause akin to the era's better known liberation movements.

Much of what Singer wrote concerning the prevention or reduction of animals' suffering was in harmony with The HSUS's objectives. Among other things, Singer's philosophy did not rest upon the inherent rights of animals. His principal concern, like that of The HSUS, was the mitigation and elimination of suffering, and he endorsed the view that ethical treatment sometimes permitted or even required killing animals to end their misery. Singer's work also influenced independent activist Henry Spira, with whom The HSUS would closely ally itself from the late 1970s onward.

Guy Hodge joined the staff of The HSUS in 1971.

While acknowledging that the new philosophical discussions differed from earlier notions of animal welfare and concern for animals, many at The HSUS saw them as "old wine in new bottles." They did not promise to change anything in the organization's legal strategy, which used wildlife-related, anticruelty, and environmental statutes that afforded relevant protections—without invoking a language of rights.[70]

The HSUS was concerned with the development of well-conceived policies about what constituted cruelty to animals and what ought to be done about it. Robert Welborn led the way in drafting a revised Statement of Beliefs and Principles, adopted by the Board of Directors on October 11, 1974.[71] Hoyt tried to make the statement of principles a "living document" by asking staff members to differentiate carefully between uses of animals when trying to determine whether The HSUS should undertake expenses "to improve the efficiency, humaneness, or respectability of such utilizations." For example, while it seemed clear to him that The HSUS "should be very much involved in helping to improve technology and procedures (better slaughtering equipment and methods, development and utilization of tissue culture methodologies, improved research facilities, improved livestock transportation, etc.) toward the end of relieving animal suffering both in degree and quantity," that premise seemed "a self-defeating function" in regard to efforts to make an activity like trapping or rodeo "more acceptable and respectable," and thus to further perpetuate an "activity we wish to eliminate."[72]

Professionalization, Scientific Proficiency, and Staff Development

From the first, The HSUS sought to establish a professional identity and stature for itself. Fred Myers and Helen Jones were highly proficient in their respective fields of journalism and public relations, which helped The HSUS to reach millions of Americans with its message in the early years. By the 1960s staff members were making national television appearances, and the organization's program of media outreach was robust. Jones's publicity work on humane slaughter was crucial to passage of the Humane Slaughter Act in 1958, and Myers's efforts to identify The HSUS with the debate over laboratory animal use resulted in his appearance on NBC-TV's *Today* show in 1962.[73]

At the same time, The HSUS had attracted some very good people to work in educational outreach, field activities, investigations, publications, and office management. In an era when everyone was expected to demonstrate multiple competencies and to be ready to assume any task, Marcia Glaser, Dale Hylton, Frank McMahon, Dixie Morgan, Patrick Parkes, Phyllis Wright, and others wore many hats in the service of the organization.

Frederick "Doc" Thomsen in 1960.

In its early years, The HSUS also relied on the voluntary assistance of technical specialists, like "Doc" Thomsen, a retired agricultural economist with a commitment to scientific detail and a penchant for accuracy. The organization's dozen or so staff members were very dedicated people, yet there were no staff scientists. The charge that The HSUS was driven by emotion rather than the facts of any given issue—a common accusation in that era—drove the push toward professionalization of its technical staff.[74]

By 1970, when Hoyt assumed office, The HSUS had begun to reap the benefits of its hard work during the 1950s and 1960s. By the late 1960s, some of its early supporters had begun to pass away and leave bequests. This gave The HSUS of the 1970s an advantage that the organization had not enjoyed in past decades—substantial testamentary gifts with which to build and expand programs and staff. Important bequests from early supporters like Luella Jeffery, Mrs. Jay S. Hartt, and Elsa H. Voss laid the groundwork for the successes of the new decade.[75]

Hoyt was determined to deploy these new assets in areas outside The HSUS's traditional concerns—such as wildlife issues—and to strengthen its capacities with additional professional and technical staff. In the 1970s, under his leadership, The HSUS became the most talent-rich organization in the history of animal protection. Having taken root under the direction of Fred Myers, it blossomed under the leadership of John Hoyt.

In 1971 Hoyt hired naturalist Guy Hodge (1944–1999) to assume daily responsibility for handling technical inquiries from the public and from government and other authorities. Hodge also performed a lot of the data research needed to make The HSUS's inventory and assessment process credible. As director of data and information services, Hoyt recalled, "Guy was our encyclopedia." Hodge developed special knowledge of emergency relief measures to help animals during disasters. In addition, he served as the organization's point man on dozens of "orphan" issues, penning articles on poisonous substances that could hurt companion animals; providing advice on how to remove raccoons, bats, and other animals from chimneys and attics; and offering hints for helping orphaned wildlife. He provided information on travel with companion animals, consulted with local governments and societies on the control of pigeon populations in urban areas, and campaigned against inhumane mousetraps. He also wrote the pioneering edition of The HSUS's book on careers working with animals.[76]

Hodge was one of several people Hoyt hired that year for technical and/or scientific expertise. Hal Perry, a well-known opponent of predator control programs, and Sue Pressman, a zoo expert, joined The HSUS in 1971 as well. These appointments marked the beginning of The HSUS's commitment to expand its activity into wildlife problems. Hoyt used the occasion of Perry's hiring as wildlife representative to articulate The HSUS's three objectives in the field of wildlife protection: "to prevent cruelty to all wild animals, to preserve all species still in existence, and to help restore the balance of nature that man has thrown out of kilter."[77]

Delos E. Culver (left), director of the National Humane Society, watches as then Vice President Richard Nixon hangs up a "Give Wildlife a Brake" poster in 1955.

Robert Bay, a veterinarian and early winner of the Animal Welfare Institute's Albert Schweitzer Medal, joined the staff in 1972 to work on a wide variety of concerns from the West Coast Office managed by Mel Morse. Among other duties, Bay accompanied HSUS investigators to the site of the seal harvest on the Pribilof Islands. In 1973 The HSUS created a

Staff and officers attending the 1973 HSUS national conference in Salt Lake City included John A. Hoyt, Frantz Dantzler, Mel Morse, Patrick Parkes, Marcia Glaser, Guy Hodge, Dale Hylton, Moneta "Dixie" Morgan, Bernie Weller, Doug Scott, Sue Pressman, Frank McMahon, John Dommers, and Phyllis Wright.

veterinary advisory committee under Bay's authority, comprised of eight veterinary scientists.[78]

Not all of the crucial hires during this era involved scientific specialists. Ben Hayes, who had served The HSUS on behalf of an outside membership fulfillment company for more than five years, came on board in 1971 to centralize that operation in-house. John Henderson also arrived in 1971, eventually overseeing publication fulfillment and mail room operations. John Dommers, a science teacher with an interest in developing educational materials on animals and the environment, came to work in the New England Regional Office in 1972. In 1973 Hoyt hired Dommers's friend and collaborator, Charles F. Herrmann, III, an editor of children's publications for Xerox Education Publications, to coordinate HSUS education programs. In time Herrmann would assume editorial responsibility for The HSUS's major publications, including *HSUS News, NAHEE Journal,* and *Shelter Sense.*

Hoyt also engineered some significant reassignments within The HSUS in these years. After Frank McMahon died in 1974, Frantz Dantzler assumed principal responsibility for investigations. In 1975 The HSUS's longtime general counsel, Murdaugh Madden, agreed to direct a new legal department full time, to expand The HSUS's role in prosecuting cruelty cases, litigating in state and federal courts to ensure enforcement of animal protection laws, and participating in administrative proceedings of importance. John Dommers served sequentially as an educator in the HSUS Connecticut branch, director of The HSUS's humane education division, the National Association for the Advancement of Humane Education (NAAHE), director of the HSUS New England Regional Office, and after 1980 as coordinator of multimedia materials.

It was the Bicentennial Year of 1976 that would prove to be the annus mirabilis of staff recruitment for The HSUS, however. During that year, Hoyt brought Patricia Forkan, Paul G. Irwin, and Michael W. Fox, D.Sc., Ph.D., B.Vet.Med., MRCVS, into the organization. All three would come to play important roles in The HSUS's long-term evolution.

Forkan came from The Fund for Animals, where she had worked as national coordinator. She brought six years of experience as a campaigner against whaling and thus became The HSUS's first specialist on the issue. However, her background in trapping and fur and wild horse and tuna/dolphin concerns brought additional assets to The HSUS. As program coordinator, reporting directly to Hoyt, she oversaw a broad range of program areas, coordinated the organization's interactions with government officials, and expanded its capacity for

Marcia Glaser and Charles F. Herrmann, III, in the late 1970s.

responding to legislative opportunities and challenges. Her appointment was a timely one, because changes in the federal tax law in 1976 permitted organizations like The HSUS to exert greater pressure and influence on the passage of legislation, without jeopardizing their tax-exempt status. In 1977 Forkan launched the Action Alert Program, a means for informing HSUS member participants of the need for quick action on legislative and other matters. The following year, she was named vice president for program and communications.[79]

Irwin joined the organization after an outside consultant, The Oram Group, examined The HSUS's management and administrative structure. The Oram review identified membership growth as one of the organization's most urgent needs. A United Methodist minister with a background in the nonprofit sector, Irwin became vice president of a newly formed Office of Development that sought to coordinate and enhance fund-raising activities. His hiring marked the advent of a new era in long-range development planning for The HSUS.[80]

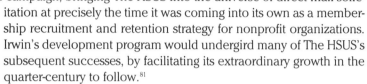

The 1974 HSUS national conference brought together (from left)—Douglas M. Scott, Michael W. Fox, Guy R. Hodge, Frantz Dantzler (newly placed in charge of investigations), and Dale Hylton. Fox would join the HSUS staff two years later.

There were signs of Irwin's willingness to set high expectations and then work hard to reach them in his first full presentation to the HSUS board. At the time, in April 1976, The HSUS had about 30,000 constituents. Irwin proposed to triple the number by January 1978, within just eighteen months. He did it by pursuing a judicious but intensive direct mail campaign, bringing The HSUS into the universe of direct mail solicitation at precisely the time it was coming into its own as a membership recruitment and retention strategy for nonprofit organizations. Irwin's development program would undergird many of The HSUS's subsequent successes, by facilitating its extraordinary growth in the quarter-century to follow.[81]

Murdaugh Stuart Madden, pictured here at the 1978 annual conference in Dearborn, joined the HSUS staff in 1975.

Hoyt's decision to hire Fox marked The HSUS's transformation from an organization of well-intentioned humanitarians into a credible professional advocacy group. An Englishman who graduated from the Royal Veterinary College (1962), Fox earned a doctorate from London University and came to the United States in 1962. His research on animal behavior, especially in relation to wolves, earned him a serious academic reputation, and he was an associate professor of psychology at Washington University in St. Louis. In addition to his scholarly work, Fox gained a wide public following with books like Understanding Your Dog and Understanding Your Cat and a regular column in McCall's, "Ask Your Animal Doctor."[82]

By 1975 Fox had grown increasingly uncomfortable with the politics of the university and was looking for ways to become a more effective voice for animals and nature outside of that setting. He knew very little of The HSUS and other organizations, although he had begun to write on animal protection issues while still a college professor. The movement did know him, however. Fox's published work and public commentary had made him a celebrity, and he made dozens of appearances on the Tonight Show with Johnny Carson.

Even before Fox's arrival, The HSUS had taken steps to seek financial support for the creation of an Institute for the Study of Animal Problems (ISAP). A major proposal for such a center had been part of the organization's submission to the executors of the Whittell estate in 1972, orchestrated by Mel Morse and Murdaugh Madden. This extraordinary competitive process began in 1970, after a testator's vagueness in specifying a proper beneficiary (George Whittell had left $6 million to the "National Society for the Prevention of Cruelty to Animals") led a California court to solicit proposals for support from qualified organizations. The HSUS's plan for ISAP was approved to receive $1 million,

Paul G. Irwin, John A. Hoyt, and Patricia Forkan in 1976.

more than any other humane organization that qualified.[83]

Upon joining The HSUS, Fox became ISAP director. ISAP's mission was to harness the work of scholars and scientists to address specific problems in animal welfare. Under ISAP's aegis, The HSUS would try to apply technical and practical knowledge to the real world of animal pain and suffering. From its inception ISAP became the center of The HSUS's research activities.

As Hoyt later recalled, The HSUS received a lot of criticism for hiring a veterinarian. For a variety of reasons, the veterinary profession did not have a good reputation among humane advocates. For his part Fox suffered the disapproval of professional colleagues in ethology and veterinary science, who disparaged his decision to join his talents with the humane movement—whose concerns and policies they often dismissed or resented.[84]

By his very presence, Fox insulated The HSUS against the charge that there was no one on its staff who really knew what he or she was talking about. "We now had someone who knew the language, we now had the competency," Hoyt recalled. This was particularly valuable as the organization moved into such new arenas as wildlife protection and the campaign against intensive rearing of animals for food.[85]

Andrew Rowan joined The HSUS for the first time in 1978.

Several years later, in 1978, The HSUS hired Andrew N. Rowan, D. Phil., a Rhodes scholar and Oxford-educated South African biochemist who had spent four years at the Fund for the Replacement of Animals in Medical Experiments (FRAME), a nonanimal research methods charity and think tank in Great Britain. Rowan joined Fox as associate director of ISAP. Under their direction, ISAP prepared reports on euthanasia of companion animals, factory farming, and the attention accorded to animal welfare in federal grant applications for animal experiments.[86]

In January 1980 ISAP launched the *International Journal for the Study of Animal Problems*, to disseminate the results of scientific work directed toward the promotion of animal welfare. This included engagement with some of the most urgent issues facing animal protectionists, including appropriate euthanasia technology, intensive farming of animals, nonanimal methods in research, and species extinction. The community of scholars that coalesced around the journal helped to legitimize animal behavior as an applied science for evaluating animals' welfare and behavioral needs. Recognizing the validity of emerging philosophical arguments about the rights and interests of animals, ISAP's journal also became an important forum for discussion of the legal and moral implications of animals' treatment. Both the ISAP journal and its successor, *Advances in Animal Welfare Science*, extended the organization's commitment to provide a forum for the dissemination of ideas and research concerning animal welfare science. What most distinguished them was their direct attention to animal welfare issues, which were still receiving mostly peripheral coverage in existing veterinary and animal science journals. By creating outlets for publication, these journals helped to stimulate further research and analysis.

Development and the Shift to a Divisional Model

With the addition of more technical and scientific staff, an expanding workload, and a growing membership and budget, The HSUS began to improvise new organizational arrangements. By 1977 there were separate departments devoted to sheltering and animal control issues, wildlife protection, field service and investigations, research and data services, legislation and program coordination, communications, youth activities, development, and legal affairs.[87]

These were exciting times, too. Not only were the issues coming to occupy greater media attention, but there were also signs that humane concerns were being taken more seriously. "The barometer of this country's sensitivity can be seen in the legislative process," investigator Frantz Dantzler remarked in 1977. "Whereas one or two animal welfare bills were introduced twenty years ago, sixty to eighty measures may come before Congress now." [88]

It was also an exciting time to work at The HSUS. Michael Fox, Patricia Forkan, Charles Herrmann, and others were grateful for the latitude their positions provided. It was easy to get hired, it sometimes seemed, because of the enthusiasm Hoyt demonstrated whenever he encountered someone he thought would be a good addition to the staff. Longtime employees joked that one might bid Hoyt farewell on a Friday afternoon as he left for a weekend engagement and then return to the office on Monday to find someone the HSUS president had met the day before on an airplane or at an animal protection conference sitting at the next desk. At the same time, Herrmann recalled, "You had to make your position," and those who succeeded in doing so went on to long careers at The HSUS. [89]

By 1978 The HSUS was providing national leadership for campaigns to promote spay-neuter of companion animals, to eliminate the high-altitude decompression chamber for euthanasia of companion animals, to address the cruelties of farm animal husbandry and slaughter, and to end the choke hold hunters and trappers had on federal and state wildlife agencies. That year Hoyt enumerated some additional cruelties then occupying The HSUS's organizational agenda:

> The HSUS has called for a boycott of Russian and Japanese products because of the extensive killing of whales by these two countries. We have urged you and others not to purchase tuna products because of the killing of large numbers of porpoise by the tuna industry. We have urged that no fur products be purchased because of the extreme cruelty to animals associated with trapping. We have and shall continue to oppose rodeos, animal coursing, hunting for sport, roadside zoos, cockfighting and dog fighting, bull fighting—bloodless or otherwise—and many other uses of animals which involve a suffering and abuse negating the economic or social benefits when viewed from a moral-ethical perspective. [90]

The agenda Hoyt articulated was an ambitious one and involved the development of robust program work on all of the major issues. Trying to do more meant having to raise more funds, and the right methods for meeting that goal were important topics at staff meetings during the late 1970s. One of the most successful instruments for recruiting members and gaining membership reports was the *Close-Up Report*, a four-page, full-color publication that targeted one specific cruelty in great detail and provided the reader with a list of suggested actions. Paul Irwin had first proposed the *Close-Up Report* in 1976 as a solution to The HSUS's need for refined fund-raising material. It turned out to be much more, however, as Patricia Forkan and other program staffers found that a four-page, full-color publication featuring detailed accounts of specific cruelties could also serve the organization's evolving needs for better program and campaign material. The *Close-Up Report* neatly tied together the imperatives of membership development and fund-raising with The HSUS's programmatic mission of education and outreach. Between the late 1970s and the late 1980s, The HSUS sent out the *Close-Up Report* four times a year. [91]

In composing the *Close-Up Report*, staff members could draw upon the several hundred animal cruelties addressed by The HSUS, highlighting the results of a new investigation, taking advantage of a rise in public concern about a specific issue, putting the publication in the service of an ongoing legislative campaign, or creating an activist tool. Each *Close-Up Report* attempted to draw the reader toward action on behalf of animals. Forkan usually decided upon the topics and oversaw content development for the reports. In the early years, Forkan and Charles Herrmann wrote them; after Deborah Salem joined The HSUS in 1981 as editor of the *HSUS News*, she and staff member Julie Rovner also played important roles in their production. [92]

HSUS staff (with RSPCA staff in Great Britain) in September 1980 included John Hoyt (1), Patricia Forkan (2), Michael Fox (3), Phyllis Wright (4), Mel Morse (5), Frantz Dantzler (6), Sue Pressman (7), Kathy Savesky (8), Patrick Parkes (9), and Andrew Rowan (10).

By 1979, Hoyt estimated, The HSUS was mailing out one million pieces of literature and other material annually. The HSUS had eighty employees, and Hoyt was proud to note that since his assumption of the presidency in 1970 not one person with program or administrative responsibilities had left the staff for other opportunities. HSUS membership had reached 115,000, its annual budget approached $2 million, and its board had grown from fifteen to twenty members.[93]

Another sign of The HSUS's coming of age came in September 1980, when ten staff members traveled to Great Britain to meet with their counterparts at the Royal Society for the Prevention of Cruelty to Animals (RSPCA), the world's first and largest animal welfare society. While noting many differences in structure, tactics, and style, HSUS participants were pleased to find it such a meeting of equals.[94]

Nineteen eighty was the first year of the Reagan administration, which would prove alternately indifferent or hostile toward humane concerns and whose deficiencies Hoyt and others would cite frequently in their writings. Most significant, the new administration stood on the principle of opposition to government interference in the lives of citizens. This approach, as applied to animal welfare concerns, seemed to spell the end of any effort to control the use and abuse of animals by government agencies and private enterprise. Such a philosophy ran counter to the programmatic goals of The HSUS as an organization that saw and understood the need for government involvement in a number of areas where animals were under serious threat.

Hoyt devoted a substantial portion of his 1981 *President's Report* to the adverse impact of the Reagan administration, which brought with it the threat of reduced funding for enforcement of existing animal protective legislation and regulatory measures. This lack of support threatened the Animal Welfare Act (AWA) as well as legislation protecting wild horses, marine mammals, and endangered species. The HSUS spent a significant amount of time in the decade building congressional alliances to thwart the administration's lack of commitment, best exemplified by the president's fiscal year 1986 budget, which zero-budgeted the AWA.[95]

Recognizing that the battle over programs that either helped or hurt animals would be fought on the basis of budgetary lines, not on the authorization of new programs, The HSUS went so far as to employ legislative staff with special experience and expertise in the intricacies of Capitol Hill funding processes. Moreover, realizing that the funding game could cut in two directions, The HSUS launched its first efforts to eliminate subsidies for programs that resulted in animal suffering and abuse during this era.[96] The organization also enhanced its legislative capabilities outside the nation's capital, appointing a coordinator for state legislation, Ann Church, a former Hill staff member, in 1983. In an inhospitable federal climate, it was all the more important that The HSUS make a stronger commitment to promoting state-level initiatives.[97]

At the same time, The HSUS tried to penetrate the policy networks that would allow staff members to influence decision making in the federal government. In 1981, for example, Fox and Hoyt met with the Secretary of the U.S. Department of Agriculture (USDA) to discuss farm animal welfare concerns. All five regional directors of USDA's Animal Plant and Health Inspection Service (APHIS), along with their Washington supervisors, visited HSUS headquarters to meet staff specialists and to learn about the evidence that had developed concerning enforcement problems.[98]

The selection of James Watt to head the U.S. Department of the Interior was a particular provocation. Watt's apocalyptic, "Earth-rejecting" personal theology—which Hoyt learned about firsthand in a dinner conversation with Watt—fueled the brash and relentless appointment of unapologetic representatives of the hunting, trapping, mining, lumbering, and ranching industries to positions of influence in the government. Watt and his confreres posed special threats to the humane movement's hard-won gains in wild horse protection, predator control, and marine life.[99]

By the time of the Watt-led offensive, the six main sections of The HSUS (under four vice presidents) were Program and Communications (Patricia Forkan), Cruelty Investigations and Field Services (Patrick Parkes), Finance and Development (Paul Irwin), Legal Affairs (Murdaugh Madden), the Institute for the Study of Animal Problems (Michael Fox), and Administration and Education (John Hoyt).[100]

Although staff members like Forkan, Guy Hodge, Sue Pressman, and others had all worked on select wildlife concerns during the 1970s, and it was obviously a matter of great interest to HSUS supporters, the organization lacked a well-focused effort on behalf of wild animals as it entered the 1980s. By then, however, with wildlife concerns rapidly expanding beyond the relatively limited scope of the humane movement's traditional activity, and membership and broader public interest in such issues rising, The HSUS moved to cover the field more thoroughly. In January 1982 The HSUS incorporated all of its wildlife programs and environmental concerns (with the exception of marine mammals and legislative affairs, both of which remained in the portfolio of Forkan) into a new section for Wildlife and Environment. Hoyt chose John W. Grandy, Ph.D., formerly executive vice president of Defenders of Wildlife, to head the section as vice president for Wildlife and Environment. Grandy's appointment marked the transition toward the modern divisional structure of The HSUS. He came into the organization at a senior level and was given oversight of an entire program area, with the charge of expanding its influence and stature both within and outside of the organization.

John W. Grandy, Ph.D., was appointed to head a new section, Wildlife and Environment, in 1981.

In the coming years, The HSUS would follow this model in establishing new program divisions and transforming older ones. The Department of Sheltering and Animal Control, descended from one of the major founding programs of The HSUS, became the Companion Animals section in 1983. In an extended process that was not complete until the late 1980s, ISAP gave way to divisions devoted to animal research issues and the welfare of farm animals. Field Services, Education, Marketing, Publications, Public Relations, Government Affairs, and Administration and Data Services eventually were organized along the same lines.

With such a differentiation of labor and talent available, The HSUS was able to provide most of the guests for *Pet Action Line*, the weekly television program it began to co-sponsor in 1984. Accepted for broadcast by 150 of 180 public television stations the year it debuted, it represented a new chapter in the history of The HSUS—its breakthrough into mass media markets.[101]

By the early 1980s, with many of the previous generation's disputants retired

HSUS President John A. Hoyt (right) receives a check for $65,450 from actresses Vicki Lawrence (left) and Betty White during an episode of the quiz show Dream House, *hosted by Bob Eubanks (center).*

or deceased, and the two organizations closer to agreement on many issues that had once divided them, the deep-seated animus between The HSUS and AHA had also faded away. Hoyt made a special point of acknowledging AHA President Martin Passaglia as a special guest at the 1984 annual conference of The HSUS. By then, too, there was an established pattern of employees leaving one group to join the staff of the other.[102]

The HSUS and the Animal Rights Movement

The 1980s witnessed an extraordinary flourishing of concern about animals and a proliferation of new organizations. Many of them were grassroots groups motivated by the philosophies of Peter Singer, Tom Regan, Ph.D., and other thinkers who had helped to raise the question of animals' treatment within the fields of moral and environmental philosophy. With the flourishing of an animal rights philosophy, which in its purest form rejected any human use of animals, and with the emergence of groups motivated by animal rights and animal liberation ideologies in the 1980s, The HSUS faced new challenges. The organization born in antiestablishmentarian politics now found itself broadly acknowledged—and sometimes criticized—as the "establishment" group of record.

The crowd was enthusiastic at the Mobilization for Animals rally in Boston, one of several rallies held simultaneously nationwide in 1983.

There was hardly any animal organization that did not have to come to terms with the influence of the new approaches. For the most part, Hoyt saw them as a positive force, providing new energy and urgency to the struggle for animals, recruiting countless new persons to the cause, sparking the formation of new organizations at all levels, and helping The HSUS to better identify its own goals and priorities. Growing interest in animals and their well-being also promised to bring unprecedented social power, with philosophers, attorneys, educators, politicians, scientists, and other influential professionals coming into the work. Hoyt wanted to place The HSUS at the heart of the effort to channel the interest of these new constituencies into further progress for animals. He was enthusiastic about Richard Morgan's Mobilization for Animals, and The HSUS was a major supporter of the primate center rallies staged by the Mobilization in 1983. At least one staff member, Michael Fox, frequently expressed his philosophical affinity with animal rights, and Tom Regan received the Joseph Wood Krutch Medal in 1986, in recognition of his outstanding intellectual contributions to the work. The HSUS benefited in many ways from the extraordinary spread of concern for animals, and Hoyt was comfortable talking about the potential for collegial endeavors, referring to the groups collectively as those "in the animal welfare/animal rights" movement."[103]

At other times and in other respects, however, the complexity of the new landscape was less encouraging. HSUS staff members shared in the broader disillusionment that followed in the wake of the Mobilization rallies, which saw virtually no follow-up. Hoyt admitted to some uncertainty about The HSUS's proper relationship to the thousands of grassroots activists taking to the streets and participating in direct action rallies. He was, moreover, skeptical about the degree to which the new dogmas would take hold within the broader society and deeply concerned about the implications of acts like the direct liberation of animals and civil disobedience. Among other things, he believed, widespread alienation of possible allies and a wicked backlash from opponents were sure to result from extralegal tactics.[104]

At the same time, cooperation with avowed animal rights groups was not always productive or satisfactory. Some of the groups with which The HSUS forged temporary alliances proved to be difficult partners, and this also shaded opinion within The HSUS concerning the wisdom of cooperation with such organizations.

Finally, Hoyt admitted, in the era of the animal rights movement's rise, it was important for The HSUS "to pause, assess, and define just where, as an animal-protection organization, we are." With the rise of challenging new philosophies, he told the audience at The HSUS's 1988 conference,

> Those of us who had been working for the protection of animals for decades were [now being] viewed with both suspicion and disdain. We were castigated because the change we were seeking was not all-encompassing; we were censured for our willingness to accept compromise, even though such compromise often resulted in achievement; and we were condemned for being successful, for realizing both organizational growth and financial success. We were made to feel guilty and, all too often, we permitted ourselves to feel guilty.[105]

In such a changing environment, Hoyt told another audience, it was important for The HSUS "to continue to be The HSUS." Perhaps the organization would "not be the shining star in the new dawn's light, nor the darling of those who would alter the course of history in a moment's time." Nevertheless, for decades The HSUS had been "affirming loudly and clearly the ethical and moral dimensions of animal protection." It would continue to do so, "growing both internally and externally, both spiritually and materially, while ever maintaining a compassion for both animals and people."[106]

While The HSUS did not embrace the philosophy of animal rights, its articulation helped to prompt a shift toward holism in The HSUS's language and perspective. Hoyt supported Fox's efforts to synthesize environmental concern with regard for animals in a worldview Fox termed "humane stewardship," an antidote to the misconstruction of Judeo-Christian stewardship and the dominance of Cartesian thought that many believed had harmed animals' situation in the world. An ecologically sensitive humaneness would include consideration for all nonsentient creation as well as for animals. Fox sometimes framed the argument as a question of rights. In a 1978 interview, entitled "Animal Rights—An Ethical Examination," Fox told a reporter that animals had three rights, "the right to exist," "the right to minimal or no suffering," and "the right to fulfillment," by which he meant the opportunity to indulge their most basic behavioral and biological requirements. At the same time, Fox continued, "Rights are always relative; they can never be absolute." When the interests of animals and humans conflicted, animals' rights ended.[107]

While staff members stopped short of arguing that animals had a legal personhood, they clearly expressed their belief that animals were "entitled to humane treatment and to equal and fair consideration." There was an "ethical imperative to work toward the legal recognizing of their rights and respect for their intrinsic worth and interests."[108] The organization's approach was encoded in a new mission statement drafted in 1997 and revised in 2002: "The HSUS envisions a world in which people satisfy the physical and emotional needs of domestic animals; protect wild animals and their environments; and change their interaction with other animals, evolving from exploitation and harm to respect and compassion."

One place Hoyt sought to spread the message during these years was the veterinary community. For a time he served on the Board of Managers of the University of Pennsylvania School of Veterinary Medicine, and the school's dean served on the board of The HSUS. At a gathering held at the school, Hoyt admonished future members of the profession that

> [if] the veterinarian should imagine that he or she can ignore or remain isolated from this movement and its implications for human/animal relationships, it is a delusion pure and simple. For it is you, and especially you as the healers and ministers to animal suffering, who will be called upon to stand front and center in the challenges this movement will ultimately generate.[109]

As it happened, this attempt to forge a closer relationship with the veterinary medical profession foundered when Dean Robert Marshak, D.V.M., proved himself to be an opponent of reforms espoused by The HSUS. A better bridge emerged after ISAP Associate Director Andrew Rowan left The HSUS to accept a dean's position at Tufts University School of Veterinary Medicine. There, under Dean Franklin Loew, D.V.M. (1939–2003), a veterinarian with a strong commitment to scholarly and technical approaches to improving animal well-being, a climate conducive to cooperation emerged. At the Tufts Center for Animals and Public Policy, Rowan sponsored *Anthrozoös*, an academic journal devoted to animal welfare concerns; tried to enhance the network of scholars and scientists who had once worked mainly through the now-defunct ISAP journal; and initiated a master's degree program in animals and public policy that by the 1990s was regularly placing students within the junior-level staff ranks of The HSUS and other organizations. When Loew joined the HSUS board in 1999, it marked the culmination of a long-standing goal to recruit a suitable and committed veterinary professional into The HSUS at the board level.[110]

Without question, the most serious liability posed by the explosion of concern for animals in the 1980s was the willingness of some people to pursue illegal and even violent actions against users of animals. Here, The HSUS faced the inevitable hazard of guilt by imputation, as critics from the medical, agricultural, millinery, and outdoor recreation fields sought to tarnish the reputation of The HSUS with unfounded claims about its affiliation with the perpetrators of illegal action.

The HSUS met this threat in 1981 by articulating a set of antiviolence principles, as Hoyt stressed the need to "do battle in ways that will not only serve the well-being of animals, but at the same time preserve and advance our own dignity and decency." This conviction guided The HSUS's response to many of the tumultuous events of the 1980s. In 1991, Hoyt collaborated with the ASPCA's John Kullberg and MSPCA President Gus Thornton, D.V.M., on the development of a set of "Joint Resolutions for the 1990s," inviting five thousand animal advocacy groups to ratify them; the document included a prominent endorsement of nonviolence.[111]

The rise of the animal rights movement certainly helped to transform the landscape in which The HSUS had to operate. "We had to identify against what they said and did," Hoyt recalled, speaking of the challenges posed by the newer groups. There were, moreover, a handful of staff resignations or dismissals that reflected differences in opinion about the way forward. There were also changes in emphasis brought about by the fact of robust competition and more aggressive campaigning by other groups. There were some instances, as in the decision to develop a stronger response to Project WILD (see chapter 6), where the activities of other groups spurred The HSUS to commit itself more seriously to a given campaign. Such a shift in emphasis also occurred in relation to the HSUS position on vegetarianism. Although many vegetarians had supported the organization throughout its history, the majority of its constituents were not vegetarian. Until the 1990s the organization was very reticent on the topic, and it received only the most halting endorsement or mention by HSUS officials. The HSUS moved beyond this impasse by including vegetarianism broadly within the pluralist framework of a Three Rs (reduction, replacement, and refinement) approach to the pain and suffering of farm animals (see chapter 2).[112]

The **Animal Activist Alert** *was founded in 1983.*

Generally, however, in the midst of the philosophical and practical firestorms that characterized the 1980s and 1990s, The HSUS hewed to its basic, long-term strategies, seeking to bring substantive, long-lasting change in the ways that animals were regarded, used, and cared for. Board and staff navigated the challenges raised by the advent of the animal rights movement well. Changes in program and policy followed the evolution of scientific and practical insights about animal welfare and strategic determinations that took account of the broad landscape of opportunity in the political, social, and cultural realms.

Heightened competition for the animal protection dollar from the early 1980s onward certainly drove The HSUS to nurture an increasingly public campaign strategy. The organization created staff positions for monitoring the AWA, coordinating the Henry Spira-led Draize test initiatives, and other specialized assignments. In 1983 The HSUS enhanced its legislative alert system through the introduction of the *Animal Activist Alert*, a quarterly publication designed to reach motivated advocates with timely news concerning legislation for animal welfare. The following year The HSUS launched a campaign department to organize its staff resources around selected issues of interest. As Patricia Forkan, who oversaw many of the relevant sections, observed, program experts were not always practiced or adept at mounting campaign-based initiatives. The organization of a campaigns department with such longtime personnel as Kathy Bauch and Pat Ragan made it possible to bring together the knowledge, experience, and assets of staff members from different sections, for the purposes of mounting targeted campaign initiatives. Over the years, this would result in such actions as Peter Lovenheim's shareholder resolution on foie gras, the Beautiful Choice™ campaign on cosmetics testing, and The Shame of Fur™, all of which showcased The HSUS's growing ability to project itself more forcefully into the public eye, while cultivating a dignified but morally energized posture of disapproval toward some of the era's most conspicuous cruelties.[113]

Defining Cruelty

One of The HSUS's most historically significant contributions has been its instrumental role in the development of a modern understanding of cruelty. In its early years, The HSUS board and staff were burdened by a dilemma that still endures—the fact that the term *cruelty* could encompass "a broad range of human behaviors and motivational states," including sadism, neglect, expedience, lack of knowledge, and "normative" juvenile behavior (like harming insects). Having to advance the cause within the framework of hundred-year-old anticruelty statutes—sometimes quite rudimentary, and often unchanged since the nineteenth century—complicated the work of 1950s-era advocates just as it continues to frustrate the goals of their successors today.[114]

Nowhere was this more challenging than in the case of broad-scale institutional uses of animals, like those that occurred in agriculture and in research, testing, and education. Quite often, these arenas of use were explicitly exempt from coverage under anticruelty statutes, so that there could be no resort whatsoever to the law in securing any measure of protection for the animals used. It was not a coincidence that The HSUS made its first legislative priorities the passage of a humane slaughter law and an act to regulate the use of animals in research.

Even so, as an early copy writer for the *HSUS News* put it, echoing the adage of Matthew 10:29, "The HSUS concentrates on major national cruelties to animals but finds time almost every day to see the sparrow's fall." While The HSUS had no police powers or law enforcement authority of its own, years of experience with crimes involving animals, and the fact that they could be deputized as agents of a local authority if need be, gave regional and headquarters staff substantial expertise and credibility that made them valuable partners for police, prosecutors, magistrates, and judges. From the 1950s, when Fred Myers and other staff members swore out complaints against rodeo cowboys, Tennessee Walking Horse enthusiasts, pound keepers, and medical scientists from Washington, D.C., to Los Angeles, California (see chapters 3 and 7), to the early twenty-first century, when headquarters and regional staff members testified as expert witnesses in judicial trials and legislative proceedings in literally every state, The HSUS was at the heart of evolving conceptions of cruelty in law, psychology, biology, philosophy, history, religion, sociology, and other fields. Between 1954 and 2004, HSUS investigators, field workers, attorneys, and program specialists were involved in hundreds of cases where they helped to explain to judges and juries the nature of the cruelty charge at hand, to clarify the evidence presented in its support, and to provide advice and assistance in postconviction and postacquittal hearings whenever the custody

of animals was at issue. During its second quarter-century, the organization became an internationally important source of data and information concerning the many forms of abuse, neglect, and exploitation of animals that come under the designation of *cruelty*.[115]

Like their predecessors as far back as the nineteenth century, post-1954 advocates were forced to acknowledge the numerous contradictions in the social, cultural, and legal definitions of cruelty and to face the inevitable clash of interests that could occur whenever animal protectionists sought to resolve them in favor of animals. For The HSUS, at times, this involved negotiating the meaning of cruelty in some very sensitive contexts, most notably in the cases of ritual slaughter for food and ritual animal sacrifice.[116]

An important development in this decades-long effort to advance public conceptions of cruelty was the appointment of Randall Lockwood, Ph.D., an assistant professor of psychology at the State University of New York, Stony Brook, as head of a new HSUS division, Higher Education, in 1984. Lockwood had earned his Ph.D. under Michael Fox at Washington University in St. Louis and shared Fox's deep interest in ethology. At The HSUS, Lockwood pursued his corollary interests in the epidemiology of dog attacks, the interaction of people and animals in child-abusing families, and the association between cruelty to animals and violence against humans. In ensuing years, he became the key player in The HSUS's interactions with law enforcement and social work agencies. In the late 1990s, this resulted in the formation of The HSUS's First Strike™ initiative (see chapters 4 and 6), a signature HSUS program that raised awareness of and provided empirical evidence for the links between cruelty to animals and harmful and violent interpersonal relationships. Lockwood and other HSUS staff members firmly established the link—which had been an anecdotal perception since the early modern era, when John Locke, among others, noted its significance—as a demonstrated truth of modern social science. In doing so, they did more than validate the importance of cruelty to animals as a marker of human social deviance—they also led social service, law enforcement, prosecutorial, and judicial personnel to think about and treat cruelty to animals more seriously because of the harm it did to those animals. This directly buttressed efforts to upgrade a variety of cruel behaviors to felony status throughout the United States.[117]

Building Bridges with Environmentalism

During the 1980s The HSUS very consciously initiated steps to place the question of animals' well-being and treatment within the broader context of environmental concern. One impetus for The HSUS's attempts to position itself vis à vis the broader environmental movement

flowed from its many years of experience on whaling, sealing, and wildlife trade issues. Its concerns in these areas frequently brought staff members into close interaction with representatives of environmental groups.[118]

At the same time, The HSUS began to focus on the deepening crisis of rainforest destruction, which, among other consequences, was eliminating millions of acres a year of animal habitat. Its campaign against the international trade in wild birds, and its concern about the use of rainforest acreage for raising cattle for the American fast-food market, also heightened awareness of the general plight of the world's tropical environments. The HSUS became a supporting member of the Rainforest Action Network and active in its efforts to press for reforms at the World Bank and other institutions whose policies often resulted in rainforest destruction.[119]

Such concerns led to the creation of the Center for the Respect of Life and the Environment (CRLE) as a division of The HSUS in 1986 to promote regard for nature and an ethic of compassion toward all sentient life. Similar commitments inspired the decision of The HSUS to affiliate with the Interfaith Council for the Protection of Animals and Nature. Through these organizations, The HSUS sought to sustain initiatives aimed at religious institutions and institutions of higher learning, to promote the philosophical and practical foundations of a humane and sustainable society. As it developed CRLE provided secretariat support for a set of global initiatives sponsored jointly with other institutions. It also promoted commitments to sustainability in academic institutions and attempted to lead organized religious institutions to embrace ecocentric, as opposed to anthropocentric, thinking.[120]

The CRLE logo was created in 1986.

In 1989 The HSUS's humane education division, NAAHE, took a new name consonant with the broad strategy of realignment in relation to environmentalism. It became the National Association for Humane and Environmental Education (NAHEE), a name that not only acknowledged the interdependence of concern for animals and environment, but also accurately reflected the division's long-standing integration of environmentalism and humaneness in its program materials.

In 1991, one year after playing a major role in the celebration of the thirtieth annual Earth Day, The HSUS launched another spin-off entity, EarthVoice, as its global environmental arm. "Part of what we wanted to do [by creating our own environmental group]," Hoyt recalled, "was to get the environmental movement to be more animal protection conscious." Under EarthVoice's auspices The HSUS tried to promote an ethic of the earth to decision makers and institutions in the United States and elsewhere, to position the organization as a global environmental leader, and to ensure its participation in environmental diplomacy.[121]

Patricia Forkan and actor Woody Harrelson celebrated Earth Day in 1990.

When Paul Irwin assumed the presidency of The HSUS, he pressed to establish the organization as one that would protect land. Having observed the importance of protecting land in Africa, he was convinced that The HSUS should create an affiliate to preserve land for wildlife both domestically and abroad. In 1993 the board of directors approved the establishment of the Wildlife Land Trust (WLT), which allowed donors to extend protection to animals through the creation of "shelters without walls," another sign of this expansion of scope. To head the division, The HSUS chose John F. Kullberg, Ed.D. (1939–2003), formerly president of the ASPCA. By 2003 the WLT owned or held protective covenants for seventy properties in twenty-one states and four foreign nations, encompassing approximately sixty thousand acres.[122]

John F. Kullberg, former president of the ASPCA and Guide Dogs for the Blind, joined the HSUS Wildlife Land Trust in the early 1990s.

The HSUS also placed its weight behind the Earth Charter, launched in 1994 as a post-Rio Earth Summit initiative to promulgate a set of principles for guiding human relationships with other forms of life on the planet. To the Rio Summit's efforts to promote global support for a sustainable development and environmental conservation program founded on holistic principles, the Earth Charter sought to add, in John Hoyt's words, "a concern for the value and integrity of individual animals in the larger Earth community. For the first time within such a document, *individual* animals are accorded appropriate recognition and consideration."[123]

At the turn of the twenty-first century, The HSUS's successes in building bridges with the environmental movement lagged behind the organization's demonstrated accomplishments on behalf of animals. Despite The HSUS's outreach program, mainstream environmentalism still generally rejected the concern for individual animals and their suffering that gave birth to organized animal protection and remained aloof from the broad range of humane concerns. There was no major environmental organization seriously or consistently committed to the humane treatment of animals. It was not for lack of effort on the part of The HSUS, however.

The HSUS purchased 700 Professional Drive, Gaithersburg, Maryland, as its operations center in 1991 and moved the majority of its staff there in 1992.

Toward the Twenty-First Century

During the 1990s The HSUS—an organization formed to instigate change—itself became the subject of rapid transformation. It was, above all, an organization of almost unequaled size and sweep in the field of animal protection. The HSUS's reputation and resources allowed it to recruit outstanding staff members from other organizations, including AHA, Defenders of Wildlife, The Fund for Animals, the MSPCA, the ASPCA, People for the Ethical Treatment of Animals (PETA), the RSPCA, the World Society for the Protection of Animals (WSPA), numerous local humane societies throughout the country, and institutions of higher learning.

The result was a staff of unparalleled strength, comprised of professionals from a variety of backgrounds, including animal behavior, wildlife science, public policy, social science, trade economics, veterinary medicine, disaster relief, the legal profession, law enforcement, and the private sector. By 2003 The HSUS constituted a virtual "learned faculty" of animal protection, with more than fifty professional staff, some half of whom had either doctoral or other higher degrees. The organization encompassed over three hundred animal issues within its remit. In the case of larger issues—like the incorporation of poultry under the protective aegis of the Humane Slaughter Act, the reduction of pain and distress in animal research, or the continuing encroachment of hunters and trappers on America's National Wildlife Refuges—not so readily resolved, The HSUS's engagement was durable and continuing. Even so, staff members kept their eyes open for the "silver bullet" issues—like the use of cat and dog fur in garment production or the distribution of "crush" videos catering to the fetish for stiletto-heel animal deaths—where quick, well-timed, or assertive action could either cripple or extinguish a specific cruelty.

By the 1990s the HSUS headquarters could no longer accommodate a rapidly expanding staff, and the organization began to explore the prospects for a move to a larger building. A generous bequest from board member Regina Bauer Frankenberg (d. 1991) made it possible to relocate most of the staff to a suitable facility in the outlying Maryland suburbs in 1992. At the same time, The HSUS was able to retain ownership of 2100 L Street, in Washington, D.C., which remained the principal place of business for key executive, legal, legislative, and other staff.

Of the many personnel changes that occurred during the decade, the most important centered on the HSUS presidency itself. In 1992 Treasurer and Chief Financial Officer Paul G. Irwin became president, while John Hoyt retained the title of chief executive officer. At the same time, longtime Vice President for Program and Communications Patricia Forkan became executive vice president. In 1997 Irwin assumed the mantle of CEO when Hoyt retired. That same year Andrew N. Rowan returned to The HSUS as senior vice president for Research, Education, and International Issues after almost fifteen years as a dean at the Tufts University School of Veterinary Medicine. Nineteen ninety-seven was also the year that Tom Waite joined The HSUS as treasurer and chief financial officer. The era's other important hires included Wayne Pacelle (Fund for Animals, 1994), Dennis White (AHA, 1995), Martha Armstrong (MSPCA, 1996), Neil Trent (WSPA, 1997), Mike Appleby (University of Edinburgh, 2001), and Gretchen Wyler (Ark Trust, 2002).[124]

Change was occurring at the board level as well. In 1989 K. William Wiseman succeeded Coleman Burke as chairman. In 1995 Wiseman was followed by O.J. Ramsey, Esq. In 2000 David Wiebers, M.D., succeeded Ramsey as chairman. A professor of neurology at the Mayo Institute, Wiebers was a founding member of the Scientific Advisory Board created in 1991 to assist the work of the Animal Research Issues section.[125]

The major growth of The HSUS took place in the heyday of direct mail solicitation, and as the architect of The HSUS's membership expansion for over a quarter-century, Irwin had facilitated its steady incorporation of strong talent from both within and outside the organized animal protection movement as well as the creation of the organizational infrastructure necessary to sustain staff members' work. In 1994, under Irwin's leadership, The HSUS set its sights on having five million constituents within five years, a goal it would realize ahead of schedule. Between 1994 and 1997, its constituency grew from 2.2 to 5.7 million supporters, and by 2003 The HSUS's constituent base reached 7.6 million people. Between 1983 and 2003, The HSUS's annual budget grew from $3.5 million to $70 million, and the number of full-time staff increased from about 60 to 280.[126]

As direct mail fund raising became more expensive and less effective by the mid-1990s, The HSUS, like other organizations, began to search for other ways to produce income. A catalog featuring popular animal-related items—artwork, calendars, clothing, crafts, scarves, ties, and more—proved to be especially successful, as did licensing agreements that placed The HSUS's name on a select few items sold in commercial outlets. After The HSUS went on-line in 1996–97, it began to explore the potential of e-commerce as a revenue-building source as well.

After assuming the positions of CEO and president in 1997, Paul Irwin launched an intensive strategic planning process designed to strengthen The HSUS's performance in all respects. Staff members at all levels participated in the development of mission statements for their respective departments and analyzed their work in light of identifiable assets, weaknesses, opportunities, and threats. The HSUS relied on focus groups to refine its outreach to members and other supporters. This resulted in the decision to replace the HSUS News, which had carried substantial reports and updates on the organization's activities, with All Animals, an AOL Time Warner-produced publication that better served the organization's interest in reaching those who wanted to help but who did not necessarily want to receive detailed and sometimes graphic reports of The HSUS's cruelty and investigations work. In 1999 The HSUS introduced the Humane Activist to replace its Animal Activist Alert. This and a series of newsletters published by specific divisions helped to deliver timely action notices to supportive individuals.

As might be expected in the case of an organization in the midst of rapid and unprecedented growth, The HSUS had its share of personnel-related challenges. In the mid-1990s, Irwin initiated an employee evaluation program, assigning staff members Kay Benedict and Randall Lockwood to devise a system appropriate to The HSUS. In 1996 the necessity for a modern scheme of performance review; complaint administration; recruitment and retention; employee development; wage, salary, and benefit structures; and employee training and development led to the establishment of a human resources division.

The HSUS website www.hsus.org had more than 2.3 million visitors in 2003.

In the 1990s The HSUS began to experiment with new media. Among other things, it moved to create a department for video technology projects, with in-house production capability, to produce and distribute broadcast-quality programming, to assist staff members with their videotape and photographic documentary needs, and to further the organization's educational mission. After 1997 the department was also involved in enhancement of The HSUS's website, making background literature and videotaped material available to the public in accessible and instant formats. The HSUS's collaboration with RealNetworks and the Glaser Progress Foundation resulted in Animal Channel (1998), which permitted The HSUS to reach millions worldwide with broadcast-quality webcast material.

In 2002 The HSUS gained another valuable avenue for promoting its visibility and program concerns within the major media by incorporating the Ark Trust and its annual Genesis Awards ceremony. Founded by Gretchen Wyler and annually televised (first on Discovery Channel, then on Animal Planet), the Ark Trust event recognized outstanding work in electronic and print media that contributes to the advancement of animal protection. As The HSUS's Hollywood office, it would continue its efforts to promote and recognize animal-sensitive programming in a variety of cultural forms.

As the century came to a close, The HSUS also made plans to strengthen its stature and influence in the field of animals and public policy. In 2001 the organization launched *The State of the Animals*, a biennial series from The HSUS's new book imprint, Humane Society Press. Its goals included the development of new perspectives on particular issues, the identification of ways to measure progress in the field, the dissemination of better statistical analysis and assessments of current trends and proposed strategies, and—broadly conceived—the maturation of a public policy wing of the society. The inaugural volume included essays on the history of animal protection, changing public policy perspectives on cruelty, a survey of social attitudes toward animals, reviews of program areas involving the use of animals in agriculture and medical research, the status of captive and urban wildlife populations, the science of wildlife contraception, and the impact of the World Trade Organization on international animal welfare concerns. The essays in *The State of the Animals II: 2003* reflected The HSUS's increasing focus on the appraisal and resolution of problems of international scope.

By 2004, to a significant extent, day-to-day management within The HSUS had passed to its vice presidents, who covered four program areas (companion animals, wildlife, laboratory animals, and farm animals), investigations, research, education and international concerns, communications and government relations, research and educational outreach, field and disaster services, administration, information services and technology, and human resources. In fact, the organization's growing complexity necessitated the creation of a class of senior vice presidents, reflecting not just longevity of service but also added responsibilities, including supervision of other senior staff.

There was an increased differentiation of responsibility and function at other levels of the organization as well. Program specialists worked on a variety of issues, and it was rarer for them to be involved in discussions

Gretchen Wyler, Genesis Awards founder and vice president of the HSUS Hollywood Office (middle), joined cohosts Eric Roberts and Gena Lee Nolin at the 2003 Genesis Awards.

GETTY IMAGES

about policy and approach in areas for which they were not responsible than had been the case as late as the mid-1980s. At the same time, while individual divisions tended to be focused more inwardly, they continued to collaborate on specific issues or campaigns calling for a multidisciplinary approach. In 1996, for example, the Farm Animals, Investigations, and Wildlife sections collaborated on a report on the promotion of an exotic meats industry in the United States. Similar cross-departmental collaboration occurred in campaigns to restrict federal monies for experiments on wild-caught primates (Animal Research Issues and Wildlife), and on the SafeCats™ program, which addressed the long-standing issue of the harm outdoor cats caused to bird life (Companion Animals and Wildlife).[127]

Ballots over Bullets

An important hallmark of Irwin's tenure was the revitalization of The HSUS's Government Affairs department. Once constrained by the limits of financial and staff resources, the department came into its own during the late 1990s, and by 2000 it was leading the animal protection field in its provision of information and services to constituents, grassroots activists, community leaders, and government officials and their staffs. In the early years of the new century, HSUS government affairs staffers were responsible for securing increased funding for enforcement of the Humane Slaughter Act and the AWA and were beginning to succeed in efforts to "de-fund" objectionable programs like animal damage control and the mink farmers' subsidy.

Wayne Pacelle directed successful ballot initiatives in the 1990s.

Another way in which the department distinguished itself during this period was its successful use of referendum and initiative to address the failure of democratic process in state and federal legislatures. After Wayne Pacelle joined the staff in 1994, The HSUS began to reassess the viability of referendum and initiative campaigns in select states. While working at The Fund for Animals, Pacelle had been involved with three initiatives, two of which had succeeded. At The HSUS, however, memory ran long concerning the Ohio antitrapping referendum loss in 1977. Saturation advertising campaigns by the hunting and trapping lobbies in the 1970s and 1980s led to humane movement losses in Oregon and South Dakota in 1980 and in Maine in 1983. More recently, the ProPets coalition, of which The HSUS was a principal supporter, had lost a number of local referenda concerning pound seizure. Resistance to the referendum process within The HSUS was strong.[128]

That resistance faded, however, as Pacelle guided The HSUS through two successful ballot initiatives in 1994. In the first Arizona voters banned trapping on their state's substantial public lands. In the second Oregon voters supported a prohibition of black-bear baiting and the use of hounds in hunting black bears and cougars. In the wake of these successes, the referendum and initiative movement hit its stride, and the proliferation of ballot measures leading up to the 1996 election cycle led the *Los Angeles Times* to declare 1996 the "Year of the Animal."[129]

Sympathetic voters certainly delivered, supporting animal-friendly measures in six of eight states, in the face of a $4 million spending frenzy by the National Rifle Association and other hunting and trapping organizations. In supporting the measures, citizens eliminated several kinds of egregious hunting and trapping practices at the state level, introducing an unprecedented element of democratic process to wildlife management, long dominated by parochial interests that rarely denied hunters and trappers their demonstrated wishes and still more rarely honored the wishes of those who objected to repugnant and unsporting practices.[130]

The majority of the initiatives focused on wildlife issues. Polling attitudes about specific practices in hunting or wildlife management, The HSUS built local and regional coalitions that drafted initiative language, gathered signatures, and pressed for public and political support. In most of these campaigns, as distinct from many similar organizations working through the referendum and initiative process, The HSUS spent almost no funds on professional signature- and petition-gathering services.[131]

In response to the setbacks they suffered, consumptive use interests worked with legislators to place countermeasures before the electorate in some states. The HSUS did not bother to contest the handful of hunter-supported initiatives that simply added "the right to hunt" to state constitutions, regarding these as symbolic and vacuous measures. On the other hand staff members vigorously contested four antidemocratic proposals that attempted to make it virtually impossible to use the initiative process, defeating three of them.[132]

The HSUS's successes even inspired a backlash campaign from the U.S. Sportsmen's Alliance, a consumptive exploitation lobby that originally formed as the Wildlife Legislative Fund of America during the 1977 Ohio antitrapping campaign. In 2003 the Alliance launched efforts to interfere with The HSUS's commercial partnerships with major corporations. It was a campaign born of frustration, for the Alliance had suffered crushing defeats in the referendum and initiative campaigns in which it sought to intervene, despite spending millions of dollars in the affected states.

The initiative and referendum process brought tangible benefits to the humane movement, benefits that went well beyond the ratification and implementation of reforms and the alleviation of animal suffering in specific contexts. It brought tens of thousands of citizens into the movement's scope, as petition signers, voters, volunteers, and campaigners. It also helped to shape coverage of organized animal protection at a time when some observers worried that the cause was drawing less, and usually less sympathetic, attention. It was, finally, a vital new outlet for the idealism and energy of those who cared about making a difference for animals.[133]

Between 1990 and 2002, humane advocates involved in statewide ballot efforts triumphed in twenty-four of thirty-eight campaigns. In campaigns where The HSUS was centrally involved, Pacelle estimated, the record was seventeen wins and five losses. Animal protectionists won five of eight measures on trapping, four of six on hound hunting and baiting, three of three on cockfighting, and two of two on airborne hunting. They had also won measures to prohibit gestation crates, canned hunts, and horse slaughter.[134]

One of the most encouraging aspects of the referendum and initiative campaigns was their reliance on direct democracy—the clear expression and fulfillment of the public's desire to protect animals from cruelty. While the post-World War II humane movement frequently benefited from strong and fair-minded cooperation of politicians of every political persuasion, there were also many instances of heavy-handed and disingenuous sabotage of legislative, judicial, and administrative decrees favorable to animals. In the U.S. Congress and the state legislatures, such subterfuge typically involved the obdurate members of wildlife and agriculture committees—legislators deeply vested in or committed to the commercial, political, or ideological interests that encompass the broad universe of animal exploitation. In 2002 such interests demonstrated both their potency and their readiness to thwart public opinion and the equitable procedures of congressional politics by "skinning" the federal farm bill, which contained an unprecedented number of amendments that members of both the House and Senate had approved. In defiance of stipulations that conferees work only to reconcile the differences between House and Senate versions of the bill, members of the House "agrigarchy"—a handful of farm-state legislators working behind closed doors—scuttled House-approved amendments that would have closed serious loopholes in federal laws restricting animal fighting, requiring the euthanasia of downed animals at stockyards, and compelling proper enforcement of the decades-old Humane Slaughter Act. They also gutted a Senate-approved amendment that would have brought an end to the trade in ursine gall bladders and parts, at the time taking a terrible toll on North America's bear population. The House conferees also forced the abandonment of the Senate-backed Puppy Protection Act, which called upon commercial breeders to permit their dogs greater socialization and to limit breeding practices according to animals' age or estrus cycle.[135]

The House conferees did not stop there, either, moving to dilute and undermine existing statutory and administrative regulations that ensured animal welfare. Acquiescing to his proposal to amend the AWA, they helped their retiring Senate colleague Jesse Helms (R-NC) make his final public legacy the permanent denial of the AWA's minimal-care protections to birds, rats, and mice. In doing so, they ignored entreaties from former Senator Bob Dole (R-KS) and other legislators who had long been constructively engaged with the issue as well as from major corporations with strong commitments to animal welfare science in their own corporate testing programs. It was an abrupt and bitter end to more than thirty years of negotiation, legislation, administrative and judicial rulings, and public debate about the desirability of extending such protection to all of the species used in research, testing, and education.

Patricia Forkan and John Grandy listened to English translations of speakers at the CITES meeting in 1994.

Through hard work and intense political engagement with legislators from both major parties, The HSUS had hoped to make the 2002 farm bill the vehicle of unprecedented good for animals. Instead, in the hands of a few unrestrained legislators determined to impose their will not only upon their colleagues but also upon the American public, it became emblematic of the breakdown in democratic process that left the United States lagging behind other developed nations in efforts to address some of the worst examples of indifference to the pain and suffering of animals.[136]

The Globalization of Humane Work

The HSUS began participating in international campaigns for animals in the 1950s. From an early stage, the organization operated from the assumption that many issues—and their solutions—transcended national boundaries. In their turn, Fred Myers, John Hoyt, and Paul Irwin all served in official capacities within WSPA, supporting campaigns that sought to project the collective influence of member societies into situations where animals suffered or died as a result of human cruelty or neglect. Especially after 1980 staff members were far more active participants in meetings of international bodies such as the International Whaling Commission (IWC) and the Convention on International Trade in Endangered Species of Wild Fauna and Flora (CITES).

This said, the determination to make The HSUS an internationally significant organization and to project its influence globally coalesced in the 1990s and gained ever-increasing importance within the organization's program areas. Issues once thought of as wholly or mostly domestic rapidly acquired international dimensions and necessitated the revision of conventional lobbying and political techniques to meet the emerging challenge. In a few instances, The HSUS had to recapitulate—on a worldwide basis—public awareness and political campaigns undertaken years earlier in the United States.[137]

The original HSI logo (above) and the current logo (below).

In 1991 the organization enhanced its capacity to address such concerns and to actively promote humane work in other nations by establishing its own international arm, Humane Society International (HSI), to provide direct relief to those trying to assist animals in other nations.[138] The idea was not to replace WSPA, but to go places where WSPA was not going—to places where there was great need, as in Russia, Romania, and Mexico. "We wanted to be an ally for WSPA, not a competitor," John Hoyt recalled.[139]

By 1998 HSI had developed a full program agenda that concentrated on extending The HSUS's existing assets—resources, personnel, and expertise—toward the resolution of identifiable needs in other nations. At the same time, The HSUS continued its support for WSPA, with Paul Irwin and Andrew Rowan serving on the WSPA board and HSUS/HSI staff supporting WSPA colleagues in a variety of situations.

In 2001, following several years of exploring such a partnership, The HSUS came together with Professor David W. Macdonald of Lady Margaret Hall (LMH) and the Wildlife Conservation Research Unit at Oxford University to establish a center at LMH focusing on wildlife welfare and the political, economic, and cultural barriers that prevented concern for wild animals' well-being from becoming a subject of wider discussion in most of the world. The central aim of the initiative was the development of ideas and arguments that would allow organizations like The HSUS to press constructive animal welfare proposals (incorporating a recognition of human needs) in the many countries where people also struggle for survival and minimal personal security and welfare standards. The center, intended as a multidisciplinary venture, was situated within a college—LMH—rather than as an academic department at the university. While The HSUS provided seed funding for the project, on the eve of its golden anniversary, The HSUS was still trying to develop a long-term funding base and a roster of partners to support a more substantial budget for the center.[140]

Even as The HSUS committed itself to an expanded role in the international arena, a revolution in global political and commercial affairs was underway. Animal protection work that once had had a national focus now became deeply embedded within international agreements, the complex workings of multinational corporations, and free-trade perspectives. Opportunistic nations now sought to evade or eviscerate legal restrictions against the wild-bird trade, the traffic in ivory, the capture of dolphins in purse-seine nets used in tuna fishing, and the leghold trap. Decades of humane progress were in jeopardy.[141]

Together with such threats, the necessity of monitoring developments concerning the array of treaties, including the IWC, CITES, the Law of the Sea (LOS), the International Standards Organization (ISO), and the Convention on Biological Diversity (CBD), led The HSUS to create a U.N. and Treaties department. The department assumed responsibility for the analysis and observation of international legislation, regulations, and agreements and coordinated appropriate organizational action when necessary. The HSUS gained consultative status at the United Nations, permitting it to develop its ties further with nongovernmental organizations in other nations. In the era of the Global Agreement on Trade and Tariffs (GATT) and the World Trade Organization (WTO), it was necessary for The HSUS to cultivate a global strategic consciousness.[142]

In 2003 the HSUS board of directors approved the first strategic plan for facilitating expansion of The HSUS's international outreach and advocacy. In keeping with The HSUS's steadily expanding commitment to international work, the plan adopted a goal of $10 million for allocation to international programs. The HSUS was one of the few organizations whose work encompassed concern for both animals and the natural environment, and its senior leadership viewed its entry into international campaigns as essential to the safeguarding of animals' well-being within decision-making bodies worldwide. As Paul Irwin, perhaps the strongest supporter of such positioning, observed, "Many times we are the sole voice in defense of animals, even when environmental groups are lobbying in the same forum. We are not deterred when we must stand alone, however. Any international agreement is a bad one if it perpetuates animal exploitation and cruelty."[143]

The HSUS at Fifty

In 2002 Irwin charged now Senior Vice President and Chief of Staff Andrew Rowan with responsibility for coordinating The HSUS's second strategic plan. The objectives Irwin identified were the need for increased visibility, the expansion of the HSUS constituency, the desirability of more "hands-on" relief work, a heightened emphasis on companion animal issues, the promotion of greater program integration, and the extension of educational and public policy outreach. Staff participation included the furnishing of data concerning the number of estimated contacts with the public through personal interaction, press coverage, HSUS publications (including *All Animals, Animal Sheltering, HumaneLines, Kind News,* and *Wild Neighbors News*), websites, and direct mail. This process revealed a rapidly diversifying range of HSUS outreach efforts.

Fred Myers's daughter Tamara Myers Field and Patricia Forkan in spring 2003, at the HSUS operations center in Maryland.

In some ways the plan laid the groundwork for important transformations in management structure and style as well as for changes in The HSUS's program priorities. However, while it included important new strategic and programmatic innovations, the plan sought to build upon the organizational strengths that hundreds of HSUS staff and board members had helped to cultivate during five decades of work for animals: The HSUS's credibility as a source of information, expertise, and action; its ability to reconceptualize and resolve the perceived conflict between human and animal interests in a variety of situations; its capacity to acquire, harness, and disseminate knowledge and advice as a stakeholder in public policy debates concerning animals; and its ability to mobilize staff members, partners, and constituents for concerted action to reduce animal suffering in the world.

A core element of the strategic plan involved the designation of signature programs that would transcend departmental boundaries and become identifiers of The HSUS's capacities and major themes. The programs chosen by the staff to represent the organization were: Pets for Life®; Wild Neighbors™: Living with Wildlife; Animals in Crisis; and Humane Leadership: Taking Action, Shaping Change. These programs encompass, respectively, protection of and regard for pets, the humane management of human-wildlife interactions, a focus on rescuing animals from cruelty and disasters, and attention to The HSUS's role in influencing and promoting policy initiatives and humane education programs.

As The HSUS neared its fiftieth anniversary in 2004, it could count two staff members from the 1960s still in its ranks—Frantz Dantzler (1962) and Dina McDaniel (1968). Personnel from the 1970s and early 1980s—Nina Austenberg, Kay Benedict, John Dommers, Patricia Forkan, Janet Frake, John Grandy,

James Herriot Award Recipients

1987 Paul Harvey
1988 Betty White Ludden
1989 H.I. "Sonny" Bloch
1990 Walter L. Cronkite, Jr.
1991 Roger A. Caras
1992 Thomas Berry
1993 Albert Gore, Jr.
1994 Prince Sadruddin and Princess Catherine Aleya Aga Khan
1995 Lauren Shuler Donner and Richard Donner
1996 Maurice F. Strong
1997 Gretchen Wyler
1999 Oleg Cassini

Special James Herriot Award Recipient

1987 J.A. Wight

THE HSUS/MCNULTY

Ben Hayes, Paul Irwin, Roger Kindler, Murdaugh Madden, Andrew Rowan, Eric Sakach, Deborah Salem, and Ellen Truong—were still with The HSUS as well. While The HSUS was in many ways a different organization from the one that had first employed them, the crucial elements of its founding vision were still in place. It was fully engaged with significant national cruelties, seeking to extend its influence throughout the United States and beyond, and promoting the highest standards of animal care in every conceivable context. The founders' early blend of selfless and pragmatic idealism, nurtured by many others in successive decades, was still the guiding ethos of The HSUS.

Fifty years after its modest beginnings, The HSUS was also the most successful organized expression of humane values in North America, providing virtually unmatched service and expertise and helping to make innovative approaches and technologies available to hundreds of animal care and control organizations throughout the nation and the world. Its encouragement of a moral and spiritual ethic for industrial and postindustrial society; its contributions to the professionalization of concern for animals through the recruitment of qualified, dedicated, and resourceful staff; its steadily expanding participation in relevant policy networks; its encouragement of a sophisticated and modern conception of "cruelty"; its embrace of a responsible, fact-based pursuit of advances in animal protection; and its reliance on an applied science of animal welfare to the issues—all of these characteristics made it an outstanding example of voluntary association in the United States. That it was dedicated to the extension of human moral concern beyond the limits of the species barrier made its success all the more striking.

In 1959 The HSUS produced People and Pets, *its first sound/slide filmstrip to teach children humane values and responsible companion animal care.*

Strength Through Unity

One of the founders of The HSUS and the organization's first executive director, Fred Myers had an early vision that is embodied to a remarkable degree by The HSUS's many programs today. His "Lust to Kill" article—written under the pen name Jonathan Fieldston in 1952—details the inhumane nature of so-called sport hunting and is as applicable today as it was when first published.

From The HSUS's founding in 1954, the organization has created publications to educate the public and promote the protection of animals in homes, in shelters, and in research laboratories.

U.S. Senator Harry F. Byrd, Jr.—flanked by Virginia State Delegate Lucas D. Phillips, HSUS President Oliver Evans, and Loudoun County, Virginia, supervisor William P. Frazer (left to right)—broke ground in 1966 for construction of The HSUS's National Humane Education Center in Waterford, Virginia.

HSUS President John A. Hoyt (right) presented author James Herriot—
the pen name of Yorkshire veterinarian J.A. Wight—with the Joseph
Wood Krutch Medal in 1986 to honor his significant contributions
toward the improvement of life and the environment.

HSUS President Paul G. Irwin (left) and Executive Vice President Patricia Forkan (right) presented actress, founder of The Ark Trust, Inc., and presenter of the annual Genesis Awards Gretchen Wyler (center) with the Herriot Award at the 1998 Animal Care Expo to recognize her efforts to promote and inspire an appreciation of and concern for animals among the public.

THE HSUS/DANTZLER

HSUS President John A. Hoyt presented journalist and radio show host Paul Harvey with the inaugural Herriot Award as Angel Harvey, the Harveys' son Paul Aurant, and Mrs. Edward M. Boehm (left to right) of Boehm Porcelain—designers of the award—looked on in 1987 at The HSUS's Annual Conference.

THE HSUS/KUSTRON

HSUS President Paul G. Irwin (left) joined actor, motivator, and television talk show host Montel Williams (right) to present the Herriot Award to world-renowned couturier Oleg Cassini (center) in 1999 at the Evening of Elegance HSUS benefit gala.

GLENWOOD JACKSON

The National Association for Humane and Environmental Education (NAHEE)—The HSUS's youth education division—produces KIND News™, an award-winning and colorfully engaging classroom newspaper for kindergarten through sixth grade students to promote respect for animals, the environment, and one another, as well as many other activity books for children and publications to help teens become involved with humane issues.

For several years The HSUS has taken humane education courses to children without any other access to them through its regional offices and Native Nations and Rural Area Veterinary Services (RAVS) programs. Here children at the Rosebud Sioux (Sicangu Lakota Oyate) Reservation in South Dakota learn dog-bite prevention strategies.

Actress Betty White, Roger Caras of the ABC television network, actress Ana-Alicia, HSUS President John A. Hoyt, and actress Loretta Swit (left to right) joined the star-studded audience to pay tribute to Jane Goodall, Ph.D., in 1991 at Gombe 30, an event to commemorate the thirtieth anniversary of the beginning of Goodall's research on the behavior of wild chimpanzees in Africa.

THE HSUS/FORKAN

THE HSUS/DANTZLER

Then HSUS Midwest Regional Director Wendell Maddox (left) and HSUS President Paul G. Irwin (right) met at the Tri-Regional Conference in 1993 to discuss the organization's ongoing efforts.

THE HSUS/CANNON

Former HSUS president John A. Hoyt joined former Arizona governor Bruce Babbitt, HSUS board member and Joseph Wood Krutch Medal recipient Amy Freeman Lee, Litt.D., and HSUS President Paul G. Irwin (left to right) at The HSUS's 1992 Annual Conference.

From its beginning, The HSUS has campaigned to reduce the number of wildlife-automobile collisions, first producing a poster in 1956 (above, top) and publishing a brochure in 1997 (above) and updated brochures and bumper stickers in 1999 (above and top right) to alert the public to this threat to both animals and motorists and explain the most effective ways to avoid such collisions before they happen.

THE HUMANE SOCIETY OF THE UNITED STATES

The HSUS launched the successful Shame of Fur campaign in 1988 to educate the public about the cruelties of the fur industry through kiosk displays (above), posters on buses (right) and subways, and advertisements in major cities across the country—including New York City (in Times Square)—and with an ongoing program to cooperate with local organizations to post billboards (top right). The organization's efforts continued in the late 1990s as the Fur-Free 2000™ campaign and as the Fur-Free Century™ campaign after the turn of the century.

www.StopPuppyMills.com

THE HUMANE SOCIETY
OF THE UNITED STATES. 2100 L Street, NW, Washington, DC 20037

The HSUS's very first brochure in the mid-1950s advocated the spaying and neutering of pets to fight the burgeoning pet overpopulation in the nation. The organization's efforts to combat mass dog and cat breeding facilities—known as puppy mills—*continue to this day, with a new website launched in 2003 and promotional materials such as bumper stickers devoted to educating the public about the facilities' often inhumane conditions and the needless suffering they cause.*

The previous pages showcase a few of the thousands of publications The HSUS has produced during the last 50 years.

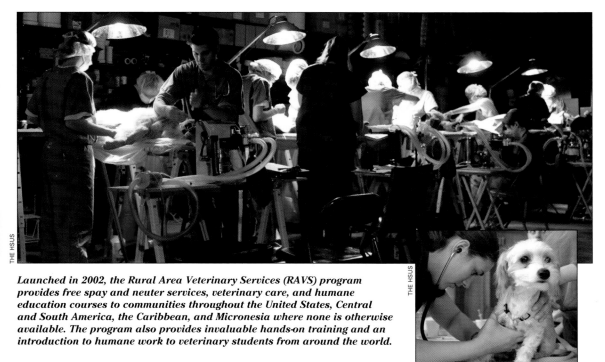

Launched in 2002, the Rural Area Veterinary Services (RAVS) program provides free spay and neuter services, veterinary care, and humane education courses to communities throughout the United States, Central and South America, the Caribbean, and Micronesia where none is otherwise available. The program also provides invaluable hands-on training and an introduction to humane work to veterinary students from around the world.

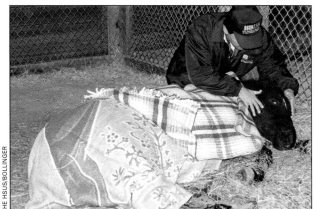

The HSUS sends Animal Cruelty Response Teams to investigate and relieve animal suffering and abuse wherever it occurs around the country. Here HSUS Gulf States Regional Director James Noe comforted Peanut, a pony with diseased feet who was rescued from a truck taking her to slaughter in New York State in 1995.

The HSUS's Disaster Services staff responds to natural and human-caused disasters around the nation, bringing expertise, food and veterinary medical supplies, and hands-on aid everywhere they are needed— from communities struck by wildfires in the West to those in the aftermath of hurricanes in the East. The HSUS also works with local, state, and national agencies to help them prepare for catastrophes before they strike to minimize the animal and human trauma they cause.

The HSUS has worked for decades to end commercial whaling, holding several anti-whaling demonstrations in Washington, D.C., in the mid-1980s (above and below). The organization maintains a prominent position at the International Whaling Commission to ensure that the current moratorium is upheld and in 2004 provided postcards for members to send Iceland's U.S. ambassador to protest the island nation's plans to resume full-scale whaling.

The owners of Talbots women's clothing stores also operated supermarkets in Japan that sold whale and dolphin meat. In 2001 The HSUS launched a campaign to protest these sales, offering members postcards to send to Talbots and urging them to write letters and make telephone calls to the clothing store chain. Due to this intense pressure, Talbots' owners complied with members' requests in 2003.

In the 1980s The HSUS targeted Canada's annual seal hunts with protests and resources such as Club Sandwiches Not Seals T-shirts. In 2002 the organization launched a renewed Protect Seals campaign with a dedicated informational website, new Do Something T-shirts, a protest rally in front of the Canadian Embassy in Washington, D.C., full-page ads in newspapers such as The New York Times, and postcards for members to mail to the Canadian prime minister, Tourism Commission, and ambassador.

The HSUS sent a humane message at several Earth Day celebrations. HSUS President John A. Hoyt conferred with actor Tom Cruise in Washington, D.C., in 1990 (above right, left to right), while actor Richard Gere discussed animal and human rights issues with HSUS Senior Vice President Patricia A. Forkan (above inset). Staff working at the HSUS tent (right) at the event distributed information to hundreds of passers-by.

HSUS Executive Vice President Patricia A. Forkan (standing, second from right) and Creative Director Paula Jaworski (right) joined HSUS staff dressed as sea turtles, who marched at the World Trade Organization meeting in Seattle in 2000, at an Earth Day celebration that year in Washington, D.C. (right). The Smithsonian Institution later requested one of the turtle costumes for its protest collection. The HSUS booths at the event (above) were a hive of activity as crowds of celebrants collected information on a wide range of humane issues.

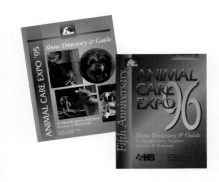

First presented in 1991 (above), The HSUS's annual Animal Care Expo is the largest educational conference and product and service exhibition in the country for the animal care and control community. Expo offers training through several dozen substantive seminars and workshops for the more than one thousand shelter and animal control professionals who attend each year, as well as networking opportunities available nowhere else.

Choose A Pal For Life

ONE OF THESE ANIMALS* could be your best friend. Each of them is looking for a home. They don't understand that for some of them, there will be no home, ever. Too many of these castoffs crowd our animal shelters, victims of a society where everything is disposable, even our companion animals. You can help. When you decide to bring a pet into your life,

give a shelter animal a home. Don't go to a pet store. Don't go to a breeder. Choose to save a life; take home a friend who will love you for life. Until there are no more healthy animals dying in our shelters, adopt a shelter pet. To join us, write The Humane Society of the United States, 2100 L Street, NW, Washington, DC 20037.

THE HUMANE SOCIETY OF THE UNITED STATES

Until There Are None-Adopt One

In 1988 The HSUS renewed its efforts to harness the power of individual consumers to the challenge of reducing the population of unwanted and homeless companion animals with the Be a P.A.L.—Prevent a Litter! campaign. The effort underscored the many ways pet overpopulation led to abuse and neglect of animals all over the country and celebrated the positive animal control accomplishments that had helped to decrease the population of unwanted animals in many communities.

Launched in 2001, the Pets for Life® program is a broad-ranging effort to keep pets with their human families in the homes where they belong. The program provides companion animal caregivers with solutions to the problems that too often cause people to relinquish their pets to animal shelters through brochures and tip sheets and an informational website.

Pets for Life also offers shelter professionals training through a National Training Center and Regional Training Centers to establish their own programs to prevent pet relinquishment. Most recently, the program provided physicians across the country with resources to educate their patients about pet ownership during pregnancy and childbirth.

THE HSUS

THE HSUS

In 1997 HSUS Mid-Atlantic Regional Director Nina Austenberg and animal companion Rusty-Bob (above) admired New Jersey's first Animal Friendly license plates. Proceeds from sales of the plates went to the state's Animal Population Control Fund for reduced-cost spaying and neutering of animals adopted from shelters and owned by public-assistance recipients. Austenberg was instrumental in initiating and pushing the program to fruition and oversees the Domestic Companion Animal Council—the watchdog committee charged with overseeing the program and its funding. Internationally syndicated Mutts® cartoonist and HSUS board member Patrick McDonnell (right) designed New Jersey's new spay and neuter license plate in 2002.

KINDRED
Spirits™

A lasting tribute
helping all animals

THE HSUS

THE HSUS

HSUS staff joined Public Broadcasting Service volunteers (above) in 1995 for a joint membership drive in Washington, D.C. Launched in 2001, Hip, Hip, Humane!™—The HSUS's living tributes program for pets and people (below)—continues to raise funds for The HSUS's vital work.

Hip, Hip, Humane!

HSUS Executive Vice President Patricia Forkan and Leader, former Senate Majority Leader Bob Dole's canine companion, shared a hug at the 1996 Annual Conference. Senator Dole and his wife, Senator Elizabeth Dole, made a generous donation to The HSUS through Kindred Spirits™, the organization's memorial program, in memory of Leader when he passed away in 1999.

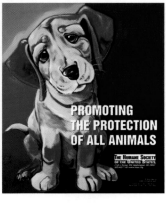

PROMOTING
THE PROTECTION
OF ALL ANIMALS

THE HUMANE SOCIETY
OF THE UNITED STATES

In Celebration
of

CHAPTER 2

There's Something Terribly Wrong:
Farm Animals and Sustainable Agriculture

he resurrection of the nineteenth- and early twentieth-century humane movement's concerns with the transportation and slaughter of animals was a significant priority for those who founded The HSUS in 1954. It was no co-incidence that the first national initiative in which they participated was the campaign for a federal humane slaughter law. With that law secured after four years of effort, The HSUS moved on to promote state-level legislation to complement and extend the coverage and scope of the federal statute and to spur the development of new technology and methods to make both slaughtering and pre-slaughter handling humane. The HSUS pursued these campaigns with heightened sensitivity to the religious constituencies concerned about attempts to regulate ritual slaughter. Despite The HSUS's careful approach, the ritual issue badly complicated state-level initiatives and inspired a new approach to the problem—the development of technical alternatives to hoisting and shackling that would be acceptable to religionists.

By the early 1970s, industrialized confinement systems—with all of their harsh impacts upon cows, pigs, chickens, sheep, lambs, and other animals—moved to the center of The HSUS's concerns. The last quarter of the twentieth century saw a massive rise in the consumption of animal products and an increasing reliance on intensive husbandry systems that denied animals' most basic biological and behavioral needs. HSUS scientists made the case against factory farming, HSUS investigators gathered evidence of its cruelty and disastrous implications, HSUS lobbyists pushed for its restriction, and HSUS publicists tried to generate public support for reform. In the 1980s, while maintaining traditional concerns with the moment of slaughter and the transportation of animals, The HSUS moved on to push for the application of animal welfare science and the Three Rs (reduction, replacement, and refinement) to the condition of the billions of animals raised and killed for food in the United States, and to raise questions about the negative consequences of the biotechnology revolution upon animals. Staff members sought to remedy the deficiencies of the Humane Slaughter Act, which did not cover chickens and did not apply to all of the nation's packing plants. The HSUS also forged links with a variety of interest groups involved in promoting ecologically sustainable agriculture and in trying to uphold organic standards. As The HSUS marked its fiftieth anniversary, the Farm Animals and Sustainable Agriculture section was engaged in concerted efforts to limit the spread of factory farming, with all of its adverse impacts on animals, the environment, workers, and consumers—even as the nation's major environmental organizations began to address intensive agriculture seriously for the first time. The HSUS also worked to cultivate a more sympathetic attitude toward animals on the part of the public. Staff members fought the negative effects of factory farming on many fronts, organizing communities, lobbying Congress, and encouraging citizens to make conscientious choices in personal consumption.

Principles and Purse Strings: The Humane Slaughter Act

From the advent of organized anticruelty work in 1866, the slaughter of animals for food was a pressing concern of humanitarians. In general, however, they did not seek to control it through legislation, but rather through the encouragement of humane slaughtering practices and technology. Legislation to regulate slaughter surfaced on several occasions in Massachusetts between 1910 and 1920, but the opposition of packers and religious authorities made its passage impossible. After this, no attempts were made at either the state or federal level to secure legislation, largely because by the late 1920s, the meatpacking industry had persuaded key humane leaders that it would take timely steps to reform itself. This did not happen, however, and the movement made very little progress on the issue during the middle decades of the twentieth century. Turning its attention to municipal animal control during the 1930s and 1940s, the movement paid less attention to the problems of cruelty in the transportation and slaughter of animals for food.

When he became editor of AHA's *National Humane Review* in 1952, Fred Myers renewed coverage of the issue, publishing several full-length pieces on the suffering of animals in food production. Myers and other advocates were especially encouraged by the emergence of a new method of anesthetizing hogs, developed by the Hormel Company of Austin, Minnesota. The Hormel system brought hogs onto a moving belt that carried them into a tank filled with carbon dioxide. The gas rendered animals unconscious within thirty seconds and conferred anesthetic effects that lasted about 25 seconds—long enough for painless slaughter.[1]

At AHA's annual convention in Denver in 1953, Myers introduced a resolution asking that the organization's leadership commission a study of the feasibility of national legislation to address the cruelties of slaughter, which the members present unanimously adopted. No action was taken on Myers's resolution during the year. However, the issue surfaced prominently at the 1954 AHA convention in Atlanta, where an intense election contest and disturbing film footage of animals being slaughtered set the stage for both the formation of The HSUS and the national campaign for humane slaughter legislation. The showing of Seattle advocate and future HSUS director Arthur P. Redman's film of conventional packinghouse practices proved to be a catalyst and spurred advocates in attendance to seek legislative action to end unnecessary cruelty to animals during slaughter. In particular, they sought to prohibit the hoisting and shackling of conscious animals and the use of sledgehammers for stunning. It became an immediate priority for both Christine Stevens's Animal Welfare Institute (AWI), founded three years before, and The HSUS, when it formed in the aftermath of the Atlanta convention. In fact, in the very first announcement of its organization, The HSUS condemned the state of slaughtering practices in the United States.[2]

Within a year of The HSUS's founding, there were bills in both the U.S. House of Representatives and the Senate, and the fledgling organization had distributed more than 800,000 pamphlets on humane slaughter. In 1955 senators Hubert Humphrey (D-MN) and Richard Neuberger (D-OR) and representatives Martha Griffiths (D-MI) and Edgar W. Hiestand (R-CA) introduced bills to outlaw the practices of hoisting and shackling conscious animals and the use of manually operated sledgehammers for stunning. USDA, led by Ezra Taft Benson, a great friend of the meat industry, opposed any legislation, arguing that meatpackers should be left to work independently on the issue. The legislation did not even get a hearing.[3]

In January 1956 Representative Griffiths introduced H.R. 8540, an improved version of her original bill (H.R. 6099), at the request of The HSUS. The new version closed some loopholes and reduced the amount of time during which packers would be permitted to reach compliance from five years to two. The HSUS responded energetically, committing itself to the mobilization of grassroots support for the measure. Among other things, it developed and distributed an illustrated pamphlet, *What You Don't Know about Hamburgers and Pork Chops*, at the rate of two thousand a day. Redman's film, exposing the extreme cruelty of hog slaughter, was widely seen, and HSUS director Joseph Sadowski underwrote a large adver-

(Left to right) Congressmen R.D. Harrison, Harold D. Cooley, Pat Jennings, and W.R. Poage watched anesthetized hogs come out of the carbon dioxide gas tunnel at a Hormel plant in 1956.

tisement in the *Christian Science Monitor*. In May 1956, after more than a year of effort, Myers and HSUS director Edith J. Goode secured the endorsement of the eleven-million-member General Federation of Women's Clubs for the bill. Staff members also worked to secure the support of religious groups for pending humane slaughter legislation.[4]

Humphrey's bill, S. 1636, became the subject of a May 9–10, 1956, subcommittee hearing, in a room jammed with supporters. Senator Humphrey kept Fred Myers on the stand for two hours after his initial testimony, to elaborate upon The HSUS's investigations concerning the packing industry. Myers pointed out that packers' claims about the prohibitive costs of humane methods were unsubstantiated and provided detailed discussion of carbon dioxide anesthetization, the captive-bolt pistol, and other methods of stunning and killing animals. When the bill left the Senate Agriculture committee, in a watered-down version striking out all mandatory clauses, it passed the full Senate by voice vote without opposition. However, the House held no hearings and took no action on any similar bill, so humane slaughter did not become a reality in the Eighty-fourth Congress.[5]

In August 1956, after the congressional session ended, congressmen interested in the issue toured slaughtering plants in Kansas, Missouri, and Nebraska, observing the poleax in use and confirming their worst suspicions about the need for humane slaughter legislation. They also witnessed the captive-bolt pistol and Hormel carbon dioxide tunnel in action. The HSUS's Helen Jones arranged for extensive media coverage of the congressional inspection.[6]

Advocates renewed the campaign for humane slaughter in 1957, with four congressional bills, introduced by representatives Griffiths (H.R. 176), Dawson (H.R. 3029), Hiestand (H.R. 3049), and George P. Miller (H.R. 2880). In the same session, senators Humphrey, Neuberger, and William Purtell (R-CT) jointly introduced S. 1497, a new version of Humphrey's bill. Under the influence of the meat industry, Senator Arthur Watkins (R-UT) sponsored a "study bill" to "authorize" the Secretary of Agriculture to examine the issue and provide a report of his findings in 1959.[7]

At an April 2, 1957, hearing in the Eighty-fifth Congress, The HSUS, AWI, AHA, a butchers' union, and several other interested groups testified in support of the legislation. Arrayed on the other side were USDA, the American Meat Institute, the Farm Bureau, the National Cattlemen's Association, the Grange, and the Union of Orthodox Rabbis. Fred Myers was not the sole HSUS witness; The HSUS also sponsored the testimony of Lt. Colonel D.J. Anthony, a British veterinary official and technical expert on slaughter methods. Myra Babcock, M.D., a Michigan anesthesiologist and HSUS director, testified, too, describing the effects of carbon dioxide and sharing her professional knowledge concerning the physiological effects of fear and suffering in animals. In addition, Arthur Redman screened his film on hog slaughter at the hearing.[8]

As their predecessors in the late nineteenth century had, humane advocates quickly ran into the challenge of Jewish food laws. "The ritual of kosher killing," journalists Paul Kearney and Richard Dempewolff wrote, "prescribes that an animal must arrive clean, whole, and unblemished at the point where the rabbi makes the final thrust." Rabbis and kosher meatpackers alike had interpreted this to mean, Kearney and Dempewolff wrote, that "the animal must be conscious, and they have insisted that the rugged shackling and hoisting alive, even of full-grown cattle, is the only practical means to comply with Hebrew law." In a compromise with rabbinical authorities, ritual slaughter, or *shechita*—which employed the shackle and hoist and demanded that the animal be conscious at the moment of slaughter—was exempted from the coverage of the proposed law. Moreover, the bill specifically defined *shechita* as humane.[9]

The legislation that emerged from the House Agriculture Committee in July 1957 was H.R. 8308, drafted by Representative W.R. Poage (D-TX), chairman of the Livestock Subcommittee and vice-chairman of the full Agriculture Committee, in consultation with The HSUS. The striking difference between Poage's bill and earlier proposals was the former's reliance on economic pressure instead of criminal penalties. It prohibited agencies of the federal government from purchasing products from any slaughterer or processor that used inhumane methods of slaughter in any of its plants. This was a potential loss of business no packing company could afford to risk. As one commentator observed, "A straight criminal law could hardly provide a penalty for violation of more than a $1,000 fine." By implication, "the Poage bill provides for a $1 million fine." Poage's bill also specified that approved methods must render animals insensible to pain, "by a single blow or gunshot or an electrical, chemical, or other means that is rapid and effective before being shackled."[10]

On the Senate side, a subcommittee unanimously voted in favor of releasing the Humphrey/Neuberger/Purtell bill. Fears that conflict over a pending civil rights bill would prevent consideration of humane slaughter proved to be unwarranted. However, it was decided to postpone action on S. 1497 until after the House had voted.[11]

The bill received a favorable report by the House Agriculture Committee, and on February 4, 1958, it passed in the U.S. House of Representatives by a large margin. However, at a June 18 Senate Agriculture Committee meeting, a majority of members dropped Humphrey's proposal in favor of Watkins's "study bill." This set the stage for a floor fight, in which Humphrey and his allies pushed for amendment of the committee bill and a roll-call vote of the full Senate.[12]

On July 29, 1958, the Senate passed S. 1497 by a vote of seventy-two–nine, after narrowly rejecting (forty-three–forty) the substitute bill. Senator Humphrey thwarted all attempts to weaken S. 1497, save for amendments exempting Jewish ritual slaughter. "I believe that we

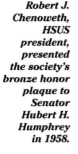

Robert J. Chenoweth, HSUS president, presented the society's bronze honor plaque to Senator Hubert H. Humphrey in 1958.

witnessed, during the campaign for slaughterhouse reform," Senator Humphrey commented, "one of those spontaneous manifestations of basic goodness and decency with which the American people every once in a while indicate that they may be worthy to lead a troubled world in progress toward peace and justice."[13]

Not wanting to jeopardize the bill's passage late in a congressional session, House conferees accepted the Senate version of the bill, and the full House passed it. President Eisenhower signed the Humane Slaughter Act on August 20, 1958, making it effective beginning June 30, 1960. A last-minute subterfuge involving the meat industry and the Military Subsistence Supply Agency of the United States Army surfaced, in which the agency ruled that it would only require compliance in contracts exceeding $2,500. This edict met determined resistance from Senator Humphrey, who received assurance of the Army's commitment to full compliance just before the date on which the law was to take effect.[14]

The Humane Slaughter Act outlawed the poleax and the shackling and hoisting of conscious animals. Its sponsors' main goal was to develop a method of rendering animals unconscious before they entered the slaughtering process, using carbon dioxide chambers, electrical stunning tools, captive-bolt pistols, and conventional firearms retrofitted with special ammunition that would stun but not kill. The law specified, "No government agency may buy meat or meat products from any packer who in any of his plants, or a plant of any subsidiary company, slaughters animals inhumanely or handles animals inhumanely in connection with slaughter." When the Humane Slaughter Act passed, the U.S. government was purchasing about $300 million worth of meat per year, and this provision affected the nation's largest packers, the government's principal suppliers.[15]

This educational folder about slaughter-plant cruelties was distributed by The HSUS in 1960.

During the law's implementation phase, The HSUS was critical of government efforts to secure compliance. Fred Myers was especially concerned that some kind of field inspection and record keeping be initiated, because, at first, enforcement depended entirely upon sworn affidavits by vendors selling meat to the government that they and their suppliers were in compliance. Some suppliers signed affidavits without realizing that they were violating the law. "Some packers and some procurement officers," Myers wrote to one Army administrator, to illustrate the problem, "seem not yet to be aware of the fact that a packer or processor must use humane slaughter methods in all of his plants and use these methods on all species of animals to be eligible to sell to the federal government."[16]

The HSUS played a crucial role in the federal humane slaughter campaign, helping to mobilize mass opinion and to promote unity of purpose on the part of humane societies, many of which had never before invested their energies in a fight that extended beyond their local communities. Myers positively gushed in his *HSUS News* report:

Congress got the greatest deluge of mail, on a single subject, within the memories of living legislators. Veteran Washington news reporters watched in amazement. "These letters," wrote one columnist, after reading many samples of the mountains of mail piling up in congressional offices, "are not the usual kind of form letters that result from pressure campaigns. These are letters that ring with the sincerity of the individuals." Even President Eisenhower told a group of congressmen: "If I relied on my mail, I would think that the country is concerned only about humane slaughter."[17]

Assessing the contribution of The HSUS to the federal campaign, Senator Stephen Young (D-OH) observed,

The paid mercenaries don't always win. The powerful American Meat Institute, which coordinated opposition to the humane slaughter bill of 1958, was shellacked by the Humane Society of the United States, which employed no paid lobbyists. The Society's three-year campaign resulted in one of the heaviest storms of mail in congressional history and succeeded in passing the bill over the combined opposition of meat packers, livestock and wool growers, the White House, the Departments of Agriculture and Interior, and the Budget Bureau.[18]

Looking back in the aftermath of victory, Myers expressed his conviction that "the humane slaughter victory could have been won a quarter of a century ago." Myers lamented the decision animal protectionists made in 1929 to cooperate with packers, who—he and some of his contemporary colleagues contended—had lulled the animal protection movement into complacency by promising to do something to reform themselves. The four-year campaign, Myers asserted, "proved that major national cruelties are ended by *hot* wars, not *cold* wars—and *certainly* not by neutrality."[19]

Humane Slaughter: Extension, Research, and Invention

In the wake of the Humane Slaughter Act—the humane movement's first federal success in seventy-five years—The HSUS began to push for the passage of laws in a number of state legislatures to require the use of humane methods in the commercial slaughter of livestock in

packing plants. In 1959 Fred Myers testified at legislative hearings on humane slaughter in California, Tennessee, Connecticut, Ohio, Wisconsin, and New Jersey, the only representative of a national organization to do so. HSUS director Arthur Redman testified in support of bills in Washington, where he led the campaign for the first humane slaughter law in any state, and in Minnesota, where a provisional branch of The HSUS secured the law. The HSUS was responsible for all five of the state laws enacted that year.[20]

The January 1961 issue of *Reader's Digest* carried an article, entitled "Let Us Have Mercy on These Dumb Animals," which drew heavily upon research conducted by HSUS staff members. The article contrasted the treatment of animals in the approximately 500 packing plants operating under the federal humane slaughter law with those that were not. Authors Paul Kearney and Richard Dempewolff reported "the unenviable experience…of observing a poorly stuck pig shoved into the scalding tank while still fully conscious" and seeing a slaughterhouse worker "swing his primitive sledge hammer a dozen times before he succeeded in stunning three frightened, bellowing steers."[21]

The very month in which the *Reader's Digest* article appeared, Belton P. Mouras began his work as head of the livestock division set up to meet the terms of Anna Belle Morris's substantial bequest (see chapter 1). Mouras played an important part in the humane slaughter campaigns, testifying on behalf of humane slaughter bills and helping to coordinate support for them in a number of states. Mouras also monitored technical developments that might facilitate the phaseout of shackle and hoist systems like those still being used for ritual slaughter.[22]

Since the federal legislation was limited to packing companies that sold meat or meat products to federal agencies, it covered approximately 80 percent of livestock slaughtered in the nation's packing plants. State laws were necessary because the Humane Slaughter Act did not affect packing plants that were not involved in interstate commerce or in selling their products to the federal government. Moreover, smaller meatpacking houses were not federally inspected to ensure the wholesomeness of their products and thus were subject only to state legislation. This meant that the 25 million animals killed annually in 2,500 smaller plants were not covered by humane slaughter regulations.[23]

As a rule these state-level proposals did not interfere with individual farmers slaughtering for their own use; did not affect poultry processing; did not require the hiring or retraining of personnel; and did not necessitate the purchase of expensive equipment or impose extra costs upon packers, consumers, or enforcement agencies. Even so, supporters had to respond to some of the same questions that came up in the struggle for the federal law. If the argument was that humane methods were more efficient and economical than cruel ones, why not let packers voluntarily adopt them? Answering this in one state legislature, Fred Myers noted, "many of them suffer from inertia and will continue doing indefinitely what they have always done in the past even though they might make money by changing their methods, and a few packers will certainly from time to time mistakenly feel that cruelty is cheaper than humanitarianism."[24]

In a few significant instances, meatpackers welcomed humane slaughter legislation at the state level. The Oscar Mayer Company, which had used a captive-bolt stunner since 1945 to render animals insensible, testified on behalf of a Wisconsin bill. In Kansas, humane organizations could point to the willingness of at least one packing plant not covered by the federal law to adopt humane slaughter practices. Such voluntary cooperation underscored The HSUS's contention that the passage of such laws would work no hardship on any party and that many packers would ultimately find them economical and practical as well as humane.[25]

It was a little more difficult to contend with the fact that agricultural interests in state legislatures virtually always sought to squelch humane slaughter proposals as part of a general strategy of suppressing any regulation or public scrutiny of animals' treatment. They frequently argued that the adoption of humane slaughter methods would be costly and impractical and that enforcement would create burdensome administrative costs. In many states elected officials tied to those interests saw to it that any legislation that raised questions about the treatment of animals used for food remained bottled up in committee.[26]

Although the resistance mounted by agricultural and industrial concerns was formidable, the opposition of Jewish religious organizations provided a more complex challenge to the success of state humane slaughter initiatives in the years following the 1958 passage of the Humane Slaughter Act. Orthodox rabbinical authorities were usually the most vocal opponents, but a wide variety of Jewish organizations monitored the progress of such bills and almost all of them sought to have *shechita* specifically characterized as "humane" under proposed statutes. Rabbinical authorities generally attacked prohibitions on hoisting and shackling as infringements on religious freedom, always a serious charge. Many who had lived through the Holocaust openly recalled that some of the first infringements upon Jewish liberties in Nazi Germany involved limitations on kosher slaughter.[27]

The HSUS, for its part, took the position that while religious practices and beliefs had to be respected, they could not be allowed to lead to disregard for the welfare of animals in human care. The welfare of animals before and during slaughter needed to be safeguarded to the greatest possible extent, whether or not the slaughter was carried out according to the requirements of a particular religious faith.

Like its U.S. counterpart, the Canadian humane slaughter law passed in 1959 (and effective November 1960) approved Jewish ritual slaughter as humane. In contrast, however, the Canadian law did require that kosher-slaughtered animals "be adequately restrained in a device of a means approved" by the Department of Agriculture. Necessity proved itself the mother of invention: a resourceful packing company produced an acceptable holding pen that gained rabbinical sanction. The pen produced by Canada Packers, Ltd., of Toronto enabled kosher packers to comply with religious stricture while abandoning the shackle and hoist system. Slaughterhouse workers prodded or led the animal into the steel pen, and, as the padded gate closed, it nudged him forward, leaving his head to protrude through a window on the other end. At this point, the *shochet* could make the cut effectively and cleanly. Fred Myers traveled to Toronto to inspect the pen and gave it his approval. More important, the pen received the endorsement of such eminent orthodox rabbinical authorities as Joseph Soloveitchik of Boston and Eliezer Silver of Cincinnati.[28]

As it turned out, the device approved for use by Canadian authorities could not pass muster under USDA's sanitary codes. However, acting on the belief that the shackling and hoisting method was an avoidable cruelty, humane advocates in the United States placed their hopes in the development of mechanical holding pens that would make it possible for the *shochet* to kill animals quickly and painlessly in compliance with orthodox Jewish requirements, while meeting the federal government's required health standards.[29]

In campaigns at the state level, The HSUS recommended enactment of laws that defined ritual slaughter of animals as humane. However, The HSUS resisted blanket exemptions for shackling and hoisting like that incorporated within the federal Humane Slaughter Act—which, under the Case-Javits amendment, did not impose a requirement for humane pre-slaughter handling in the case of kosher-killed animals. At the same time, HSUS representatives refused to concede that their proposals constituted an infringement of religious practice. Hoisting and shackling, they insisted, was a "packinghouse method" rather than a requirement of the Jewish faith. Moreover, as they sometimes pointed out, as a matter of principle and conviction, ritual slaughter cut in the other direction, too. Kosher meat was often sold without identification on the open market, especially in the battleground states of New Jersey and New York, making its consumption difficult for non-Jewish constituencies to avoid.[30]

In 1960 and 1961, The HSUS keyed its strategy for state-level legislation to the anticipated emergence of acceptable alternate methods of handling animals before kosher slaughter. Looking toward a future in which alternative devices would be available, The HSUS responded in state after state with compromise amendments that would have permitted a fixed short-term exemption for shackling and hoisting under the proposed statutes. Even in the event of a crippling amendment's passage, Fred Myers believed, it would be feasible to seek revision of an enacted state law once the new pens for ritual slaughter were approved and placed on the U.S. market.[31]

In the meantime, several bills failed after lively debates on whether they infringed on the religious rights of Jews. Orthodox authorities consistently sought to scuttle legislation that proposed to eliminate hoist and shackle methods. In 1962's most spectacular battle, the opposition of religious constituencies sent legislation in New York to a crushing defeat, and a significant number of states passed a kosher slaughter exemption as part of humane slaughter legislation. Rabbinical authorities sometimes testified in these hearings and typically supported those bills that did not interfere with *shechita*. By 1963 fourteen states had enacted such legislation, and another half dozen were considering similar proposals.[32]

The prospects for resolving the impasse between humane groups and rabbinical authorities improved in 1964, when the ASPCA secured a patent on a holding pen that received the approval of the Rabbinical Council of America. This led The HSUS to renew its efforts to explore the prospects for legislation to eliminate the ritual slaughter exemption in the federal law. It certainly strengthened the case against an exemption in the state laws and in some instances it did lead Jewish organizations to drop their active opposition to such bills.[33]

On the other hand, enduring difficulties in securing complementary state legislation continued to frustrate HSUS staff members working on the issue. In 1965, with the backing of many rabbis and Jewish laymen in the state, the Pennsylvania legislature passed a humane slaughter bill that prohibited the shackling and hoisting of conscious cattle before slaughter. Later that year, however, a group of orthodox rabbis from Pittsburgh attempted to cripple the law just weeks after it had taken effect. Oliver Evans beseeched Governor William Scranton to resist the proposal, pointing out that the shackling and hoisting of animals for ritual slaughter was "a packinghouse practice that has nothing to do with the actual humane kosher ritual itself. It is a modern, speedy system that was certainly unknown to Moses or the sages of the Talmud." Evans also pointed out that the state of Israel not only forbade hoisting and shackling but declined to accept American kosher meat handled that way. The rabbis' initiative subsequently died in committee.[34]

HSUS director Grace Conahan (later Korsan) (d. 2002) led the fight to secure passage of humane slaughter legislation in Missouri. There, the bill landed in the rurally dominated agriculture committee five years in a row. In 1969 Conahan succeeded in having the bill, containing a ritual slaughter exemption, assigned to the Criminal Jurisprudence Committee, where it got a fair hearing.[35]

The battle in New York continued into the late 1960s. In that state, however, movement disunity, controversial legislation, and advertisements sponsored by Alice Herrington's Friends of Animals badly polarized the situation. The bill Herrington favored did not specifically define *shechita* as humane and raised a swell of opposition from Jewish groups. Despite long-standing efforts to see humane slaughter legislation passed in New York, it never happened. Still, the number of states backing the federal law with legislation of their own grew to nineteen by 1968 and twenty-three by 1972. At that point, however, humane advocates began a more determined search for technological innovations that might help to remove rabbinical objections to outlawing hoisting and shackling.[36]

The Council on Livestock Protection

In the years following passage of the federal Humane Slaughter Act, The HSUS continued to study methods of humane slaughter, including the use of carbon dioxide to immobilize animals before slaughter, electrical stunning, and the modification of a veterinary "bull leader." Staff members read the *National Provisioner* and other meat industry publications and kept abreast of relevant advances in health sciences, physiology, and design engineering, ordering scientific and technical papers about which they heard or read. They also monitored technical and scientific developments that might prove to be helpful in mitigating the pain of castration, docking, branding, and dehorning, paying special attention to studies of the evaluation of pain in animals as well as the relationship between pre-slaughter stress and the quality of meat produced.[37]

The most pressing technical challenge reformers faced, however, remained kosher slaughter. In the states where ritual slaughter comprised a significant portion of the total amount of meat processed—like New Jersey and New York—the kosher meat industry generated intense opposition to humane slaughter legislation. Longtime campaigners gradually accepted the fact that resolution of the ritual slaughter issue had to be the first priority.[38]

By the early 1970s, scientists active in the field were in agreement that shackling and hoisting by the hind leg was stressful to animals. They had observed animals quivering and shaking in this position and measured the effects of shackling through the study of brain wave patterns, heartbeat, and blood acidity. At the same time, an increasing number of activists had become convinced that further efforts to secure federal or state legislation relating to kosher slaughter could not succeed without an intensive campaign of education within the Jewish community.[39]

American advocates remained confident in their assertions that shackling and hoisting was a packinghouse method rather than a religious requirement. As part of their case, they cited the fact that slaughterers in Israel either cast animals to the ground or held them in the Weinberg pen, a Danish invention, before the *shochet*'s cut. American packers, advocates believed, disdained the Weinberg pen as "slow, cumbersome, and costly."[40]

American sanitary laws constituted another obstacle. In the United States, animals could not be cast to the ground before cutting, on the grounds that disease from an infected animal might be transmitted to a healthy one if the head and throat had touched the floor. This necessitated focusing on a holding pen.[41]

For a few years, The HSUS channeled most of its efforts on this front through the Council on Livestock Protection (CLP)—a partnership of groups that included The HSUS, AHA, the MSPCA, and others. The CLP, formed in 1971 under the leadership of John C. Macfarlane (1974 Joseph Wood Krutch Medal recipient), sought to support research into finding better methods of handling livestock prior to slaughter—with the goal of eliminating hoisting and shackling once and for all—and to investigate the potential of narcosis for use in the slaughter of livestock. It was also active in efforts to seek better methods of loading and unloading live-

John Macfarlane (right) is congratulated by Dr. Amy Freeman Lee and HSUS president John Hoyt upon receiving the HSUS Joseph Wood Krutch Medal in 1974.

stock and better methods of transporting animals from farm to market. John Hoyt, a member of the CLP's governing board throughout its existence, invested considerable time and effort in the CLP's goals during the 1970s.[42]

The CLP did its best to avoid antagonizing rabbinical authorities, who remained vigilant in their efforts to scuttle initiatives they judged would limit religious freedom. With the development of an alternative to shackling and hoisting, the CLP maintained, it would be possible to revisit the 1958 federal exemption given to ritual slaughter, widely known as the Case-Javits amendment. The Case-Javits amendment exempted from the Humane Slaughter Act's provisions not only the act of ritual slaughter itself, but also the pre-slaughter handling practices commonly found in kosher slaughtering plants, including the shackling and hoisting of conscious animals.[43]

The CLP and its member societies did not join in the lawsuit filed by Henry Mark Holzer that argued that the exemption was not only inhumane but also violated the principle of separation of church and state. For its part, The HSUS responded to the Holzer lawsuit by restating its support for repeal of the Case-Javits amendment to the federal Humane Slaughter Act. The CLP avoided any explicit condemnation of *shechita* but maintained that the shackling and hoisting of a conscious animal prior to the knife cut was not a necessary part of the ritual.[44]

Unfortunately, the ASPCA pen for restraining large animals had not proved entirely satisfactory for kosher slaughter, and several of the technical experts who studied its use had their doubts about its humaneness. For one thing, it involved a series of physical manipulations that, while not injurious, seemed to involve some psychological distress. It also required a highly skilled operator. In the hands of a careless person, it could result in excessive pressure to an animal's backbone and neck and cause more harm and carcass damage than shackling and hoisting.[45]

During 1972 and 1973, the CLP provided $55,067 to University of Connecticut researchers working to devise a machine to restrain conscious smaller animals like calves and sheep in an upright position before slaughtering. Professors Ralph Prince and Donald Kinsman developed a conveyor belt system that made it possible to avoid shackling animals by their hind legs and hoisting them into the air head down.[46]

Eventually the CLP received the support of the American Jewish Committee for its efforts. However, like the ASPCA initiative before it, the CLP's proposal became mired in the heavy costs of the research. More decisively, no slaughtering plant was willing to take a chance on implementation of the pen as designed.[47]

For some years persistent confusion about whether the CLP and its constituent groups were trying to regulate the moment of slaughter also hindered progress. Through the early 1970s, the official position of The HSUS was that *shechita*—the actual slaughtering of an animal—was humane. However, the organization was firmly against the shackling and hoisting of an animal prior to ritual slaughter, maintaining that ritual slaughter's reliance on shackling and hoisting was rooted in the slaughtering industry's conventional practice and was not an integral part of *shechita*.[48]

The CLP marked the beginning of The HSUS's association with Temple Grandin, a consultant and designer of livestock facilities. While admitting that the human factor would always exert the strongest impact on the humaneness of any system, Grandin championed the view that well-designed equipment influenced by knowledge of livestock behavior could substantially reduce animals' stress and that humane handling of animals made both moral and economic sense.[49]

The Connecticut pen was ready for commercial construction by 1975, and several Jewish organizations offered suggestions for its modification after visiting the experimental project at the University of Connecticut or viewing slides of the apparatus. Progress toward its adoption flagged until a resolution at the 1978 annual meeting—introduced by Brooklyn trade unionist, tenant rights advocate, longtime kosher slaughter campaigner, and 1985 Joseph Wood Krutch Medal winner Max Schnapp (1904–1995)—rekindled The HSUS's effort to promote its approval and use. In November 1978 John Hoyt and other members of the CLP met with representatives of the Joint Advisory Committee of the Synagogue Council of America and the National Jewish Community Relations Advisory Council.[50]

The CLP then focused its energies on the development of a conveyor system that would obviate the perceived need for shackling and hoisting of animals. In 1986 Temple Grandin modified the Connecticut pen prototype with a new entrance design that positioned calves on a moving double-rail conveyor. The successful testing of this device and Grandin's modification of a V-conveyor restrainer played important roles in the decline of hoisting and shackling in larger plants.[51]

At this point Henry Spira, then beginning to apply to farm animal welfare issues the strategic principles he had advanced so competently in relation to the use of animals in research, testing, and education (see chapter 3), saw Grandin's work on kosher slaughter devices. Spira's efforts to mediate the long-running debate with representatives of the rabbinical community convinced him it was the wrong approach. Instead, Spira made contact with a meatpacker with a demonstrated reputation for progressive-mindedness on slaughtering issues and a representative of the American Meat Institute's committee on worker safety, two men he believed would be open to the opportunities that Grandin's work had introduced for improving both the handling of animals and the security of the workplace. This crucial work underway, Spira then moved to discuss the issue with major kosher meat suppliers, persuading them that expanding public awareness of shackling and hoisting (another objective he was actively pursuing) would not serve them well in terms of their bottom line. By 1994 the last of the major kosher slaughtering facilities in the United States adopted the Grandin system. The impasse that had perpetuated shackling and hoisting for decades was at an end.[52]

The Humane Slaughter Act of 1978

In 1967 Representative Joseph Y. Resnick (D-NY), who sat on the House Agriculture Committee, commissioned an HSUS survey on food packers' compliance with the 1958 Act. Two investigators made unannounced observations at thirty-two plants in twelve states and concluded that the Act's provisions were being respected, but that innumerable cruelties continued due to callous attitudes and conduct on the part of stockyard and packing plant employees in herding the animals.[53]

"Doc" Thomsen of Humane Information Services was one of those who kept the humane slaughter issue alive in the ensuing years. In 1971, pointing to the dramatic reduction in cruelty that such a bill might accomplish, Thomsen proposed that the humane movement seek a legislative prohibition of imported meats produced at a high cost of suffering to animals in other nations. Thomsen reasoned that American cattlemen would support the bill, out of their conviction that their foreign competitors, "already enjoying the advantages of lower labor and other costs, should not be allowed the additional advantages of freedom from humane slaughter requirements."[54]

Michael Fox observed that slaughter personnel need constant supervision in handling and slaughter methods: here, an electrical stunner is placed improperly on a pig. Such placement would cause paralysis but not unconsciousness while the animal is shackled, hoisted, and slaughtered.

In reality such a proposal also promised to redress the growing problem of meat producers who transferred their operations to other nations to flout or circumvent the Humane Slaughter Act. In 1973 Representative Bill Gunter (D-FL) introduced H.R. 8055, requiring foreign packing plants to use humane slaughtering methods. "Doc" Thomsen estimated that five million head of cattle already came as imports every year and that the figure was on the rise. American consumers had a right, he asserted, to know that the beef they ate was coming from countries that observed a humane slaughter requirement.[55]

Thomsen's continuing efforts to bring the issue back onto the national agenda resulted in an improved bill, H.R. 9658, introduced in 1975 by Representative George Brown (D-CA). H.R. 9658 would have required that all federally inspected slaughterhouses and all foreign slaughterhouses sending meat to the United States use humane methods of handling and slaughter, as called for in the 1958 Act. At that time, Brown estimated that some 275 slaughterhouses (those that did not sell to the federal government or engage in interstate commerce) in the United States continued to use inhumane methods.[56]

Brown's bill went nowhere in the Ninety-fourth Congress, but he introduced an identical measure in the Ninety-fifth, on January 6, 1977. Responding to requests to support the bill, The HSUS undertook a detailed study of enforcement and compliance. HSUS researchers judged that more than 100 slaughterers then under federal inspection standards were not in compliance with the Humane Slaughter Act.[57]

Patricia Forkan presents a certificate of appreciation to Senator Robert Dole, who was active in the passage of legislation implementing the Humane Slaughter Act.

Before long Senator Robert Dole (R-KS) introduced a companion bill, S. 3092, actively endorsing the need for legislation to create effective enforcement mechanisms for the Humane Slaughter Act. Patricia Forkan and HSUS attorney Roger Kindler worked with Senator Dole's drafting lawyer to address The HSUS's concerns. Like the 1958 legislation, the bills did not address kosher slaughter or the shackling and hoisting of fully conscious animals prior to ritual slaughter, however. Politicians preferred that The HSUS continue its efforts "to work privately with the Jewish community to effect change." In their final versions, H.R. 1464 and S. 3092 required that humane methods of slaughter and pre-slaughter handling be employed in all slaughterhouses under the jurisdiction of the Federal Meat Inspection Act. This would have subjected some three hundred additional slaughterhouses to the requirement to handle and slaughter animals humanely.[58]

HSUS director Robert Welborn and staff members Forkan, Michael Fox, and Margaret Morrison testified before either House or Senate committees considering the legislation. Welborn's testimony reflected The HSUS's judgment that enforcement of the Humane Slaughter Act had become "non-existent" and that there was no reliable way to know what methods were being used by which slaughtering facilities.[59]

A strong and unified lobbying effort led by The HSUS and AWI ensued. The U.S. Senate passed S. 3092 on August 7, 1978, and the House followed shortly thereafter with approval of H.R. 1464. On October 10 President Jimmy Carter signed into law the Humane Methods of Slaughter Act. The law relied on the authority of meat inspectors to withhold inspection until cruel practices were corrected. The law also required that meat imported from foreign sources be derived from animals slaughtered in plants that met the standards of the Humane Slaughter Act. It thus excluded access to the American market by foreign slaughtering interests that did not comply.[60]

Michael Fox, Robert Welborn, and Margaret (Peggy) Morrison testified before House and Senate subcommittees in 1977 and 1978.

Against Factory Farming, for Humane Husbandry

While The HSUS had pursued improvements in the treatment of animals in transportation and slaughter since its founding, it confronted a new challenge by the mid-1970s: the suffering and deprivation of animals in intensive confinement systems. Factory farming—the automated, capital-intensive, high-volume production of animals for food—was causing more distress, suffering, and susceptibility to disease than any slaughtering or pre-slaughter handling procedure.

Michael Fox testifies before Congress.

The humane movement was well aware of the dramatic transformation taking place in American agriculture during the 1960s and 1970s. Ruth Harrison had sounded the tocsin worldwide with the publication of *Animal Machines* in 1964, and "Doc" Thomsen and other American advocates had followed her lead in calling attention to "the world's greatest humane problem." For a variety of reasons, however, organized animal protection made very little progress in directing its attention to the intensive husbandry of animals for food.[61]

Within The HSUS, the situation changed with the hiring of Michael Fox. The treatment of animals used for food became an important priority of the Institute for the Study of Animal Problems (ISAP) after it formed in 1976. As ISAP director, Fox became an outspoken critic of industrial animal husbandry and was often featured in industry journals or in public forums where he advanced the animal welfare position and sought to break down prejudices against the humane movement. "There's something terribly wrong with this system if we have to dock pigs' tails to prevent other pigs from biting them off," he told one reporter. "Are we going to cut off their legs when they start biting those next?"[62]

Intensive livestock husbandry practices were documented by Fox in the 1970s and 1980s.

During the late 1970s, Fox's photographic essays introduced *HSUS News* readers to the "Brave New World" of factory farming. Fox traveled extensively—sometimes undercover—visiting factory farms and slaughterhouses, interviewing employees, taking photographs, and observing animal suffering firsthand. "It left a very deep emotional wound, it'll never heal," he recalled a quarter-century later. The sacrifice was not in vain, however, for The HSUS was responsible for a substantial increase in media coverage accorded to the farm animal issue. The HSUS scored an important breakthrough in reaching the broader public in 1980, when David Nevin's profile of Fox and his investigations appeared in the April issue of *Smithsonian*. Nevin followed Fox around on a tour of factory farming facilities and helped to acquaint Americans with what Fox called "the five freedoms"—or basic rights—that should be guaranteed to all animals used in food production: "the freedom to be able easily to get up; lie down; turn around; stretch; and groom or preen."[63]

The following year, Representative Ronald Mottl (D-OH) sponsored a resolution, H.J. Res. 305, proposing the establishment of a Farm Animal Husbandry Committee to investigate all facets of the factory farming industry for a report to the United States Congress. The farming community, the meat industry, and a range of producer associations attacked Mottl and his proposal, but factory farming had become the subject of federal legislative debate for the first time.[64]

Under Fox's leadership, the Farm Animals section targeted industry claims that humane reforms were unnecessary and that modern intensive confinement systems could not be profitable if they jeopardized animals' overall health and welfare. As a contributor to the 1981 report of the Council for Agricultural Science and Technology (CAST), Fox worked to legitimize the study of farm animals' well-being as an area of scientific inquiry. The final report reflected the stronger influence of animal-production scientists with ties to

agribusiness. Nevertheless, it resulted in a $380,000 USDA grant to several universities engaged in the study of stress in animals raised for food, a tacit acknowledgment that The HSUS had raised issues worthy of investigation.[65]

Seeking to build broader support for reform, The HSUS produced several audiovisual products to acquaint the public with the problems of intensive farming. In 1980 it published *Factory Farming* and in 1981 a slide show and cassette, "Humane Concerns of Factory Farming." In 1983 Fox authored a booklet, *Farm Animal Welfare and the Human Diet*, and in 1984, a full-length book, *Farm Animals: Husbandry, Behavior, and Veterinary Practice*. The HSUS also placed its energies be-

By March 1982 The HSUS had distributed 200,000 "No Veal This Meal" cards.

hind the first legislation to target intensive farming practices, H.R. 3170, introduced by Representative James Howard (D-NJ) in 1983.[66]

That same year, the American Farm Bureau and its Utah state affiliate attacked HSUS humane education specialists for their attempts to raise the factory farming issue in the curriculum that the National Association for the Advancement of Humane Education (NAAHE) (The HSUS's youth education division), was developing. The attack in Utah was promoted under the banner, "How Can You Keep Them Down on the Farm After They've Seen NAAHE?"[67]

Farm groups responded very defensively to the extensive publicity The HSUS's educational efforts generated. The livestock industry, one representative insisted, "supplies consumers with a nutritious and plentiful meat supply. No one knows better than the livestock producer that sick, malnourished, or suffering animals are less productive. Realistically, no one is more interested in the well-being of livestock than the producer." In response to such claims, Fox cautioned that factory farming interests' focus on productivity "as an indicator and guarantor of farm animal welfare" was a misleading approach. In practice, the goal of maximizing productivity did not usually result in a high standard of animal welfare.[68]

The HSUS was one of the first animal organizations to adopt the use of shareholder resolutions to raise public awareness of the need for reform of food production practices. In 1983 HSUS Counsel for Government and Industry Relations Peter Lovenheim, Esq., zeroed in on another of factory farming's most egregious cruelties, the force-feeding of ducks for foie gras, by organizing a stockholder resolution at the annual meeting of Iroquois Brands, Ltd., a company that imported paté from France. Lovenheim's resolution proposed that the company investigate the practices of its supplier and report on any cruelty discovered. The proposal gained more than 5 percent of the votes cast by shareholders at the Iroquois Brands, Ltd.'s annual meeting, and Lovenheim put it forward again in 1984. This time Iroquois declined to include the proposal under a Securities and Exchange Commission exemption permitting the exclusion of shareholder resolutions "not significantly related to the issuer's business." Since the paté trade represented only a small part of the company's business, Lovenheim took the matter to federal court in an effort to secure a ruling that the proposal concerned a significant ethical issue and thus could not be dismissed as trivial.[69]

On March 27, 1985, Judge Oliver Gasch issued a preliminary injunction requiring the inclusion of Lovenheim's resolution in Iroquois's mailing to shareholders. The court noted that humane laws had already established cruelty as a significant social concern and that animal welfare organizations in the United States generally opposed force-feeding. While Lovenheim's resolution received less support than it had the previous year (gaining just 4 percent of the votes cast), Iroquois subsequently announced its decision to sell its stake in paté.[70]

As foie gras began to occupy a so-called niche market in American gourmet stores, giving rise to several production sites in the United States, The HSUS went on the attack. In 2000 The HSUS continued to challenge paté in the marketplace, gaining substantial publicity for its protests against the staging of a foie gras extravaganza by the Smithsonian Institution.

One of the factory farming issues on which the humane movement made the greatest progress in the 1980s involved the mistreatment of calves in veal production. Its conspicuous cruelty, humane advocates charged, revealed the degree to which modern agricultural science had come to ignore the most basic biological and behavioral requirements of animals. Under the standard confinement system, young calves were kept chained or closed up in a wooden crate on a slatted floor without bedding, often in semi- or total darkness, for sixteen weeks before slaughter. They were given almost no room to move and fed an iron-deficient diet to keep their flesh tender and pale.[71]

The HSUS's "No Veal This Meal" campaign, launched in early 1982, helped fuel concern about this worst of all husbandry practices; by year's end, over 300,000 cards addressed to restaurateurs had been distributed to diners nationwide. In preparing the campaign, The HSUS conducted an extensive survey of milk-fed veal operations in the United States. "Think Twice" (before ordering a veal entrée) advertisements, describing the lives of veal calves in intensive confinement, appeared in city magazines in some of the nation's top restaurant markets, including those in Boston, Chicago, Los Angeles, New York, and Philadelphia. Fox believed that the campaign was the first step toward "a major revolution in public attitudes towards farm animals and the ways in which they are raised."[72]

In 1984 The HSUS publicized a disturbing study—that USDA had sought to suppress—in which a government-sponsored researcher determined that most veal and dairy calves in the United States were raised under stressful conditions. The HSUS played a central role in promoting knowledge of the alternative systems then gaining ground in the United Kingdom.[73]

In 1989 the Veal Calf Protection Act, introduced several years before by Representative Charles Bennett (D-FL), gained a hearing in Congress, the first farm animal welfare bill to do so in about a decade. While the Bennett bill went nowhere, it was an important register of the degree to which public concern over veal had forced its consideration within the nation's highest legislative bodies. One marker of that concern was the fact that, by 1993, veal consumption had declined to less than one pound per capita, from its peak of 3.5 pounds.[74]

The HSUS also launched a direct attack on egg and pork production, with its "Breakfast of Cruelty" boycott in 1987, that targeted the suffering that underlay America's bacon-and-egg repasts. HSUS members flooded the offices of the United Egg Producers and the National Pork Producers Council with boycott pledge cards, and both organizations responded with public relations efforts designed to address The HSUS's criticisms. Real reform, however, never made it onto the table.[75]

The 1986 fight over face branding of cattle destined for slaughter under a herd reduction program provided one of the decade's other benchmarks in relation to the mistreatment of animals used for food. The district court's decision provided a historically significant example of judicial acknowledgment of the necessity to avoid unnecessary cruelty in the execution of public policy decisions. HSUS legal staff members were enthused about the value of this prece-

Michael W. Fox was one of a number of protestors who were symbolically branded during a protest against the dairy cow hot-iron branding decision at the USDA building in 1986.

dent-setting decision, which marked the acceptance of a legal theory sometimes advanced but never before accepted—"that a humane public policy by itself mandates or requires government programs to choose among the most humane alternatives."[76]

The Biotechnology Revolution

Michael Fox's eye for emerging threats also put The HSUS in the vanguard of opposition to the genetic engineering of animals, as scientists began experiments with human growth genes inserted into mice, sheep, and pigs to accelerate their maturation, size, and weight. Fox recognized the problematic character of the early research in this arena and its future ramifications for humane work and tried to bring such concerns onto The HSUS's agenda. The Farm Animals section became the center of the organization's efforts to focus the attention of the humane movement and the general public on the serious implications of the biotechnology revolution on animal welfare. The HSUS collaborated with the Foundation on Economic Trends in a lawsuit charging that the new studies represented a "new and insidious form of cruelty toward animals by robbing them of their unique genetic makeup." Fox offered some of the earliest warnings about the care and welfare of genetically manipulated animals and led the movement's campaign against patents on animals, the first of which was granted in 1986. Such research, as he pointed out, was "not being regulated and taking place in an ethical vacuum."[77]

Beginning in 1987 The HSUS backed bills by Representative Charlie Rose (D-NC), Senator Mark Hatfield (R-OR), Representative Ben Cardin (D-MD), and others that called for a moratorium on the granting of patents until such time as the complex ethical and regulatory issues raised by genetic engineering could be addressed properly. The HSUS continued to seek legislation, even after the first patent was granted in April 1988, but without ultimate success.[78]

The HSUS was also in the forefront of efforts to challenge the adoption of bovine growth-stimulating hormone (BGH) to increase milk production. As part of The HSUS's campaign work in this arena, Fox testified in 1986 against the approval of BGH technology. Treatment with the hormone, The HSUS charged, would accelerate and expand production pressures on dairy cows, pushing them to the limit and turning them into biological machines that wore out in three to four years. The widespread adoption of BGH, Fox also asserted, would increase milk production by 20 to 40 percent, with the undesirable result of reducing the number of dairy farms in the country by a similar degree. Apart from the animals, who would fall prey to production-related diseases and suffering, the losers would be small and mid-size family dairy farms, central to a diversified, ecologically sound, and democratic agriculture. In summer 1993 The HSUS testified before the U.S. Food and Drug Administration (FDA) in opposition to the authorization of BGH use in cattle. However, the agency did not heed The HSUS's counsel that products from BGH-treated cows be so labeled.[79]

In 1997, when British researchers announced the successful cloning of an adult mammal, Dolly the sheep, The HSUS weighed in with its concerns about the exploitation of sentient animals through cloning biotechnology. Staff members publicly discussed the likelihood that cloning would increase animal suffering by "accelerating the expansion of factory farming," "preempting the development of humane production technologies," "facilitating the exploitation of animals as involuntary organ donors," "facilitating the replication of sick animals," and "rendering animals more susceptible to infectious and other diseases." Asserting the public's right to a full review of the new technology's ramifications, Michael Fox deplored the lack of concern demonstrated by the bioethicists consulted by the federal government.[80]

Eating with Conscience: Humane Sustainable Agriculture

A crucial element in The HSUS's strategy to fight factory farming involved its effort to forge partnerships with other interests critical of intensive livestock agriculture and livestock rearing in ecologically unsustainable environments. Even as The HSUS began to project its influence worldwide, its principal advocate for humane and ecologically sound agricultural practices worked to draw attention to the link between the growing worldwide taste for beef and the serious global environmental problems such a trend caused. Fox called upon the public to reduce its reliance on animal products to alleviate animal suffering, prevent the grave environmental harm being caused by intensive confinement livestock husbandry, and preserve the stake of small farmers who wanted to practice traditional agriculture. By doing so, he argued, "we can do more to help the animal kingdom than by any other single act." [81]

Whatever progress The HSUS had helped to secure on the factory farming front by the 1980s, it had not squarely confronted the rising public demand for meat and other animal products, with all of the demand's implications for animal welfare. It began to do so with greater vigor at the end of the 1980s, even as animal rights organizations like Farm Sanctuary advanced the issue with creativity and innovation. Never a vegetarian organization, The HSUS now sought greater ties to the sustainable agricultural movement, which tended to share the philosophical orientation of the humane movement about how animals used for food ought to be raised. [82]

In 1988 The HSUS promulgated a set of humane guidelines for raising livestock, poultry, and dairy animals humanely, the organization's first serious step toward the development of minimal housing and husbandry standards in the United States. The guidelines called upon producers to provide adequate living space and a nutritious diet, better handling and care, periodic access to the outdoors, the maintenance of animals in groups, and the use of anesthesia when performing surgical husbandry procedures. [83]

During the 1990s, under the leadership of Melanie Adcock, D.V.M., who succeeded Fox as head of the Farm Animals section, The HSUS launched a series of campaign initiatives focusing on the treatment of animals used for food. One, "What's Behind These Bars?" focused on the plight of hens in battery cages and encouraged consumers to avoid purchasing eggs produced under such conditions. This marked the beginning of The HSUS's first serious attempts to address the mistreatment of poultry, never covered by the Humane Slaughter Act and forced to endure some of the worst excesses of intensive animal husbandry practices. In 1993 the section launched a campaign to get eggs from uncaged hens into the nation's supermarkets. Joining forces with consumer, environmental, farmer, and animal-protection groups in numerous communities, the campaign encouraged consumers to "shop with compassion." By 1995 the campaign could claim success in eight cities. [84] In 1999 the Farm Animals section hired its first poultry science specialist, enhancing its efforts to address the numerous cruelty concerns associated with poultry production and allowing The HSUS to play a role in legislative initiatives to end that suffering. [85]

In 1994 The HSUS launched an additional campaign, Eating With Conscience™, premised on encouraging Americans to change their diets to support the development of a food production system that provided consumers with options that suited their ethical convictions. The campaign sought to encourage and enhance distribution systems that allowed people to purchase organic and compassionately produced foods in their localities. The HSUS set itself a goal of reaching beyond the humane movement to inform and energize other constituencies in efforts to meet the animal welfare, environmental, and health threats of factory farming.

Adopting the same strategic principles that The HSUS had adopted in relation to the laboratory animal issue, the Farm Animals section began to apply the principle of the Three Rs (reduction, replacement, and refinement) to its work. Eating With Conscience™ marked the formal incorporation of the Three Rs into The HSUS's farm animal welfare program. The campaign's literature asked consumers to reduce their consumption of animal products; to replace such products with grains, fruits, and vegetables; and to refine their food purchases by supporting small-scale, community-based agriculture and choosing healthy, organic, and free-range foods whenever possible. Eating With Conscience™ received sharp criticism from agricultural interests wedded to factory farming methods.[86]

It was notable that vegetarianism fit nicely into the reduction and replacement dimensions of the Three Rs paradigm. Grace Conahan Korsan, an original board member, was a vegetarian when The HSUS began in 1954, and an increasing number of those who joined the staff in the 1980s and 1990s were, too. That said, HSUS policy and program had always been guided by a pluralist perspective that recognized that not all parties to the work or the debate over animals' treatment were or would become vegetarians. John Hoyt acknowledged the validity of vegetarianism in 1983, and The HSUS actually asked supporters to "eat less meat" as early as 1988. Even so, the case for a pluralist approach could have been articulated more strongly and clearly than it generally was, and the Three Rs framework made possible a more graceful acceptance and incorporation of vegetarian constituencies than earlier responses to the subject had ever accomplished.[87]

Factory Farming and the Organics Standard

During the 1990s, The HSUS worked to support a more level playing field for humane sustainable agriculture by identifying and challenging factory farming practices and expressing strong support for organic and sustainable production. The Farm Animals section also participated in numerous conferences on sustainable agriculture and development to ensure that the humane treatment of animals received its proper due in deliberations and policy statements. The HSUS did its best to capitalize on the opportunity provided by the passage of the Organic Foods Production Act as part of the 1990 farm bill. The act called for the establishment of national standards for organic products. Among other contributions, HSUS staff members lobbied for the federal funding needed to launch the National Organics Standards Board (NOSB).[88]

In 1995 and 1996, the Farm Animals section persuaded the NOSB, a group of appointees responsible for the standards of USDA's National Organic Program, to include humane husbandry practices as a criterion for products carrying the "organic" label. Through its participation in the broader coalition of the Campaign for Sustainable Agriculture, The HSUS further advanced the same goal. Throughout the second term of the Clinton administration, the section fought off agribusiness lobbyists' controversial proposals for a redefinition of the USDA standard for organic certification—proposals that would have permitted factory farming into organic food production. Forging a coalition to fight the inclusion of genetically engineered, irradiated foods grown on land fertilized with municipal sludge and animal products produced on factory farms within the designation "organic," The HSUS undertook substantial efforts to monitor the outpouring of citizen outrage over the proposal and to recruit those who protested to USDA into a broad-based campaign to preserve the integrity of the "organic" label.[89]

Factory farming lobbyists continued their assault after George W. Bush took office, seeking to dilute the integrity of the organics standard by removing its requirement that birds raised for food must have access to the outdoors. In May 2002 The HSUS's testimony before the NOSB resulted in a twelve–one vote in favor of outdoor access. Assuming that eternal vigilance would be the only real guarantor of such principles, however, protecting the integrity of the NOSB standard now became a permanent responsibility of the Farm Animals section and Government Affairs department.[90]

Downers and Transportation

Until the emergence of the downed animal campaigns of the early 1990s, the question of animal handling and treatment in transportation languished. Although humane organizations cared about the mistreatment of animals being shipped to slaughter, they did very little to spur reforms of objectionable practices. In their early years, HSUS staff members investigated the problem of livestock shippers' noncompliance with the Twenty-Eight Hour Law, hoping to make an 1873 law directed against rail transportation applicable and enforceable in the case of animals transported by motor vehicle. By 1957, advocates estimated, 60 percent of the nation's livestock traffic moved by truck and some 90 percent moved partway by truck. A 1961 study by USDA re-

Investigator Frantz Dantzler inspects "pig parlor cars" on a train carrying hogs to slaughter.

vealed that the death rate of hogs in truck shipments was nearly double that by rail. In 1964 Representative George M. Rhodes (D-PA) sponsored H.R. 10026 to extend the provisions of the Twenty-Eight Hour Law to the transportation of livestock by truck. It failed.[91]

The issue surfaced again in the 1970s, with livestock truck hauls becoming ever longer, when national livestock dealers and the American Trucking Association sought the movement's counsel concerning ways to improve the transport of livestock in trucks. This was a positive measure, although the two organizations lacked authority to make truckers comply with the guidelines. In 1971 Representative William Dickinson (R-AL) introduced H.R. 9086 to amend the Livestock Transportation Act to include common carriers by motor vehicle. The HSUS weighed in on subsequent congressional bills designed to enact measures to stop the death and suffering of livestock being transported by truck, citing one study claiming that over 200,000 full-grown hogs died annually in transit, from overcrowding, unsuitable weather, bad handling practices, and improper loading.[92]

In the mid-1980s, HSUS investigator Paul Miller found livestock beaten with clubs, hauled in unsuitable vehicles, and held in improperly maintained facilities, and The HSUS told members in a special *Close-Up Report* that the meat industry and USDA "tolerate a certain level of injury, death, and abuse. Economically, that loss has been built into the profit structure of the meat-producing industries." By this time other organizations were beginning to sharpen their focus on transportation cruelties and on the related problem of downed-animal abuse, the result of mistreatment and indifferent handling procedures at auctions and stockyards.[93]

The HSUS also weighed in on the plight of "downers"—animals too weak, sick, or disabled to move on their own. During 1991 and 1992, five HSUS investigators found that downed animals were the victims of abuse and neglect at 73 percent of the thirty-one livestock markets and stockyards they visited. Downed animals were trampled by their healthier penmates or winched and dragged by their necks, ears, legs, and tails. Auctioneers and meatpackers carried on a low-bid trade in "downers," making a mockery of the livestock industry's professed commitment to elimination of downed-animal misery. In 1992 The HSUS testified before the House Agriculture Subcommittee on Livestock, Dairy, and Poultry and proposed remedies to the problem that were based on its own investigative findings.[94]

In the late 1990s, The HSUS joined Farm Sanctuary and other groups in petitions to the FDA and USDA to classify meat from downers as adulterated, a designation certain to remove incentive for owners to prolong the agonies of already suffering animals.[95] The more important collaboration with Farm Sanctuary came in 2001, however, when The HSUS made heavy commitments to have downed-animal legislation incorporated into the farm bill. In their gutting of the farm bill's animal welfare provisions, the House conferees created a "study" bill to review the situation of "downers," subverting the wishes of the thousands of citizens who had communicated their desire to see this needless cruelty ended.[96]

Factory Farming and Public Health

In the early 1980s, The HSUS began to raise objections to another disconcerting trend—the excessive use of antibiotics in animal feed, to counter the ill effects and disease conditions that overcrowding of animals created. In 1985 The HSUS was a co-signatory on the Natural

Resources Defense Council's petition to Secretary of Health and Human Services Margaret Heckler, requesting a suspension of approval for any new animal drug applications. At hearings held by the FDA, HSUS officials recommended a prohibition on the subtherapeutic use of penicillin and tetracycline in animal feeds, on the grounds that their ubiquitous presence in such products would encourage the growth of organisms resistant to these critical medical drugs, with serious consequences for public health. Factory farming environments that relied on the routine administration of potent drugs with proven value in human medicine, The HSUS argued, were inimical to animal well-being, which could best be guaranteed by the removal of animals from overcrowded conditions that caused extreme stress.[97]

By the mid-1990s, the adverse impacts of factory farming were gaining unprecedented levels of attention. Michael Fox and other staff members had been warning the public about intensive animal agriculture's massive pollution, inhumane working conditions, damage to rural community life, and food safety concerns for several decades, but many other interest groups were now aware of the problem. Media scrutiny of factory farming focused on the pollution of waterways and drinking water, fish kills, and the emergence of *Pfiesteria* in tributaries of the Chesapeake Bay and in North Carolina. The Farm Animals section responded by producing a video in collaboration with the video services department of The HSUS.

The campaign to highlight factory farming's inherent dangers also gained from government action to recall contaminated meat. The link between bovine spongiform encephalopathy (BSE, or "mad cow disease") and the practice of feeding rendered animal protein to cattle in confinement systems made it possible to call into question the viability of factory farming methods. After the controversy over BSE erupted in March 1996, staff member Howard Lyman, appearing on the syndicated television talk show *Oprah*, touched off a firestorm by warning that the presence of animal parts in cattle feed posed a risk to humans. Texas cattlemen sued under their state's "food disparagement" statute. The trial vindicated the free speech rights of both host Oprah Winfrey and The HSUS.[98]

The HSUS's concern over routine use of antibiotics in animal feed finally gained broader attention at the century's end. In 1997 the World Health Organization called for a ban on the use of antibiotics to promote animal growth, and the European Union prohibited antibiotics commonly used in human medicine from being included in animal feed. The HSUS supported federal legislation to "keep antibiotics working" in human medicine by limiting their use in animals. The HSUS sought to illuminate the factory farming industry's rampant dependency on subtherapeutic antibiotics to promote growth and control the numerous disease outbreaks common to the factory farm environment.[99]

A Closer Look at Animals

If Michael Fox's co-workers in the early 1980s sometimes marveled at his prescience concerning trends in the field of animal agriculture, about one matter—his insistence that more and more Americans could be educated to accept the view that animals used in agriculture were complex emotional beings—colleagues had their doubts. By 1997, the year Melanie Adcock became vice president of the Farm Animals and Sustainable Agriculture section and Fox assumed his new role as HSUS senior scholar of bioethics, The HSUS had launched several campaign initiatives working to realize Fox's vision. The most important, A Closer Look at Animals™, explicitly focused on the transformation of public attitudes about farm animals and tried to inculcate a deeper appreciation of farm animals as feeling beings with emotion. As part of the initiative, The HSUS published a number of full-length essays that showed animals as complex, sensitive, and social individuals, against the technological paradigm that cast them mainly as "meat and milk machines."[100]

The HSUS annual celebrations of National Farm Animals Awareness Week, launched in 1992, frequently honored efforts to make people more aware of farm animals and their needs. The division also sponsored the care, shelter, and sanctuary of several animals who made occasional public appearances with staff members. In the wake of the 1995 box office hit film *Babe*, The HSUS placed special emphasis on the pig, drawing a stark contrast between that animal's intelligence and the harsh treatment the animals received under intensive confinement. Staff specialists also sought to focus attention on cruelty cases involving farm animals, especially in those instances where law enforcement and judicial personnel might not be inclined to take them seriously.[101]

"No Counsels of Despair"

In 2001, in *The State of the Animals: 2001*, HSUS president Paul G. Irwin proclaimed the welfare of farm animals in the United States "shameful." With more than eight billion animals killed for food every year in the United States, it was hard to claim that the humane movement had successfully promoted the case for according better protection to animals used for food. It was a hard time for the Farm Animals section, too, as high staff turnover and the decisions of Melanie Adcock and her interim successor, Gary Valen, to take positions with other organizations active in humane and ecologically sustainable agriculture slowed the section's progress.[102]

The HSUS placed special emphasis on the plight of pigs on factory farms in the 1990s.

It was also a time for taking stock. In The HSUS's early years, and especially during the campaign for the Humane Slaughter Act, the organization was able to locate a few fair-minded politicians on the congressional agricultural committees that control the fate of relevant legislation. By the 1980s this had changed, and an unyielding "agrigarchy"—congressional committees stacked with politicians heavily tied to factory farming and hostile to genuine principles of humane treatment—blocked all animal protection initiatives, making progress through Congress an unrealistic objective. As The HSUS reached its fiftieth anniversary, it was this "failure of democracy" that left the United States badly lagging behind Western Europe in addressing the worst features of animals' confinement in industrial agriculture.[103]

Despite this restriction on the possible avenues of reform, The HSUS gave evidence of its determination to halt the spread of factory farming in the new century and to wage the campaign for animals' humane treatment on a number of other fronts as well. As Michael Appleby, B.Sc., Ph.D., who left his position as senior lecturer on animal behavior at the University of Edinburgh to become vice president for Farm Animals and Sustainable Agriculture in 2002, observed, The HSUS "should yield to no counsels of despair."[104]

The years 2000–2003 saw The HSUS launch at least three initiatives to confront the excesses of industrial animal agriculture and slaughter. Each reflected the moral indignation Irwin had expressed in his *State of the Animals* assessment. All three bore the marks of the enhanced organizational capacities that characterized The HSUS during Irwin's presidency.

Taking stock of the agricultural committees' approval of the "race to the moral bottom" that characterized intensive animal husbandry in the United States, The HSUS resorted to the state ballot and initiative process to secure a striking victory that revealed and capitalized upon Americans' desire to improve the lot of animals raised for food. Together with Farm Sanctuary and other groups, the HSUS Government Affairs department coordinated a significant effort to delegitimize factory farming by placing a ballot initiative before Florida voters in

2002. By a 55 percent to 45 percent count, Floridians approved Amendment 10, a proposal to ban the use of gestation stalls, so-called crates of cruelty, two feet by seven feet in dimension, in which pregnant sows could not turn around and were forced to spend every minute of their lives in their own feces and urine. Agricultural interests, not brazen enough to argue that the crates were humane or appropriate, instead sought to scuttle the initiative by arguing that it was unsuitable for consideration as an amendment to the Florida constitution. They failed.

The HSUS also sought to invigorate Humane Slaughter Act enforcement, a neglected concern since the 1980s. Neither The HSUS nor other organizations had worked hard enough to enhance funding and support for inspection regimes since the 1978 amendments. In fact, things had gotten much worse, and there was considerable evidence of animal suffering in slaughter. Among other factors, deunionization had allowed the slaughtering industry to speed up kill lines so much that animals were being hung up on hooks, skinned, dismembered, disemboweled, and boiled while still alive and conscious. While empowered to do so, inspectors were rarely instructed or given an opportunity to halt production lines after observing humane slaughter violations, and some plants had erected visual barriers that rendered such oversight unfeasible in any case. After a 1997 USDA-commissioned survey of federally inspected slaughterhouses revealed numerous violations of federal laws, including the Humane Slaughter Act, the Government Affairs department made such objectionable practices a priority. The HSUS was not alone in its outrage, as Senator Robert Byrd (D-WV)—a young congressman during the humane slaughter battle of the 1950s—took to the floor of the U.S. Senate in 2001 to express his indignation at press reports of horrendous treatment of animals and human workers in the nation's slaughterhouses. Wayne Pacelle, senior vice president for Communications and Government Affairs, immediately enlisted Byrd's help with reform, and Byrd led the fight for supplemental funds in 2001 to hire inspectors to monitor unloading, handling, stunning, and killing practices. The fiscal year (FY) 2002 Agriculture Appropriations bill contained a substantial increase for enforcement activities, and, for FY 2003, Byrd and a bipartisan roster of 39 senators and 132 representatives sought a $5 million increase from the Appropriations Committee for oversight activities. Sponsors expected that the new inspectors would work solely on humane slaughter enforcement.[105]

HALT HOG FACTORIES

The Humane Society of the United States

Finally, in 2002, The HSUS's Farm Animals and Sustainable Agriculture section rolled out Halt Hog Factories™, a campaign drawing attention to the devastating impact of confined animal feeding operations on animal well-being, human health, and the environment. The HSUS launched its efforts in Iowa, which had more than six hundred hog confinement operations. Staff members worked with local activists and citizens' groups to make the fight against factory farming a genuine grassroots struggle. "By directing our attention to Iowa," Michael Appleby declared, "we can make a real difference in the battle against large-scale confinement operations and have a 'trickle-down' effect in other top producing states."[106]

Fred Myers and other HSUS campaigners of the 1950s undoubtedly would have been horrified by the numerous and conspicuous cruelties that characterized modern food production at the dawn of the twenty-first century. They would just as likely have found encouragement, though, in the range of efforts—like the federal legislative drive to enhance humane slaughter enforcement and eliminate the suffering of downers, the Florida ballot initiative, and the campaign to reach America's heartland with the ugly truth about factory farming—that characterized The HSUS's twenty-first-century program of action. In its efforts to curb the myriad abuses of factory farming, The HSUS followed in the spirit of its founders' very first campaign, continuing to make the abuse and suffering of animals used for food the subject of a broad-based and democratic debate.

CHAPTER 3

To Find Other and Better Ways:
Animal Research Issues

he HSUS emerged, in part, from tensions surrounding the use of pound and shelter animals in research, and it formed at a time of significantly expanding government-funded scientific research, much of it relying on animals. In the ensuing years, public support for animal experimentation, the entrenched position and influence of institutions tied to the practice, and the increasing complexity of animal use made it a vexing and difficult issue to address.

When The HSUS began its work, staff members labored mainly on the federal humane slaughter campaign. Even so, The HSUS had a well-defined but limited agenda in relation to animal research—to keep pound, shelter, and stolen animals out of the laboratory; to campaign for the humane handling and treatment of animals used by scientists; and to develop the facts about conditions in the nation's laboratories. The HSUS was not an antivivisection society, as Fred Myers explained in a 1958 *HSUS News* article. Rather, it stood for the principle that "every humane society…should be actively concerned about the treatment accorded to such a vast number of animals." It also believed that "every individual person, and particularly everyone who endorses the use of animals in research, has a moral obligation to know the facts and to do all that can be done to protect the animals from preventable suffering." At The HSUS's 1958 National Leadership Convention, Myers reminded his audience that "the animal that will die six seconds from now, the animal that is dying now, the [millions of] animals that will die this year—these animals cannot wait." For these animals, he argued, people of goodwill needed "to do now what can *now* be done."[1]

Nor did the founding staff and board members seek to make an enemy of the scientific community. In 1961, explaining why The HSUS had not been organized as an antivivisection society, Myers told one correspondent that the organization believed that scientists needed encouragement "to find other and better ways of accomplishing the ends that animals now serve," and that it was "possible to improve the care of animals in many laboratories and that, through careful design of experiments it would be possible to reduce the number of animals necessarily used." By the time Myers wrote this, William Russell and Rex Burch had published their seminal work, *Principles of Humane Experimental Technique* (1959), and Frederick "Doc" Thomsen recalled that the book had served as Myers's bible as he prepared The HSUS's first legislative initiatives concerning the humane treatment of animals in laboratories. Consistently and throughout its first half-century, The HSUS associated itself with the principles embodied in this work—that scientists, policy makers, and the public should agree upon an active program of reduction, replacement, and refinement—the Three Rs—to alleviate the suffering and, where feasible, to eliminate the use of animals in experimentation.[2]

In the years following Myers's death in 1963, The HSUS pushed for federal legislation to protect animals in research, testing, and education. Its investigations of the laboratory animal trade provided crucial momentum for the passage of the Laboratory Animal Welfare Act, and staff members worked to promote subsequent legislative amendments designed to extend substantive protection to animals in laboratories. Although The HSUS had sought other goals, it nevertheless threw its full support behind passage of the amendments that transformed the Laboratory Animal Welfare Act into the AWA.

In the 1970s, after John Hoyt became president, The HSUS recruited professional staff to work on laboratory animal issues and sought to boost the status of nonanimal methods research through the formation of ISAP. By the 1980s, with the use of animals in research, testing, and education receiving tremendous public attention, the Animal Research Issues section placed its support behind the passage of the Dole-Brown amendments and appropriate implementation. It also pushed for administrative reforms within USDA and other supervisory authorities to enhance and extend the coverage of the AWA. At the same time, The HSUS continued to protest weak enforcement by USDA and took a variety of measures to enhance government accountability, successfully petitioning for regulatory coverage of farm animals (when used in biomedical research); filing an administrative petition to secure the inclusion of mice, rats, and birds under the Act; and attempting to strengthen legislative and regulatory backing for the Three Rs.

During the same period, The HSUS extended its efforts to promote a strategic approach to the development, validation, and acceptance of nonanimal methods in research. By 2004 The HSUS was pursuing a program of action very much in accord with the one it had forged in relation to animal research in its earliest years. The Animal Research Issues section was the humane movement's strongest promoter of the integration of the Three Rs approach into both government and corporate strategies for reducing human reliance on animal use in laboratories. With its pain and distress initiative, The HSUS attempted to set the pace and tenor for a campaign that directly addressed the question of animals' actual suffering and sought to remedy such suffering through concerted action.

The Post-1945 Context of Animal Use

Before 1954 animal protectionists had very little impact on the conduct and course of animal use in research, testing, and education in the United States. Close to a dozen antivivisection and vivisection reform societies had formed by the early years of the twentieth century, and a variety of legislative proposals surfaced in state legislatures like those of California, Illinois, Massachusetts, New York, and Pennsylvania. There were half a dozen antivivisection societies operating when The HSUS formed, but they were virtually irrelevant entities with no serious influence beyond the occasional bit of publicity. Animal experimentation in the United States flourished without any legislative restriction whatsoever.

Until 1960 or so, almost all of the bills relating to laboratory animal use that came before any legislature centered on the seizure of animals from pounds and shelters. This was an especially controversial issue within the humane community, for it struck at the heart of the mission most advocates associated with pound and shelter work—to provide animals with either a second chance at life or a dignified and painless death. Moreover, such bills generally resulted from the initiative of biomedical research interests, seeking to legalize and simplify access to dogs and cats from pounds and shelters. In the post-World War II period, with research booming and demand for animals on the rise, the medical research

Investigators found overcrowded pens—holding 50–75 dogs each—on the premises of a Pennsylvania dealer who supplied animals to laboratories.

community pushed hard for pound access laws. In 1948 and 1949, researchers in Minnesota and Wisconsin succeeded in pushing through strict seizure laws, forcing shelters operated entirely by charitable funds to supply animals for experiments.[3]

In one laboratory more than five thousand white mice were found in 1958 kept in tiny plastic boxes like these.

Biomedical researchers' aggressive efforts to secure pound and shelter animals antagonized humane workers, who saw these attempts as a betrayal of the basic charge of an animal organization. Responding to the situation, with a gambit that proved to be controversial, AHA President Robert Sellar attempted to negotiate with the National Society for Medical Research (NSMR), which represented the biomedical research community in these interests, hoping to secure a deal in which researchers could seek to acquire animals from publicly subsidized or operated pounds and shelters but would refrain from attempts to secure them from privately subsidized facilities of any kind. However, Sellar's attempt to resolve the threat posed by seizure legislation to the morale and smooth functioning of the shelter community became controversial when news of the negotiations leaked out to antivivisectionists. Sellar's subsequent death ended serious efforts to address the issue through negotiation, and the surviving AHA leadership—dominated by the leaders of large humane societies—found it difficult to resolve the ongoing tensions.[4]

In 1952 the representatives of member organizations at AHA's national convention approved a resolution to develop nationwide resistance to the NSMR's efforts. However, AHA management backed away from engagement with the issue, leading to still greater discord. Hired by Sellar to edit the AHA's publication, the *National Humane Review*, Fred Myers vigorously attacked the NSMR for its policy and conduct. In short order, he clashed with AHA's post-Sellar management, which favored a less direct and less confrontational challenge. The subsequent debate over censorship of his articles led to the showdown that resulted in Myers's departure—along with three other AHA staff members—to found the National Humane Society, the organization that became The HSUS.[5]

In the years immediately following The HSUS's formation, pound seizure was at the heart of the organization's program activity, as it assisted local organizations in legislative and public awareness battles that pitted them against research institutions across the country. The HSUS's efforts were handicapped by the acquiescence of several major organizations—including the ASPCA—to researchers' demands for pound access. The HSUS worked hard to defend the interests of humane societies that did not want to operate under the burden of pound seizure requirements, helping to defeat legislation that might have required them to turn over animals to laboratories.[6]

Apart from these early skirmishes over pound seizure, the broader familiarity of The HSUS with laboratory animal issues came from investigations undertaken by staff members and other humane workers. In 1957 Fred Myers and Helen Jones visited medical school animal quarters in three states, observing experiments and postoperative care. In 1958, after a three-year campaign, their reports and activism concerning shipments of monkeys—dead, dying, and mutilated—coming through New York's Idlewild (now JFK) Airport persuaded the government of India to adopt stricter guidelines for transportation and care of animals destined for use in polio research. In 1959 another animal advocate, Ann Cottrell Free, exposed the terrible conditions in which caged dogs were kept by the FDA in its Washington, D.C., facility. Free's revelations raised concern about the prevalence of substandard treatment, housing, and care—even in a federal laboratory setting.[7]

During 1958 and 1959, The HSUS also sent animal caretakers to seek positions inside several California research facilities to gather evidence. The investigators took photographs and kept diaries to record the work of the scientists who employed them. Their efforts revealed gross neglect, and it was "claimed and proven," as HSUS director Jacques Sichel wrote to one

Fred Myers presents testimony before Congress during his tenure at The HSUS.

U.S. senator, "that animals were left unattended to die after the completion of painful experiments, that live animals were thrown into garbage containers, [and] that animals were kept in their quarters and permitted to suffer without any attempt at post-operative care." The HSUS began to prepare evidence for a complaint under the California anticruelty statute, because the California Board of Health, charged with the statute's enforcement, failed to hold a public hearing on the matter, although it claimed to have investigated the charges thoroughly. In 1960, after The HSUS took an appeal to the California Supreme Court, three doctors sued the California branch for $240,000, alleging that The HSUS's charges had libeled them. Interpreting the researchers' actions as an expression of the NSMR's recently announced strategy to destroy any humane organization that sought to promote reforms in the institutional use of animals, The HSUS fought back. Among other actions, it published a collection of the depositions. HSUS officials looked forward to the chance to see their charges of cruelty publicly aired, but, ultimately, the case went away because no decision was handed down against the branch. Even as the case disappeared, however, the widespread publicity it generated helped to create momentum for reform.[8]

The HSUS was active on other fronts as well. In 1961 a $10,000 grant from the Doris Duke Foundation made it possible to perform a statistical analysis of grants made in support of animal experimentation. Myers hired Westat Research Analysts to conduct a study of reduction of animal use through improved experimental design and statistical methods. In a sample of 173 research projects involving animals, reported in the 1961 *Index Medicus*, Westat found that 129 of them—close to 75 percent—could have reduced their use of animals through proper statistical design. Moreover, Westat concluded that only 4 percent of the 173 projects written up had been well designed and properly analyzed.[9]

The following year, HSUS director James T. Mehorter, a psychologist at Berkshire Community College in Massachusetts, collaborated with two medical doctors to conduct an attitudinal survey of fifteen hundred prominent opinion makers on animal use in laboratories. A majority of those surveyed supported the view that painful uses of animals should be limited and probably controlled by law.[10]

The Push for Federal Legislation

As it moved to establish a broad policy position on the use of animals in research, testing, and education, The HSUS set its sights on the passage of federal legislation modeled after the English Cruelty to Animals Act of 1876, which put a rudimentary system of oversight in place. Other organizations, especially Christine Stevens's AWI, also sought to make the case for a system of regulation and restraint. From the start, however, there was a serious question about whether the movement would be able to unite around a proposal for federal legislation. Unity was necessary, many argued, to overcome the overwhelming forces that would array themselves against such a bill. Nevertheless, there were significant differences of opinion about the provisions such legislation should contain.

For a few years in the 1950s, The HSUS believed that it might be possible to prosecute laboratory workers for cruelty under ordinary state statutes. Proposals for the regulation of animal experiments began to surface in the U.S. Congress in the late 1950s. However, the emphasis placed upon the passage of humane slaughter legislation at both the federal and state levels prevented animal protection organizations from devoting their full energy to reforming laboratory animal use.[11]

In May 1960 Senator John Sherman Cooper (R-KY) introduced the first serious federal bill on the topic in over half a century. S. 3088 established basic record-keeping requirements, mandated comfortable and decent housing and nourishment, and called for pre- and postprocedural anesthetic relief when it would not interfere with experimental outcomes. Painful experiments could not be conducted without proper licensure. Twelve other senators co-sponsored the bill, which was drawn up by Abe Fortas. The following month Representative Martha W. Griffiths (D-MI) introduced a companion bill, H.R. 1937, in the House.[12]

The HSUS did not support the Cooper-Griffiths bill, placing the organization at odds with Christine Stevens. The Cooper-Griffiths bill proposed to place enforcement authority within the U.S. Department of Health, Education and Welfare (HEW), the same agency dispensing grants to researchers through the National Institutes of Health. The HSUS doubted that enforcement would be vigorous under the proposed arrangement and felt vindicated by its observations of the response of the FDA and HEW to the inadequate conditions Ann Cottrell Free had uncovered in an FDA laboratory.[13]

> **Cruelty Retards Medical Research**
>
> THE HUMANE SOCIETY OF THE UNITED STATES
> Washington 36, D.C.

The HSUS's experience in the California episode also influenced its rejection of the Cooper-Griffiths legislation. There, The HSUS spent thousands of dollars on investigations, court action, and educational outreach to the public and to legislators. The California law that purportedly protected animals in laboratories had never been enforced, and The HSUS thought the statute's delegation of enforcement authority to the wrong agency (the state's Department of Health) was the reason.[14]

A 1963 HSUS pamphlet urged support for H.R. 4856, the Randall bill.

Instead of HEW, The HSUS wanted to explore and promote other enforcement options that did not leave oversight in the hands of any agency or department that would itself be regulated by the proposed legislation. Several subsequent bills sponsored by The HSUS (like Representative Claude Pepper's H.R. 8077 in 1963) sought to place enforcement power within a proposed Agency for Laboratory Animal Control, a scientifically oriented agency of the Department of Justice.[15]

In 1961 The HSUS backed H.R. 3556, introduced by Congressman Morgan Moulder (D-MO). This bill was a little more restrictive than the British act upon which the Cooper-Griffiths bill had been based. Among other things the Moulder bill specified that "no unanesthetized animal shall be burned, scalded, or subjected to perforation of the abdominal viscera, or to any similarly acutely painful procedure," and that "animals used in surgery or other procedures causing pain or stress shall be given pain-relieving care." In a single month, The HSUS sent out more than 100,000 folders about the Moulder bill to humane societies and advocates.[16]

In 1962 both bills received a hearing, and Fred Myers presented extensive testimony before the House committee overseeing the legislation. Myers told of "seeing dogs in cages so small they could not stand, cats in cages with wire mesh floors so widely spaced they could not walk, stand or lie down in a normal manner, animals left unattended after surgery, or treated in 'pigsty conditions.'" At the hearings and on national television, Myers demonstrated working models of the Blalock Press and the Noble-Collip Drum, devices used to create injuries, pain, and shock during laboratory procedures.[17]

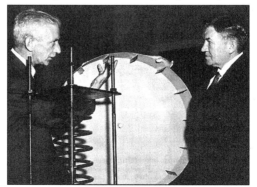

In 1962 Fred Myers (left) demonstrated the Blalock press and Noble-Collip drum in front of a jam-packed roomful of spectators.

Because it, too, proposed to place enforcement authority for ensuring laboratory animal welfare within HEW, The HSUS withheld its support for the senate bill co-sponsored by senators Joseph S. Clark (D-PA) and Maurine Neuberger (D-OR) in early 1963. Instead, The HSUS promoted H.R. 4856, the legislation it drafted for Representative William J. Randall (D-MO), and H.R. 8077, the bill introduced by Pepper later the same year. These bills required that research projects use the fewest possible animals and none at all when a substitute method was available, that animals be fully anesthetized except when it could be fully demonstrated that anesthesia would interfere with the experiment, that animals likely to suffer prolonged pain or distress in experiments be killed painlessly immediately after their completion, and that animals be kept in comfortable, clean quarters and given postoperative care comparable to that enjoyed by human patients undergoing significant procedures. The HSUS thought the Pepper and Randall bills retained all of the virtues of the Moulder legislation.[18]

Even as the debate over federal legislative proposals continued, The HSUS extended its public outreach efforts. HSUS director Cleveland Amory's June 1 and August 3, 1963, *Saturday Evening Post* articles leveled a serious indictment of laboratory animal care in the United States. The HSUS also produced literature that made the case for oversight, like *Cruelty Retards Medical Research* and *Proof of Cruelty to Laboratory Animals*, adopting a careful approach of providing no horrifying accounts or disturbing photographs. This was part of a strategy to avoid antagonizing sensitive supporters and the scientific community it hoped to influence.[19] With as many as eight competing bills on the subject in the Eighty-eighth Congress, the movement could not muster the same degree of unity and cooperation it had managed for the Humane Slaughter Act. Congress was also engaged in crucial debates on civil rights legislation, which pushed many other matters off of the congressional agenda. Federal protection for animals in laboratories would have to wait its turn.[20]

The struggle continued on several other fronts. From 1960 on The HSUS collected statements from scientists and experimenters who were willing to speak frankly about avoidable pain and suffering in the laboratory and the limits of experimental methodology. The pointless infliction of pain and the suspect character of results gained from using badly stressed and neglected laboratory animals became important arguments during the campaign for federal protection for laboratory animals.

In early 1964 Amory, HSUS President Oliver Evans and investigator Frank McMahon made unannounced visits to a number of animal laboratories in New York State and took photographs to document what they saw. Several animals lay dead in their cages. Others were emaciated. Cages were overcrowded, and many animals lacked food and water. Sanitation was poor, and animals recently subjected to surgery received insufficient attention and care.[21]

Public pressure resulted in significant developments within the scientific community. The NIH published its first *Guide to the Care and Use of Laboratory Animals* in 1963. The American Association for Accreditation of Laboratory Animal Care (AAALAC) was established in 1965, in part as an effort to shore up the claim of self-regulation. The April 1965 report of Great Britain's Littlewood Committee, appointed by the Home Office to reevaluate the control of experiments under the British Cruelty to Animals Act of 1876, also encouraged American humanitarians. HSUS spokesmen underscored the British report's emphasis on the need for increased governmental inspection, greater restrictions on the infliction of avoidable pain, and unnecessary duplication or replication of experiments.[22]

Frank McMahon (right) and Dale Hylton examine rabbits living in filthy conditions at a Pennsylvania laboratory-supply operation in the mid-1960s.

The HSUS's unique contribution to the campaign for regulation was its five-year investigation of animal dealers who supplied laboratories. With the laboratory animal issue heating up in the early 1960s, field investigators intensified their efforts to expose the system that took animals from such random sources as dealers, auctions, pounds, and assorted other sites to medical or commercial laboratories. After Frank McMahon joined The HSUS as director of field services in

1961, he began aggressive investigations of dog dealers in a number of states, trying to generate support for a federal law to prevent cruelty to laboratory animals and the repeal of pound seizure laws like New York State's Metcalf-Hatch Act. McMahon's arrival marked the start of five years of intensive investigative work tied to the goal of federal and state regulation, during which time The HSUS was instrumental in securing convictions for illegal acquisition of animals, cruelty, filthy conditions, and neglect in feeding, watering, and control of disease at dealers' establishments. In 1962 McMahon participated in the arrest of Lester Brown, a Whitehall, Maryland, animal dealer, who was later convicted of cruelty to animals. This set the stage for a more fateful encounter with Brown four years later.[23]

Antipathy to the Metcalf-Hatch Act led The HSUS to extend its investigations to New York State. In October 1963 McMahon and investigators from a local humane society entered the premises of Rock Mountain Valley Farm, near High Falls, with a magistrate's warrant. McMahon arrested the proprietor, who was managing a colony of animals recovering from experimental surgeries in dirty and overcrowded conditions. Rock Mountain Valley Farm purportedly housed experimental dogs for Columbia, Cornell, and New York universities as well as for several New York City hospitals.[24] While the complaint was dismissed on a technicality, The HSUS pointed to the case as evidence of the need for federal legislation to prevent cruelty to animals in laboratories and for revision or repeal of Metcalf-Hatch.

Many of the dealers who supplied laboratories operated in Pennsylvania, and HSUS investigators spent a lot of time there working with Fay Brisk of the Animal Rescue League of Berks County and other campaigners seeking to reform the traffic in animals. In

Frank McMahon (left) comforts Teenie, with her owner, Garland Lloyd, after her rescue from an NIH kennel in Maryland.

1964 The HSUS collaborated in a series of investigations of Pennsylvania dealer John Dierolf, charging that hundreds of animals on his farm were housed and fed improperly. McMahon, Brisk, and several colleagues, deputized as agents of the Animal Rescue League of Berks County, entered the Dierolf premises with a search warrant. Besides the unbelievably horrendous conditions in which the animals lived, dozens of the animals were seriously ill. Other humane society investigations revealed the state as the main crossroads of a spirited traffic in animals for research, many badly cared for by negligent dealers. McMahon was also monitoring Pennsylvania's dog auctions, where large numbers of animals were sold without any proof of ownership.[25]

Testifying before representatives of the Pennsylvania Department of Agriculture, McMahon observed, "Animals held in this Commonwealth for resale to various institutions are kept under the most repugnant and appalling conditions imaginable." Among other measures The HSUS strongly backed an enhanced dog law for the state, which McMahon called a "clearinghouse for cruelty." In late 1965 a bill to stiffen penalties for cruelty to animals by kennel operators and others passed the Pennsylvania legislature. HSUS officials hailed Pennsylvania's new dog law as a model for the nation. Even so, it was very difficult to get a state's attorney to work energetically on such cases, and cruelty convictions, when secured, had limited effect. In most instances the dealer paid a $450 fine and court costs and could resume his operation unchanged.[26]

By the time the Pennsylvania bill passed, The HSUS's efforts to track the traffic that sent pets to laboratories had also attracted the attention of federal legislators. The case of Teenie (or Tiny), a small black and white setter purchased by NIH from a Pennsylvania dealer, was a catalyst in the drive toward federal reform. Fay Brisk traced ownership of the dog to a Virginia man who had reported Teenie stolen in August, but NIH would not release her, claiming she was the property of the U.S. government. At that point Frank McMahon, Dale Hylton, and HSUS attorneys traced and verified the sequence of dealer transactions that had brought

Teenie to NIH, demonstrating that not even the nation's federal research laboratories bothered to keep adequate records of the animals it acquired for experiments.[27]

The HSUS remained vigilant in Pennsylvania, even as federal attention to the subject increased. McMahon continued to uncover "shocking abuses and cruelty" at dog auctions, cooperating with Brisk to bring together evidence and testimony from sheriffs, policemen, dealers, informers, doctors, veterinarians, and humane agents to make the case for an act to protect dogs, cats, and some other animals being supplied to laboratories.[28]

A shelter manager returned dogs to his Long Island shelter in 1964 following the arrest of an animal dealer who attempted to buy the animals for resale to research laboratories.

The Laboratory Animal Welfare Act

In spring 1965, with events unfolding rapidly in both Pennsylvania and the U.S. Congress, The HSUS placed its support behind new legislation, H.R. 10049 and H.R. 10050, sponsored by Claude Pepper and Paul Rogers (D-FL), respectively, and largely drafted at The HSUS by "Doc" Thomsen and others. Rogers was influential within the House Subcommittee on Health and Public Safety, which planned to hold hearings on laboratory animal use, and chaired a committee investigating general HEW practices. For the first time, The HSUS supported the establishment of an Office of Laboratory Animal Welfare within HEW, independent and insulated from political pressure. The Pepper-Rogers legislation also required measures to achieve reduction, replacement, and refinement, encompassed laboratories and dealers not targeted by earlier bills, and proposed ineligibility clauses for violators. In September 1965 Senator Thomas McIntyre (D-NH) introduced S. 2576, a companion bill to Rogers's H.R. 10050, and it, too, gained The HSUS's endorsement.[29]

By that time, however, the campaign for legislation to regulate animal use in laboratories had taken a fateful turn, and a new approach quickly pushed older ones aside. Public outrage over the theft of animals for sale to medical research facilities led to a recasting of the debate. It was the trade in animals, not their treatment in laboratories, that would become the primary subject of legislation.[30]

On September 2, 1965, Representative W.R. Poage, champion of the Humane Slaughter Act, held a public hearing on H.R. 9743, a bill introduced on July 9 by Representative Joseph Y. Resnick (D-NY) to ban interstate shipment and sale of stolen pets. Resnick had conscripted USDA attorneys to help him craft a bill that would bypass congressional health committees. Senators Warren Magnuson (D-WA) and Joseph Clark (R-PA) immediately introduced a companion bill.[31]

Resnick became incensed about dog stealing after investigating the alleged theft of a family dog for sale to a Bronx research facility. Pepper, a dalmatian, disappeared from her backyard in July and was later identified in a photograph of animals being unloaded by a Pennsylvania animal dealer from his truck. Discovering that the dog had been sold to a dealer in Resnick's home state, New York, the family appealed to him after being denied access to the facility. Resnick's bill proposed making it a federal crime for any facility to purchase or transport dogs or cats in interstate commerce without a license from USDA, and requiring research facilities to purchase animals from licensed dealers.[32]

Frank McMahon was a crucial witness in the hearings on the Resnick bill. In his testimony he gave details of a sting operation in which he helped Nassau County, New York, police convict a dealer who bribed shelter employees on Long Island for access to impounded pets. HSUS President Oliver Evans testified, too, making a few additional recommendations. The HSUS entered a detailed record of its five-year investigation of animal dealers into the record.[33]

McMahon and Fay Brisk also produced a confessed dog stealer who testified for one hour before the assembled congressmen. The thief answered McMahon's questions about methods of stealing, vehicles used, auction practices, and interstate transportation. "The HSUS has given invaluable assistance in all of my efforts to obtain enactment of this bill, especially in locating this man who has been in the dog racket," Resnick said as the hearing closed.[34]

Representative Poage sponsored H.R. 12488, the bill that emerged from the committee hearing, and the research community opposed it with vigor, arguing that the proposed legislation would fatally diminish the supply of needed laboratory animals and impede medical progress. But the course of events made it impossible to overcome the momentum building toward its passage. In late January 1966 Frank McMahon, together with the Maryland State Police, organized a raid on the facilities of Whitehall, Maryland, dog dealer Lester Brown, who had been arrested for cruelty to animals four years earlier. Investigators found more than a hundred dogs, sick, injured, and starving, and—in one case—frozen to death. The veterinarian on the raid recommended immediate euthanasia of fifteen animals, and Brown was charged with twenty-nine counts of cruelty. The raid on this "Concentration Camp for Dogs" received coverage in *Life* magazine. The *Life* piece, with accompanying photographs by Stan Wayman, generated extraordinary public concern and an outpouring of constituent response.[35]

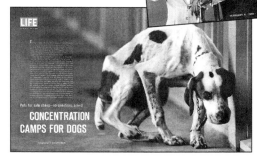

Life *magazine's exposé, "Concentration Camp for Dogs," generated a huge public response in 1966.*

With the Poage bill still pending, another HSUS investigator, Declan Hogan, revealed the results of a six-month investigation of dog dealers and laboratory animal suppliers. Hogan, who posed as a potential buyer and seller of dogs, cats, and other animals, worked his way into the vast, unregulated network of wholesale dealers in laboratory animals. In a few instances, his reports provided information used to bring cruelty charges against specific dealers. However, The HSUS also used Hogan's field notes to illustrate the need for remedial legislation at additional hearings held in March.[36]

Cultivating a shabby appearance and presenting himself as having a checkered background, Hogan had nevertheless been able to secure an interview with an NIH official to discuss a contract to supply animals. The NIH animal procurer gave Hogan a set of minimum standards that The HSUS already knew was not being followed by the majority of NIH suppliers and recommended a man who had been charged with cruelty to animals as having an "ideal setup" that Hogan would do well to emulate. Later on, visiting the parking lot to examine the aluminum camper that Hogan and Dale Hylton had rigged out as a disguised animal transport vehicle, the NIH man said, "Beautiful! The Humane Society will never suspect you're an animal supplier!"[37]

On April 29, 1966, the U.S. House of Representatives approved an amended version of the Poage bill, with a 352–10 roll call vote. Stripped by congressmen acting at the behest of the research community, the bill covered only dogs and cats. It did not provide for mandatory inspection of dealers, and it did not extend to the laboratory environment itself.[38]

Now action shifted to the Senate, where Warren Magnuson made clear his intention to see a bill released from the Senate Commerce Committee, which he chaired. Opponents of protective legislation successfully stripped the Senate bill of any reach into the laboratories,

President Lyndon B. Johnson (right) presents HSUS investigator Frank McMahon with one of the pens the President used to sign the Laboratory Animal Welfare Act into law in 1966.

CHASE LTD

but Senator Mike Monroney (D-OK) proposed an amendment to restore coverage of animals in research institutions. A heated hearing occurred on May 25.[39]

The HSUS thought Monroney's proposals for regulating usage were inadequate and feared that their adoption would "foreclose for a number of years the additional legislation which would be needed for adequate coverage of all of the problems involved." Staff analysts were also disappointed that Monroney's initiative removed Magnuson's proposal to outlaw auctions—notorious sites of cruelty and illicit trade in animals. Thus, The HSUS favored the Magnuson bill without the Monroney amendments and pressed for two separate pieces of legislation, one covering animal dealers, the other designed to protect animals in research laboratories. This strategy did not find favor, and the Magnuson-Monroney proposal was reported out of the committee on June 15 and passed by the Senate on June 22 by a vote of eighty-five–zero.[40]

Although The HSUS had sought to strengthen or eliminate the laboratory provisions, it celebrated the passage of Poage-Magnuson. President Johnson signed the bill into law on August 16, 1966, with HSUS investigator Frank McMahon receiving a ceremonial pen. The Laboratory Animal Welfare Act was not limited to dogs and cats but extended its provisions to monkeys, guinea pigs, hamsters, and rabbits. The Act did exempt animals from coverage "during actual research or experimentation." It placed enforcement power within USDA, which had about eight hundred veterinarians in its Animal Health Division at the time. While the Act focused on the prevention of pet theft and empowered the Secretary of Agriculture to license dealers who buy and sell dogs or cats, it also required that research facilities register with the Secretary of Agriculture, that dogs and cats be identified, and that dealers and research facilities keep records of their purchase, sale, transportation, identification, and previous owners' shipment of the animals. In addition, it set standards for housing, feeding, and veterinary care for dogs and cats and sanitation, ventilation, and separation by species.[41]

McMahon represented The HSUS at meetings convened by USDA to discuss implementation. USDA officials asked for input on proper methods of transporting, caging, and identification of animals. The agency also asked for access to The HSUS's files on dealers, and the organization complied, providing information on more than four hundred dealers, accumulated during five years of investigation. Several months later The HSUS provided detailed comments on USDA's proposed regulations for administration and enforcement.[42]

At the same time, The HSUS did not feel that the Laboratory Animal Welfare Act went far enough, pointing out that it would protect only a small percentage of the millions of animals being used in research. After the Act's passage, The HSUS pushed hard to secure prosecutions of violators, cracking down on unauthorized release to laboratories by pounds and shelters and on unlicensed dealers. Dealers fought back, sometimes with lawsuits.[43]

The HSUS worked hard to fend off a serious postenactment threat, the denial of congressional funding for enforcement. Time ran out on its efforts to secure legislation to extend protection into the laboratory during that session. However, at the start of the Ninetieth Congress in 1967, Oliver Evans made clear The HSUS's intention to seek legislation that ensured reform within the research laboratories themselves.[44]

Because The HSUS had spent almost five years gathering evidence of misconduct and animal misery in the animal dealer trade, and because the prosecution of cases sometimes took years to complete, HSUS field representatives continued to be highly active as investigators and court witnesses, even after passage of the Laboratory Animal Welfare Act. McMahon and other agents also pursued efforts to have civil service status attached to the position of dog warden in key states like Pennsylvania, where agents of the Agriculture Department sometimes appeared in court to help exonerate animal suppliers from cruelty charges.[45]

Field representatives also continued to cooperate with local humane authorities in raids on animal suppliers as part of The HSUS's efforts to demonstrate that inadequate congressional appropriations for administration and enforcement of the Laboratory Animal Welfare Act were rendering it ineffectual. The HSUS used raids in Missouri and New Jersey—which revealed diseased and malnourished animals being held under conditions that failed to comply with the Act—as evidence for its argument that the government should discontinue licensing dealers before rigorous inspection of their facilities.[46]

With the Laboratory Animal Welfare Act secured, The HSUS focused its efforts on extending protection to the treatment of animals during experimentation. In 1967 it supported legislation introduced by Representative Paul Rogers (D-FL) and Senator Jacob K. Javits (R-NY) that attempted to enlarge the scope of the Act. This legislation had twenty congressional and seven senate sponsors. It would have expanded the Laboratory Animal Welfare Act to include protection for all warm-blooded animals, in nearly all laboratories, and throughout any experiment in which they were involved. The Rogers-Javits bill also required the improvement of facilities, the use of anesthesia and pain-relieving drugs (where it did not defeat the purposes of the experiment), good postoperative care, and the substitution of non-sentient and less developed forms of life for higher mammals. It called for an institutional animal care committee at each laboratory and proposed assigning responsibility for enforcement to HEW. Under the proposal, mechanisms for enforcement would have been coordinated with accrediting bodies within the scientific community.[47]

"Doc" Thomsen shared The HSUS's view that USDA was not the logical agency to administer an act dealing with medical research. It was one thing for the agency "to administer an act regulating dog dealers, who commonly operate from farms, and with provisions relating only to the housing and care of animals." But USDA was not properly equipped "to deal with the most important provisions of a laboratory bill." In 1967 Thomsen and others could well recall USDA's active opposition to enactment of the Humane Slaughter Act a decade earlier; the agency did not exactly inspire confidence in its desire or its ability to oversee standards of animal welfare in the complex world of laboratory animal use.[48]

Sponsors and supporters of the Rogers-Javits bill, however, had not reckoned with the opposition of Christine Stevens of AWI, who was determined to block transfer of responsibility from USDA. Once an advocate of placing jurisdiction within HEW, she was firmly against it by 1968. While the Rogers-Javits bill had an unprecedented 38 House and Senate co-sponsors, Stevens used her considerable political influence to get it buried in committee.[49]

In his postmortem commentary on the 1967–1968 campaigns, Thomsen admonished opponents of the Rogers-Javits bill for the misrepresentations they had made and the disharmony they had engendered. His defense of the bill emphasized its codification of an alternatives strategy, its proposal for oversight committees, and its attempts to improve housing and care. Thomsen also noted Rogers's successful efforts to gain

An HSUS investigator photographed a dealer removing dogs from a Midwestern shelter in the mid-1980s.

THE HSUS/GREYHAVENS

broad approval from affected departments of the government, many humane groups, and important scientific constituencies.[50]

In 1969, attempting to satisfy discordant factions within the humane movement, Representative Rogers wrote his new version of the bill in such a way that, if enacted, it would not interfere with Public Law 89-544, the Laboratory Animal Welfare Act. The HSUS was not naïve about the prospects for enforcement within HEW but thought it would be possible to push for independent administration of the Act with the support and oversight of the bill's legislative sponsors. The organization also pointed to cases in which USDA veterinarians had come to the defense of laboratory animal dealers on trial for cruelty.[51]

In the meantime HSUS investigators continued to generate evidence that the Laboratory Animal Welfare Act as it stood was not being enforced properly, and *HSUS News* carried accounts of substandard dealers still in operation, serving as dog wardens and animal control officers, buying animals from pounds in states where it was prohibited, securing USDA licenses with ease, transporting animals under horrible conditions, and carrying on a vigorous business at auctions and "trade days" around the country.[52]

While convinced that Rogers-Javits was the stronger bill, The HSUS was realistic when confronted with evidence that continuing political roadblocks would forever forestall a vote on its merits. The HSUS did not reciprocate with opposition when the legislation Christine Stevens favored was proposed in 1970 by representatives William Whitehurst (R-VA) and Thomas Foley (D-WA). Instead The HSUS threw its full support behind Foley-Whitehurst, offering suggestions for its enhancement and working effectively with legislators to ensure its passage.[53]

The bill that eventually resulted, H.R. 19846, was the subject of hearings on June 5 and 6, 1970, and passed the House on December 7. A Senate version was approved the next day, and, on Christmas Eve 1970, President Nixon signed the legislation into law. The Laboratory Animal Welfare Act became the Animal Welfare Act (AWA). Now the law regulated more dealers, exhibitors, and others who handled live animals and provided for enhanced housing, care, sanitation, and veterinary care for animals in laboratories, including the use of pain-killing drugs, tranquilizers, and analgesics. The 1970 law required that institutions provide pain-relieving drugs and analgesics and report their use or lack of use. Another important addition to the law was its requirement for an annual report by the Secretary of Agriculture on the administration of the AWA, "to include recommendations for legislation to improve the administration of the Act or any provisions thereof."[54]

Everyone in the HSUS orbit agreed that the AWA was a big step forward. However, it still exempted animals mistreated in numerous categories of activity, and it did not extend its protection to those animals actually undergoing an experimental process or procedure in a laboratory.[55] Moreover, there was one component in the Rogers-Javits bill that the Foley-Whitehurst legislation did not perpetuate: a provision for replacement techniques like cell and tissue culture, computer simulation, and physicochemical (or physiochemical) analysis. The HSUS would lead the way in pushing such nonanimal methodologies in the years to come.[56]

1970–1990: Alternatives, Animal Liberation, and Accountability

In the 1970s new factors began to influence the debate on animal use. First was the emergence of the philosophies of animal liberation and animal rights, which provided compelling arguments for those who sought to challenge animals' use in research and fueled some of the animal protection movement's earliest applications of strategy and tactics characteristic of the civil rights and women's movements. At the same time, the development of nonanimal methodologies began to flourish, fueling the claim that there were—increasingly—alternatives to at least some animal use. Some of the earliest proposed amendments to the AWA provided for the collection and dissemination of information to reduce duplication of experiments and promoted the development of substitutes for animals in testing and refinement of protocols to alleviate suffering.[57]

After the 1970 amendments, deliberations concerning expansion of the AWA's coverage began to shift toward the air transportation of animals to supply the pet trade. However, occasional public scandals continued to infuse debate on the AWA's application to laboratory animals. In 1973, for example, thousands of Americans wrote to elected officials in protest of the U.S. Air Force's use of two hundred debarked beagle puppies for pollution studies.[58] As it turned out, both the Air Force and the U.S. Army were using beagles in experiments. John Hoyt wrote letters to Secretary of Defense James Schlesinger and other officials seeking information on military use of animals. The replies he received, Hoyt told *HSUS News* readers, made clear that the Department of Defense "does not feel obliged to justify the morality of its actions."[59]

HSUS legal staff initiated proceedings under the Freedom of Information Act to force release of the facts concerning experiments at the Army's chemical warfare research facility at Edgewood Arsenal in Maryland. In June 1975 The HSUS's inquiries resulted in a restricted tour. As HSUS staff member Phyllis Wright (a one-time inspector of animal research facilities in the District of Columbia) quickly realized, Army facilities didn't even come close to the AWA standards. Wright observed "deplorable" conditions for housing animals at the Army's Edgewood, Maryland, installation. Among other things Wright found beagles kept in cages with wire grid floors in an unventilated building whose interior temperature exceeded 100 degrees and rhesus monkeys quarantined in cages fifteen by twenty-two by twenty-two-inches. Although they lacked enforcement authority, USDA inspectors subsequently confirmed Wright's assessment, noting that while Edgewood and other federal facilities were exempt from the AWA's provisions, the 1970 amendments did require that federal facilities maintain equivalent standards.[60]

The issue gained further ground in the public arena with the 1975 publication of Peter Singer's *Animal Liberation*, which singled out questionable examples of animal use in research, testing, and education. That same year the National Academy of Sciences sponsored a symposium to explore ethical, philosophical, and legal aspects of biomedical research.[61] John Hoyt sounded the note of accountability that would guide The HSUS's policy on the issue. "For too long, scientists have enjoyed the luxury of 'doing their thing' behind closed doors and most often they are doing it with public monies. Neither their objectives nor their techniques have had to stand the test of public scrutiny. Consequently, only rarely are they required to apply to their work ethical and moral standards other than their own."[62]

Even before the Air Force beagles episode, The HSUS had begun to explore the creation of a staff position specifically devoted to laboratory animal welfare. Robert C. Bay, D.V.M., a laboratory animal veterinarian and the first recipient of AWI's Albert Schweitzer Medal in 1955, joined The HSUS in the early 1970s to work on program issues from the California office run by Mel Morse. Personality clashes with Morse made Bay's tenure a short one, and The HSUS carried on for a few years more without a full-time staff position focusing on animal research.[63]

It was the establishment of the Institute for the Study of Animal Problems as a research division within The HSUS that laid the groundwork for its future contributions in this arena. When Michael Fox joined The HSUS as ISAP director, he was able to trade on his academic contacts to gain access to a number of laboratories where he could continue to learn about and monitor developments in the use of animals in research, testing, and education. While at Washington University, he had been appointed to two committees of the National Academy of Sciences that focused on laboratory use, and he was able to continue on these for a time. In 1976, after Henry Spira (1927–1998) launched his first lab animal initiative, a targeted campaign against experiments conducted at New York's Museum of Natural History, Fox visited Lester Aronson, Ph.D., head of the research project at the museum. Later he recalled that Aronson's defense of "knowledge for knowledge's sake" transformed his own approach to the issue.[64]

HSUS President John A. Hoyt and Vice President Patricia Forkan (center) were pleased with the case presented against Edward Taub in 1981 by Assistant District Attorney for Montgomery County Roger Galvin (right). Montgomery County (Maryland) Detective Sergeant Rick Swain (left) who was the investigating officer, later became HSUS vice president of Investigative Services.

With interest and opportunity in the field of alternatives growing, John Hoyt hired Andrew Rowan, D.Phil., as associate director for ISAP in 1978. Rowan had spent two and a half years as scientific administrator at Great Britain's Fund for the Replacement of Animals in Medical Experiments (FRAME) and had advanced this issue in a number of academic papers, including one that addressed the reduction of primate use in vaccine development. Now Rowan became The HSUS's leading spokesperson on the potential of nonanimal methods. "I would say that you could reduce the use of animals by 30 to 50 percent and not retard the progress of research very much," he told the *New York Times* in 1981.[65]

Just after Rowan's arrival, ISAP conducted a review of animal use in research, testing, and education to (1) test the effects of the AWA, (2) review the degree to which scientists addressed animal welfare concerns in submitting their grant applications, and (3) establish guidelines for peer review boards. The thirty-two-page report concluded that applications for research support provided review committees with insufficient information to make informed judgments about whether the proposals were in compliance with NIH guidelines for the care and use of animals in laboratories.[66]

The HSUS was also a critic of research at the nation's federal primate centers, its attention having been directed by a few sympathetic primatologists to unflattering internal federal critiques. ISAP representatives provided congressional testimony and scientific review, and in 1984, building on its own assessment of the limited utility of research being conducted at the nation's primate centers, The HSUS proposed that Congress divert funds from the centers to establish National Centers for the Development of Alternatives.[67]

These activities were characteristic of the steps taken to fulfill ISAP's charge to "meet the development of laboratory animal science or laboratory animal medicine with the science of animal welfare." As ISAP advisory board member Franklin Loew, D.V.M., noted, "This has involved expanding human understanding of non-human animals' requirements for space, social interaction, and other environmental components on the one hand, and on the other, an increasing realization by scientists that in certain fields, animals may no longer be the best means of obtaining scientific information."[68]

From the outset of Spira's efforts, The HSUS provided crucial support to the architect of the Coalition to Ban the Draize Test and several other campaigns that targeted laboratory use. The HSUS covered numerous incidental costs associated with Spira's campaigns and hired a Draize test coordinator to provide additional support. Rowan and other staff members gave technical and strategic advice that proved to be essential to Spira's success, and they helped to gather much of the material used to document the test's deficiencies and the true potential for the development of alternatives.[69]

The relationship with Spira was a dynamic one that exemplified the desire and willingness of HSUS officials to pursue mutually agreeable objectives with independent advocates motivated by the writings of Peter Singer (*Animal Liberation*), Tom Regan (*The Case for Animal Rights*), and other intellectual leaders of the growing social movement devoted to animals' interests. Spira had taken Singer's course at New York University in 1974 and consciously sought to apply the principles he learned in a succession of mid-twentieth-century social justice movements to a new cause—the elimination of animal suffering.[70]

Spira's strategy and practice introduced a sophisticated reliance on the private sector's dynamic potential, once mobilized, turning it into an instrument of change. His approach, emphasizing preliminary research and strategic preparation, precise definition of practical and achievable objectives, readiness to negotiate, determination of arenas for compromise, and magnanimity and fairness in acknowledging any positive concessions made by the targeted institutions, found favor within The HSUS. It was a model of action that appealed to key staff members and one that many would adapt for other issues in the years that followed.

The HSUS was also approached by Alan Goldberg, Ph.D., director of the Johns Hopkins Center for Alternatives to Animal Testing (CAAT), to join its advisory board. The CAAT had its origins in the agreements reached by the cosmetics testing industry and the Spira-led coalitions. For the first time, serious financial, scientific, and practical resources were being directed toward the identification and validation of alternatives to animal use in research, testing, and education. More important, through CAAT, the issue penetrated to the heart of the toxicology establishment.[71]

The technological developments of the 1980s resulted in the proliferation of educationally and economically advantageous alternatives. Political pressure, public concern, and an appreciation of the scientific possibilities inherent in nonanimal methods research also led to an Office of Technology Assessment (OTA) study on nonanimal methods in 1986. HSUS pressure resulted in the inclusion of four animal welfare advocates on the advisory panel, and Representative Doug Walgren (D-PA) held hearings devoted exclusively to alternatives.[72]

In the mid-1980s The HSUS completed a survey of nearly six hundred companies to verify which of them conducted animal tests. This survey formed the basis of a campaign encouraging consumers to purchase cosmetics and household products produced by companies that eschewed animal tests.[73] Launched in 1990, The Beautiful Choice™ highlighted companies and brands whose products did not involve animal ingredients or animal testing, featuring a list of "The Beautiful Twenty-Six" in *Cosmopolitan* and a widely circulated HSUS *Close-Up Report.*[74]

The HSUS's Michael Fox (left) and Heather McGiffin and PETA's Alex Pacheco (right) leave the Montgomery County District Court after testifying in the Silver Spring case.

The Road to Dole-Brown

By the late 1970s and early 1980s, bills promoting the dedication of federal funds to the investigation and validation of nonanimal alternatives surfaced regularly. The HSUS, working with director Robert Welborn and Bernard Rollin, Ph.D., a philosophy professor from Colorado State University, was helping to lead the push for alternative methods of testing, specifically those that reduced laboratory animal pain and distress. As always it remained committed to advancing the humane care of laboratory animals until such time as replacement alternatives could be developed. The 1980s saw an invigorated campaign to promote additional amendments to the AWA, even as the Reagan administration sought to zero-budget inspection funding under the AWA every year. The HSUS worked with members of the Agriculture Appropriations Subcommittee to restore these funds. The cause was helped by a General Accounting Office report that revealed deficiencies in enforcement practices on the part of USDA.[75]

In October 1981 Congressman Doug Walgren (D-PA) held hearings in his Science, Research, and Technology Subcommittee to consider animal use in research and testing. Walgren invited input from a variety of parties, including colleagues who had introduced legislation concerning alternatives or—in the case of Representative Pat Schroeder (D-CO)—measures to minimize painful experiments, establish oversight committees, and add rats and mice to the list of animals protected under the AWA. Both Fox and Rowan testified at the Walgren subcommittee hearing.[76]

As it happened, the Walgren hearings took place just after the sensational controversy surrounding Edward Taub, Ph.D., and seventeen monkeys at his lab in Silver Spring, Maryland, came to public attention, and this case dominated the two-day hearings. The Silver Spring monkeys case—brought to light by Alex Pacheco and Ingrid Newkirk, who used it to launch their organization, People for the Ethical Treatment of Animals (PETA), to national prominence—seemed to render some legislators more open to the claim that abuse could and did occur in laboratories regulated by the federal government. Fox testified as an expert witness in the trial of Taub and his assistant, after each was charged under Maryland state law with seventeen counts of inflicting unnecessary pain and suffering on primates. Before the verdict in the trial came in, HSUS attorneys filed suit against USDA to require better enforcement of the AWA. The suit, eventually dismissed, contended that numerous serious violations of primate care standards had been present the very day that a USDA inspector had visited Taub's Institute for Behavior Research laboratory. A further setback occurred in August 1983, when Taub's conviction for cruelty to a laboratory animal was overturned by the Maryland Court of Appeals.[77]

The emergence of PETA and other animal rights groups in the early 1980s introduced many new voices and approaches to the controversy surrounding animal experimentation. These organizations also tended to campaign more aggressively than The HSUS—sometimes to good advantage, sometimes not. At its best, the work of the newer organizations did render further evidence of the failure of research institutions to maintain their compliance with required standards of due care under the AWA and of a disturbing lack of commitment by NIH and USDA to promote and enforce compliance with determination.

While The HSUS did not play the central role in any of the era's most significant animal care scandals, its staff members did provide crucial support and technical counsel to individuals and organizations attempting to identify breaches of the AWA and other questionable laboratory practices. Michael Fox was one of five experts PETA asked to view and provide a deposition on conditions in Taub's facility. In 1984 Fox and investigator Marc Paulhus accompanied Tallahassee, Florida, police on an authorized search of a Florida State University laboratory where cats were reportedly being deprived of water as part of an ongoing experiment.[78]

President Reagan's October 1984 veto of the Walgren amendments to the NIH reauthorization bill set the stage for the struggle to enhance the AWA to ensure greater protection for animals in American laboratories. Walgren's bill, the result of a long and complex conferencing process in the House and Senate, had been approved by Congress, but the president rejected the authorizing legislation twice, citing its attempt to "exert undue political control over decisions regarding scientific research."[79]

On October 30, 1985, President Reagan again vetoed provisions to protect laboratory animals—with the full support of the NIH—embedded in the NIH reauthorization and the Manpower Act. This was an ominous sign of the many fights that lay ahead. While advocates heralded congressional passage of additional humane standards some fifteen years after the last passage of relevant legislation on laboratory animals, the president rejected them as "overly specific requirements for the management of research."[80]

Fortunately, animal protectionists had opened the struggle on another front, one that proved to be more difficult for the administration to circumvent. The decisive moment came when Robert Dole (R-KS), Senate majority leader and—with Representative George Brown (D-CA)—cosponsor of legislation on the use of laboratory animals, attached the laboratory animal measure he was sponsoring to the Senate version of the 1985 omnibus farm bill. The Dole-Brown legislation bore some similarity to the NIH reauthorization initiatives, and Brown had introduced a bill with these provisions in the earlier session with little success. The matter took off in the Ninety-ninth Congress, however, because Dole enjoyed controlling influence over the farm bill. Moreover, since USDA administered the AWA, the farm bill was a plausible vehicle for amendments. The 1985 Dole-Brown amendments mandated improved standards for lab animal care and institutional animal care committees to assess research proposals and address animal welfare problems within those institutions and encouraged alternative methods—especially those that reduced pain and distress. The legislation also compelled NIH to establish plans for research into methods of experimentation that adhered to the Three Rs—reduction and replacement to lessen the overall numbers of animals used and refinement to produce less pain and distress than methods currently in use. In addition to animal care committees and a program for the evaluation of nonanimal research methods, the amendments directed researchers to avoid repeated operations on the same animal, to consult with a veterinarian to evaluate strategies and methods for pain relief to reduce animal distress, and to use an information service at the National Agricultural Library to ensure that they avoided unnecessary duplication of experiments.[81]

The Dole-Brown legislation had some teeth, in that it authorized the assessment of fines for unchecked violations and provided for the suspension of funds to facilities that failed to correct identified deficiencies. Senator John Melcher (D-MT), a veterinarian, also saw to it that Dole's proposal included stipulations that primates' psychological well-being would be addressed through facilities improvement. The debates over environmental enrichment for primates and the exercise needs of dogs in laboratories were not easily resolved and would last well into the twenty-first century.[82]

The Dole-Brown amendments enjoyed the united support of both The HSUS and Christine Stevens's AWI, which had not seen eye to eye on all aspects of the 1966 and 1970 legislation. Although some other organizations' and individuals' opposition to the measured character of the Dole-Brown amendments was intense, the strong support of these two established groups helped to ensure their passage. As in 1966 aroused public concern helped to override the usual protests from some quarters of the research community. Similarly, the passage of the 1985 amendments owed much to the catalytic impact of the Silver Spring monkeys case (1981) and a subsequent University of Pennsylvania Head Injury Clinical Research Center scandal (1984–1985), cases exposed by PETA but publicized by a wide variety of groups during an intense round of activism that encompassed the period of debate over the Dole-Brown bill. Between the two, animal advocates conclusively demonstrated that substandard treatment of animals could and did occur in the nation's laboratories.[83]

After Dole-Brown

The Dole-Brown amendments to the AWA brought significant but not very visible gains. These were bolstered by similar provisions in the Health Research Extension Act of 1985, which led to the issuance of the Public Health Service Policy on humane care and use of laboratory animals. Working within the framework established by these legislative changes, The HSUS sought to advance the cause of laboratory animals by undertaking a range of initiatives designed to buttress that framework. While some elements in the biomedical research community resisted reforms, The HSUS tried to promote greater understanding of the new requirements and sought to influence the promulgation of appropriate regulations for implementation.

By the 1980s research demands for chimpanzees and other primates for use in studying AIDS, hepatitis, and other diseases, combined with the dwindling supply of animals from the wild, pushed the use of primates squarely onto the humane agenda. Their use became even more controversial after NIH announced plans to launch a program for breeding chimpanzees in centers throughout the country. The HSUS was critical of the plan for its failure to address the heightened ethical implications of using animals so genetically close to human beings. The NIH plan failed to address alternative options, appropriately designed and enriched housing standards, provisions for mother-infant contact, and other concerns.[84]

The HSUS worked hard to advance the case for administrative regulations that set minimum standards for implementation of the 1985 amendments, which were designated the Improved Standards for Laboratory Animals Act. In 1990 the organizations charged that USDA had let five years pass without promulgating standards, and that regulations, once issued, were riddled with loopholes concerning cage-size requirements. In October of that year, after congressional pressure forced the publication of USDA's draft regulations, staff members from five departments helped to compose The HSUS's 150-page commentary on the proposals.[85]

In autumn 1992 The HSUS filed an administrative petition seeking an overhaul of USDA's reporting system, which was woefully behind those of other nations that used laboratory animals extensively. The petition called upon USDA to employ a "pain scale" with meaningful categories, a classification of experiments by purpose, and a system for confirming which animals were obtained from pounds, shelters, or the wild or were bred for research.[86]

The HSUS also sought to promote greater accountability in those government agencies where there had generally been very little. In mid-1986 The HSUS pushed congressional representatives to amend the Alcohol, Drug Abuse, and Mental Health Administration (ADAMHA) authorization, thus bringing that agency under the provisions of the recently passed Dole-Brown legislation.[87] A still more impressive result ensued from The HSUS's initiative to bring military experiments under the aegis of the AWA. This campaign coincided with two congressional oversight hearings, in 1992 and 1994, and The HSUS played a central role in shaping the language and tone of the resulting report. The HSUS recommended that the Department of Defense submit an annual report on its animal use, embrace an aggressive alternatives development program, appointment an ombudsman for humane concerns at each of its research facilities, and include animal protection advocates on its animal care committees.[88]

The Dole-Brown bill's establishment of a requirement for institutional animal care and use committees (IACUCs) at all institutions that used animals set the stage for another positive oversight scheme. The legislation required that each IACUC include one member not directly affiliated with the institution (although Patricia Forkan and Christine Stevens had strenuously lobbied for two outside members). The Animal Research Issues section did its best to educate and instruct IACUC members in the principles of humane experimental technique and confronted IACUCs in cases where they failed to diligently and vigorously implement the AWA's mandates.

The HSUS's pursuit of sound public policy and adherence to the federal standards took place within the context of shrill backlash from some sectors of the research community, especially from interest groups with a stake in the status quo. Drawing on accounts of threats or acts of sabotage conducted against animal researchers and their institutions, and sometimes on prejudicial reports of specific incidents, the research lobby tried to smear The HSUS as a "terrorist" organization. Against these baseless charges, John Hoyt, Martin Stephens, Ph.D., who oversaw the section beginning in 1986, and other staff members consistently underscored The HSUS's absolute commitment to nonviolent moral suasion in letters to journals and periodicals, in congressional testimony, and over the airwaves. The Joint Resolutions for the 1990s, to which The HSUS was a principal signatory, absolutely condemned "threats and acts of violence against people," and "willful destruction and theft of property."[89]

The HSUS's Martin L. Stephens testified on the military's use of animals in 1992.

The issue of whether rats, mice, birds, and farm animals ought to be included within the protective framework of the AWA went back to 1970, when Congress broadened the scope of the act to include all mammals and birds. Through the years, pleading lack of resources and relying on linguistic evasions of the AWA's requirements, USDA specifically excluded farm animals, birds, rats, and mice from coverage.[90]

On November 15, 1989, The HSUS joined with the Animal Legal Defense Fund (ALDF) to petition USDA for the extension of the AWA to *all* birds and mammals used in laboratories.

Such a move would provide protection to mice, rats, birds, and farm animals, species that together comprise almost 90 percent of vertebrate animals used in research. The exclusion of these animals was a result of USDA's questionable interpretation of the language in the 1970 amendments to the AWA, which had as their purpose the extension of statutory protection to all warm-blooded animals used in research. Despite the evidence provided that it did not have the discretion to deny such protection, USDA had failed to alter its policy of exclusion.[91]

HSUS President Paul G. Irwin (right) congratulated Russell and Burch Award winner Robert Van Buskirk, Ph.D., at a 1995 awards ceremony in Washington, D.C.

In April 1990 USDA announced that it would extend the provisions of the AWA to all farm animals used in biomedical research. However, USDA responded to the other elements of the petition by reasserting its position that the Secretary of Agriculture had discretion to determine which animals used in research ought to be covered by the AWA. On August 7, 1990, The HSUS and ALDF joined forces again, this time in a lawsuit that sought to compel USDA to take steps to protect birds, mice, and rats used in biomedical research. On April 1, 1991, a federal district court denied USDA's motion to dismiss the suit. The parties had "standing" to sue because they had been denied the right, as contemplated by the 1970 amendments, to disseminate comprehensive and accurate information and data concerning laboratory animal use to their members.[92]

On January 8, 1992, the U.S. District Court in Washington, D.C., ruled that USDA was in violation of the AWA, having failed to take administrative measures to incorporate all warm-blooded laboratory animals within the protective aegis of the legislation, as required in 1970. The court strongly rebuked USDA for its intransigence and ordered the agency to reconsider the 1989 petition that plaintiffs had filed for the inclusion of birds, rats, and mice in the AWA regulations.[93]

Unfortunately, an appeals court reversed the decision, ruling that The HSUS, the ALDF, and other plaintiffs lacked legal standing to bring suit.[94] In the late 1990s, the Alternative Research and Development Foundation, a project of The American Anti-Vivisection Society, met a court's test for standing, and then-Secretary of Agriculture Dan Glickman voiced support for a settlement that set the stage for rules that included mice, rats, and birds. Before it went any further, however, the National Association for Biomedical Research, an animal use lobby, persuaded senators to block USDA from spending any funds from the FY 2001 agricultural appropriations budget on implementation. The following year, Senator Jesse Helms (R-NC) successfully amended the Senate's version of the 2002 farm bill to permanently deny AWA protection to mice, rats, and birds.[95]

Advancing Alternatives

During the 1980s and the 1990s, HSUS staff members testified at virtually every congressional hearing concerning animal testing, placing special emphasis on the potential of nonanimal methods. In a movement increasingly enthralled by the promise of alternatives, The HSUS sought to provide realistic perspectives on what was possible. In 1986 this commitment resulted in the publication of *A Layman's Guide to Alternatives to Animals in Research, Testing, and Education* by Martin Stephens. *A Layman's Guide* was designed for legislators, journalists, humane advocates, and others interested in a brief survey of the promise as well as the current limitations of such methodologies.[96]

In 1991 The HSUS inaugurated its Russell and Burch Award to honor those scientists who—in the tradition of the two men who produced the founding document of the field—

made a significant contribution to the development and advancement of humane experimental technique that resulted in reduction, replacement, or refinement. Initially awarded annually, and, later, every three years, the honor had gone to scientists outside the United States on four occasions by the time The HSUS celebrated its fiftieth anniversary—testament to the broad international scope of the so-called fourth wave in alternatives development.[97]

Nineteen ninety one was also the year that Hoyt, Stephens, HSUS director Eugene W. Lorenz, and David O. Wiebers, M.D., established The HSUS's Scientific Advisory Council (SAC), recruiting physicians, psychologists, veterinarians, and other scientists as part of an attempt to further the embrace of nonanimal methods in research. In 1994 three academic physicians, all members of the SAC—Wiebers, Jennifer Leaning, M.D., and Roger D. White, M.D.—published a letter in the British medical journal *Lancet*, asking fellow medical scientists to work to improve the status quo in animal use, above all by actively embracing the Three Rs. Wiebers, Leaning, and White encouraged their colleagues to avoid "reflexive, parochial attacks, based in part on untenable positions," in favor of an approach that recognizes the animal protection community as a positive stimulus "for change that would otherwise be unlikely to occur."[98]

By 1995 The HSUS's efforts to cooperate with major corporations involved in product development led to a partnership with the Gillette Company, directed toward research and validation of nonanimal methods. That year the program disbursed $100,000 in support of scientific work concerning skin and eye irritation. The HSUS also helped fund a 1995 workshop to evaluate the results of a three-year assessment of alternatives to rabbit-eye irritancy testing, which drew representatives from government, industry, and other stakeholders.[99]

An important measure of the degree to which The HSUS had successfully crossed the threshold of the policy networks in which crucial decisions about animal use were made was the invitation Stephens received to participate in the early deliberations of the Interagency Coordinating Committee on the Validation of Alternative Methods (ICCVAM), formed as a result of 1993 legislation requiring the development of validation and regulatory strategies within the National Institute of Environmental Health Science (NIEHS). Stephens was the only representative of an animal-protection organization invited to attend, although Andrew Rowan—then at Tufts University—eventually joined the NIEHS Federal Advisory Committee on Alternative Toxicology Methods, which provided guidance and counsel to ICCVAM.[100]

Another marker of The HSUS's rise to prominence as a partner in the worldwide search for identification, development, and validation of nonanimal methods was its increasing involvement with the triennial World Congress on Alternatives and Animal Use in the Life Sciences. The HSUS played a central role in the organization of the fourth World Conference, held in New Orleans in 2002, which drew almost five hundred participants from several dozen countries, representing the full range of stakeholders in the field. The HSUS also edited the conference proceedings for eventual publication, as part of the broader effort to disseminate the knowledge and insights that emerged from the event.

The Pain and Distress Report began as part of Animal Research Issues' 2000 initiative.

The Pain and Distress Campaign

In the late 1990s, The HSUS began an intensive review of policies and practices concerning animal pain and distress at the nation's research institutions. The Animal Research Issues section initiated a careful analysis of available statistics on pain and distress. In 2000 the section launched a refinement initiative focused on pain and distress.

The HSUS's campaign coincided with USDA's July 2000 solicitation of comments on the regulation and reporting of pain and distress under the AWA. The HSUS also asked constituents to contact USDA to ask that the agency demand stricter accountability from reporting institutions and take active steps to promote understanding and awareness of animals' pain and distress. More than 2,500 public comments were received.[101]

The HSUS's insistence on an accurate USDA reporting system was a core element of the Pain and Distress Campaign. While better statistics and record keeping in and of themselves would not relieve animals' pain and suffering, they would, as earlier regulations concerning other aspects of animal use in the laboratory had, lead to more focused attention on the question of how to effectively assess, prevent, or alleviate distress.[102]

The HSUS acted with the knowledge that enforcement of the federal reporting requirements concerning pain and distress, mandated under the AWA amendments of 1970, had been poor. Investigation and inquiry revealed that scientists frequently cited a lack of data and information on "how to recognize, assess, alleviate, and prevent pain and distress in research animals as a rationale for either not reporting pain and distress or not acting to mitigate it—which leads to tremendous animal suffering."[103]

As part of the campaign, the section contacted every research institution in the United States, soliciting support for a concerted push to eliminate significant pain and distress in the laboratory by the year 2020. The campaign sought to generate more attention to the detection of pain and distress in animals, better approaches to the identification and measurement of pain in animals, and greater momentum toward the elimination of these conditions. The HSUS placed substantial emphasis on gaining endorsements for the initiative from professional associations and government agencies and sought to secure their cooperation with efforts to promote workable definitions of animal distress as well as with efforts to eliminate it. Another objective was the allocation of funds from the NIH budget for the identification and alleviation of pain and distress in animal research subjects.[104]

Conclusion

When The HSUS formed, animal protectionists enjoyed only the slightest influence on the course of animal research in the United States. Scientists were largely able to do whatever they wanted to laboratory animals, and the standards of care provided in many laboratory animal facilities were limited. Laboratory animal use grew from around 17 million a year in the mid-1950s to more than 60 million a year in the early 1970s. By the turn of the twenty-first century, the number of laboratory animals used annually had dropped by 50 percent, to less than 30 million, standards of care had been improved dramatically in both theory and practice, and researchers were obliged to justify their proposed projects before IACUCs. Even though the IACUCs' enforcement of USDA regulations varied widely, it was clear that many fewer animals were being used, that animals used in laboratories were receiving better care, and that all projects involving animals required more careful justification than was the case fifty years before.[105]

Fifty years after The HSUS's constructive early engagement with the question of animal use in research, testing, and education, the organization was an important participant in relevant policy networks within both the public and private sectors and had played a major role in the improvements in laboratory animal welfare. The HSUS championed the incorporation of the Three Rs approach into national law and policy and helped to make the drive for alternative methods a self-sustaining process. The scope of the Animal Research Issues section's activities extended well beyond the boundaries of the United States, as staff members also took part in the deliberations of a number of international bodies where animal research issues were considered.

Whatever the deficiencies of the AWA in 2004, a fair assessment should acknowledge its contributions to improved animal well-being over four decades. Because of the 1960s campaigns and subsequent revisions, many unprincipled dealers who once operated with impunity were forced out of business. Under pressure from The HSUS and other organizations, the AWA expanded to include more species, and more environments in which animals are used have come under its aegis. New levels of oversight, like those embodied by the IACUCs, were put in place, and these, too, improved the situation. The AWA was the instrument of needed reforms in the transport of animals and in the protection of animals outside the arena of laboratory use. It was also, especially after 1985, the frame of reference for debates over evolving definitions of animal well-being, pain and distress, and environmental enrichment in the laboratory setting. For its part, The HSUS was where its founders intended it should be—at the heart of those debates.

CHAPTER 4

The Best Care Possible:
Companion Animals

hen the HSUS formed, the animal care and control community consisted of numerous poorly financed groups—many of them run on a volunteer basis—and perhaps a dozen or so well-heeled societies, mostly in the nation's larger cities. The field also included countless municipal pounds—bleak, dismal places, run on low budgets and quite often by uncaring employees. These hundreds of organizations focused on myriad issues and approaches and were frequently not even aware of, let alone cooperating with, one another. In 1954 the humane field comprised a chaotic universe, and there were essentially no efforts underway to create order and stability. Euthanasia practices were often badly improvised, and the level of professionalism within animal care and control work was not high in most communities. Pounds and shelters were coming under terrific pressure to turn their animals over for use in research, testing, and education. This was the situation that the founders of The HSUS hoped to change, by laboring to enhance the moral and practical quality of work undertaken at the local level.

This was also the reason that early HSUS staff positions focused on field services and technical support. Fred Myers and his colleagues saw local societies and animal shelters as the central institutions of humane work, with all programs—like humane education, cruelty investigations, spay/neuter promotion, and others—revolving around them. Their staffs, their boards of directors, and their members represented the primary constituency of The HSUS. They were the people who HSUS staff members wanted to serve as well as the people upon whom the organization relied for its own growth and support. It was an important part of The HSUS's founding vision to provide technical assistance and advice on all aspects of animal control, to help local societies to improve their facilities and their operations, to enhance the training of humane society employees, to promote the use of humane techniques and state-of-the-art equipment, and to assist communities throughout the country to draft effective animal-control ordinances.

From this early vision of service emerged the main goals of the Companion Animals section: the professionalization of animal care and shelter work at all levels, a strategy for reducing the surplus of unwanted and homeless animals, the reform of euthanasia practices, the restriction of abuses by the pet shop and commercial pet breeding trades, and the elimination of miscellaneous cruelties that cause harm to companion animals. Several generations of leadership supported these goals through public education, training, research, legislation, and media outreach.

By 2004 the Companion Animals section was one of the world's most important sources of information and action on the wide range of companion animal issues and a steadfast advocate for appropriate reforms in shelter management, euthanasia practices, and animal control operations. During its first fifty years, The HSUS had played a crucial role in bringing heightened attention and respect to animal care and sheltering concerns. For half a century, too, The HSUS had celebrated the human-animal bond, even as it sought to encourage responsible stewardship of companion animals.

Learning, Doing, Teaching: The Early Years

Abatement of the nation's surplus of unwanted dogs and cats was one of The HSUS's earliest priorities. It was a strong personal concern of all four original staff members and of many of The HSUS's first board members. According to "Doc" Thomsen, when The HSUS launched its work, organizers encountered considerable ambivalence about both spay-neuter and euthanasia among humane supporters. As it happened, however, Fred Myers was a realist, determined to set the organization he led on a path that emphasized the long-term prevention of animals' suffering and death through aggressive and pragmatic action. The HSUS's first publication, *They Preach Cruelty*, focused on the tragedy of surplus animals, as did subsequent brochures, titled *Puppies and Kittens—10,000 Per Hour* and *From Cause to Effect*, the last of which included a space for local societies to rubber-stamp their own names and appeals. From the start, HSUS staff members emphasized the importance of spay-neuter approaches, public education, and euthanasia in dealing with the tragedy of animal surplus. Recognizing the power of example, Fred Myers once protested to Pat Nixon, wife of then-Vice President Richard Nixon, that her cat was having too many kittens. "Until we are able to sell the public on the neutering and spaying of pets," Myers once said, "our shelters can never be anything but slaughter houses." [1]

Among other challenges, the movement had to develop ways to contend with the owners' reluctance to have their animals altered. The subject was plagued by misconceptions

An HSUS poster discouraging the surplus breeding of puppies was available to humane societies at low cost in 1959.

and shibboleths about its effect on animals' weight, temperament, and overall health. Then there was the issue of cost. Many owners simply didn't bother to deal with spaying or neutering their animals, while others balked at veterinary fees. [2]

The HSUS made the transformation of shelter policies nationwide a priority goal, reasoning that adoption procedures and related policies did affect the surplus animal population. In 1958, with the help of a dedicated grant from the Lyondolf Fund, The HSUS initiated production of its first audiovisual aids, consisting of a five-minute film and a slide set that dramatized the suffering resulting from animal overpopulation. The very same year, facts presented in The HSUS's earliest folder reached an estimated thirty million Americans, fans of the comic strip *Peanuts,* who followed a four-strip series in which Charlie Brown read the publication's contents aloud to Lucy and the eavesdropping Snoopy. [3]

Not all of the major shelters were stepping up to confront the surplus animal problem at this time, and The HSUS was not reticent in its indictment of confused or indifferent counsel. In 1956, when New York's Bide-a-Wee Home Association advised citizens to let their dogs mate several times a year to prevent "sexually frustrated male dogs," The HSUS moved quickly to condemn this advice and to remind Americans of the great tragedy of surplus animals. In 1964 The HSUS scored the ASPCA for similar indifference and pressed the nation's first humane society to require spaying of all female dogs and cats before release to new owners. [4]

Another difficult challenge stemmed from the hostility of veterinarians, who, in the 1950s and 1960s, sought injunctions to prevent humane societies from sponsoring the practice of veterinary medicine (and especially of spay-neuter surgery) in their shelters. In 1959 in Missouri, a group of twenty-one veterinarians sought to prevent the operation of an animal clinic with a bill in the legislature and a petition for injunctive relief. The HSUS retained legal counsel in St. Louis to assist the Humane Society of Missouri and won permission to appear in the case as a friend of the court. The veterinarians' attempt failed. [5]

The HSUS's most important general contribution to the field of animal care and control was its fifty-year commitment to assisting organizations and communities operating pounds and shelters all over the country to improve their services. Whatever the intentions of government officials and humane society organizers in many communities, their pounds and shelter operations sometimes proved to be appallingly deficient. In the pre-1975 years, especial-

In 1958 fans of the comic strip **Peanuts** *learned the facts about dog and cat overpopulation from Snoopy, who quoted an HSUS brochure.*

ly, many societies were using jury-rigged and ineffectual systems for euthanasia, inadvertently or intentionally causing greater harm and suffering to animals. Their housing systems were impossible to clean and disinfect, and their outdoor areas offered no protection. They were also forced to employ untrained staff. With so few outlets for proper training, attendants were often careless, lackadaisical, or ignorant in regard to basic procedures, and low-paying positions did not always attract the best applicants to pound and shelter work. There was not a single aspect of pound and shelter work that The HSUS did not seek to improve through education, counsel, training, lobbying, and other measures.

Although its founders deliberately strove to raise the humane movement's sights to the pursuit of a broad range of issues from a national perspective, The HSUS's involvement with local animal control work was always very direct. In fact, founder Larry Andrews's main activity as director of field services involved personal interaction with the operators of local humane societies and public pounds. Andrews traveled extensively, much as he had done for AHA, visiting facilities, assessing their needs, meeting with staff and boards of directors, and providing education and training for shelter operation, adoption policies, euthanasia procedures, humane education, cruelty investigation, and promoting the use of HSUS educational materials.

In the late 1950s, The HSUS experienced a noticeable increase in pleas for technical assistance and aid from municipalities facing the challenges of local animal control. Taking these early inquiries seriously and determined to support the development of improved animal care and control services at whatever level, The HSUS intervened in a number of local and regional contexts. In August 1959, for example, Fred Myers and Director of Organization Albert B. Lawson, Jr., collaborated with the commissioners of three southern Maryland counties to develop plans for a new animal shelter and animal control program for a region that had none. The three counties (Calvert, Charles, and St. Mary's) committed $50,000 to the construction of a shelter in Hughesville, Maryland, with ambulance trucks and advanced equipment and agreed to pay the new society $24,000 to cover operations in its first year. Incorpo-

Fred Myers and his staff worked to improve animal shelters to bring to an end the days of abysmal public pounds like this one at city dumps across the country.

rators of The Humane Society of Southern Maryland included Myers, Service Department Director John Miles Zucker, and HSUS director and benefactor Elsa Voss. In 1962 Myers offered to provide similar assistance for the construction of a proper animal shelter in the nation's capital, offering to commit The HSUS to a $250,000 fundraising campaign for the project.[6]

In several emergency situations, created through death, dereliction of duty, or corruption, HSUS staff members also stepped in to manage local facilities. In 1962 Director of Affiliates Philip T. Colwell temporarily took charge of the Champaign County Humane Society in Illinois after the untimely death of its principal officer. The following year The HSUS assumed provisional control of the Camden, New Jersey, pound in the aftermath of a scandal surrounding the illegal sale of animals to a

Ohio State Senator Charles J. Carney (left) accepts the annual Fred Myers Humane Award from Paul E. Stevens, general counsel for the Youngstown (Ohio) Animal Charity League, an HSUS Affiliate, in the 1960s.

wholesale dog dealer who supplied them to medical school and pharmaceutical company laboratories.[7]

Animal destruction and euthanasia practices also received early scrutiny from The HSUS. In 1958, acting in his capacity as a representative of a Maryland humane society, Fred Myers swore out a complaint against the dog warden of Rockville for firing four pistol shots into a dog and allowing the animal's suffering to continue for thirty minutes until county police officers came and ended the animal's agony with a single bullet. Less than one year later, The HSUS persuaded officials at the District of Columbia pound to abandon a carbon monoxide euthanasia chamber in favor of sodium pentobarbital administered by a city veterinarian. In the spring of 1960, The HSUS successfully petitioned to enjoin the public shooting of dogs on the streets of Lorain County, Ohio.[8]

The identification of the most humane methods of euthanasia was a steady priority in the early years. The HSUS's Committee to Study Euthanasia Methods investigated technologies used by the meatpacking industry as part of efforts to identify potential methods of destroying companion animals painlessly. In February 1961 John Miles Zucker, by then director of branches and affiliates, contacted a hog slaughtering plant for information on carbon dioxide, used to anesthetize animals before slaughter, to see whether it might be used as an active agent in a euthanasia system. In June 1961 The HSUS purchased an Electrothanator, an electrical cabinet that had been widely adopted in Great Britain. This device relied on electrical current, passed first through the brain and then through the body, to destroy animals. Myers had it installed at a shelter operated by the Southern Maryland Humane Society. In 1963 Lewis Timberlake corresponded with a manufacturer about other electrocution units that might be adapted for euthanasia.[9]

At about the same time, The HSUS commissioned the development of a mobile euthanasia unit. It took a van equipped with an Electrothanator (which Fred Myers usually called an "electrical euthanasia" device) for demonstration to local societies and pounds. Frank McMahon drove the van all around the country, sharing his knowledge with shelter workers.[10]

The selection of euthanasia methods by the shelters actually operated by The HSUS in its early years suggests the pace of its decision to endorse sodium pentobarbital as the best method of euthanasia. In January 1963, when Frantz Dantzler first began working at the Boul-

Frank McMahon drove The HSUS's mobile euthanasia unit (here in Washington, D.C.) around the country for demonstration to local shelters and pounds.

der County Humane Society, a special affiliate of The HSUS, the organization employed water-cooled, filtered carbon monoxide in its shelter. When Dantzler moved to Salt Lake City the following year to assume the position of supervisor at the shelter operated by The HSUS's Utah State branch, he discovered that sodium pentobarbital was well established as the euthanasia method of choice. The branch had already tried and discarded an Electrothanator, which Dantzler remembered seeing in a storage area.[11]

In the early- to mid-1960s, much of The HSUS's outreach on companion animal control concerns fell to Director of Field Services Frank McMahon and to field representatives working with him. Together, staff members presented comprehensive workshops under the sponsorship of local humane societies, reviewing equipment, handling procedures, shelter and pound upkeep, animal control practices, ordinances, contract negotiation, and public relations. Through these events, The HSUS was able to directly influence the abandonment of gunshot euthanasia and/or the replacement of antiquated destruction chambers with newer methods.[12]

During this same era, The HSUS established an affiliates' program, certifying humane societies that met approved standards of policy and program, allowing them to represent its interests in addressing specific animal control problems in their localities, and collaborating closely with them in investigations, raids, and other endeavors.[13] The HSUS also made available an "economy shelter" kit, with full blueprint plans and specifications, to enable the construction of basic facilities wherever they might be needed. Several of these were built.[14]

Some of the earliest audiovisual products sponsored by The HSUS sought to enhance the reputation of local animal control agencies and to raise the level of appreciation for their work. A few months before his death in 1963, Fred Myers contracted for a motion picture script "aimed at putting across the theme that 'good humane societies make better communities.'" The following year The HSUS produced a twenty-one-minute film, *Help at Hand*, that emphasized

Beginning in the late 1950s, The HSUS offered "economy shelter" kits for constructing humane animal facilities like this one.

humane education programs, animal rescue, and adoption services and described the challenges of dealing with animal control ordinances, surplus animal breeding, and cruelty investigation. Several years later another film, *My Dog, the Teacher*, financed by ALPO and featuring HSUS President Oliver Evans, tracked the story of a partially deaf boy who learns humane values through his adopted beagle puppy. At the same time, it depicted the transformation of a badly operated municipal pound into a properly run animal shelter.[15]

Waterford and the National Humane Education Center

Fred Myers had longed to create a center for humane education and training, one that would include a shelter operation. With the promised support of two HSUS stalwarts, HSUS director Edith Goode and Alice Morgan Wright, the organization moved toward realization of Myers's dream. In 1963 Goode and Wright donated a 140-acre farm in Loudoun County, Virginia, to The HSUS. After its development in 1965, it became the National Humane Education Center (NHEC), complete with demonstration animal shelter and other training facilities. The original vision of the sponsors centered on a model shelter that would serve as a training center for the care, housing, and euthanasia of animals. Staff members and supporters hoped that the shelter would demonstrate the superiority of certain practices, like the free housing of cats, twenty-four-hour outdoor access, and the use of sodium pentobarbital.[16]

With the development of the Waterford facility, The HSUS became directly involved in Loudoun County's animal control work, as the NHEC accepted animals taken up by local dog wardens. In its first two years of operation, the Waterford facility spayed or neutered 2,467 cats and dogs, at a subsidized rate for area residents who could not afford standard veterinary fees. During the period 1969–1972, the Waterford clinic performed almost five thousand spay and neuter operations.[17]

Dale Hylton and Phyllis Wright (then at the Washington Animal Rescue League) served with various HSUS directors on a committee to investigate suitable methods of euthanasia for Waterford and other facilities. In time the group concluded that the Electrothanator was not appropriate for use under any circumstances, and discussions of its viability directly shaped The HSUS's long-standing policy that euthanasia methods that either obviously traumatized animals or

John Hoyt and Phyllis Wright (right) introduced Loudoun County civic leaders, such as Mrs. J.F.M. Stewart of Upperville, Virginia, to the Waterford facility.

left any doubt in the mind of a human attendant or observer that it was painless could not be recommended. Euthanasia was already well recognized as the leading cause of employee "burn-out" or "compassion fatigue" in animal shelter operations.[18]

The Waterford facility did have a Euthanaire decompression chamber, but, while it was shown to students and its operating concept was explained to them, it was not used for any actual euthanasia work. Although it planned to have one on the premises, The HSUS specifically did not contract for construction of a carbon monoxide euthanasia chamber by outside parties, since it was determined "to demonstrate (right from the outset) the practicality and feasibility of having it developed by local talent." Hylton conscripted his secretary's husband to locate an automobile engine, water tank, and gas filtration system, which they then used to build a euthanasia chamber. This unit, too, was used for training purposes, not for actual euthanasia.[19]

During its relatively short life span, The HSUS's Waterford animal shelter was responsible for a number of innovations. The HSUS also devised a limited-contract arrangement with a local veterinarian, who came by the shelter regularly to address any problems of illness noticed by staff.[20]

Together with Mel Morse, who made regular visits during his brief tenure as HSUS president, Hylton also made Waterford (the first shelter ever to his knowledge) require neutering of male dogs. The shelter had already moved to require spaying of all female cats and dogs and neutering of male cats. Early in the Waterford years, the new policy led to a memorable episode. One day a dog warden brought in a fine-looking black Labrador. Hylton decided to keep the dog around for longer than the prescribed holding period but eventually neutered him and adopted him out to a retired couple. About a month later, a farmer came around looking for a valuable stud dog who had gotten away from him some weeks before—the very dog, as it turned out, neutered by clinic professionals a few weeks earlier. Before the man could act upon his anger, however, his children found a scruffy-looking collie they wanted to take home with them.[21]

Whatever its impact as an animal shelter, as a training program, the Waterford initiative proved to be ineffectual. An insufficient number of humane society employees from other parts of the country were ready or able to travel to Virginia. Within a few years, moreover, the animal control program at Waterford quickly began to absorb staff and funding resources that might otherwise have gone toward addressing the problems of cruelty at a national level. Key administrators and board members began to question the wisdom and propriety of The HSUS's management and subsidy of an essentially local animal shelter, even in its home region. Although some board and staff members dissented, feeling that Waterford had unmet potential that—with stronger programmatic and fund-raising commitments—could still be realized, their view did not carry the day. The HSUS discontinued the shelter, which it had been subsidizing at the rate of $50,000 per year. Plans to convert the property into a nature center did not materialize, and, finally, in 1974 the HSUS Board of Directors voted to sell the property and its shelter facility. Loudoun County, Virginia, acquired the land and buildings, which became the center of county animal control operations.[22]

While it had not fulfilled original expectations, Waterford was by no means a failure, for it was there that staff members like Dale Hylton expanded their knowledge of and experience with appropriate shelter operations, gaining insights that they would share with countless other animal care workers in the years to follow. The Waterford experience proved to be useful when The HSUS moved in the direction of sponsoring workshops on shelter management and operation around the country in the 1970s.

The Professionalization of Animal Care and Control

For two decades the mainspring of The HSUS's programs in companion animal care was Phyllis Wright, who had run a boarding kennel, taught dog obedience classes, and operated several animal shelters in the Washington, D.C., area after serving as chief of dog training for the U.S. Army during the Korean War. Wright joined the staff of The HSUS in January 1969, and by 1975 she was The HSUS's chief liaison with the animal sheltering community. For a time she even had her own television show in the Washington, D.C., market. Under Wright's legendary leadership, The HSUS consistently articulated the differences between itself and other organizations regarding euthanasia, spay-neuter, shelter management, veterinary care, and related issues.[23]

Wright's "pull no punches" approach made her one of the most quotable HSUS officials. "We are striving to put ourselves out of business," she told one audience. "Until that happens, when there is no longer a cruelty or overpopulation problem, I intend to continue inspecting every shelter in this country and to help them provide the best care possible for the animals." On another occasion, at a humane society banquet in North Carolina, she declared, "The animal facility in this county is not fit for a dog."[24]

While Wright was alive, the nation's animal shelters had no greater defender or advocate. She was a stern critic of uninformed disparagement or disapproval of individual shelters and their practices. At the same time, Wright believed that there were some criticisms that all good animal shelters had to heed, and she was not afraid to pose the question, "How humane is your society?" Wright liked to tease workshop participants with the admonition, "You might as well tell me what you've been doing [wrong], because if you don't, someone else in this business will."[25]

By 1969, the year Wright joined The HSUS, the crisis of cat and dog overpopulation in the United States was reaching its worst proportions. The increasing popularity of keeping animals had given rise to an entire industry of pet-related enterprises, including mass breeders who serviced pet store chains with utter indifference to the mounting numbers of homeless and unwanted animals. These new ventures exacerbated the challenges that animal care and control organizations had to confront by driving the population of surplus animals to new heights.[26] By 1971 The HSUS estimated that, collectively, private charities and public facilities were expending approximately half a billion dollars annually on the euthanasia of unwanted dogs and cats. Several years later an HSUS survey placed the number of dogs and cats killed annually in American shelters at 13.5 million.[27]

The HSUS consistently pushed spay-neuter programs during this era, with public service advertisements, support for subsidized or lowered-fee programs, and other public outreach measures. Everyone involved with the problem at the national level, however, knew that it would take much more to bring the situation under control, and The HSUS began to investigate stronger and more comprehensive approaches. This search led inevitably to heightened scrutiny of the nation's weak animal control laws, which, historically, had imposed nominal licensing fees and had operated with inadequate enforcement mechanisms.[28]

In 1973 the National League of Cities identified the proliferation of dogs, cats, and their waste as a threat to public health as well as "an assault on urban aesthetics, a pollutant, and a safety hazard." In some cities there were packs of stray and feral animals running at large. Yet local governments, despite their concern, usually refused to provide adequate funding to animal control operations, public education, and other useful measures. One of the most serious problems animal care and control agencies faced nationwide was the ineffectual support they generally received from the municipalities in which they were active. The HSUS sought to position itself as a catalyst for change and a source of rock-solid data on animal-related problems, and staff members hoped to fortify local efforts to secure increased municipal support and funding. In 1977, for example, Guy Hodge authored *The Reign of Dogs and*

A Trip to the Spay Clinic Changed My Life

Born to Lose

There are so many puppies and kittens born in this country that few of them find permanent homes. The rest of them lead lonely, suffering lives—often cut short under the wheels of a car or in the death room of a pound.

Don't be responsible for more suffering and needless death. Have your pet spayed or neutered.

The HSUS made spay/neuter posters available, for use in schools, shelters, and public buildings, in 1972.

Cats, a special report on contemporary approaches to animal control, for the International City/County Management Association (ICMA), as part of an outreach program to municipal managers. It was the first of four HSUS-authored, ICMA-published reports.[29]

William Hurt Smith oversaw the HSUS Animal Control Academy.

Efforts to revamp animal control programs around the country coalesced under the approach that Phyllis Wright designated as LES—legislation, education, and sterilization. The HSUS promoted adequate licensing fees, broad community education, and sterilization programs. Under the influence of "Doc" Thomsen, The HSUS began to promote local ordinances that relied on enforcement of responsible pet ownership rather than on public persuasion. The growing conviction that effective animal control ordinances were the only realistic means for ending the surplus of companion animals underpinned the staging of national conferences in 1974 and 1976. The latter event produced a model ordinance that The HSUS circulated widely.[30]

Basic to the animal control ordinance backed by The HSUS were requirements that dogs and cats be licensed, with tags affixed to their collars; that there be a differential licensing arrangement for intact and neutered animals; that animals be kept under control at all times; that breeders be subject to licensing and regulation; that animals adopted from public and private shelters be sterilized; and that there be a tracking system to facilitate the immediate return of free-roaming animals whose owners could be identified.[31]

Even as animal care and control workers around the country confronted the escalating surplus of unwanted animals, The HSUS sought to extend its efforts to promote professionalism in philosophy and practice. The affiliates program, designed to forge links between The HSUS and local animal welfare organizations, rested upon the willingness of those groups to accept HSUS policy on animal welfare issues as well as their adherence to standards of program and sheltering procedure. However, the program received little attention after 1968, in part because the integrity of most local operations rested mainly upon a handful of key personnel. Once those people moved on to other organizations or agencies, there was no guarantee that the societies would continue to be run properly.

In 1974 The HSUS launched an accreditation program that encompassed several of the goals that had driven the affiliates system. Using well-developed criteria for the evaluation of

Phyllis Wright (in the late 1980s) was a familiar face to readers of The HSUS's magazine for animal shelter professionals, Shelter Sense.

animal welfare and animal control organizations, the accreditation process recognized quality animal care, humane education, sensible animal control, professional investigation methods, responsible administrative practices, and outstanding public relations capacities. The HSUS issued accreditation certificates to animal shelters to encourage higher standards for animal welfare and control practices, to develop lines of communication between organizations and agencies working in the field, and to promote greater public respect and support for professional and responsible operation. The program also involved an annual reaccreditation process.[32]

As part of its outreach to local shelters throughout the country, The HSUS staged traveling leadership workshops, "Solving Animal Problems in Your Community." Each of these two- and three-day events, which began in 1971, drew at least 100 registrants to participate in sessions on public relations and humane education outreach, adoption standards and procedures, euthanasia methods, cruelty investigations, and the philosophy and strategy of animal control programs. The workshops not only helped The HSUS to forge ties with local societies, but they also strengthened the relations among organizations in a specific region. Wright liked to involve local humane workers where appropriate and usually set time aside for their direct participation, but the program almost always included

HSUS personnel like John Hoyt, investigator Frantz Dantzler, and education specialists John Dommers, Charles Herrmann, and Kathy Savesky. Regional office staff members were often important participants in the workshops, too, and frequently handled preliminary preparations and promotional efforts.[33]

The workshops offered at these events changed with the field itself. In the early years, they focused on how to clean a shelter or how to conduct cruelty investigations. They subsequently expanded to include sessions highlighting new developments in rabies control, the handling of wildlife, and the use of information technology. The conferences also featured experts, such as former prosecutors and state health department personnel. Finally, the conferences helped to relieve the sense of isolation that wore so heavily upon shelter workers.[34]

In 1979 The HSUS enhanced its educational capacities in the realm of companion animal care by launching an Animal Control Academy in conjunction with the University of Alabama. There, under the direction of William Hurt Smith, instructors helped to train law enforcement and humane society personnel in proper methods of investigation, shelter operation, animal care, and euthanasia. By the end of 1983, the Academy had produced eighty-two graduates.[35]

Workshops such as this one, held in Little Rock, Arkansas, in 1980, helped to relieve shelter workers' sense of isolation.

By that year Phyllis Wright's HSUS area of oversight had also taken on its modern appearance. In 1977 Wright's title was director of the department of animal sheltering and control. Six years later, the section she oversaw was known as Companion Animals, and its responsibilities included the operation of the Animal Control Academy and the Accreditation Program and the publication of *Shelter Sense* ten times a year. Three staff members conducted on-site evaluations of animal control and humane society operations, visiting approximately fifty shelters a year. The section's personnel testified at state and local hearings concerning ordinances and other matters and fielded a broad range of public inquiries.[36]

The signing of a joint statement of agreement on the guiding principles of animal care and sheltering with AHA and the National Animal Control Association in 1985 signaled a new era of cooperation toward the goal of an effective strategy for addressing companion animal overpopulation and other problems. The agreement reflected the organizations' common belief that the challenges in the field were larger than any one organization, national, regional, or local, could solve and underscored the necessity of cooperation and communication to further progress. All agreed on the need for better public education, professionalization of staff, higher standards of service and practice, improved public health and safety programs, and full support for appropriate legislation and law enforcement work.[37]

Despite the good intentions that motivated its launch in 1974, The HSUS's accreditation program had its limitations. In ten years of operation, just twenty-two of eighty organizations had succeeded in achieving the rigorous standards in the time required. Many agencies and organizations did not even attempt to apply for accreditation, knowing they could not implement the necessary improvements in a timely way. Personnel changes within societies also hindered the implementation of appropriate policies and practices. Finally, although the shelters paid a nominal fee for the service, it took up a large share of staff time whenever an organization was seeking to be approved. HSUS officials concluded that the program was not properly serving the majority of animal control and sheltering agencies and that it was placing unreasonable burdens upon staff.[38]

Accordingly, in 1985 The HSUS launched its PETS (Professional Education and Training Services) program, to encourage broader participation by organizations seeking to improve their operations. Instead of requiring that specific standards be met, the new program

emphasized training for executive directors and shelter managers. Once these individuals successfully completed the training, their organizations were given an opportunity to commit themselves to professional standards established by The HSUS. The new program emphasized the professionalism and development of staff members rather than the accomplishments of organizations and agencies.[39]

In subsequent years, The HSUS sought to assist local shelters to improve their work through its "E- [for Evaluation] Team" and then, after 1999, its Animal Services Consultation (ASC) program. The ASC involved HSUS staff specialists and outside professionals in a full-service review and audit of a given animal care or control agency's operations and practices. The consultation involved extensive preliminary assessments based on documentary records and data and consultation with key personnel to establish the agency or organization's expressed needs and objectives. After completing its review, including an on-site visit, the HSUS team provided its client with an evaluation report that examined its operations within a broad context, taking into account dozens of variable and contingent factors that can affect the fortunes of an animal care or control organization. In some cases, the ASC report could become a central strategic document for the entity's future development.[40]

In 1991 The HSUS launched Animal Care Expo, which quickly became an annual responsibility for the Companion Animals section, by 1996 under the leadership of one of Phyllis Wright's most accomplished protégés, Martha Armstrong. An international event, part trade show, part educational conference, Expo generally drew at least one thousand participants and several hundred exhibitors every year. The HSUS offered certificate courses and workshops on a wide range of topics, while allowing participants ample opportunity for networking and the examination of new animal products in the exhibit halls.[41]

In 1999 The HSUS initiated a new program for the training and education of shelter professionals, designed to avoid and eliminate the deficiencies of the certification and accreditation approach. The Pets for Life National Training Center, run in partnership with the Dumb Friends League of Denver, Colorado, now became an important part of the Companion Animals section's ongoing commitment to professional training for animal care and control personnel. Through Pets for Life, shelter staff could learn how to improve and implement behavior modification programs in their shelters. Students also received instruction in how to operate a behavior assistance and training program in their own communities. As of winter 2003, more than three hundred shelter employees from 210 shelters in fifty states, Canada, and Hong Kong had completed the program. By then, too, The HSUS had taken the Pets for Life training program on the road, launching regional training centers to provide assistance to shelter personnel across the country.[42]

The Challenges of Spay-Neuter

In the early 1960s, The HSUS shifted its emphasis from simply discouraging surplus breeding of animals through restraint and quarantine during their seasons of heat—the basic advice that circulated through the 1950s—to a more aggressive program of promoting spay-neuter as the solution to companion animal overpopulation. With lingering medical concerns about the effect of organ removal upon animals resolved, with the surgical option more widely available through veterinarians and sometimes at shelters and clinics, and with people increasingly disposed to spend more money on taking care of their animals, it became a more realistic and effective proposition to advance. Under the circumstances, it was ironic that, once the humane movement began to introduce its own spay-neuter clinics and subsidy programs, it would find its greatest and most tenacious opponent to be the veterinary profession. Even in the face of such antagonism, The HSUS and many local societies pushed for laws to require spaying and neutering of animals adopted from their facilities or for differential licensing arrangements that charged higher fees for unaltered animals. "We are in competition with the euthanasia room, not the veterinarians," Phyllis Wright emphasized.[43]

The hostility of veterinarians to subsidized spay-neuter programs lasted for decades, and it was one of the reasons that federal legislation to provide low-interest loans for the construction and launch of municipal spay-neuter clinics went nowhere. While the issue pitted concern for the prevention and suffering of unwanted animals against the claimed privileges of private enterprise, institutional prerogatives, and professional qualifications, veterinarians' major accusation was that subsidy programs constituted a form of unfair competition. At its most shrill, the veterinary community denounced subsidized spay-neuter as "the first step in socialized medicine." At other times representatives belittled the impact of spay-neuter on the overall problem of animal overpopulation. These fights lasted into the 1980s and 1990s, with crucial decisions handed down in Louisiana, Michigan, and Virginia.[44]

The opposition from professional veterinary authorities proved to be troubling, as they even sought to prevent individual practitioners from cooperating with lowered-fee or subsidized spay-neuter initiatives. In 1974 a ruling by Ohio's attorney general on the legality of humane organizations' providing subsidies for spay-neuter conduct-

A protégé of the late Phyllis Wright, Martha Armstrong, shown here with her dog, Angus, took the helm of the HSUS Companion Animals section in 1996.

ed by veterinarians found that such activity did not constitute solicitation of business on behalf of those veterinarians (Opinion no. 74-064). The opinion concerned a program launched by HSUS founder Larry Andrews through his organization, United Humanitarians. Veterinarians who had agreed to cooperate with the program were threatened with loss of licenses on the ground that humane groups offering this subsidy were "soliciting business" in violation of the state's veterinary medical practices act.[45]

However, in October 1984 the Internal Revenue Service (IRS) ruled that the Michigan Humane Society's three full-service veterinary clinics comprised an essential part of its charitable, humane activities and did not constitute a trade or business. The IRS made a similarly encouraging determination in regard to a spay-neuter clinic operated by the Humane Society of Huron Valley, accepting the premise that the control of animal overpopulation through spay-neuter work did prevent cruelty to animals and thus did constitute a charitable activity. In this decision, HSUS attorneys reported, the IRS also diverged from the earlier understanding that "charitable veterinary services must be limited to treating stray, abused, or abandoned animals, or the animals of indigent owners." The decision seemed to recognize that responding to *any* animal's medical needs, regardless of whether that animal has a human being responsible for it or is able or willing to pay for services, is inherently charitable. Michigan veterinarians made a fight of it, getting legislation introduced in the state legislature to suppress full-service clinics operated by humane societies.[46]

In 1986 the American Veterinary Medical Association (AVMA) asked the U.S. Congress to impose taxes upon nonprofit organizations that operated any form of business not directly tied to their mission. The specified business activities included spay-neuter surgeries and vaccinations at humane society-operated clinics. The next year John Hoyt was one of the humane advocates who testified before a subcommittee of the House Ways and Means Committee in support of tax-exempt status for charitable hospitals and spay-neuter clinics. Fortunately, the committee took no action.[47]

Spay-neuter was not the only option pursued by those concerned with controlling the population of unwanted animals. Not surprisingly, the era of the pill and the sexual revolu-

tion produced a new alternative to surgical sterilization. Since the late 1950s, The HSUS had followed
scientific reports of investigations into chemical
sterilization, like those conducted by Leon F. Whitney, D.V.M., at Yale University. Whitney's study of
Malucidin, a yeast extract that caused the reabsorp-
tion of embryos, provided an early sign of the potential of such approaches.[48]

By 1970 a number of pet food and drug manufacturers were engaged in research toward the development of a drug to prevent estrus or conception
if estrus occurred. Corporate giants Upjohn and Ral-
ston-Purina were aware of the potential market for

*A carbon monoxide gas chamber—
an ancient crate with an intake hose
attached—in a Midwestern pound.*

safe and effective chemosterilants but could not seem to overcome the obstacles, which included the necessity of daily administration, adverse medical effects, genetic damage, trans-
species differentiation, and FDA concerns about human consumption of pet food. The
search for reproductive inhibitors was also frustrated by other obstacles and mishaps. A federal program that developed one such inhibitor for use in deer populations abandoned the
work when a hunter's wife who had eaten deer meat complained of a miscarriage.[49]

Veterinary medicine was also lukewarm on the shift toward chemosterilant alternatives,
because spay-neuter operations generated a portion of individuals' incomes within the profession. Veterinarians believed (probably incorrectly) that a shift toward alternatives would
have resulted in a significant reduction if not elimination of income from this practice, although it was well known that the profit margins on vaccines and other injectable drugs was
higher than those attached to surgery. For their part, humane officials worried that, once scientists had successfully developed a one-time injectable that safely and permanently sterilized animals, the organized veterinary community would do its best to persuade state officials that only veterinarians could be authorized to provide the shots, a concern amply vindicated by subsequent experience.[50]

After The HSUS launched ISAP in the mid-1970s, a study of chemical birth control for animals was an early priority. Mel Morse, one of ISAP's founders, was in regular contact with
corporations working on implants and other methods. When Michael Fox became ISAP director in 1976, The HSUS launched a serious review of the possibilities of chemosterilization
in the male dog.[51]

For a time, with generous support from the Geraldine R. Dodge Foundation, The HSUS
donated some funds to the research of Colorado State University's Lloyd Faulkner concerning chemical sterilants for male dogs. Faulkner was investigating contraceptive implants and
a vaccine immunization that inhibited reproductive function. The animal health products division of at least one major pharmaceutical firm was also conducting research on vaccine
compounds. But sterilants did not become the panacea that scientific professionals had asserted, and chemical vasectomy remained an elusive goal. The search for the "silver bullet"
continued, however, and in 2003, almost forty-five years after the first mention of such a product in *HSUS News*, the FDA approved the chemosterilant Neutersol for use in male dogs between three and ten months old.[52]

As The HSUS continued to monitor developments in the field, the Companion Animals
section developed a list of characteristics that a chemo- or immunosterilant must have to constitute a genuine alternative to surgical spay-neuter for shelters and in animal population control efforts in developing nations, where The HSUS and its international affiliate, HSI, were becoming more involved. According to the document, the sterilant must not cause harmful or
unpleasant side effects; must be administrable without the need for anesthesia; must not require repeated injections and/or boosters; and must cause permanent sterility in animals.[53]

Euthanasia

Throughout its history The HSUS has framed the euthanasia of unwanted animals as an unfortunate aspect of a problem whose resolution required a more comprehensive solution. While acknowledging the unavoidability of euthanasia as a response to companion animal overpopulation, The HSUS has insisted on the identification and adoption of the most compassionate options available. In The HSUS's first several decades, staff members confronted the problem of crude, inefficient, and cruel methods of destroying animals in local shelters, called for research into new approaches, and pushed for comparative studies of extant alternatives. The organization was an early critic of mechanical means of animal destruction, such as chambers in which gas, electricity, or rapid decompression were used to euthanize unwanted animals as well as such crude methods of killing as strychnine, drowning, and gunshot. The HSUS also played an instrumental role in the shift toward lethal injection by trained and caring personnel as the standard means of euthanasia in well-managed shelters and animal care facilities.[54]

Euthanasia of surplus animal populations in the United States dates from the 1870s, when the nation's first shelter substituted the use of carbonous oxide gas for drowning and clubbing of animals by mid-nineteenth-century municipal agents. Sadly, the options available remained much the same for the next ninety years, and when The HSUS formed, humane societies were choosing among a limited range of methods that included electrocution, carbon monoxide, carbon dioxide, cyanide, and nitrogen. Over the years, the cruelties and deficiencies of each of these methods became manifest. Nevertheless, animal care and control organizations continued to rely upon them, as convenience, lack of capital, and other factors ensured their survival into the modern era.

For years The HSUS responded to persistent requests for investigations and inquiries concerning euthanasia practices and related abuses at pounds and shelters around the country. In 1967 Dale Hylton traveled to Brownsville, Texas, to assist HSUS member Evelyn Yates in her campaign to replace a crude, makeshift carbon monoxide shed in use at the city pound. Attendants piped in exhaust fumes—unfiltered and uncooled—from a truck, and the inefficiencies of the structure prolonged the animals' painful death.[55]

On another occasion Hylton went to visit a municipal pound near Asheville, North Carolina, during an investigative tour of other southern states. Discovering that the local health department and its contractor had failed to follow plans provided by The HSUS for a chamber that used cooled and filtered carbon monoxide gas, Hylton worked with local humane advocates to lobby county supervisors for an immediate halt to construction. As a result, the county board contracted with another local firm to build a chamber that conformed to HSUS specifications.[56]

The HSUS even went so far as to sue local governments in an effort to force the adoption of appropriate means of destroying animals. In 1972 a review of euthanasia practices at the San Antonio, Texas, pound led to a lawsuit, when HSUS staff members noted that it sometimes took as long as an hour for animals to die in the facility's gas chamber. "If you can't kill an animal in two minutes, then don't call it euthanasia. Call it slaughter—call it anything you want, but don't call it euthanasia," Phyllis Wright commented.[57]

By the early 1970s, controversy over the decompression chamber dominated discussions of euthanasia. The high-altitude, low-pressure chamber was a widely adopted technological spin-off from Air Force research concerning the physical reaction of pilots and others to rapid decompression. Decompression destroyed animals by reducing the oxygen content in the chamber

In 1973, The HSUS's Phyllis Wright examined an opening in an animal shelter wall in Chesapeake, Virginia, where exhaust from a truck was piped in to kill surplus animals.

through an exhaust pump, creating a near vacuum. For many years, this method had strong defenders within the humane community. It was in broad general use, and before 1957 it even enjoyed the approval of The HSUS. The decompression chamber could be operated without much training by nonveterinary personnel and could euthanize several animals at a time. Over time, however, it began to attract greater scrutiny and disapproval, and critics argued that animals suffocated and experienced loss of lung tissue and excruciating pain as a result of the pressure change.[58]

The HSUS was one of the earliest, if not the first, major critic of the decompression method. However, "Doc" Thomsen's searching analysis of the rapid decompression chamber in 1972 was a benchmark in the effort to abolish its use, bringing together a broad range of facts and findings that helped to substantiate doubts about the method's humaneness. Thomsen spoke for many in the field when he observed, "Intense pain for even a very short time should not be tolerated by humanitarians if there is any alternative."[59]

Executive Vice President Mel Morse, with forty years of experience in the movement, helped to focus The HSUS's response to the issue. Morse was familiar with virtually all methods in use and had unparalleled knowledge of the numerous factors infusing the debate. While convinced that decompression was not humane, Morse insisted that The HSUS needed to come up with a strong alternative. If not, he cautioned, "people will go back to using the old monoxide truck backing up to a tank type of thing." Morse also underscored the importance of striking a balance between humaneness to animals and safety for the operator. Discussions Morse held with HSUS attorney Murdaugh Madden resulted in the selection of euthanasia technologies as a suitable topic for investigation by ISAP, then being planned. In 1972 The HSUS put money toward serious evaluations of the decompression chamber and the nitrogen flushing chamber as an alternative. This inquiry collapsed, a casualty of movement politics, John Hoyt thought. However, The HSUS was already focusing on sodium pentobarbital as the best and most humane method in sight. Nevertheless, it, too, presented a problem. As a barbiturate, it was a controlled substance under federal law, and that presented substantial obstacles to its use. Madden thought that scientific analysis of the options would help the case: "The more data we have the more we can push for sodium pentobarbital to be approved for widespread usage."[60]

On this as on many animal welfare issues, organized animal protection was ahead of the veterinary community. In 1962 an AVMA panel withheld its approval of decompression, acknowledging the "serious objection" that animals may suffer excruciating pain for a short time. In 1972, however, a second panel judged the method "humane" and recommended it as satisfactory, "provided the equipment is properly constructed, maintained, and operated." Finally, in 1978 a third AVMA panel, citing general lack of understanding of decompression's physiological effects, stated that "other methods of euthanasia are preferable." Nevertheless, the 1978 panel proclaimed rapid decompression a "satisfactory procedure for euthanasia."[61]

The grassroots campaign against decompression got off to a dramatic start in 1971, when Florida opponents of the chamber actually stole a unit from one humane society. Legislative initiatives to prohibit its use followed in subsequent years, and in 1976 Arizona and Massachusetts became the first states to ban the chamber. Phyllis Wright, Michael Fox, and other HSUS personnel testified before state legislatures and community councils in several campaigns. The HSUS celebrated John Kullberg's decision to drop use of the decompression chamber at the ASPCA once he became that organization's president in 1978. Further opposition to its use resulted in a prohibition on use of the decompression chamber in twenty-eight states by the end of the 1980s.[62]

Sodium pentobarbital was not the only method proposed as a substitute for decompression. T-61 and Succostrin frequently surfaced in discussions of the topic, too. T-61 was a compound that comprised a fast-acting local anesthetic to minimize the pain of injection, a narcotic agent designed to produce loss of consciousness and paralysis of the respiratory appa-

ratus, and a curariform drug that exerted a strong paralytic effect and induced circulatory col-
lapse. T-61 was introduced in Europe in the early 1960s, but it did not enjoy widespread use
in the United States until the 1970s. At that time, surveys indicated its increasing adoption as
a euthanasia agent. One perceived advantage was that it did not present the same amount of
red tape and difficulty of acquisition that attended sodium pentobarbital.[63]

Succostrin (succinylcholine chloride)—another curare-like drug—produced death by im-
mobilizing the respiratory organs, causing fatal suffocation. However, since it exerted no depres-
sant action on the brain, an animal would suffer severe pain without even being able to com-
municate that suffering. After Michael Fox became director of ISAP in 1976, The HSUS intensified its warnings about the hazards and inhumane use of Succostrin and T-61 for euthanasia.[64]

By the mid-1970s, The HSUS was leading the push for universal adoption of barbiturates
like sodium pentobarbital for euthanasia. This solution posed some challenges, because laws
had to be altered to permit humane societies to purchase barbiturates and lay personnel to
administer them. The injection method minimized potential for error but brought technicians
into close contact with the animals they euthanized and placed unusually heavy emotional
burdens upon the individuals charged with responsibility for the task. For this reason sessions
on the emotional dimensions of euthanasia work were crucial elements in the training program of the Animal Control Academy, founded just as the shift toward sodium pentobarbital
gathered momentum. While The HSUS's training programs acknowledged that providing a
physically painless death could be a psychologically painful experience for technicians
charged with carrying out euthanasia, the organization strongly endorsed methods that required close contact with the animals. The Companion Animals section sought to develop
consensus that euthanasia methods be dignified as well as humane, that equipment be properly maintained, and that those responsible for euthanasia be suitably trained.[65]

Pet Shops and Puppy Mills

Breeding and supply for the pet industry market has long been an issue of concern to The
HSUS. The routine sale of sick animals by pet stores emerged as a serious concern in the mid-
1960s. In Washington, D.C., during the Christmas holiday season in 1966, an estimated fifty to
seventy-five dogs sold in pet stores had to be euthanized due to illness. The HSUS testified at
a hearing by the District of Columbia commissioners on the matter and pointed out that pet
stores in the nation's capital, virtually unregulated in comparison to those in other communities, exhibited some of the most unsanitary and inadequate conditions in the country.[66] In
1967 a California pet wholesaler sued The HSUS after its California branch confiscated animals from him.[67]

The HSUS also supported state-level legislation to restrict retail sales of household pets by
individuals and stores for which it was not a principal business. Such legislation targeted variety stores and other outlets that used such marketing as a gimmick or an impetus to increase
sales volume. The HSUS argued that employees of such stores were almost always unquali-
fied in the humane care and treatment of animals. As part of the broader campaign to restrict
such commerce, Frank McMahon persuaded Sears to abandon its plan to sell dogs.[68]

Both the national office and branches sought to prohibit the sale of baby animals for the
holiday entertainment of children, a common practice at Easter. There were many cruelties attached to this practice, and nearly all of the chicks, rabbits, ducklings, and other animals died
shortly after the holiday from improper nutrition, starvation, abuse, overhandling, or plain neglect. In 1965 members of the California branch picketed a discount store that was giving away
15,000 baby chicks, in an effort to drum up support for prohibitive legislation. The HSUS provided a model ordinance to campaigners and assembled medical data establishing a link between salmonella infection and animals sold in the Easter trade, based on U.S. Public Health
Service surveys from half a dozen states and individual doctors' reports. By 1966 eleven states
and more than one hundred communities had enacted legislation to outlaw the trade.[69]

The HSUS was sometimes successful in persuading government agencies to ban the sale of other animals. In 1975, after a year-long campaign waged by The HSUS and Consumers Union, the FDA restricted the sale of turtles after they proved to be transmitters of infectious salmonella to children. But five years later, turtle sales continued in some states, and pet shops and dealers marketed them with impunity.[70]

HSUS officials used the description, "puppy mill," as early as 1965, when they participated in the arrest of Joseph P. O'Neill, a Princeton, New Jersey, kennel operator, for cruelty to animals. O'Neill's operation purchased puppies from all over the country and then advertised purebreds for sale in leading newspapers. O'Neill pled guilty to charges of cruelty in Williamsport, Pennsylvania, after Frank McMahon and a local humane agent kept him under continuous observation for almost twenty-four hours while he picked up puppies in four Pennsylvania communities. During that time O'Neill provided no food, water, or attention to the animals in his truck.[71]

In time the term "puppy mill" came to describe certain commercial dog-breeding establishments selling wholesale to the pet industry. The HSUS pushed to see amendments made to the AWA in 1970 that required all such businesses to be licensed and inspected regularly. In 1974 The HSUS held conversations with pet shop industry representatives about the viability of self-regulation by the industry. At that time the American Kennel Club (AKC) reported about 2,500 complaints yearly against pet shops. Concerns included the buyers' inability to obtain papers for purebred animals they purchased, the condition or health of the animals, and the sellers' determined resistance to return or replacement.[72]

Despite these efforts, unfortunately, puppy mills flourished during the 1970s. In those years America's heartland—its Midwestern states—also became known for harboring substandard mass breeding operations that produced purebred animals wholesale for the pet store market. Concentrated in rural areas where land was cheap and pet food an easily available by-product of livestock agriculture, puppy mills gained popularity as a "second crop" for many farmers, with the encouragement of USDA. In 1977 nearly three thousand of the nation's six thousand animal dealers lived in Iowa, Missouri, and Kansas.[73]

During the mid-1970s, HSUS investigators Ann Gonnerman and Frantz Dantzler went into the field to document the deplorable conditions of Midwestern puppy farms. Their work provided background for Roger Caras's 1976 feature report on puppy mills for ABC-TV News. Some of the worst facilities they visited had received USDA licensure, a fact that badly undercut efforts to prosecute. While Dantzler believed that conditions were so horrendous that on-the-spot arrests for cruelty to animals were warranted, prosecutors faced the challenge of convincing judges and juries that cruelty had occurred in facilities that were "USDA approved."[74]

In 1980–1981 puppy mills became the subject of an extended investigation by HSUS investigator Bob Baker, who spent five months researching them. "Breeders usually enter the business after hearing of a relative, neighbor, or acquaintance who is earning a substantial

HSUS Chief Investigator Frank McMahon inspected makeshift cages from which 135 animals were removed at a Pennsylvania puppy mill.

Dog dealer Joseph P. O'Neill watches as Lycoming County SPCA agents transfer puppies to a waiting ambulance.

amount of money in his or her spare time raising dogs," Baker reported. "The single most distinguishing characteristic of [puppy mill owners] is their desire to produce puppies at minimum cost with minimum effort, regardless of what is best for the animals. The only apparent concern affecting the dogs' welfare is their desire for a high enough survival rate to ensure a profit." [75]

A pet-shop pup carried a high price in the 1980s.

In the case of puppy mills, Baker charged, the AWA simply was not being enforced. Most inspectors were veterinary and animal health professionals who spent the majority of their time looking for brucellosis in cattle, "who considered the enforcement of regulations against dog breeding operations to be an imposition on their work schedules." Baker found that 44 percent of the facilities surveyed had "chronic and persistent deficiencies as noted by the USDA inspector, and yet no disciplinary action had been initiated." [76]

A General Accounting Office (GAO) investigation of puppy mills in 1984 confirmed The HSUS's allegations of major deficiencies in the enforcement of the AWA regulations concerning puppy mills. Very little changed, however, and Representative Manuel Lujan, Jr. (R-NM), led efforts to press USDA to examine its effectiveness in ensuring compliance. The HSUS continued its public awareness efforts, even setting up information booths at AKC events in the 1980s. In 1989 USDA's Animal Plant and Health Inspection Service (APHIS) formed a new division, the Regulatory Enforcement/Animal Care Program (REAC), to work exclusively on animal welfare concerns, but it accomplished very little on the problem of puppy mills. [77]

In May 1990, after a decade of frustration over the lack of enforcement at all levels, The HSUS launched a nationwide boycott of puppies from the six worst puppy-mill states—Missouri, Kansas, Oklahoma, Arkansas, Iowa, and Nebraska. In time Pennsylvania was added to the list. The goal of the campaign was to spur the states to enforce those animal welfare regulations already in place and to pass appropriate legislation where none existed. Bob Baker appeared on numerous national television programs, and he and Gail Eisnitz took a film crew from ABC's *20/20* television news magazine to document conditions at a puppy mill owned by a USDA inspector. A decline in pet shop sales of puppies in California, a major market, signaled the positive impact of the boycott. In a few instances, too, the publicity campaign spurred enhanced efforts to enforce the laws. [78]

The publicity campaign also led to renewed action at the federal level. Representative Ben Cardin (D-MD) and a dozen colleagues responded to the HSUS investigation by sponsoring the Puppy Protection Act, H.R. 3718, in November 1991 to provide strong legal recourse to those who purchased animals from pet stores and commercial breeders. [79]

The HSUS's Legal and Government Affairs staff joined with members of the Companion Animals section in intense efforts to improve the situation in 1994 and 1995. In June 1995 Senator Rick Santorum (R-PA) led a signatory campaign in which more than one hundred congressional representatives and senators asked USDA secretary Dan Glickman to protect puppy mill animals. The initiative gained a degree of bipartisan support unmatched by virtually any other animal issue, as elected politicians who had heard so many complaints about puppy mills came forward to sign the letter. [80]

Subsequent regulatory changes failed to impress HSUS staff members who had participated in public meetings and negotiations, however. Santorum and his colleague, Richard Durbin (D-IL), and representatives Sam Farr (D-CA) and Ed Whitfield (R-KY) subsequently introduced the "Puppy Protection Act" to improve USDA enforcement of

Investigator Bob Baker found substandard conditions in puppy mills across the Midwest in the 1980s.

the AWA at commercial breeding operations by requiring greater socialization of animals, enhancing their suitability as household companions, placing a limit on the frequency with which females could be bred, and a "three strikes and you're out" rule that denied licenses to three-time violators. The House bill drew 150 sponsors, and the Senate version passed as part of the 2002 farm bill. Unfortunately, the Santorum initiative and related measures were scuttled by the opposition of breeders, led by the AKC.[81]

The puppy mill tragedy had profound and wide-ranging implications. Animals from such facilities were often more susceptible to disease than other animals, because of poor breeding and health care and the stress of long-distance transportation at an early age. Kept in cages, they frequently lacked crucial socialization and developed behavioral problems that made them unsuitable companion animals. Puppy mill animals frequently surfaced among pound and shelter relinquishments. Even as it caused incredible animal suffering, the puppy mill system exacerbated the already staggering problem of animal overpopulation. It was still causing The HSUS and the worldwide humane community tremendous difficulties in the early twenty-first century. In the late 1990s, The HSUS refocused its puppy mill campaign by conducting a survey of consumers who purchased animals from pet stores. While Bob Baker, Frantz Dantzler, and other investigators had documented terrible conditions at hundreds of puppy mills in the 1980s and 1990s, government action did nothing to ameliorate the situation. The new approach involved addressing the attitudes of the public toward animal shelters and pet stores through continuing broad-based education campaigns.[82]

The shipment of puppies by air in unsafe and inappropriate containers, such as produce crates, was a major factor in the passage of the Humane Transport Act in 1976.

The Humane Transport Act

In addition to its obvious adverse impact on the effort to reduce companion animal overpopulation, the rise of the puppy mill industry created other urgent challenges for the humane movement. Chief among these was the terrible conditions under which animals were transported via air. This problem ensued directly from the proliferation of Midwestern puppy mills, and it was no coincidence that Kansas City was "the hub of the nation's puppy traffic" during the 1970s.[83]

The lack of training of airport workers, and the general indifference of the carriers, resulted in numerous difficulties and sometimes even the death of animals in transport. Many of the consignors were pet shops and puppy mills that showed little concern for animals' welfare and often shipped dogs in lettuce crates and other substandard containers. Companies like the Railway Express Agency (REA), which was alone responsible for over 90 percent of commercial animal shipments in North America transported animals under a system better suited to freight than to living creatures.[84]

The major airlines, for their part, were eager to compete for a share of the trade and did very little to address the terrible neglect and suffering of animals that was manifest in terminals around the country every day. As Frank McMahon told one reporter, "Airlines have no obligation to give food, water, exercise or periodic inspections to animals, regardless of the length of flight. The problem is complicated by the fact that many air express employees are paid by commission and are therefore willing to accept anything, regardless of the condition of either the animal or the shipping crate."[85]

Nor were airlines and shippers concerned about the effects of extreme temperatures on animals being shipped. As The HSUS pointed out, airlines were satisfied to let passengers and others believe that animals in baggage compartments were getting the same benefits as people traveling in the passenger cabins. Animals on longer flights sometimes suffocated or died of heat exhaustion. There were numerous tragic incidents involving those who had entrusted their companion animals to air carriers. Aggrieved citizens commonly transmitted such stories to The HSUS's offices.[86]

The situation was inextricably bound up with the history of the AWA. As passed in 1966, the AWA had established humane standards for the treatment of animals while housed in scientific institutions, on the premises of animal dealers, or in transit. The 1970 revision amended its coverage to include nonlaboratory animals being transported, bought, or sold for "teaching purposes or for use as pets." But while animal dealers, circuses, zoos, and other exhibitors were now required to meet the AWA standards, there was a loophole that exempted the coverage of animals while they were being transported by common carriers in interstate commerce.[87]

Representative Lowell Weicker, Jr. (R-CT), introduced a bill in 1970 requiring the humane treatment of animals transported by air and persuaded a Senate colleague to sponsor a companion bill. While this legislation failed, it led to greater interest in the issue. HSUS investigations in Connecticut and Washington, D.C., provided crucial evidence of improper identification, poorly constructed containers, inadequate health certification, and animal injury. The organization also filed a December 1973 petition with the Civil Aeronautics Board (CAB) requesting positive action to address the situation. A congressional hearing on the matter took place the same year, and in 1974 Representative Thomas Foley (D-WA) introduced amendments to the AWA to assign responsibility for the regulation of animal transport by common carriers to USDA. The HSUS provided expert testimony and a special report, *Shipping Animals by Air*, that spelled out the numerous threats to animals' well-being that were routine in the carrier industry.[88]

Foley's bill passed in 1976 as the Humane Transport Act. In February 1977 an administrative law judge endorsed many of the contentions The HSUS had made in its CAB petition, and the following September, USDA's animal air transport regulations went into effect. They set a minimum travel age for puppies and kittens, promulgated standards for shipping containers, imposed a maximum limit on the amount of time that animals could remain in transit, mandated health certification of animals, established humane facilities in air terminals, and required shippers to post care and handling instructions on containers used to ship animals.[89]

USDA did succeed, however, in lessening airlines' responsibility to transport animals humanely. The agency amended two provisions of its AWA regulations, the first allowing the airlines to approve the use of all shipping containers a dealer asserted to be in compliance with USDA standards, and the second creating a serious loophole in the temperature range specifications. The HSUS was able to head off the latter measure, which lowered the minimum temperature at which animals might be held in airport facilities from forty-five to thirty-five degrees. This proposed relaxation of standards came at the insistence of commercial animal dealers who sought to limit interference with their lucrative Christmas season trade.[90]

The next decade's experience with air transportation of animals saw continued complaints about conditions, especially after deregulation of the airline industry in 1983. Two years later Phyllis Wright estimated that deregulation had resulted in at least a 50 percent increase in complaints to The HSUS. Animals continued to arrive dead in carrying crates and sometimes did not arrive at all, as carriers sent them to the wrong airports in the wrong cities. With the 1976 AWA amendments in place, however, staff members were at least able to follow up with USDA officials after turning over the information needed to investigate incidents and grievances that citizens brought to their attention.[91]

Responding to pleas for action in spring 1987, Representative Tom Lantos (D-CA), a strong supporter of animal welfare concerns, convened a meeting with airline industry representatives, government officials, and HSUS staff members to discuss the rise in complaints.

Unsafe conditions, inadequate handling procedures, and delays and misrouting remained all too common, and Lantos counted on the likelihood that a strong expression of congressional interest would make USDA and other agencies more attentive to the problem.[92]

From Pound Seizure to Pet Protection

One of the most important sources of tension within the humane movement in the 1950s involved pound seizure or mandatory surrender of animals, especially after passage of New York State's Metcalf-Hatch Act in 1952. This legislation required New York municipal pounds to supply hospitals, medical research facilities, and commercial laboratories with unclaimed animals. Metcalf-Hatch provoked bitter controversy and determined opposition from some of the state's humane organizations, many of which did not oppose research with animals but "could not countenance experimentation with animals which had once been pets."[93]

The legislators who acquiesced to the research community's demand for access to pound and shelter animals by passing such legislation were not typically sensitive to the function and charge of humane societies. They were generally private organizations, supported by endowments and individual donations. In most communities, the humane society usually saved the taxpayers money by assuming the responsibilities once borne by the dismal municipal pound. Whatever public subsidy a society received for animal control never covered the actual costs involved in the gathering up of strays and related activities, not to mention the range of overhead costs necessary to maintain a proper organization, with veterinarians, educators, equipment, ambulances, literature, property, and other costs.

Whether or not humane societies were running a public pound, most were governed by a sense of responsibility to the animals in their care. If possible, humane workers hoped to return animals to the homes from which they had been lost or strayed or help to find suitable new homes for them. Failing these outcomes, or in cases of serious disease and injury, they were committed to ensuring a merciful and painless death of the animals in their charge.

There was also the issue of public trust—that people would hesitate to relinquish animals to shelters for fear that those animals would be used for research. Such perceptions could undermine a shelter's role as a haven for unwanted animals. As a consequence, the animals not relinquished to shelters might face worse fates.

Like many of their colleagues in organized animal protection, the founders of The HSUS were opposed to pound seizure. As a result, the protection of animals—lost, stolen, or strayed—from the threat of being taken for laboratory experiments has been a priority since the organization first incorporated. Much of the founders' outrage focused on the ASPCA, which was responsible for municipal animal control in New York City. Myers and others charged that the ASPCA had acquiesced to pressure from Governor Thomas Dewey and members of the New York legislature in the early 1950s—backed up by a $1 million licensing and animal control contract—and failed to resist Metcalf-Hatch. By accepting public money, the ASPCA was required to surrender dogs and cats to scientific institutions—and it did.[94]

The issue came up regularly during the 1950s and early 1960s, and The HSUS tried to provide strong support to humane societies attempting to fend off pound surrender ordinances. Fred Myers testified against pound seizure before state legislatures and local councils, advancing the view that research, teaching, and commercial laboratories should not be permitted to take animals from pounds and shelters. The HSUS not only argued that pound seizure laws aggravated the challenge of developing humane solutions to the surplus animal problem. It also advanced the view that such laws encouraged neglect of animals in laboratories by making an unlimited source of dogs and cats available at very little cost.[95]

Sometimes, the matter went to the courts. In July 1963 The HSUS's Utah State branch challenged a new pound seizure law in the Utah Supreme Court as unconstitutional. HSUS officials announced that they would submit to arrest rather than release animals from the branch's shelter. The HSUS's national office backed the branch fully, with both legal counsel and financial support.[96]

Investigation was another way in which The HSUS sought to make its case. By focusing on wholesale dog dealers who mainly supplied research institutions—after buying up animals at pounds and shelters—field agents exposed the mistreatment and neglect of former pets on their way into the laboratories. During the period 1963–1966, Frank McMahon, Dale Hylton, and other investigators filed charges of cruelty against a number of dealers keeping animals in inadequate and unsanitary conditions. In time such investigations revealed the activity of dealers who routinely bribed pound and shelter employees for access to animals, sometimes against the explicit policies of the shelters' boards of directors. The HSUS also sought to persuade local communities to execute animal control contracts with humane societies rather than private operators who—unmotivated by humane feeling—made very little effort to find homes for healthy, well-adjusted animals, preferring to sell them to laboratories or medical schools.[97]

During the 1960s, while pound seizure remained objectionable, it took a backseat to the epidemic of pet stealing that attended the laboratory animal trade. While the practices were related, it was pet stealing that helped to catalyze public concern in the effort to reform the traffic in laboratory animals. As part of this shift in focus, on August 11, 1965, 350 members of The HSUS, in all states but Delaware, New Hampshire, Hawaii, Wyoming, and Alaska, counted the number of dogs and cats advertised as lost and found in their local newspapers. The HSUS estimated that the nationwide traffic in stolen dogs generated at least $50 million in income annually and that two million dogs disappeared every year to become laboratory subjects.[98]

But pound seizure still surfaced as a controversial problem, as it did in California just weeks after the passage of the AWA. In that crucial state, the HSUS California branch led a successful campaign of opposition to a statewide pound seizure initiative, while losing its battle to prevent the San Diego pound from contracting for the sale of impounded animals to the University of California. Another skirmish ensued in New Jersey, where HSUS branch president Jacques Sichel and executive director Donald Maxfield collaborated with the national office to defeat a mandatory pound seizure law in 1967. The following year The HSUS played a strong role in helping members of the Dane County (Wisconsin) Humane Society overcome an attempted takeover of that organization by University of Wisconsin medical school personnel determined to ensure a supply of shelter animals for use in laboratories.[99]

Although keeping lost or stolen pets out of the laboratory trade was a principal goal of the original AWA, by the 1980s it was clear the AWA had not succeeded in doing so. Class B dealers, licensed by USDA and permitted by the statute to gather animals from random sources, commonly acquired and sold animals stolen or procured through deception from households (like answering "free to a good home" advertisements); purchased or brokered through auction "bunchers" without proper records; or "adopted" from pounds, shelters, and other sources under false pretenses. On some occasions, USDA inspectors consciously ignored violations of federal law, including falsification of records—the best check against pet theft.[100]

In the 1980s, under the leadership of John Hoyt, The HSUS renewed its engagement in the issue of pound seizure. In 1984 The HSUS pushed for a government report on the use of random source animals in American laboratories. The HSUS also provided crucial leadership for the ProPets coalition, which sought to secure pound seizure prohibitions at the local level. ProPets drafted a model state bill for use at local and state levels and targeted communities of promise or special urgency. The coalition operated on the basis of The HSUS's long-standing convictions that, as Hoyt put it, "Making animals available for such purposes is contrary to the purpose and proper function of a public or private shelter," and that "making animals available for such purposes aggravates the problems of animal control and protection." [101]

Nevertheless, the coalition's record in its chosen strategy of supporting community-level referenda on the subject backfired in the wake of several significant losses. This led to a change in strategy, and in May 1986, the pound seizure ban went national, as Representative Robert Mrazek (D-NY) introduced H.R. 4871, the Pet Protection Act, to prohibit the use of federal funds for the purchase of animals taken directly or indirectly from animal shelters. This would have amounted to an absolute ban, since the NIH gave out virtually all monies for medical research involving cats and dogs. With shelter animals comprising an estimated 1 percent of the total number of animals used in research, testing, and education, researchers nevertheless attacked the Mrazek bill with energy.[102]

By 1987 Senator Wendell H. Ford (D-KY) introduced another approach to the problem, one that tried to eliminate once and for all the problem of pet theft. In August 1988 the U.S. Senate approved Ford's bill, which made it an offense for Class B dealers under the AWA to procure "random source" animals from sources other than publicly operated shelters and humane societies as well as individual breeders. The bill required that shelters and pounds hold cats and dogs for at least one week before turning them over to dealers. The measure eliminated the sale of animals at auctions, prime venues for the disposal of stolen animals.[103]

Unfortunately, Ford's Pet Theft Act collapsed in the Senate, as the research community mobilized in opposition to its passage. A diluted version of the bill was added to the 1990 Food, Agriculture, Conservation, and Trade Act. This amended the AWA to require that animals in shelters and pounds be held for a minimum of five days—including a Saturday—before being sold to research facilities and that all relevant records follow the animal through every move and transfer.[104]

While efforts to address the problem of pet theft continued into the 1990s, the struggle to eliminate pound seizure subsided. Fewer and fewer research institutions wanted to use pound animals or face the intense negative attention such use brought with it. In 1954 pound seizure, seen as a terrible provocation to humane societies, had helped to precipitate the schism that gave birth to The HSUS. At one time, some fourteen states and hundreds of communities required municipally owned and operated shelters to provide unclaimed animals for research. By 1991 fourteen states had prohibited pound seizure, and many municipalities had dropped the practice, convinced that it was a public relations nightmare for local shelters.[105]

(From left) Representative Dean Gallo, The HSUS's Martha Cole Glenn and John A. Hoyt, and Senator Alan Cranston celebrate the passage of "National Prevent-A-Litter Month."

Coming to Terms with the Companion Animal Surplus

In the late 1980s, The HSUS began to explore ways to harness the power of individual consumers—which had proved to be such a powerful tool in the campaigns against fur—to the challenge of reducing the population of unwanted and homeless animals. In 1988 The HSUS launched its first effort of this kind under the battle cry, "Be a P.A.L.—Prevent A Litter!" The campaign underscored the many ways in which companion animal overpopulation led to abuse and neglect of animals all over the country and celebrated the positive animal control accomplishments that had helped to decrease the population of unwanted animals in some communities. Award categories honored a variety of contributions to the field. Representative Thomas Foley (D-WA) and Senator Robert Dole (R-KS) sponsored resolutions to raise public awareness by designating April 1988 as "National Prevent a Litter Month."[106]

In 1991 The HSUS extended its efforts to end the euthanasia of healthy animals languishing in the nation's animal shelters by launching a corollary campaign, Adopt One, under the slogan "Until There Are None, Adopt One!" Finally in March 1993, President Paul Irwin called

for a temporary, one-year national moratorium on the breeding of dogs and cats. This brought The HSUS into a direct struggle with professional breeders and the AKC, whose practices had been, at least indirectly, exacerbating the homeless animal crisis for many decades. In the year of the moratorium alone, the AKC registered 1.5 million new dogs.[107]

While none of these initiatives was launched with the realistic expectation that it would actually end the tragedy of surplus animals, they reflected the organization's desire to raise awareness concerning the multifaceted dimensions of the problem and the need for a variety of approaches to its solution. They also showed The HSUS's determination to challenge all parties to *do more*.[108]

The message of these various initiatives was a simple one: dogs and cats died in shelters because there were too

During the 1992 Animal Care Expo, The HSUS's Kate Rindy explained the call for a one-year moratorium on the breeding of companion animals as Paul Irwin, HSUS president, listened attentively.

many of them, and to resolve this tragedy it was necessary to reduce the number of births. The HSUS considered the moratorium campaign a marked success not so much because it resulted in any measurable decline in animal births, but because of the intense dialogue and publicity it engendered.[109]

Taking Cruelty Seriously: Felony Status and First Strike™

In the mid-1980s Phyllis Wright and Randall Lockwood began to discuss the need for a comprehensive campaign to ensure that law enforcement and social services agencies took individual cases of cruelty to animals seriously, for their inherent viciousness as well as for what they might say about the perpetrator's potential for further misdeeds, including further violence against animals or human beings. After years of experience in conducting raids, HSUS investigators were in a position to confirm that law enforcement officers took dogfighting very seriously in states where it was a felony. This led the organization to push harder for "upgrade" (from misdemeanor to felony-level offense) campaigns. Investigators Bob Baker, Eric Sakach, and others testified before many state legislatures and were key figures in the assignment of felony status to such crimes.[110]

Wright watched these developments with interest, for she had been having a lot of trouble getting law enforcement agencies to treat individual cases of cruelty seriously. On occasion, she noted, even the most shocking instances of cruelty failed to move local authorities, and they frequently failed to pursue such cases with any vigor. This was enormously frustrating to Wright.[111]

Staff members agreed that a thorough campaign would involve education, legislative initiatives, and enhanced networking with law enforcement agencies. In 1986 Lockwood and Guy Hodge authored an award-winning piece in *HSUS News* that highlighted "The Tangled Web of Animal Abuse"—"the link between cruelty to animals and other forms of violent or anti-social behavior." This landmark article marked the first step in the campaign to sensitize the humane movement to the need for serious efforts to integrate its concerns with those of law enforcement and social service agencies.[112] This first step taken, Lockwood and other members of his Training Initiatives staff initiated a program, termed First Strike™, of outreach to law enforcement and social services agencies. The HSUS hired a social worker to coordinate some of these relationships, and Lockwood undertook a heavy schedule of lectures, training, and documentation efforts to support the program.

Within a decade of these initial steps to develop broader outreach, The HSUS was in regular contact with congressional offices, representatives of the FBI and the Department of Justice, and other law enforcement agencies. It was collaborating in efforts to promote awareness and education within law enforcement circles, which began to view prosecution of animal cruelty cases as an important part of threat assessment and another way of getting dangerous individuals into the legal system. With more successful animal cruelty prosecutions on the record, humane societies and law enforcement personnel would find themselves better equipped to address future threats to animals or people by the same individuals.[113]

Staff members from government affairs, regional offices, companion animals, and other sections and departments, following the initiative of longtime legislative specialist Ann Church, also worked to support the program, pushing for legislation to upgrade deliberate animal cruelty from misdemeanor to felony status. In 1999 The HSUS was responsible for the passage of seven such laws, and by 2004 The HSUS had pushed the total number of states in which such acts could be prosecuted as felonies to forty-one.[114]

Dangerous Dogs

One of the most serious offshoots of dogfighting in the 1980s (see chapter 7) was the alarming rise of vicious dog attacks and fatalities. As the problem of dangerous dogs came to increased public attention, it began to occupy a greater proportion of staff time and organizational resources within The HSUS. Public preoccupation with the topic reached an unprecedented peak in 1986.[115]

The dangerous dog problem presented animal control organizations and government agencies throughout the country with a serious challenge. For many years the local societies The HSUS serviced had been keeping statistics on the problem, sometimes as a legal responsibility under the terms of animal control agreements. However, the programs they managed had been designed to address issues associated with rabies, and they were less well equipped to handle other concerns. As investigation and research revealed, however, by the mid-1980s the dangerous dog problem had its roots in the irresponsible breeding and use of vicious dogs for fighting, protection, and other purposes.[116]

As community after community moved to consider breed-specific bans and other regulatory measures, The HSUS established itself as a preeminent source of sound data and counsel. This was another area in which Randall Lockwood worked closely with staff members in the Companion Animals section. From 1986 on The HSUS collaborated with the U.S. Centers for Disease Control to track fatal dog attacks. The year 1990 produced an all-time high of twenty-four such deaths. In 1995 The HSUS joined forces with the U.S. Postal Service to stage National Dog Bite Prevention Week.[117]

Limited-Admission and No-Kill Operations

The HSUS has always endorsed euthanasia over indefinite and substandard confinement and careful screening over indiscriminate placement in its work. Even as the "no-kill" movement gained momentum and popularity during the 1990s, The HSUS hewed to the perspective its founding figures had articulated and opposed the warehousing of animals. In its public comments on the issue, The HSUS reframed the debate as one between open- vs. limited-admission facilities and underscored its view that there are worse things than death for an animal, including not only disease and neglect but also a life of physical and or psychological deprivation and distress. In the tradition of Phyllis Wright, The HSUS championed the work of good shelters and did not turn its back on them in light of the no-kill challenge.[118]

In responding to the no-kill movement, The HSUS found a compass in its original mandate—to strengthen and enhance the general work of the humane movement—the whole movement. At the same time, the organization hewed to a firm view, encompassed by the following statement:

> The HSUS believes that keeping old, sick, aggressive, or otherwise unadoptable animals caged in the shelter for months, years, or lifetimes to avoid euthanasia is not in the animals' best interests—and would not be even if every shelter had unlimited space and resources. The HSUS is strongly opposed to the long-term, institutional

housing of companion animals because it may deprive animals of adequate human attention. Every dog, cat, and other companion animal deserves—and ultimately belongs in—a lifelong home with attentive, responsible caregivers.[119]

The HSUS's long-standing policy had, of course, been shaped by an earlier era's deep shock at the state of no-kill facilities. "I have found that while an animal shelter offers a genuine temporary refuge for homeless animals, as a permanent abode such confinement produces misery and frustration for most dogs," one early supporter wrote. Mel Morse, while speaking sympathetically of the intentions of those who ran no-kill operations, nevertheless noted, "Those of us who have been in this movement very long have seen the results—an accumulation of animals either imprisoned for life in kennel runs or running at large where disease is rampant. Many of us investigating such premises see miserable animals—some tied to trees, others chained to dog houses, many with sores, some dead among the living." Then, Morse observed, "where do you say no to the next animal when all the facilities are full....How about the hundreds to follow? There comes the time inevitably when the decision has to be reached—euthanasia."[120]

At the same time, The HSUS was never complacent about euthanasia. Fred Myers frequently admonished colleagues that "any humane society that runs a 'slaughter house' without simultaneously fighting unceasingly to get at the roots of the need for wholesale euthanasia is not entitled to be called a humane society." Myers admired those colleagues who, "while courageously taking on themselves the miserable and deeply distressing task of euthanasia, [also] labor prodigiously against the necessity."[121]

The HSUS strove to remind all parties to the debate that earnest and dedicated shelters and humane workers should not be blamed for the overpopulation crisis and the euthanasia policy. "The whole community, not just the shelter and its caring staff, bears the responsibility for euthanasia of unwanted animals," Martha Armstrong said in 1998. Armstrong even proffered the example of one shelter that sought to underscore this point in its own community by reporting "how many unwanted animals the community generates instead of stating how many animals the shelter euthanatizes."[122]

Celebrating the Companion Animal Bond

While facing up to many of the worst threats to the well-being of dogs, cats, and other companion animals, and drawing important distinctions between what humans want to do with animals and what is actually in animals' interests, The HSUS did not fail to celebrate the bond between humans and companion animals in its programs and out-reach. In developing its programs, The HSUS relied on the goodwill and support of those who cared about animals, many of whom kept animals in their own homes. The HSUS did its best to acquaint new supporters with a broader range of animal-related concerns, in keeping with the vision of its founders to focus the attention of those who cared about dogs and cats onto the wider universe of animal suffering.

An HSUS brochure from the 1950s discussed the needs of species adopted from animal shelters and other facilities.

The safety and security of companion animals was a priority from the day The HSUS opened its doors, and the organization placed special emphasis on the prevention of animal theft. In 1956 The HSUS called for a national law to make the transportation of stolen dogs across state lines a federal crime, and Fred Myers asked staff members to explore cooperation with private companies on the development of a foolproof method of identifying dogs to minimize the large numbers lost, stolen, or abandoned. The campaign for the Laboratory Animal Welfare Act during the 1960s became, in part, a war against petnapping, and The

The HSUS welcomed the 1966 issuance of a U.S. five-cent commemorative stamp dedicated to the "Humane Treatment of Animals."

HSUS was relentless in its efforts to halt the traffic in animals, assigning more staff investigators to the problem than any other organization.[123] The HSUS also targeted inferior labeling standards for animal food products in its early years. After the first federal guidelines on the subject were issued in the early 1960s, The HSUS pointed out that the FDA had long failed in its efforts to enforce good practices. The HSUS called upon the states to institute more rigorous requirements that would frustrate the use of adulterated or filler products in pet foods. Successful state testing programs in a few states had done much to discourage false and exaggerated claims and misleading designation of product ingredients.[124]

As an organization formed to promote the adoption of homeless animals from pounds and shelters and to encourage responsible guardianship and care, The HSUS welcomed the 1966 issuance of a U.S. five-cent commemorative stamp dedicated to the "Humane Treatment of Animals." The stamp, issued in honor of the one hundredth anniversary of the humane movement, featured a mongrel dog.[125]

Throughout its history, The HSUS has vigorously challenged characterizations of animals as a social nuisance and dismissed works that depict devotion to them as a symptom of social alienation.[126] Against such demonization of companion animals and those who care about them, The HSUS has highlighted the vital contribution that animals make to human mental and physical health, as part of appropriately managed animal-assisted therapy, and, more commonly, as part of a healthy family and home life.

In those cases where individual renters could establish their ability to properly care for animals, The HSUS supported and fought to preserve their freedom to keep companion animals. As early as 1976, The HSUS backed legislation to prohibit federal assistance to rental housing projects in which tenants were forbidden to keep animals and to local governments that do not permit animals in rental housing. In 1983 staff members worked for the passage of legislation to allow the elderly and the handicapped to have pets in all federally subsidized housing. The HSUS helped to scuttle attempts by the U.S. Department of Housing and Urban Development (HUD) to limit P.L. 98-181's coverage to individuals living in housing built exclusively for occupancy by the elderly and handicapped. By 1995 this campaign developed even further, providing such a guarantee for anyone in federally subsidized housing; this measure passed in 1999. At about the same time, The HSUS launched its Rent with Pets™ program (*rentwithpets.org*), which helped people to locate suitable housing where they could live with companion animals and worked proactively to persuade property owners and homeowners' associations that those who kept animals in a responsible way were excellent tenants.[127]

After its formation in 1975, the HSUS Legal Department was a staunch defender of the principle that people should be able to make suitable arrangements for the care of animals following the deaths of their human guardians. In 1976 HSUS General Counsel Murdaugh Madden made a submission to a Florida court that expressed concern with the callousness of banks and trust officers in observing the wishes of individuals who had attempted to make such provisions. Madden also penned articles on the subject from time to time, exploring the pitfalls and challenges of such situations, encouraging readers of *HSUS News* to work out suitable arrangements with family members and friends willing and able to respond appropriately and to avoid "elaborate legalistic approaches" involving legal and financial institutions. "Lawyers rarely, and banks and courts *never*," Madden warned, "act effectively in a situation where what is needed is quick action, compassion and understanding, and a warm and friendly hand." [128]

The HSUS has also been attentive to opportunities for celebrating the human-animal bond through special events, contests, and programming. In 1986 Phyllis Wright served as one of the judges in Purina Dog Chow's "Search for Capitol Hill's Great American Dog." In 1993 The HSUS was the beneficiary of proceeds from a "Socks Appeal" contest to find a cat that most resembled President Clinton's. In 1996 The HSUS co-sponsored a public debate between journalists from *Dog World* and *Cats* magazines, on whether a dog or a cat was best qualified to represent the nation's companion animals. In 1999 former Senator Robert Dole (R-KS) and his wife, Elizabeth, entered the name of their dog, Leader, into The HSUS's *Book of Kindred Spirits*, established to pay tribute to departed loved ones. On three different occasions, The HSUS underwrote the broadcast of the James Herriot series, *All Creatures Great and Small*, on a Washington, D.C.-area public television station. [129]

In 1993 eleven animal-related organizations, including The HSUS, joined together to launch the National Council on Pet Population Study and Policy to gather and analyze data on the keeping of animals, to promote responsible stewardship, and to develop programs for the reduction and elimination of the homeless and unwanted animal overpopulation. In 1996 The HSUS convened a twelve-member National Companion Animals Advisory Group, comprised of respected shelter administrators from around the country, to assist in shaping the goals and programs of the Companion Animals section. The group met twice a year to review policy and programmatic concerns and regularly consulted with staff members on a variety of sheltering issues. [130]

By the end of the twentieth century, research efforts examined the problem of companion animal overpopulation as a multifaceted question, one that called for sound quantitative analysis to determine which animals were being handed over to shelters and by whom, economic comparisons of the relative costs of animal control versus other programs, and sociological investigations of the human-animal relationship and its value. Practical and scholarly attention to the problem of relinquishment increasingly focused on the ostensible "failure" of human-companion animal relationships, manifest in such phenomena as abandonment, neglect, surrender at shelters, unrestrained reproduction, and wandering. On the assumption that better bonds would reduce the range of problems that result in animal suffering and death, The HSUS committed itself to fostering greater understanding of the psychological and biological needs of animals and to promoting a broader public responsibility toward animals.

The HSUS created "Renting with Pets," an on-line resource for rental-housing managers and pet owners.

The HSUS did not join those organizations attempting to spur a transformation in the treatment of companion animals by pushing for the substitution of the word, "guardian," for "owner" in legislation and ordinances. While generally supportive of the view that the keeping of animals encompassed far more than simply a right of property, for a variety of reasons, The HSUS did not support the legal change in terminology to guardianship, instead endorsing and promoting use of the term, "caregiver." [131]

However, the organization remained as committed as any to the idea that people should make their commitments to individual animals lifelong, that such commitment should not be broken for frivolous or resolvable reasons, and that humans were obligated to provide for their companions not only during their lives, but also—as they grew older—with a humane death. These convictions formed the core of a new signature program introduced in the early twenty-first century, Pets for Life®, which had as its goal the cultivation of successful bonds between humans and companion animals and, through the sustenance of better relationships between humans and the animals with whom they shared their lives, the reduction of shelter relinquishments.

Conclusion

As the new century dawned, taking advantage of The HSUS's own publishing and distribution capacities, the Companion Animals section commissioned or cowrote a number of full-length works, including *The Humane Society of the United States Complete Guide to Dog Care* (published by Little, Brown and Company), *The Humane Society of the United States Complete Guide to Cat Care* (published by St. Martin's Press), *Community Approaches to Feral Cats*, and *The Humane Society of the United States Euthanasia Training Manual*. These and other publications helped thousands of animal care and control professionals to meet the daily challenges of their work and millions of people worldwide to better care for their companion animals. The HSUS's Video Services department also advanced the goals of companion animal protection through the distribution of one-minute segments on companion animals twice weekly to more than one hundred news stations around the country. As a source of information on companion animal care, The HSUS had few equals by 2004.

While relations with the veterinary community continued to run hot and cold—according to the issue—The HSUS did not stop trying to forge appropriate links. In the late 1990s, program staff began to focus on the development of materials suitable for informing veterinarians about the issues of dogfighting, community animal control, the epidemiology of animal health, and maintenance of the human-companion animal relationship. In 2004 The HSUS was planning to publish a diagnostic guide to encourage veterinarians to identify and report signs of cruelty that may signal domestic abuse or other problems within a family. The organization set its sights on the professionalization of animal shelter medicine and the creation of a shelter medicine curriculum in the nation's veterinary schools. The HSUS also supported a summer fellowship program launched by the Geraldine R. Dodge Foundation, which supported approximately thirty veterinary students per year in their pursuit of a range of projects to improve companion animal care through the nation's shelters and in other contexts.[132]

Nor did The HSUS shy away from controversy in confronting cruelty to companion animals. In 1991, after being queried on The HSUS's position concerning the Iditarod long-distance sled-dog race, HSUS President Paul Irwin directed staff members to investigate the practices of mushers and others associated with that year's race. That same year four-time Iditarod winner Susan Butcher stated, "We [Iditarod competitors] wouldn't, as a group, pass anybody's idea of humane treatment of animals." The HSUS denounced the event in 1994, after investigations revealed that dogs had died in the race every year since its 1973 inception, their deaths routinely reported alongside information about weather conditions and other race statistics. The HSUS's action adversely affected the race's corporate sponsorship, as several prominent corporations ended their association with the Iditarod.[133]

The Companion Animals section worked closely with regional offices of The HSUS, and field representatives frequently represented The HSUS in relations with local societies. While The HSUS had no legal enforcement powers, on occasion field representatives would sign individual complaints in aggravated cases, just as any citizen might. While The HSUS did not become directly involved with the thousands of local investigations and prosecutions going on at any given time throughout the country, staff members frequently furnished advice, guidance, and (sometimes) financial and legal support for such activities. On those occasions when an issue or incident appeared to have national importance or showed potential as a vehicle for advancing the cause through test cases or other initiatives, The HSUS might become more actively engaged. After 1985 or so, the same was true in large-scale cases like those involving animal hoarders, in which The HSUS sometimes did become involved with rescue operation support, the delivery of equipment and training, and appropriate networking among responsible agencies.

In keeping with the organization's increasingly international outreach, the Companion Animals section was also involved in efforts to promote higher standards of animal care and control work abroad. In some parts of the world, the deficient practices in use harkened back to those that characterized nineteenth-century America in their inadequacy and crudeness. There was hardly a country in the world that did not face the challenge of having to deal with a surplus animal population, and The HSUS's international arm, HSI, was well able to draw program staff from the Companion Animals section into the arena of international work.[134]

Above all, however, staff members in the section continued to cover the dozens of issues involving companion animal well-being that had come within their remit. The section regularly dealt with such concerns as fad pets, collectors and hoarders, puppy mill breeding, the handling of feral cat populations, euthanasia techniques, greyhound racing, and questions of veterinary care. The section maintained an active portfolio of casework, helping shelters with their efforts to secure funding, conducting pound and shelter inspections, working on legislation to facilitate the licensing of shelters to use controlled drugs for euthanasia of animals, mediating disputes over rabies control policy, assisting with investigations, and providing hands-on relief in the case of disaster or failure of physical plant systems around the country.

In 2004 no one associated with humane work could overlook the fact that millions of domestic animals were still homeless and abandoned to uncertain fates each year. Still, there were encouraging signs of progress in the field. Humane societies had made significant gains in their efforts to reduce the numbers of animals euthanized because they were not wanted. They were attempting to meet new challenges, especially the population of stray and feral cats. Most important, however, they were addressing their work with better information, expertise, and precedent.

From The HSUS's inception, a deep concern for companion animal welfare was a hallmark of its programs. By the time of The HSUS's fiftieth anniversary, the Companion Animals section was The HSUS's largest section, reflecting its commitment to the health and well-being of companion animals, the concerns of the humans who loved and cared for them, and the needs of the many private organizations and community agencies that served, guaranteed, and protected their interests. Fred Myers saw local humane institutions as The HSUS's central constituency, and Phyllis Wright and her colleagues did their best to nourish this vision through decades of service and devotion. During The HSUS's first half-century, the animal care and shelter community in the United States evolved to an extent that would have gratified 1950s-era advocates, who had long had to contend with the unflattering implications of being "just dogcatchers" for several generations. The physical facilities and veterinary medical capabilities of humane societies and animal control agencies had vastly improved. Their stature in their respective communities had grown, and to an increasing degree, their policies on animal overpopulation, dangerous dogs, veterinary care, and other matters had become more preventive than reactive in character. It was not a coincidence that this evolution in the field closely paralleled the emergence and development of The HSUS itself. Not only could it celebrate the increasing professionalism of the field; it could also lay a substantial claim to some measure of credit for having helped that process along.

The Great Chain of Life:
Wildlife and
Marine Mammals

hen The HSUS formed, it had a philosophical commitment to wildlife and marine mammal protection, but it lacked the resources to pursue those issues with vigor. The main focus of The HSUS during its first decade was on animals used for food and in research. Still, it made some tentative steps toward incorporating wildlife and marine mammals into its range of concerns. Opposition to hunting, mismanagement of animal populations by state wildlife agencies, lethal predator control in the interests of agriculture, the clubbing of seals, and the harpooning of whales all emerged as target issues once the organization acquired the resources to address them.

By 1970, the year John Hoyt joined The HSUS, the era's burgeoning environmental consciousness had brought the plight of some animals, including whales, seals, dolphins, bears, wolves, and numerous endangered species, to greater public attention. One of the first things Hoyt did after coming to The HSUS was to create a wildlife issues program. During the 1970s Hoyt hired a number of specialists to work on wildlife and marine mammal issues. Guy Hodge, Hal Perry, Sue Pressman, Michael Fox, Patricia Forkan, and Natasha Atkins all helped to advance the program in those years. They witnessed some stunning victories in the realm of wildlife protection: the ban on DDT in 1971; enactment of the Marine Mammal Protection Act and the ban on predator poisons in 1972; and the signing of the CITES treaty and the passage of the Endangered Species Act (ESA) in 1973. As one HSUS staff member noted, however, these were battles that would not stay won.[1]

In 1981, with the Reagan administration's policies threatening wildlife, marine mammal, and environmental protection gains on virtually all fronts, The HSUS moved to establish a program specifically devoted to these concerns. Hoyt chose wildlife scientist John W. Grandy, Ph.D., to head a newly established department of Wildlife and Environment as a vice president. Grandy had six years of experience at Defenders of Wildlife and broad knowledge of predator control programs, federal wildlife policy, and the CITES treaty. He also brought a network of political and legal contacts that would prove to be useful to The HSUS in the years to come.[2]

Building upon its first principled expressions of concern for wild animals, The HSUS developed one of the most comprehensive wildlife-oriented and marine mammal advocacy programs in the world. A quarter-century after its establishment within The HSUS, the section labored on behalf of numerous species. Its concerns ranged from wildlife death tolls on the highway to disreputable hunting practices in the fifty states, from the peril of endangered species to the challenge of living with wildlife in the nation's suburbs, from the clubbing of seals to the display of captive animals at roadside zoos, from the depravity of the "canned" hunt of confined wildlife to the calculated destruction of the drift net. Strong support for The HSUS's wildlife and marine mammal protection programs gave the organization an opportunity to establish itself as an influential and credible force, bringing together good science, good principles, and the full panoply of legal and legislative remedies available for ensuring animals' interests.

Wildlife and Marine Mammal Issues and The HSUS before 1970

The early- to mid-twentieth-century humane movement's engagement with wildlife and marine mammal issues was a limited one. For many years advocates associated with AHA and other groups campaigned for a humane trap and protested the use of fur. Humane publications deplored hunting but did not mount any serious challenges to it. Even after The HSUS formed, inadequate funding and higher-priority program commitments made it impossible for the organization to devote much time or resources to wildlife and marine mammal concerns before 1970. The HSUS did, however, make selective contributions that made clear its dedication to the protection of wild animals and marine life and set the stage for the emergence of a full-fledged program of related advocacy.

At least one original board member, Delos E. Culver (1954–1958), had a strong interest in wildlife issues, with roots in the movement that extended back to the Anti-Steel Trap League (ASTL), founded by Colonel Edward Breck in the 1920s. Culver was one of the incorporators of the ASTL's successor group, Defenders of Furbearers, in 1947 and, when this group in turn became Defenders of Wildlife, Culver served for a time as president. Culver was arguing for the prohibition of the leghold trap and the need for humane alternatives years before the founding of The HSUS.[3]

In 1957 another HSUS director, Senator Richard L. Neuberger (D-OR), sponsored the first humane trapping bill ever introduced in the U.S. Congress. The bill required that trappers check their traps daily or use traps that killed animals instantly. Neuberger introduced a better version in 1959, but it did not garner much support. For one thing, its successful passage depended on the availability and acceptability of a humane trap. In addition, both the Department of the Interior and USDA opposed the bill.[4]

In 1958 Alice Morgan Wright and HSUS director Edith Goode, working with humane advocates from all over the world, secured an early victory on the marine mammal protection front, as the principle of humane treatment of sea animals won endorsement from participants in the United Nations conference on the Law of the Sea. While not compulsory, humane advocates believed that the resolution approved would signal the start of serious progress toward the adoption of humane methods of killing whales and seals.[5]

In 1956 The HSUS produced "It Pays to Give Wildlife a Brake," a poster addressing the problem of animal casualties on the nation's highways. In 1962 the organization began a five-year effort to inventory the number of animals and birds killed on the nation's highways in one day, each July 4. Twice as many birds as animals were killed, and rabbits topped the list of animals killed, ahead of rats, snakes, deer, and squirrels. The premise was to confirm or deny prevailing theories regarding preferred soil cover, foliage, and other factors along highway rights-of-way. Eventually, this program inspired efforts by the Federal Highway Administration to reduce the number of animals killed on highways through the use of fencing, repellents, and roadway design.[6]

From its founding, The HSUS also took a strong stand against hunting, whose enthusiasts, to say the very least, as Oliver Evans put it, could not cite the kinds of benefits claimed for medical and nutritional use. The HSUS's opposition went deeper than such assessments, however. As early as May 1957, the *HSUS News* shared with its readers Joseph Wood Krutch's compelling indictment from *The Great Chain of Life*: "When a man wantonly destroys one of the works of man we call him a vandal. When he wantonly destroys one of the works of God we call him a sportsman." Just a year later, The HSUS's annual report repeated Krutch's disparagement of hunting as "the pure evil of which theologians speak." By the mid-1960s, it had published pamphlets on the issue, including *Killing for Fun, A New Look at Sportsmanship*, written and illustrated by naturalist Hope Sawyer Buyukmihci (1913–2001), and *Lust to Kill*, based on Fred Myers's 1952 article.[7] The HSUS did more than just publish pamphlets. In summer 1966 the HSUS California branch strongly condemned bow and arrow hunting in testimony before the California Assembly Interim Committee on Conservation and Wildlife, and HSUS President Oliver Evans lodged a strongly worded protest with the U.S. Fish and Wildlife Service about the opening of the Aransas (Texas) National Wildlife Refuge to archery hunting for deer."[8]

The mid-1960s witnessed The HSUS's entry into the realm of predator control policy, too. It opposed government-sponsored destruction of wild animals in California and backed the Dingell bill to establish a national policy and program to curb indiscriminate predator control practices.[9]

During the 1960s wildlife concerns increasingly gained attention as a topic of internal deliberations within The HSUS. Participants at its twelfth annual National Leadership Conference, in Hershey, Pennsylvania, in September 1966, heard Mrs. Robert Arny, of Montclair State College, talk about the need for a wildlife-focused humane agenda. Arny went beyond condemnations of hunting to indict the work of the dam-building Bureau of Reclamation and the government's predator control programs.[10]

When plans for ISAP emerged in early 1970, The HSUS began a more systematic review of the contributions it might make in the field of wildlife protection. The original proposal for ISAP identified a variety of potential projects, including data collection, promotion of first aid techniques, the support and analysis of field studies focused on wildlife, review of wildlife management policies, focus on endangered species issues, monitoring of federal and state agencies, disaster relief and disease outbreak procedures, and evaluation and standardization of tranquilization and handling techniques. The HSUS also hoped to deploy ISAP's resources for the development of educational and factual materials for school distribution as well as for the evaluation of relevant legislation and its effects.[11]

Early pamphlets published by The HSUS condemned hunting.

Predator Control

Lethal predator control has been going on in North America at least since Europeans arrived in the early 1600s, and it was firmly established as a national policy by the early twentieth century. In 1931 the first federal legislation on the subject resulted in the Animal Damage Control (ADC) program. This enactment inaugurated an astonishingly destructive phase of the human war against wildlife, as Americans liberally poisoned, trapped, shot, and exterminated animals—both predators and nonpredators—by the millions. Since the 1930s, under the alternate control of USDA or the Department of the Interior, the ADC program has been the largest and most conspicuous practitioner of lethal predator control in the United States. In recent years, renamed the Division of Wildlife Services, the program killed about one million wild animals a year.

The HSUS was one of many organizations that began aggressive efforts to confront the ADC program in the late 1960s, arguing that it was indiscriminate, cruel, environmentally and ecologically harmful, and out of step with contemporary science and values. The issue of predator control surfaced still more prominently in the 1970s, as conflict between livestock interests and wildlife protection advocates increased. In May 1971 The HSUS further expanded its efforts in this area by hiring Hal Perry, a longtime campaigner against predator control programs conducted by the federal government in the Southwest. Perry started out as a wildlife specialist but then worked as a field representative out of the Rocky Mountain Regional Office, opened by Frantz Dantzler, in 1972.[12]

Even before Perry came to The HSUS, the organization had joined in a lawsuit to halt the use of Compound 1080, a poison used to kill predators. The primary target of the ADC pro-

Dick Randall was a skilled photographer and passionate critic of the ADC program.

DICK RANDALL

gram was the coyote, accused by sheep ranchers of destroying their livestock. In the process of trying to eradicate the coyote with an arsenal of poisons, however, federal agents killed hundreds of thousands of other animals, including some endangered species. In 1971 HSUS General Counsel Murdaugh Madden took the deposition of an ADC official as part of ongoing litigation targeting the Department of the Interior. Along with other evidence, the official's answers confirmed that the federal government could not substantiate sheepmen's claims of massive losses from the depredations of coyotes, had invested virtually no effort in the search for more humane and selective methods of killing predators, and had conducted the program largely to prevent ranchers from taking matters into their own hands.[13]

In 1972 President Nixon announced an immediate ban on the use of poisons for predator control on public lands, and the Environmental Protection Agency (EPA) banned the shipment of all poisons used in predator control shortly thereafter. The HSUS quickly followed up with campaigns to obtain a complete ban on the use of poisons by states and individuals, rigorous enforcement of the president's order, and training of state employees and private landowners in other methods for coyote removal and popular control.[14]

Elation over the president's executive order waned with the clarification of administration-sponsored proposals that large-scale killing would continue under the auspices of individual states and the creation of exemptions for Native American lands leased to sheep ranchers. It also quickly became apparent that sheepmen—through the National Wool Growers Association—would intensify their lobbying efforts to get the Nixon ban lifted.[15]

Challenges to predator control dragged on through the Ford and Carter administrations, as The HSUS filed suit to stop EPA from allowing ranchers to poison animals, and sheep ranchers pressured the Ford administration to approve the use of sodium cyanide. Critics of the ADC programs became bolder and bolder in their charge that federal predator control policy was the product of ranchers' greed, indifference, and sloth. For generations, private ranchers paid the smallest of fees for the right to graze ever larger herds of animals on public lands. They undertook no responsibility whatsoever for the protection of animals from disease, starvation, harsh weather, and other adversities.[16]

In 1979 President Jimmy Carter's secretary of the Interior, Cecil Andrus, articulated specific goals for the ADC program, including a phasing out of lethal preventive controls over the long term, the adoption of nonlethal, noncapture methods of control, and a concerted effort to redirect attention to the goal of "preventing predator damage rather than controlling predators." However, in 1980 a two-year government study of the use of a Compound 1080 toxic collar recommended its increased use.[17]

In 1981 The HSUS registered a big victory when EPA canceled a permit allowing the field use of Compound 1080 after an HSUS lawsuit. But the policy was reversed several years later. By that time John Grandy, who had considerable experience with the issue, had joined The HSUS and had begun to mobilize staff members and consultants in pursuit of a permanent ban. For a time in the late 1980s, Grandy served on the U.S. Secretary of Agriculture's Advisory Committee on Animal Damage Control, using the position to promote rational approaches to animal damage control and to monitor the disastrous impact of nonselective programs of predator control on animals. In 1986 The HSUS singled out ADC for particular scorn when Ronald Reagan's proposed fiscal year 1987 budget included no funds for the AWA. "$0 to Protect Animals, $10 Million to Kill Them," the *Animal Activist Alert* proclaimed, decrying the ADC budget as "one of the biggest gravy trains ever to roll out of Congress." The ADC's transfer from the Department of the Interior to USDA did nothing to change things.[18]

Dick Randall, recruited by Grandy from the Defenders of Wildlife network, where they had first become acquainted, was an important figure in The HSUS's engagement with the issue. From 1988 until Randall's death in 1997, The HSUS supported his efforts to document the irrationality and violence of the ADC program through photography, writing, and personal witness. Randall's humane epiphany came after years of working as a wildlife killer in the employ of the U.S. Fish and Wildlife Service during the 1950s. A skilled shooter and trapper, he spent five years destroying predators and rodents through poisoning, trapping, and shooting. Eventually Randall became convinced that natural forces, left alone, were sufficient to control predators and rodents. He quit ADC in 1971 to devote the rest of his life to reforming the agency. Randall's road to Damascus conversion made him a powerful witness against Compound 1080 and other disturbing predator control methods sponsored by federal and state agencies.[19]

The HSUS's Frank McMahon watches as crew members of the Maaslloyd *feed giraffes at a New York pier in 1966. Fear of hoof and mouth disease required the animals to be quarantined, but when no quarantine facility was supposedly available, HSUS efforts kept the zoo-bound animals from being dumped overboard.*

Randall's intimate understanding of ADC programs, together with his damning photographic evidence of their non-selective and highly destructive effects upon wildlife, made him an extraordinary ally. He was a walking encyclopedia concerning ADC and the lawless conduct it fostered, including the rampant destruction of bald and golden eagles by zealous ranchers in the 1970s. He helped to sharpen The HSUS's long-standing critique of ADC as a conspicuous misappropriation of federal tax revenues, secured in the interests of a minority of belligerent western ranchers by their elected representatives in Washington, and he helped Grandy and other staff members to make the case that predator control programs exert a devastating impact on ecosystem balance.[20]

In 1997, when Animal Damage Control became "Wildlife Services," The HSUS could not let the name change go without comment, publicly arguing, "the name should not change until the program does." Several years later The HSUS's Government Affairs department successfully lobbied for an unprecedented $10 million cut from Wildlife Services' budget. Although the vote was reversed, it was a sign of The HSUS's progress in advancing its agenda through the Capitol Hill funding process. [21]

Government Affairs registered a victory over Wildlife Services in 2002, when it secured a referendum victory in Washington State, where voters overwhelmingly endorsed an initiative banning the use of Compound 1080 and sodium cyanide. After USDA received unofficial approval from state officials, Washington made plans to go ahead with its poisoning regime—in violation of its own policy stating that employees must comply with applicable federal, state, and local laws. However, The HSUS persuaded the state's attorney general that USDA's response amounted to willful disregard of voters in her state, and she successfully pressured the federal agency to observe the requirements of the referendum, effectively ending Wildlife Services' poisoning and trapping activities in Washington.[22]

Captive Animal Populations: Zoos, Circuses, and Nature Parks

When The HSUS began its work, it focused on cruelties far more conspicuous than those that could be found in the nation's zoos. While zoos were not uncontroversial within the movement before 1970, they did not receive much scrutiny from humane organizations, nor did animal protectionists present a coherent or even a very public critique of keeping animals in captivity.

The HSUS did care about the welfare of captive animals though, as Frank McMahon demonstrated in a widely publicized confrontation with USDA officials over a shipload of animals in 1966. USDA had forced the *Maaslloyd*, a Dutch freighter, to halt outside New York Harbor because of fears concerning hoof and mouth disease, several cases of which had recently surfaced at two of the ship's ports of call in Africa. A Nebraska congressman asked The HSUS to intervene when USDA declared that if no overseas quarantine site could be arranged, the animals, bound for American zoos, would have to be dumped overboard. McMahon and HSUS director Edward Bostick had a stormy meeting with USDA officials, who finally admitted that the Department of Defense had offered a small island in Long Island Sound to serve as a quarantine site for the required sixty days. USDA finally relented and cleared the ship for entry into the harbor. When the *Maaslloyd* reached the docks, government officials saw McMahon—triumphant—standing on its bridge, having convinced the captain of a small boat to take him out to the ship in the middle of the night while it was still outside the three-mile limit to guarantee the outcome.[23]

The HSUS's real zoo-related activities began in 1971, when John Hoyt hired zoo specialist and veterinarian Sue Pressman from Boston's Franklin Park Zoo as director of wildlife protection. It was a timely appointment, because zoos were now subject to minimum standards enforceable under the AWA amendments of 1970. One of Pressman's first assignments was to conduct an investigation of zoos, roadside menageries, and other captive animal displays in the United States. The HSUS position was characteristically pragmatic. "The HSUS does not believe in caging animals," the article announcing Pressman's appointment declared, "but until a practical alternative is put into effect, it intends to work toward improving the condi-

Sue Pressman investigated zoos and other captive animal displays from 1971 until 1986.

tion of all caged animals." Pressman visited many zoos during her time at The HSUS, and her inspections and reports garnered significant public attention, prompting zoo officials to embark on crash cleanup strategies both before and after the exposure her visits generated. "We thought long and hard" before sending Pressman out to do such zoo surveys, John Hoyt recalled. "Zoos are like apple pie. Very rarely do you see the bad side….Some of the ones we identified did disappear. We tried to help those that wanted to improve." [24]

The HSUS first adopted a comprehensive policy position on captive animals in 1975, as its board of directors pledged to work against roadside menageries and other substandard facilities. The organization did not take a position against all zoos, however, and pledged continued support for endangered-species breeding and educational programs managed by zoos. Staff members inspected numerous roadside menageries, zoo parks, and other facilities and interceded in cases where traveling acts and shows were the source of animal misery. In such instances, The HSUS often functioned as a self-declared "goad, exposing a problem and stimulating action from law enforcement agencies." By 1983, however, HSUS staff members had inspected 363 zoos nationwide and singled out ten of the nation's worst.[25]

In 1984 the board of directors revised HSUS policy, adopting the position that animals should not be taken from the wild for public display at zoos, which, to a considerable extent, were responsible for "abuse, neglect, suffering, and death of animals." When it came to support for endangered-species breeding and educational programs, moreover, few zoos, it appeared, met satisfactory standards. There was no place for zoos that could not improve on their programs of care and education. The Wildlife section was an early and stalwart critic of ineffectual education programs, underscoring the superficiality of what passed for instruction at most zoos. Their continuing popularity, HSUS staff members asserted, rested upon their status as a relatively inexpensive recreational option, not on their claims to provide the public with an introduction to the value of ecosystems, habitat protection, and endangered-species protection.[26]

Staff members' knowledge of zoos and the needs of their captive populations sometimes

While the Lancelot Link chimpanzees appeared to travel in style and comfort, HSUS investigator Sue Pressman found their actual living quarters (see inset) dirty, barren, and inadequate.

led to happy outcomes, and The HSUS was involved in many successful efforts to relocate displaced or relinquished wild animals, beginning with Pressman's years of service (1971–1986). One of the best known of these interventions came in 1981, when Pressman addressed the situation of the chimpanzee Ham, the first animal the United States sent into space. Zoo staff had never been able to find a suitable group environment in which to situate Ham, whose unusual background had included almost no socialization whatsoever with others of his species. He had lived alone for twenty years. Pressman urged Ham's transfer to the North Carolina Zoological Park, where he was paired with a lonely female chimp of comparable age.[27]

Sometimes, such interventions could involve many animals. John Dommers intervened in 1987 when a small zoo in Connecticut closed its doors, helping to find new facilities for a group of animals, including primates. In the early 1990s, New England regional staffers Arnold Baer and Frank Ribaudo drew The HSUS into a similar situation involving Rhode Island's Slater Park Zoo, long reviled by local animal protectionists as a substandard facility. Staff members worked with city authorities to explore all options for improving the situation and ultimately influenced the Pawtucket City Council's 1993 decision to close the zoo as a cost economy. As the Wildlife section's Richard Farinato noted, there were approximately two hundred such municipally owned zoos at the time, but "few cities are getting into the zoo business and many of them will be looking to get out—for the same reasons that existed at Slater Park." The HSUS helped to relocate Slater Park's animals to more suitable facilities, including the Black Beauty Ranch and Wildlife Rescue and Rehabilitation Center in Texas.[28]

During the 1970s, recognizing that zoos were not the only places where captive animals were kept, The HSUS put Sue Pressman's talents to use in investigations of the television and movie industry. Although Mel Morse had monitored the issue on behalf of The HSUS for some years, the organization had not gotten directly involved, in part because AHA had a Hollywood office charged to look out for abuses. The movie and television western was the focus of attention for many years, and humane organizations campaigned with some success against the use of trip wires to yank the legs out from under horses during spectacular staged falls, particularly on overseas sets. However, the scrapping of a production code led to a rise of abuses by 1966, and even the trip wire made a triumphant return. Animals suffered and died (like the donkeys in *Patton*) in a spate of movies where the bullets and knives were real, and by the mid-1970s, Hollywood wasn't even sending the scripts to humane groups for review.[29]

In 1975 The HSUS decided to do more to establish the facts about the performing animal industry. Pressman went on several trips to California and spent weeks at a time undercover, observing the living quarters, training methods, and standards of care in the industry and questioning actors, actresses, producers, cameramen, script writers, trainers, and others for information concerning persistent allegations of neglect and abuse. Pressman saw animals (whose owners had in many cases reaped thousands of dollars from their performance work) confined in the worst possible housing, subjected to abusive training methods, deprived of proper nutrition and exercise, and denied any kind of preventive veterinary care. Animal trainers occupied a netherworld of deliberate cruelty, rampant opportunism, and shameless deceit in pursuit of profit. "Nine different trainers told me they owned Gentle Ben, the bear from the TV series of the same name, and almost as many people told me they owned the Mercury cougar," Pressman recalled. "It is a rare producer who knows enough about animals to know whether the animal is being cared for and treated properly."[30]

As word of the investigation spread, the ranks of The HSUS's movie industry informants swelled. A congressional sponsor of animal welfare legislation began to examine the possibilities of protection for captive animal populations. Jack Valenti of the Motion Picture Association of America took notice and warned colleagues of "the extent to which The Humane Society...is checking through undercover agents [about] such cruelty."[31]

In the 1970s The HSUS also kept an eye on circuses, because in their case, too, 1970 amendments to the AWA established requirements for adequate treatment and care. Both Frank McMahon and Sue Pressman checked out the animal quarters of major circuses whenever they got the opportunity to do so. In 1977 investigators Frantz Dantzler, Phil Steward, and Marc Paulhus joined Pressman in an investigation of traveling circuses. As a result of their efforts, one operator was arrested three times in three different states for his neglect of primates. In 1980 Pressman actually joined the circus, working undercover for several months on a cleanup crew, traveling with several troupes and observing the lives of performing animals. Especially in the smaller "mud shows," she witnessed terrible shortages of water for cleaning animals, cooling them down, and quenching their thirst; days of being chained in the heat; starvation and malnutrition; and inadequate veterinary care.[32]

By June 1997, when The HSUS launched a concerted campaign to raise public awareness of the suffering of wild animals in circuses, it had more than two decades of experience with "The Big Lie Behind the Big Top." A videotape and education kit of the same name went out to hundreds of organizations nationwide, as public misgivings about animal welfare in American circuses increased in the wake of several high-profile cases of abuse and mistreatment.

From the 1980s onward, The HSUS also worked to expose the proliferation of "game ranches," where those with the money could purchase the right to shoot just about any animal they desired—at close range and with little or no personal risk. The ranches were intimately tied to the trade in exotic animals, something which The HSUS investigated at some length during the 1980s and 1990s, sending staff members out to auctions and other sites important to wildlife exchange. In 1985 HSUS West Coast regional investigator Eric Sakach accompanied officials of the Oregon State Police, USDA, and the Central Coast Humane Society on a raid of an exotic game ranch in Siletz, Oregon.[33] The operator of this substandard facility moved his animals to Idaho, where, in 1996, he became the subject of another HSUS-assisted investigation. This time, Northern Rockies Regional Office director Dave Pauli coordinated The HSUS's response to a tragic episode that resulted in the killing of sixteen lions who escaped from a game farm co-owned by the man whose Oregon operation The HSUS had helped to shut down. This time, The HSUS's testimony helped to ensure that the shocking negligence of the operators not only earned them prison sentences (not long enough, in the opinion of many observers), but barred them from any further contact with animals for eight years.[34]

At century's end the section focused its efforts on framing the problem of captive wildlife as a circular or interconnected process, in which zoos, circuses, auctions, animal traders, hobby breeders, exotic meat purveyors, canned hunt operators, animal parks, pet shops, and other individuals and institutions comprised an intricate network for animal exchange. While they advanced differing rationales for their activity, all of these participants bore some responsibility for animals' suffering and death. Inhumane and abusive conditions prevailed in many facilities, and the often underhanded means by which the traffic was carried out made it difficult for humane advocates to track.[35]

Given the transnational scope of so many of the issues it had to confront, the Wildlife section also developed an ever stronger role in promoting responsible and humane management of captive wildlife in other nations. HSUS representatives assisted South African humane organizations in the highly publicized case of the Tuli elephants, in which a court of law ruled that traditional elephant training methods were cruel, and a number of the animals were set free in protected parklands in South Africa.

It was fitting that more than thirty years after The HSUS undertook its first extended investigations of captive wildlife cruelties, Richard Farinato, HSUS director of captive wildlife, was quoted in *Newsday* (28 July 2003) and the *Washington Post* (16 March 2003, 9 December 2003) about a series of animal deaths at Washington, D.C.'s National Zoo. If zoos made any progress during the last quarter of the twentieth century, it was due in some measure to the steady surveillance, criticism, and constructive input that The HSUS had provided since 1970. Public skepticism about the legitimacy and quality of zoos grew substantially during this period, as media exposés revealed gross neglect, impenetrable secrecy, and the zoo community's reluctance to accept thoroughgoing mechanisms of regulation to prevent abuse and suffering.

Hunting

"In these United States," Fred Myers observed in 1952, "an attack upon the tradition-hallowed sports of hunting and fishing is likely to bring down on one's head as much abuse as hostile criticism of Motherhood [or] the Fourth of July." Myers and his colleagues assumed that risk, however, placing The HSUS squarely against recreational hunting from the very first. They saw it as a particularly demoralizing

HSUS director Gisela Karlan (left) and regional director Nina Austenberg talked to a CBS-TV reporter during a 1983 protest at the Great Swamp deer hunt.

form of cruelty—"propagandized as a sport"—that undermined what they took to be a fundamental tenet of humane conviction. "Cruelty, like kindness, is indivisible," Myers wrote. "Children and men cannot be taught simultaneously to take pleasure from cruelty to some living things and to abhor cruelty to others."[36]

While The HSUS had a clear view concerning the morality of hunting, however, the organization had a harder time developing a program strategy to address it. In the early years, hunting usually came up in discussions of demoralization of youth through their observation of or participation in cruelty. On occasion The HSUS or one of its state branches might level a protest against a particularly egregious practice. However, lack of funds and a preoccupation with more urgent priorities kept The HSUS from doing much about it.

By 1970, when John Hoyt came to The HSUS, this had begun to change. The ratio of hunters to the total American population had begun to decline. At the same time, The HSUS was beginning to learn more about the available means for challenging it through legal, legislative, and other strategies.[37]

The most obvious line of attack was to challenge hunting on publicly owned lands. In 1971, with the help of Senator Gaylord Nelson (D-WI), a board member, The HSUS worked for a bill to prohibit aerial hunting over any U.S.-owned public lands. The next year, the organization mobilized quickly when a number of western states began to take advantage of a loophole to wage aerial warfare against wildlife on their own authority.[38]

In the early 1970s, The HSUS and its New Jersey branch also began what became a long campaign to block public hunts at the Great Swamp National Wildlife Refuge in Morris County, New Jersey. In 1970 federal judge John Sirica granted a temporary restraining order to halt the hunt, which was upheld in the circuit court. "It is a small but significant step," John Hoyt commented, "toward the day when decisions affecting the nation's animals will be considered and dealt with humanely and intelligently....The Interior Department's plan was basically intended to give pleasure to hunters, and this, by any standard, is not a legitimate purpose in a government conservation project."[39]

In 1973 Judge Charles Richey rejected The HSUS's lawsuit against the Department of the Interior to stop hunting at Great Swamp. Richey ruled that private hunting was permissible in federal game preserves, that hunting was one of the public recreations for which the refuges were established, and that "public hunting is not inconsistent with sound wildlife management."[40]

In successive years during the late 1970s, the HSUS New Jersey branch filed suit in federal court to prevent the annual deer hunt at Great Swamp. The lawsuit challenged habitat management practices at the refuge in an effort to show that the Department of Interior was itself responsible for the increase in deer population that (it alleged) made a hunt necessary. The HSUS suit failed.[41]

The HSUS's approach to hunting during the decade also broadened beyond the Great Swamp fight. Among other actions, The HSUS sought to force the federal government to use humane methods of wildlife control on national wildlife refuge grounds. The organization sued to prohibit public hunting with bow and arrow on the refuges, contending that humaneness ought to be declared to be part of an explicit public policy.[42]

The HSUS sent representatives to meet with wildlife and fishery management officials to share its views, too. John Hoyt frequently represented The HSUS before such groups. "It is wrong for animals to be reduced to animate targets, with no meaningful purpose in their deaths, save one of personal pleasure and satisfaction of the hunter," Hoyt told one audience of wildlife managers in 1975. Speaking opportunities increased after the appearance of the CBS documentary *The Guns of Autumn*, broadcast nationally on September 5, 1975, which generated unprecedented public exposure of hunting's seamier side.[43]

HSUS staffers also took aim at hunters' claims that they paid their own way through fees and taxes. Studying the revenues from Pittman-Robertson, the Federal Aid in Wildlife Restoration Act, the Migratory Bird Conservation Account, the Federal Duck Stamp Program, and other income streams, The HSUS advanced its view that hunters were not self-sustaining conservationists but self-interested influence brokers with disproportionate sway over wildlife management policy at both the state and federal levels.[44]

Such accusations formed the core of efforts to protest against Project WILD, a conservation education program emphasizing utilitarian and consumptive approaches to wildlife management, while glossing over animal welfare and ecological concerns that might have created a fuller picture. Project WILD characterized wild animals as renewable resources and cast hunting, trapping, and lethal predator control as essential wildlife management tools. The HSUS joined forces with other groups in late 1984 to oppose the use of public monies for the distribution and dissemination of the curriculum.[45]

During the 1980s The HSUS continued its long campaign to make the national wildlife refuges true places of sanctuary for animals. As it turned out, animals on the refuges were almost never safe from hunting, trapping, cattle grazing, timber cutting, mining, pesticide spraying, motorboating, waterskiing, and other human activity. By 1985 staff members estimated that more than half of the 424 refuges in the National Wildlife Refuge system were open to hunting and that at least 400,000 animals were killed or wounded on those refuges every year.[46]

In November 1984 The HSUS filed a lawsuit alleging that the U.S. Fish and Wildlife Service (FWS) had violated numerous federal laws through its administration of hunting programs on refuges. Above all, The HSUS charged, FWS had failed to prove that hunting programs were compatible with the original purposes of the Refuge System Administration and Recreation Acts. In addition, FWS had been negligent in failing to take proper action to protect endangered species on the refuges, had improperly delegated authority for their management to state agencies, and had disregarded its responsibilities for full consideration and disclosure of the impact of the decision to permit hunting on refuges. However, this litigation to prevent hunting on the National Wildlife Refuge System fell short when a court ruled that The HSUS did not have standing to sue.[47]

On the other hand, The HSUS did manage to stop hunting in a few instances, like at Laxahatchee National Wildlife Refuge in Florida in 1985, where The HSUS worked as part of a successful coalition effort to cancel a planned hunt by the Fish and Wildlife Service. The same year, director O.J. Ramsey represented The HSUS in a lawsuit against the state of California, to halt Placer County's killing of mountain lions.[48]

Activists protest as a hunter leaves refuge grounds with two carcasses tied to the roof of his car. For many years HSUS members converged on New Jersey's Great Swamp Refuge to picket the slaughter of white-tailed deer.

OBSERVER-TRIBUNE, RECORDER COMMUNITY NEWSPAPERS

The HSUS led all organizations in calling for the resignation of Ray Arnett as assistant secretary for fish, wildlife, and parks in the Department of the Interior, in strongly worded statements that identified Arnett's responsibility for policy reversals and initiatives that opened up more refuges to hunting, trapping, and commercial uses like timber cutting and mining.[49]

At about the same time, the fight to give meaning to the designation "national wildlife refuge" moved to the U.S. Congress. In 1987 The HSUS took a leadership role in urging introduction of the Refuge Wildlife Protection Act, sponsored by Bill Green (D-NY). The HSUS was also a mainspring in the Wildlife Refuge Reform Coalition, a coalition of thirty-five organizations determined to restore integrity to the management of the National Wildlife Refuge System.[50]

The next year The HSUS won an appeal of its four-year-old lawsuit concerning hunting programs in the National Wildlife Refuge System. The U.S. Court of Appeals for the District of Columbia ruled that The HSUS did have standing to file a legal challenge to the Department of the Interior's policy concerning the opening of wildlife refuges to hunting. HSUS members, in the words of the Court, had "classic aesthetic interests, which have always enjoyed protection under standing analysis," and while not explicitly stated in The HSUS's charter, the human appreciation of other living beings was an "unstated but obvious side goal of preserving animal life."[51]

As it happened, ultimate success on this front proved to be elusive, because The HSUS was never really able to gain the support necessary from the Department of the Interior or Congress. The hunting lobby, moreover, was simply too strong.[52]

The HSUS was somewhat more successful in its efforts to influence the process by which the federal government annually set hunting seasons and bag limits on migratory birds. Unlike most other forms of hunting, duck hunting attracted wealthy individuals who hunted not for sustenance but purely for recreation. The HSUS judged it especially shameful that any species should fall into decline simply to satisfy a nonessential interest. By the early 1980s, for example, the nation's black duck populations (a favorite target of hunters) had declined precipitously throughout much of their range, yet the federal government continued to permit hunters to kill large numbers of them. The HSUS's efforts to force the federal government to give this species the protection it needed took the form of public education and litigation. Although the government reduced allowable kills under pressure, bag limits remained too liberal in the early twenty-first century to permit the species to rebound.[53]

In the mid-1990s the federal government's proposals to reduce by as much as half the population of the magnificent snow goose—purportedly because high numbers were damaging their Arctic breeding grounds—brought heavy protest from the animal protection community. Led by The HSUS, snow goose advocates asserted that the reduction program was driven, not by habitat concerns, but by state pressure to ease hunting restrictions on an abundant species to increase hunting license sales and shore up declining hunter numbers. Although the killing was eventually permitted, the most egregious proposals to achieve population reduction goals were rejected. The HSUS succeeded in its campaign to substantially reduce the number of gulls poisoned by the federal government in an effort to protect nesting shorebirds in a Massachusetts wildlife refuge and influenced a federal decision to reject a proposal to poison millions of blackbirds to determine whether such draconian measures increased commercial production of sunflower seeds. By the late 1990s, The HSUS was actively opposing demands by sport and commercial fishing and aquaculture interests to lift restrictions on the killing of double-crested cormorants, and as the new century dawned, The HSUS was also fighting for the recovery of imperiled trumpeter swan populations and arguing in favor of nonlethal control of the introduced mute swan.[54]

In the 1990s, the humane movement's attempts to challenge hunting took another tack, as The HSUS and other organizations resurrected a time-honored American tradition, the referendum and initiative process, to advance an agenda of wildlife protection at the state level. This resort to the democratic legacy of the Progressive era proved to be eventful and resulted in decisive victories against hunting and trapping interests. The HSUS played crucial and often central roles in the passage of these initiatives, all of them benchmark victories in the struggle to give nonhunters a voice in the determination of wildlife policy.

In 1992 Colorado voters endorsed a ballot measure to prohibit the baiting and hounding of black bears and the hunting of black bears by any means during their spring nursing season. In 1994 voters in Oregon supported Ballot Measure 18, a ban on the baiting of bears and the hounding of black bears and mountain lions. Intense efforts by the National Rifle Association and other shooting lobbies, and opposition from the Oregon Department of Fish and Wildlife, failed to stop the measure. There was no sport involved in the practice, Wayne Pacelle charged. "Baiting and hounding are the moral equivalent of shooting an animal in a cage at a zoo."[55]

The Government Affairs department also worked to defeat hostile ballot measures, like California's Proposition 197, which proposed eliminating the protected status of mountain lions in the state and making them permissible targets for trophy hunters. In March 1996

Paul G. Irwin (left) and John W. Grandy (right) administered immunocontraceptive vaccine to an elephant in Kruger National Park in 1998.

California voters rejected Proposition 197. The HSUS led the coalition that squared off with hunting interest groups, which spent $600,000 on the initiative.[56]

The same year, voters in Oregon, unresponsive to suggestions that they had been duped by "animal-worshipping extremists," rejected the hunting lobby's proposal to rescind Ballot Measure 18 banning the baiting and hounding of bears, approved just two years earlier. Almost 60 percent of the vote was wildlife-friendly.[57]

Besides the hope it offered for tangible protection of animals, The HSUS's successful embrace of the ballot initiative strategy marked a new era in its efforts to overcome the stranglehold enjoyed by hunters, trappers, and other consumptive users of wildlife over the decision-making process concerning wildlife at all levels. Throughout the history of wildlife management in the United States, state commissions excluded the interests and participation of nonhunters, and the agencies they oversaw tended to ignore many important issues that fell outside the realm of hunters' concern. During the 1990s, especially, these ossified boards were preoccupied with encouraging women and the young to hunt (to bolster waning numbers), responding to the perceived threat from antihunting and antitrapping groups, and the protection and enhancement of established hunting and fishing areas. Myriad wildlife concerns, including habitat loss and degradation, extinction, illness, and the interests of nongame species, did not even come onto their agenda. Despite the known magnitude of the population of birding and wildlife enthusiasts who did not hunt, these commissions made no serious effort to address the interests and concerns of the nonhunting majority, let alone to harness their practical and financial support for programs and initiatives. Wildlife agencies were, moreover, disturbingly unresponsive to citizens' pleas for assistance and counsel with wildlife problems that did not relate to hunting and hunting practices. The domination of such agencies by hunting interests virtually guaranteed the permanent neglect of animal populations that were not preferred targets of hunters.[58]

The HSUS's embrace of the referendum and initiative process offered humane advocates a way to overcome this inherently undemocratic arrangement, allowing citizens with a broader view of wildlife policy to exert some influence on wildlife commissions and the agencies they oversaw. In some instances the ballot initiative could be used not simply to change an objectionable policy or practice, but to affect the very character of a wildlife commission itself. Question 1, the successful 1996 Massachusetts referendum banning the use of steel-jawed leghold traps, also abolished the requirement that hunters and trappers constitute a majority on the state's Fisheries and Wildlife Board, authorizing the governor to appoint any qualified individual to serve. It was a striking victory for the principle of democratic representation for nonhunting and nontrapping constituencies on such commissions. Two years later The HSUS registered a related success through moral suasion, when it persuaded Maryland's governor to appoint a nonhunter to the state's Wildlife Advisory Commission.[59]

Immunocontraception

Suburban development, one of the defining demographic characteristics of post-World War II America, drew The HSUS into many situations centering on the explosion of white-tailed deer populations in urban, suburban, and exurban parklands. Wildlife section staff members John Grandy, Tony Povilitis, Ph.D., John Hadidian, Ph.D., and Allen Rutberg, Ph.D., all represented The HSUS at one time or another in cases where perceived conflict between the human and deer populations led in the direction of hunts. Wildlife commissions and hunting enthusiasts were only too happy to cast themselves as the experts in population control, their solutions usually tilting toward annual deer hunts that never did resolve the problems they purported to address. The HSUS, for its part, tried to promote nonviolent resolution of these situations, with controlled hunts a last resort in all cases.[60]

There were other situations in which the perception that excessive numbers of animals in some instances posed a threat to humans or to themselves led to proposals for hunting, roundups, and other objectionable responses. In addition to its role in dozens of local skirmishes about the deer population in a variety of urban and suburban contexts, The HSUS was involved in debates over the control of excess elephant populations in African nature parks and wild horses on the American range.

Eventually, such confrontations inspired dialogue about the feasibility of wildlife contraception as means of population control for deer, elephants, wild horses, and other species. While public expectations in this arena tended to exceed current technology, the demand for nonlethal solutions did encourage experimentation and serious discussion of immunocontraception technology as a long-term goal for the management of select wild animal populations.

In the 1980s The HSUS's interest in immunocontraception led it to assume a serious role in funding and coordinating research and development in the field. The Wildlife section led the drive to develop refined, field-tested immunocontraception vaccines for use in appropriate settings. This ambitious goal involved the selection of qualified scientific collaborators, reliable manufacturing partners, and the capacity for advanced training of those who might use such vaccines. To be successful, The HSUS and its partners would have to shepherd the compounds through a lengthy and complex FDA review process. Moreover, contraceptives would have to be species-specific and demonstrably easy to control before they could ever be approved.

Even, so, the incentive to pursue immunocontraception was very strong, because it promised a nonviolent solution for a handful of issues that The HSUS had been trying to address for decades. Thus, in the early 1990s, The HSUS initiated a wild horse immunocontraception program as part of an effort to end reliance on roundups and other extermination programs while preserving the integrity of wild horse populations on America's public lands. In 1991 Grandy and HSUS consultant Jay Kirkpatrick, Ph.D., offered testimony to the Senate Appropriations Subcommittee on Interior and Related Agencies. There they pushed for the Bureau of Land Management (BLM) to adopt criteria for fertility control initiatives to aid in the management of wild horse populations. It was an old idea, dating back to passage of the Wild, Free-roaming Horse and Burro Act of 1971, and Kirkpatrick and his colleagues had worked steadily on its development. Unfortunately, the research had come to a dead halt with the appointment of James Watt as Secretary of the Interior in 1980.[61]

By 1993 The HSUS could proclaim "a new day for wild horses," however. With the political climate more favorable, The HSUS collaborated with Kirkpatrick, John W. Turner, Ph.D., Irwin K.M. Liu, Ph.D., and other colleagues to develop contraceptives suitable for the uses it advocated. In one instance The HSUS team collaborated with the BLM to test the effectiveness of several versions of the immunocontraceptive vaccine. The presence of the Assateague Island, Virginia, wild horse herds as a nonnative species but protected cultural resource in a fragile ecosystem, and historic concern with the mistreatment of wild equines in the annual round up at Chincoteague (see chapter 7), also created a distinctive opportunity for testing new approaches. After research showed that the the immunocontraceptive vaccine porcine zona pellucida (PZP) worked well to inhibit fertility in domestic mares, The HSUS helped in efforts to evaluate its effectiveness in wild horse herds on Assateague Island. These trials proved to be very successful.[62]

Another important benchmark of the drive for immunocontraceptive solutions was the elephant project launched in Kruger National Park, South Africa, in 1996 to assist authorities trying to managing elephant populations. While elephants were safe within Kruger, South African authorities were interested in developing a humane means for limiting their population in situations where wildlife-people conflicts could lead to serious controversy and illegal and violent activity on Kruger's boundaries and elsewhere. HSUS staff and consultants joined South African officials to administer PZP to eleven elephants.[63]

That same year Paul Irwin and John Grandy participated in the fourth International Conference on Fertility Control for Wildlife Management in Queensland, Australia, sponsored by The HSUS and HSI. The novelty of this emerging field was apparent: Jay Kirkpatrick's presentation was the only one based on the results of extensive field research. Irwin, Grandy, and Kirkpatrick found that much of the research going on elsewhere focused not on the control of wildlife populations in geographically limited areas, but on the limitation of nonnative species. In his presentation Grandy questioned the legitimacy of large-scale population control, especially the assumption that the suppression of nonnative species is a management imperative.[64]

By 1996 The HSUS was also involved in collaborative efforts at three field-research test sites for the control of white-tailed deer populations through immunocontraception. At one of these, the Fire Island National Seashore in New York, The HSUS's contraception research team made exceptional gains in knowledge and experience with the administration of vaccine, in a situation where the National Park Service required the team to avoid capturing, handling, or touching the animals.[65]

At the dawn of the twenty-first century, The HSUS's immunocontraception program encompassed projects involving white-tailed deer, wild horses, zoo animals, elephants, elk, water buffalo, and dogs. Virtually all of the HSUS-sponsored work in this area relied on the PZP vaccine, and with demonstrated reductions of unconfined deer populations at several tests sites under steady surveillance, and contraception studies underway in South Africa and elsewhere, The HSUS was well on its way to the validation of nonviolent methods of controlling wild animal populations.

Trapping

Trapping was a prominent concern of early twentieth-century humane societies, one that the individuals who founded The HSUS perpetuated in their work, too. The abolition of the steel-jawed leghold trap was an important early campaign and legislative priority, and The HSUS led or supported virtually every attempt to limit or eliminate its use. Popular in the fur trade because it does not spoil the value of the pelt of the animal, the leghold trap provided one of the most shocking examples of how far the United States lagged behind the numerous other developed nations that had abolished its use.

Trapping of animals was closely tied to the production of furs for the market. This issue, too, came into sharp relief during the 1970s, as public concern for imperiled species led to restrictions on the sale of clothing and items of fashion made from the skins of endangered species like leopards, cheetahs, ocelots, and jaguars. The HSUS was an early promoter of synthetic furs.[66]

Simulated furs, such as this cheetah-type coat, were beginning to win acceptance in 1970.

The 1970s also saw the reemergence of legislative efforts to ban the trap. HSUS director Senator Gaylord Nelson (D-WI) proposed a bill prohibiting use of the steel-jawed leghold trap in 1971. Five years later The HSUS testified in support of the Bayh-Anderson bill against trapping. In the aftermath of the hearings, HSUS officials judged that neither The HSUS nor other humane organizations had effectively counteracted "pseudo-scientific arguments of trapping advocates" who presented testimony. Attempting to combat the claims made by trappers and some wildlife managers about the benefits and necessity of trapping, The HSUS commissioned its own trapping study by Martha Scott Garrett, aimed at gathering support for an elimination campaign. The HSUS study underscored the fact that the removal of surplus animals by trapping does not protect wildlife against population buildups that lead to the spread of disease, starvation, and habitat destruction, as claimed by trapping's supporters.[67]

The publication came just in time for use by Margaret Morrison, Michael Fox, and Guy Hodge, who went to Ohio to work on behalf of the antitrapping referendum introduced by future Great Lakes regional director Sandy Rowland's Ohio Committee for Humane Trapping in 1977. HSUS representatives also worked closely with Senator Harrison Williams (D-NJ) when he introduced a bill to forbid importation and interstate shipment of furs from any animal trapped in a state or nation where the leghold trap was not banned.[68]

A few years later, both The HSUS and its regional office played a role in the 1984 ban on the leghold trap in New Jersey, Senator Williams's home state. The next year, after trappers filed suit to challenge the constitutionality of the ban, The HSUS threw its energies behind defending the ban, with staff members testifying in the trial that resulted in a 1986 decision upholding the ban. During the same period, the Wildlife section worked to assist those seeking to enact local bans in several counties and communities nationwide.[69]

There were no further federal hearings on trapping after the Bayh-Anderson hearings. In 1984, however, John Grandy testified

At a fur fair in 1979, John Kullberg (then with the ASPCA) and Margaret Morrison inspected a pelt suspected of coming from an endangered species.

on behalf of H.R. 1797, documenting the harm the trap caused and reaffirming "the rights of animals not to be caught in this barbaric trap." Soon thereafter The HSUS launched a major ad campaign directed against the leghold trap. Readers of *Ms.* and *Cosmopolitan* that fall saw The HSUS's full-page advertisement, "Here's the Part of a Fur Coat Most People Never See," complete with details on the trap's cruelty and the link between fur purchases and animal suffering. Through the 1990s The HSUS continued to receive and compile reports of nontarget species, including companion animals, being harmed in traps.[70]

As the hunting issue had gone, so went trapping. In the 1990s The HSUS's Government Affairs department led the humane movement's efforts to secure the passage of several anti-trapping initiatives at the state level. In 1994 Arizona voters approved a ban on the use of leghold traps and other body-gripping traps on public lands. Proposition 201 encompassed 83 percent of the land in the entire state, and passed just two years after a similar measure failed amid a massive spending campaign by protrapping forces. It was also the first successful passage of a statewide trapping measure in decades. In 1999 the department helped to ensure passage of Proposition 4, a California initiative that banned the use of the steel-jawed leghold trap, as well as the use of Compound 1080 and sodium cyanide to kill animals.[71]

The Campaign against Fur

For years those concerned about the suffering of animals trapped or ranched for fur understood the degree to which it was a consumer-driven problem. In 1988–89, the fur issue was given special emphasis by The HSUS and its Campaigns department and Wildlife section. The HSUS's Investigations Department backed the campaign with a number of investigations of fox farms in Midwestern and western states. Pat Parkes and Frantz Dantzler conducted one in Illinois, and Bob Baker and Lisa Landres did the same in Oklahoma.[72]

The Shame of Fur™ campaign became one of The HSUS's most ambitious public outreach activities, featuring Times Square light displays, billboards, celebrity participation, and numerous media appearances. Actress Candice Bergen and model Carré Otis lent their names to the campaign, which targeted affluent, career-oriented young female customers. For several subsequent years, animal protectionists saw encouraging signs that the fur industry was in demise.[73]

The HSUS tried to undercut the fur industry by attacking substantial government subsidies that supported the advertising budget of the mink industry, which raised animals in small wire cages and killed by anal execution, among other methods. In 1995 the U.S. House of Representatives voted to cut the $2 million annual mink subsidy. Senator Robert Smith (R-NH), a strong champion of the measure as it made its way through the legislative process in the U.S. Senate, observed, "where mink coats were once seen as a status symbol, now they are a symbol of cruelty," and "because we know that they are being subsidized so heavily by the taxpayers, they are a symbol of government waste. People are not interested in either one."[74]

As the fur industry began to fight back hard with efforts to repopularize fur, The HSUS reinvigorated its antifur programs with Fur-Free 2000, a multiyear effort to counter the industry's move with a new look, new research, and new statistics. The campaign took a more positive, less accusatory tack than that which characterized earlier campaigns and involved collaboration with designer Oleg Cassini, who brought out a line of synthetic fur garments and contributed some design work to the campaign. As part of a public effort to redeem the misery of fur production, the organization collected furs for distribution to wildlife rehabilitators, who put them to use in providing comfort for injured and orphaned wild animals.

HSUS analysts found cause for celebration in the dramatic reduction of animals killed in traps or kept in cages, the decline of fur farms, and the decrease of ranched mink killed for fur.[75]

Before the end of 2000, HSUS investigative campaigns concerning clothing made from dog, cat, and fetal lamb fur had hauled two more skeletons out of the fur industry's closet and frustrated its efforts to diversify and extend fur product lines through the promotion of "trimmed" accessories and garments. While the nation was not yet fur-free, it was—increasingly—free from illusions about the misery and death of animals that lay behind the fur trade.[76]

Wild Neighbors
*was published
in 1997.*

Living with Wildlife

In the booming years of post-1970 suburbanization and sprawl, encroachment upon wildlife habitat created countless crises in which The HSUS sought to help sympathetic citizens, organizations, and government agencies to stem the cycle of animal destruction. The promotion of public awareness, tolerance, and appreciation of wildlife became an important priority, and the number of queries concerning wildlife in urban settings and the resolution of conflict between people and wildlife rose steadily through the years. Responsibility for such concerns became Guy Hodge's specialty after he joined The HSUS. In one highly publicized episode of the mid-1970s, Hodge reviewed a Department of Defense plan for continued destruction of blackbirds at Fort Campbell, Kentucky. Hodge and other specialists condemned the aerial spraying operation, in which thousands of roosting blackbirds suffered lingering and painful deaths. The HSUS threatened litigation and pressed Army officials to abandon the use of Tergitol, a detergent that, when mixed with water, removed the natural insulating oils from the birds' feathers, causing them to freeze to death.[77]

For over a quarter-century, Hodge counseled callers and correspondents about wildlife-related problems, providing advice on nonlethal solutions for a variety of challenges—from bats in the attic, to raccoons in the chimney, to deer in the garden. Hodge and other staff members also participated in public debates over the removal of beaver colonies from urban and suburban ponds, the elimination of pigeons judged either too "abundant" or "threatening to public health," and other topics. In all of these situations, The HSUS sought to promote nonviolent solutions and preventive measures to the problems associated with animals' presence. In 1991 Hodge put the accumulated wisdom of several decades' experience into the much-valued *Humane Control of Wildlife in Cities and Towns*, a pocket guide that was widely used by animal control and humane society personnel as well as by the general public.

In 1996 the realm of service that Hodge pioneered blossomed into a full-fledged program directed at suburban wildlife protection. The program, overseen by John Hadidian, Ph.D., incorporated three core elements—resolution of the continuing tension of human-wildlife conflicts, enhanced public recognition and acknowledgement of the intrinsic value of wildlife in the human social world, and deeper reflection concerning the human relationship to the natural environment and its nonhuman inhabitants. By providing practical assistance, reliable information about animals and their environments, and a strong perspective on the need for guidelines and foresight in relation to human-wildlife conflicts, The HSUS sought to promote compassionate attitudes and conduct toward animals in those contexts where people and wildlife most frequently encountered one another.[78]

In 1997 The HSUS responded to the explosion of interest in wildlife commensals with a more comprehensive book, *Wild Neighbors: The Humane Approach to Living with Wildlife.* Staff members also worked with The HSUS's Video Projects staff to produce one-minute spots as part of a *Wild Neighbors* series, featuring advice and information concerning the activities and needs of wildlife in urban and suburban areas and the appropriate means of resolving potential conflict involving such animals. Many of the segments were made available on the HSUS website, *www.hsus.org.*

The HSUS's commitment to urban wildlife populations also led to its acquisition of the Urban Wildlife Sanctuary Program of the National Institute for Urban Wildlife, America's oldest urban land and sanctuary program, in the late 1990s. At that time 150 properties fell under the oversight of The HSUS, ranging in size from small residential backyards to entire municipalities. By 2003 the Urban Wildlife Sanctuary Program included some 550 members, mostly residential property owners. Members of the program received *Wild Neighbors News,* a quarterly newsletter offering practical background and habitat advice, introduced in 1999.[79]

Eventually The HSUS became directly involved in the protection of wild animals through the preservation of natural habitat and the establishment of permanent sanctuaries. The HSUS Wildlife Land Trust (WLT), formed in 1994, provided a mechanism through which donors and testators could keep designated tracts of land wild and free from hunting in perpetuity. At its launch, the WLT was the only national land trust that committed itself never to permit commercial or recreational hunting and trapping on its properties. It did so through the acquisition of easements on property it does not own, monitoring and maintenance, and other means. The organization has not limited itself to the United States but has acquired properties in other countries as well. These "shelters without walls" ensure that there will always be some places on earth where animals may live free from the threat of exploitation and death at the hands of humans.[80]

Also in 1994, through the generosity of Barbara Birdsey and the Orenda Wildlife Land Trust, The HSUS enhanced its wildlife program capability with the establishment of the Wildlife Rehabilitation Training Center (WRTC) on Cape Cod, Massachusetts, later known as the Cape Wildlife Center. The Geraldine R. Dodge Foundation underwrote a feasibility study that led to the development of a full program of classes, workshops, and seminars and a clinic and classroom framework in which to offer them.[81]

From the 1990s on, quite apart from its ambitious efforts to protect animal habitat and to provide for the rehabilitation of wildlife, the HSUS Wildlife section greatly expanded its capacity to advise and counsel individuals, associations, corporations, and government agencies on appropriate responses to a variety of challenges associated with the presence of wildlife. This enhanced level of expertise became the basis of a signature program for the twenty-first-century HSUS.[82]

Rachel Blackmer, D.V.M. (left), and Catherine M. Brown, D.V.M., M.Sc., of the Cape Wildlife Center, unveiled the new wildlife transport van at The HSUS's Back to the Wild fund-raiser in 2002.

Endangered Species, CITES, and the War on Wildlife

After The HSUS made a full commitment to expanded coverage of wildlife issues in the early 1970s, staff members became stalwarts at congressional hearings concerning reauthorization and enhancement of such enactments as the ESA and CITES. Against the endless and determined assaults on these protective enactments, The HSUS worked on its own and in cooperation with other organizations to preserve them in both spirit and practice. Guy Hodge's 1972 congressional testimony concerning the ESA was the first of many such engagements that staff members would undertake during the next three decades. During the struggle over the ESA's reauthorization in the mid-1980s, The HSUS anchored a coalition to preserve and strengthen it. After joining The HSUS, Grandy brought the organization into the fight over a status review of the bobcat for possible protection under the ESA and its listing as an Appendix II species under CITES, a long-running struggle with which he had been involved while at Defenders of Wildlife. The HSUS also helped to get the harlequin duck added to the list of endangered waterfowl species.[83]

After 1982 The HSUS also played a crucial role in the meetings of CITES, held every two years. The CITES signatory nations agree to prohibit trade in species listed in Appendix I as endangered and to strictly regulate trade in species on Appendix II, those determined to be threatened. CITES had gotten off to a fine start in its early years, when the United States evinced a serious commitment to the protection and preservation of animals. By the 1980s, however, when HSUS staff members first began to attend, CITES had become a field of battle where trophy hunters, fur prof-

HSUS vice president John W. Grandy and Associate Director of Wildlife Susan Lieberman attended a session of CITES in 1989.

iteers, exotic animal traders, and other interests tied to the destruction and use of animals fought to limit restrictions on their activities. The Reagan administration's permissiveness concerning increased exploitation of animals inspired similar laxity in other nations.[84]

The HSUS's participation in CITES politics became even more necessary in the 1990s, when the decisions of CITES Parties increasingly began to reflect the influence of protrade officials and wildlife traders who argued that wildlife must "pay its way," and that, to ensure their survival, even endangered and threatened species must render economic benefit to humans who live nearby. In the 1990s a few influential conservationists endorsed this view by supporting Zimbabwe's efforts to promote international trade in endangered species.[85]

In the late 1980s, as the plight of the African elephant worsened, opposition to poaching and the sale of ivory gained a prominent place on the division's agenda. CITES instituted a limited quota system in 1986 to permit the export of ivory from those nations making sincere efforts to suppress poaching and encourage conservation. Unfortunately, the system failed badly; a stunning proportion of the ivory traded worldwide proved to be poached. The HSUS began pushing for a worldwide ban on the trade of ivory, and in 1989 a vigorous campaign resulted in listing the elephant on CITES Appendix I, thus prohibiting any legal commerce in live specimens, parts, and products.[86]

The campaign for elephants took on a special urgency when proposals for lifting the

CITES ban on ivory surfaced. Attempting to forestall a "downlisting" of the African elephant to CITES Appendix II, HSUS investigators went to four African nations in the early 1990s to gather evidence that the continent's elephant populations could not survive a reopening of trade in elephant parts. Unfortunately, in 1999 the ivory trade resumed, as the CITES Standing Committee permitted Botswana, Namibia, and Zimbabwe to ex-

The Ivory Room at Zimbabwe National Park headquarters contained more than thirty tons of ivory in 1993.

THE HSUS/DANTZLER

John Grandy examined a recovering parrot in the temporary rehabilitation facility set up by The HSUS/HSI in Honduras in 1992.

port 107,026 pounds (fifty-nine metric tons) of stockpiled ivory to Japan.[87]

During the last several decades of the twentieth century, The HSUS became even more involved with issues stemming from the international trade in wildlife and wildlife parts. This traffic generated terrible pressure on wildlife populations in the United States and other nations, speeding extinction, generating indifference to animal well-being, and causing untold animal suffering in all parts of the world.

This issue went back to the 1970s, a decade in which The HSUS frequently confronted the elaborate machinations of the pet shop industry, which pressured the Department of the Interior to relax its restrictions on the importation of wild animals sold to the public by the industry. HSUS staff members were very familiar with the numerous problems that resulted from this traffic, because they handled a steady flow of inquiries about the removal of wild animals that people had concluded they could not keep. Animal shelters rarely had the resources or facilities for providing appropriate care, and zoos did not want these animals. Mortality rates of animals caught for the pet trade were high at all stages of the process.[88]

In 1978 ISAP conducted an investigation of the trade in wild birds, then increasing in popularity as household pets. In just a few years, the pet trade's rapid commodification of wild-caught birds had caused substantial harm and suffering. The traumas of capture and captivity led to high rates of illness and mortality among birds, whether smuggled or imported under legitimate circumstances. Many died at quarantine stations established by USDA to prevent the spread of Exotic Newcastle Disease and other perceived threats to the nation's domestic poultry.[89]

In the mid-1980s The HSUS created a full-time staff position devoted to the live bird trade, and biologist Susan Lieberman, Ph.D., played a crucial role in worldwide efforts to end the traffic in wild-caught birds. The first domino fell in New York in 1985, when legislators approved a law to prohibit the sale of wild-caught birds within the state. State campaigns in Pennsylvania and New Jersey followed in 1987. The HSUS bolstered these campaigns by publishing Lieberman's *The Wild Bird Trade: Ending Commercial Imports*, a scientific case against the keeping of wild birds as pets.[90]

In a 1991 investigation that transcended national borders, HSUS staff members generated useful evidence in support of the campaign for an immediate halt to the trade in imperiled species. The HSUS's work in Honduras demonstrated how the U.S. failure to prohibit the importation of birds consistently undermined the efforts of those nations that were making sincere attempts to halt bird exports. The HSUS went on to play a crucial role in the passage of the U.S. Wild Bird Conservation Act of 1992 (WBCA), which banned importation of parrots and other birds listed on the CITES appendices. Unfortunately, the Department of the Interior continued to permit the importation of more than one hundred species of wild-caught birds listed on CITES Appendix III (a unilateral listing by a so-called range state of its own species). The HSUS and Defenders of Wildlife joined in a successful lawsuit that forced the Interior Department to comply with the WBCA by banning the traffic in birds listed on the CITES appendix.[91]

Sustainable Use and the Slaughter of Animals

In 1972 The HSUS sent General Counsel Murdaugh Madden to the United Nations Conference on the Human Environment in Stockholm, Sweden, to see if he could place concern for animals on the agenda of the international environmental community. While at the sessions,

Madden grew disturbed over repeated recommendations that developing nations seek to attract tourists by either introducing or increasing hunting opportunities within their borders. "[When] it came to animals," Madden reported, "the only concern voiced was for the urgency to use wild animals as a means of building national economies."[92]

Two decades later the trend Madden identified had become an unmistakable threat to animals in all parts of the world. During the 1990s The HSUS became aware of rising numbers of animals, including endangered species, being killed by American hunters in other nations. In "Big Game, Big Bucks," a special report, HSUS Wildlife staff members Teresa Telecky, Ph.D., and Doris Lin tracked the alarming 71 percent rise in trophies taken between 1990 and 1993 and the shocking number of endangered animals included in those figures. A relaxed policy of acceptance by the American government and the proactive safari hunting agenda of several hunters' organizations spelled disaster for other nations' wildlife.[93]

The publication of John Hoyt's *Animals in Peril: How "Sustainable Use" Is Wiping Out the World's Wildlife* (1996) marked The HSUS's increasing focus on safari hunting dressed up as good conservation practice. The claim that trophy hunting generated income for communities in need resulted in several misguided programs that diverted badly needed U.S. Agency for Development (USAID) funds into safari hunter boondoggles as part of sustainable development approaches to helping other nations.[94]

In 1997 The HSUS launched a successful effort to end USAID support for Zimbabwe's CAMPFIRE (Communal Areas Management Program for Indigenous Resources), an initiative that promoted both trophy hunting of elephants and ivory trading as a means of generating income for local communities. HSUS Government Affairs and Wildlife staff persuaded representatives and senators to block the diversion of funds from the African Elephant Conservation Act to CAMPFIRE. The HSUS issued a special report on CAMPFIRE to document the program's known flaws and its threat to the long-term health of elephant populations and African communities. Along with the International Fund for Animal Welfare (IFAW), The HSUS sponsored the first Pan-African Symposium on Non-Consumptive Approaches to Wildlife Conservation.[95]

Animals in Peril *was published in 1996.*

In a related publicity campaign, The HSUS exposed the story of a wealthy American hunter whose trophy lust drew the Smithsonian Institution's National Museum of Natural History (NMNH), into a shocking evasion of the ESA's prohibition against the importation of trophy kills of endangered species. After accepting a $20 million donation from Kenneth Behring, the museum administrators obsequiously moved to apply for scientific permits covering the importation of his most recent rare kills. "[It is] inappropriate," John Grandy charged in a widely publicized letter of condemnation, "for the Smithsonian to contribute to the further endangerment of these subspecies." The HSUS's protests reached a nationwide audience even as the Smithsonian struck bargains that placed Behring's name not only on the NMNH's Hall of Mammals but also on the Smithsonian's National Museum of American History building.[96]

Given the attention accorded to market-driven hunting as a problem that typically depleted the endangered animal populations of other nations, there was a special irony in the fact that during the 1990s it became a serious threat to animals in the United States. As bears were pushed ever closer toward extinction in the drive to meet the lucrative market demand for traditional Chinese medicines incorporating bear gall bladders, The HSUS took the fight to the U.S. Congress, where legislators approved an amendment to the 2002 farm bill that would have effectively halted this unlawful activity. Like the other animal-friendly measures in that year's farm bill, however, it, too, fell victim to the political chauvinism of a handful of House conferees determined to scuttle animal-friendly measures irrespective of the support that congressional colleagues had demonstrated through their earlier votes in both the House and Senate.[97]

Marine Mammal Protection

One of the most important developments in animal protection in the post-1950 period was the heightened public interest in marine mammals, especially dolphins and whales. Sensitive, highly intelligent, and charismatic animals, they were the favored subject of documentaries and television programs and became iconic fixtures in American popular culture. At the same time, marine mammal species were under extraordinary pressure from commercial exploitation, pollution, trophy hunting, and government-sanctioned predator control.

The HSUS established early ties to the issue in 1957 when longtime supporters Edith Goode and Alice Morgan Wright initiated efforts to get a U.N. conference working toward a Law of the Sea treaty to adopt a conservation provision to ensure that commercial killers of marine life use humane methods of slaughter. In 1958 their effort bore fruit, as a special subcommittee of the U.N. Conference on the Law of the Sea adopted a resolution asking states "to prescribe, by all means available to them, those methods for the capture and killing of marine life, especially of whales and seals, which will spare them suffering to the greatest extent possible."[98]

While The HSUS did not pursue an active program of marine mammal protection, chief investigator Frank McMahon was among the first humane advocates to investigate the Pribilof seal cull, first going there in 1968. After McMahon's death in 1974, The HSUS continued to work to limit the cruelties of the annual slaughter he had helped to bring to light. Frantz Dantzler and John Grandy also witnessed the event in subsequent years. The HSUS would play the lead role in the seal slaughter's ultimate demise.

The HSUS developed a steadier presence in the arena of marine mammal protection after Patricia Forkan joined the staff in 1976, and she represented the organization in virtually every battle over the fate of whales, dolphins, and seals. In 1981, after three years of intense lobbying and the support of sympathetic officials, Forkan's campaign to legitimize the policy option of not exploiting marine mammals found its way into the Law of the Sea via Article 65: "Nothing…restricts the rights of a coastal state or the competence of an international organization, as appropriate, to prohibit, limit, or regulate the exploitation of marine mammals more strictly than provided for….States shall cooperate with a view to the conservation of marine mammals and in the case of cetaceans shall in particular work through the appropriate international organizations for their conservation, management, and study." From that time forward, Forkan kept The HSUS in the forefront of battles to save marine mammals worldwide.[99]

The HSUS's Patricia Forkan, John Grandy, and Naomi Rose, pictured here with Free Willy coproducer Richard Donner (left), worked on marine mammal issues in the 1990s.

In 1993 The HSUS hired its first marine mammal scientist, Naomi Rose, Ph.D., making it possible to provide not only strong advocacy but also enhanced technical and scientific expertise in support of its efforts to address issues that continued to gain status as an organizational priority. The HSUS's marine mammal program—once a dream of Goode and Wright—was engaged in a full program of advocacy for whales, dolphins, seals, and other animals.[100]

Save Whales, Not Whaling

Most of the post-1970 battles over whaling were fought within the deliberative sessions of the International Whaling Commission (IWC). Founded in 1946 to control commercial whaling, by the early 1970s, the IWC had become the center of debates over conservation, preservation, and appreciation of whales. Because the IWC had no enforcement authority, the pressure of individual governments in ensuring compliance by other nations was essential to progress.[101]

In 1971 the U.S. Congress enacted the Pelly Amendment, which gave the president the

power to place an embargo on the fish products of those nations whose citizens conducted any whaling that undermines international conservation goals. The original ESA restricted importation of sperm whales. In 1973 the ESA was amended to prohibit all exports as well as interstate commerce.

The first call for an international moratorium on whaling came in 1972, and in 1974 The HSUS board voted to endorse an economic boycott of one whaling nation, Japan. After Patricia Forkan joined the staff two years later, she regularly attended meetings of the IWC, something she had done since 1973. Most groups working on the issue, like The HSUS, sought a total prohibition on whaling. With synthetic or natural equivalents available for virtually every product derived from whales, they argued, the balance ought to shift in favor of such extraordinary animals.[102]

In 1979 The HSUS pushed hard to ensure the successful passage of the Packwood-Magnuson Amendment, which denied fishing rights within the United States' two-hundred-mile limit to any nation that failed to support the international agreement on whale conservation. In 1981 whale campaigners took encouragement from the approval of a "near-moratorium" on the taking of sperm whales. However, the whaling nations of Japan, Norway, and Iceland filed objections to the IWC's proposed 1983 phaseout of the cold harpoon for killing minke.[103]

In 1983 The HSUS participated in the first Global Conference on the Non-Consumptive Utilization of Cetacean Resources. This benchmark event introduced whale watching as an economic alternative to whaling. It drew upon the principle embodied in Article 65, the measure Patricia Forkan had championed—that a coastal nation could legitimately decide not to use marine mammals consumptively or view them as a resource to be harvested.[104]

Great Lakes Regional Director Sandy Rowland held an HSUS banner at a Cleveland JAL protest in 1985.

In 1985 The HSUS responded to the American government's deal with Japan allowing that nation's whalers to hunt sperm whales for another four years by co-sponsoring a successful lawsuit to invoke the sanctions called for by the Packwood-Magnuson Amendment. That same year The HSUS participated in the "Boycott for the Whales" campaign, an international coalition that targeted Japan Air Lines (JAL), in which the Japanese government held a 40 percent stake. HSUS Whale Campaign Coordinator Campbell Plowden toured major cities with a twenty-five-foot-long humpback whale balloon, presenting a multimedia presentation and staging protests outside of JAL ticket offices.[105]

The third prong of the 1985 campaign involved the mailing of more than one million pieces of direct mail targeting the fish products sold by the whaling nations of Iceland, Japan, Norway, and the Soviet Union. The HSUS also distributed hundreds of thousands of wallet-size cards promoting the fish boycott. There was some good news that year: the Soviet Union announced its decision to "temporarily" halt its whaling activities after the 1987 season. *Glasnost*, it seemed, had wrought a change in Soviet whaling policy.[106]

Finally, in 1986 the indefinite moratorium on commercial whaling went into effect, on the narrow basis that the IWC lacked sufficient information to manage whale populations properly. However, Icelandic whalers continued to slaughter fin and sei whales for commercial profit, under the guise of scientific research; they were, literally, studying whales to death. This set the stage for a heated debate at the 1987 IWC meeting that resulted in the passage of a resolution establishing stringent criteria for the killing of whales under research exemptions. In 1988 a consortium of organizations, including The HSUS, filed suit against the U.S. departments of Commerce and State for failure to enforce domestic laws, including the Pelly Amendment to the Fisherman's Protective Act and the ESA. The lawsuit focused on Iceland's continuing contravention of IWC prohibitions against commercial whaling. But The HSUS did not let it rest there. Counting on the fact that whaling for scientific advancement would subside if the resulting whale products could not be sold, The HSUS pushed for a boycott of Icelandic fish products. The HSUS initiated a public boycott of several major restaurant chains that led at least one of them to halt purchases of Icelandic fish.[107]

The HSUS was also active in the protests against the slaughter of thousands of pilot whales in the Faroe Islands, midway between Scotland and Iceland. The Faroe hunt was outside the jurisdiction of the IWC and expanded during the 1980s without any concern for its impact on the whale populations of the North Atlantic.[108]

HSUS President Paul G. Irwin inspects whale skeletons in Antarctica in 1996.

The HSUS called for an economic boycott of Norway in 1993, after that nation defied the IWC by killing approximately 300 minke whales. At about the same time, the U.S. Congress passed unanimous resolutions calling upon the federal government to oppose any management scheme through the IWC that proposed commercial whale hunting. Unfortunately, the optimism created by the congressional resolutions was dashed by the evidence that the Clinton administration was quietly engineering a reversal in U.S. antiwhaling policy, easing Norway's resumption of whaling by refusing to impose sanctions of any kind.[109]

Even so-called sanctuary programs threatened animals. The HSUS worked hard to challenge a 1998 proposal that would have fully authorized whaling within a country's two-hundred-mile coastal zone in exchange for the establishment of a whale sanctuary on the high seas.[110]

The HSUS opposed the proposal to resume the Makah tribal hunt of whales in 1998 because the Makah initiative did not fit the IWC criterion for aboriginal whaling. The HSUS rejected the charge of "eco-colonialism" leveled by proponents. Not to oppose it, HSUS representatives argued, would have opened the door for "cultural whaling" arguments by Japan (which gave funds to the tribe in support of its plans) and others.[111] Clinton eventually failed to impose sanctions, while chiding Japan for its pursuit of policies that undermine the developing global consensus in support of sanctuary programs.[112]

In 2000 The HSUS also went to court to force the National Marine Fisheries Service to take steps to protect the beleaguered right whale, a species whose survival was threatened by death and injury.[113]

The organization was vigilant in its efforts to keep America's marine parks from participating in the international captive marine mammal trade. The HSUS generally disputed the legitimacy of claims that marine parks serve a genuine educational function, arguing that they capitalize upon, rather than enhance and mobilize, public concern about the plight of marine mammals worldwide.

In 1991 The HSUS joined other groups in a lawsuit challenging the permit awarded to Chicago's Shedd Aquarium for the capture of four whales for public display. Less than two years later, two of the whales were dead.[114]

The HSUS's campaigns to help the plight of whales in captivity led to direct involvement with the rescue and rehabilitation of Keiko, whose circumstances in captivity came to world attention with the film *Free Willy*. HSUS support for the project focused on the development of knowledge, experience, and protocol for rescue, rehabilitation, and release of captive and stranded whales and dolphins.[115]

At the turn of the twenty-first century, marine mammal protection still required determined vigilance against international efforts to circumvent or remove prohibitions and restraints on whaling. Commercial whaling was on the rise, and The HSUS stepped up its efforts to promote strengthening of the moratorium and collaboration with other organizations committed to whale protection. Japan and Norway were still actively engaged in efforts to undermine international agreements, and the Japanese continued to exploit the "scientific research" loophole to justify the killing of whales. In 2002 The HSUS directly challenged Japan's "checkbook diplomacy" at the Shimonoseki meeting of the IWC, defeating Japanese proposals for an open season on whales. However, vote-buying did prevent whale protectionists from securing the three-quarters majority necessary for the establishment of whale sanctuaries in the South Pacific and South Atlantic oceans.[116]

Since confronting the plight of whales in the mid-1970s, The HSUS has argued consistently that the nations of the world should end their political and economic support for whaling in favor of a program of continued preservation of whales for their own sake and for the benefit of future generations. The contemporary HSUS agenda, advanced through its U.N. and Treaties department and the "Save Whales, Not Whaling" campaign, remains one of seeking to transform the IWC into a sponsor of sanctuary programs for whales, not the arbiter of quotas for their continuing destruction.[117]

Dolphins, Porpoises, Drift Nets, and Death

In 1972, under citizen pressure, the U.S. Congress passed the Marine Mammal Protection Act (MMPA), which mandated that the tuna industry reduce its kill of porpoises to near-zero within two years. The industry did not comply, and after several skirmishes in court and legislature, The HSUS joined other groups in an international boycott. In 1976 The HSUS asked members to boycott tuna products in response to the massacre of porpoises in tuna nets during the 1960s and early 1970s, during which time the annual slaughter reached upwards of three hundred thousand.[118]

In 1977 Patricia Forkan testified at Senate oversight hearings on the MMPA, reiterating The HSUS's long-standing commitment to an immediate imposition of the standard of zero mortality and injury rate on the American tuna industry. The MMPA had posited as an immediate goal that incidental killing or serious injury of marine mammals during commercial fishing operations be reduced to zero. Five years later, however, the National Marine Fisheries Service was still setting permissible kill quotas that totaled tens of thousands. During a series of 1977 hearings, HSUS attorneys cross-examined government officials on the feasibility of promulgating new methods that would ensure the drastic reduction of porpoise mortality.[119]

For some years after that, the American tuna industry fished under a special government permit, allowing no more than 20,500 porpoises to be killed each year and mandating that federal observers monitor the kill. Beginning in 1981 The HSUS pushed for federal support for a program to develop equipment and techniques designed to reduce porpoise mortality to near zero, but both this program and the mandate for federal observers came to a standstill.[120]

In 1972 the American tuna fleet was the largest of any nation's and was responsible for more than 85 percent of dolphin deaths worldwide. While measurable reduction in dolphin

Anthony J.F. O'Reilly, president and CEO of the H.J. Heinz Company, announces Starkist's policy change, which was prompted by the consumer boycott of canned tuna.

kills occurred until 1981, the tuna industry's efforts to adulterate the MMPA succeeded, and the U.S. Congress amended the act to permit an annual kill of 20,500 dolphins in tuna nets. This marked the erasure of the MMPA's original zero mortality goal.[121]

By this time, research and experience had amply demonstrated the devastating impact of drift nets on the web of marine life. Their indiscriminate plastic mesh filaments trapped porpoises, seals, sea lions, dolphins, and a variety of sea birds, especially shearwaters and puffins. In 1986 The HSUS and other organizations fought hard to limit the scope of a permit issued to Japan by the National Marine Fisheries Service. The permit covered the incidental death toll of marine mammals caused by the activity of the Japanese salmon fishing industry in U.S. waters.[122]

In 1988, after environmental advocate Sam LaBudde's videotapes of dolphins' suffering and death in tuna nets shocked the world, The HSUS renewed its call for boycotts of tuna products and adopted a "get tough" approach in its dealings with government agencies to ensure that the dolphin-kill quota be dramatically reduced to near-zero levels, that alternative methods of catching tuna be adopted, and that the United States refuse to permit the importation of tuna from any country that could not prove its compliance with U.S. marine mammal protection laws. Patricia Forkan, watching a television profile of swimmer Matt Biondi, then in the midst of winning five gold and two silver medals at the 1988 Seoul Olympics, learned that Biondi was strongly interested in dolphin protection. She contacted his manager, and, before the Olympics ended, Biondi had already written letters concerning dolphin protection to his senator, Alan Cranston (D-CA). Biondi subsequently appeared in poster material for the HSUS campaign to save dolphins and worked actively with HSUS staff in attempting to influence negotiations on reauthorization of the MMPA. The LaBudde film helped dolphin protection advocates to secure amendments to the MMPA, which set a limit of 20,500 purse-seine net deaths per year.[123]

In April 1990 H.J. Heinz, owner of the Starkist Seafood Company, the largest tuna canner in the world, announced that it would no longer buy or sell tuna products that resulted in dolphins' deaths. Bumble Bee and Chicken of the Sea followed suit, and Congress subsequently approved legislation to prohibit the use of the term, "dolphin-safe," on tuna cans if the tuna was caught with purse-seine nets.[124]

Advocates took heart in the substantial decrease in annual dolphin deaths that ensued. A new threat loomed on the horizon, however, with the advent of new opportunities for other nations to challenge animal-friendly legislation as protectionist trade practices impermissible under global trade agreements like the General Agreement on Tariffs and Trade (GATT) and the World Trade Organization (WTO). Mexico launched aggressive efforts to do so, challenging 1990's U.S. Dolphin Protection and Consumer Information Act. The European Community followed suit with a complaint that the United States' secondary embargo against Italy was a violation of free trade.[125]

In 1993 The HSUS helped to secure the passage of the International Dolphin Conservation Act, which set the stage for an international agreement with key foreign countries to end the intentional slaughter of dolphins. The addition of Naomi Rose provided not only strong advocacy but also technical and scientific expertise in support of HSUS efforts to prevent capture from the wild, trophy killing, and unrestrained predator control.[126]

The appointment was a timely one, for the Clinton administration quickly committed itself to bartering away animal protective laws to improve trade relations, and dolphins became some of the first victims of the new free-trade agreements to which the United States became a signatory. The Clinton administration worked with tuna fishermen from Mexico,

Colombia, and Venezuela to weaken dolphin protection laws. In 1995 this collaboration culminated in the Panama Declaration—a bailout of Mexico that came at the expense of dolphins, by ending the ban on dolphin-deadly tuna and revising the definition of "dolphin-safe." In the bitter fight that ensued, The HSUS and its partner organizations turned back congressional initiatives that sought to implement the Panama Declaration by amending the three major U.S. laws protecting dolphins.[127]

In 1996 The HSUS celebrated a decision in the U.S. Court of International Trade in which the American government was found to be in violation of the High Seas Driftnet Fisheries Enforcement Act for not enforcing sanctions against Italy for its fishermen's violations of drift net standards. The HSUS had been lead plaintiff.[128]

In 1997 The HSUS was unable to defeat the passage of dolphin-deadly legislation in the U.S. Congress. The International Dolphin Conservation Program Act permitted the chasing and harassing of dolphins (which results in dolphin deaths). Many conventional environmental groups backed the measure, once more underscoring the chasm that separates them from The HSUS when it comes to protecting animals' lives.

The blow was compounded in 1999, when the Clinton administration embraced significantly weakened standards for the dolphin-safe label adopted in 1990, after long years of campaigning by The HSUS and others. From then on, the dolphin-safe label was available for use by those companies marketing tuna caught by setting purse-seine nets on dolphins. The only consolation came from the announcement by three major companies—Bumblebee, Chicken of the Sea, and Starkist—that they would continue to engage in the dolphin-safe fishing practices that the dolphin-safe label originally signified.[129]

During the final decade of the twentieth century, The HSUS also became increasingly involved with the plight of captive dolphins and took a firm position against their capture for public display and entertainment. Staff members participated in two reintroduction projects, which brought unfamiliar challenges and all too familiar vexations about the commitment of other institutions and organizations to appropriate rehabilitation and release.[130]

Sealing

The HSUS first took a position against the slaughter of seals in an annual meeting resolution approved in 1960. In spring 1961 it asked the U.S. Department of State to use its influence within the International Commission for Northwest Atlantic Fisheries to reduce the killing of harp and hood seals and to push for the adoption of humane methods of killing.[131]

In 1967 the organization began to agitate actively against seal culls, organizing pressure in both Canada and the United States to influence the Canadian Minister of Fisheries to reduce and reform the annual seal slaughter in the Gulf of St. Lawrence. In 1968 HSUS experts, including Frank McMahon, joined Brian Davies of IFAW in Alaska's Pribilof Islands to explore the possibility of using humane methods to catch and destroy seals taken in an annual kill.[132]

McMahon was part of a U.S. Department of the Interior task force that went to the Pribilof Islands in search of humane methods for conducting a cull there. The group tested several methods of killing, including carbon dioxide, electricity, the Schermer concussion bolt stunner, a penetrating bolt pistol, and .22 caliber rifle fire using nontoxic pulverizing cartridges.[133] The HSUS continued to send staff members to observe the seal kills and to stop some of the abuses attending the slaughter during the 1970s.[134] The HSUS submitted reports on the hunts to the federal government in an attempt to press for immediate relief measures on the part of the Department of the Interior. While humane advocates opposed clubbing seals to death, they generally restricted their opposition to promoting reforms in the process of herding and slaughtering the animals. Under the 1911 Northern Pacific Fur Seal Treaty, the seals were protected by strict controls, and an end to the Pribilof Islands hunt would have broken the treaty, allowing pelagic sealing—the taking and killing of animals on the open seas—to resume.[135]

Sue Pressman holds a harp seal pup during a trip to the Newfoundland ice floes as an observer of the Canadian seal hunt in the 1970s.

In 1972 The HSUS urged a ten-year ban on the killing of seals and the importation of products made from them, and, happily, the clubbing of seals came under the MMPA, passed that same year. The MMPA called for a moratorium on the capture and/or killing of marine mammals and marine mammal products but included broad exemptions for scientific research, public display, and native use. While it helped to stop the importation of some seal products, the MMPA did not stop the taking of North Pacific fur seals, who were not covered by the moratorium because the international fur seal treaty covering their treatment superceded the MMPA. The U.S. Department of Commerce assisted American fur processors by issuing waivers to the moratorium.[136]

By the mid-1970s The HSUS was a principal actor in international efforts to suppress clubbing seals to death. In 1975 staff members sought to oppose the importation of pelts into the United States on the grounds that they were killed inhumanely.[137]

Sue Pressman's efforts to document the 1976 kill in South Africa provided crucial support to the campaign, as she testified before government and judicial officials. In 1977 the U.S. Court of Appeals ruled that the government's decision to waive the ban on importation of South African baby fur seal skins violated the MMPA. Pressman also monitored the Canadian harp seal hunt in 1978, gaining a rare observer permit. She was, however, denied the right to take photographs or interview any of the hunters. By 1980 The HSUS could claim the distinction of being the only animal organization in North America to have observed and evaluated firsthand the three major seal hunts conducted in Canada, South Africa, and the United States.[138]

In 1981 the 1911 treaty under which the United States, Russia, Japan, and Canada agreed to halt the practice of open sea (pelagic) sealing that jeopardized the fur seal herd to the point of extinction came up for a renewal vote in the U.S. Senate. The HSUS took on the Sierra Club, the Audubon Society, the National Wildlife Federation, and the Reagan administration in an effort to persuade the Senate to reduce the number of fur seals clubbed by native Aleuts in the Pribilofs by 70 percent. The HSUS celebrated March 1, 1981, as the International Day of the Seal, sponsoring a concert by musician Paul Winter at St. John the Divine Cathedral in New York City as part of its campaign to gain support for the congressional initiative. This celebration of the season of the seals' birth, jointly organized with Paul Winter, became an important annual ritual in The HSUS's antisealing campaigns.[139]

Patricia Forkan and John Grandy raised awareness during International Day of the Seal observances, which began in 1981.

That same year The HSUS successfully defeated an amendment to the MMPA sponsored by Representative John Breaux (D-LA) that would have permitted the importation of seventy thousand cape fur seals from South Africa. At MMPA reauthorization hearings, Patricia Forkan squared off with representatives of Fouke Fur Company, the principal processor of furs taken from seal pelts in both the South African and Pribilof culls.[140]

In 1983 John Grandy initiated a campaign to end the slaughter of North Pacific fur seals. Among the first major actions of the campaign, The HSUS prepared for and solicited participation by five other groups in a legal petition to the U.S. Department of Commerce to end the slaughter by having the fur seal declared a threatened species under the ESA. On June 15, 1984, just after the federal government announced that the seal cull would go forward that year, The HSUS joined IFAW and The Fund for Animals in a lawsuit charging that the Pribilof killings would violate the Fur Seal Act, the Marine Mammal Protection Act, the 1911 treaty that purportedly protected the seals, the National Environmental Policy Act, and the Administrative Procedures Act. The lawsuit failed; the federal district judge hearing the case ruled on June 28 that the fur seal treaty "assumes that seals will be killed."[141]

HSUS staff members form part of the living ring of seal petitions encircling the Commerce Department building.

Days later Grandy went to the Pribilof Islands for the first time to observe the slaughter firsthand. Grandy spent a large part of his time interacting with Aleut leaders and trying to understand their view that the killing represented useful and productive work for their people. Even so, an economic analysis of the Commerce Department's arrangement with the Aleuts left him convinced that the slaughter was mainly a form of "thinly veiled social welfare."[142]

In 1985 The HSUS placed special emphasis on the North Pacific fur seal. On March 1, 1985, the fifth annual Day of the Seal, The HSUS organized a demonstration against the American seal hunt. Staff members and supporters surrounded the U.S. Department of Commerce with petitions containing one hundred thousand signatures from citizens who supported a prohibition on sealing on the Pribilof Islands. Later that year The HSUS retained former U.S. Senator Paul Tsongas to lobby on the issue; his help ensured the support of forty-four senators for a letter to the Secretary of State denouncing the North Pacific Fur Seal Treaty. Two HSUS vice presidents testified before the Senate Foreign Relations Committee in opposition to the renewal of the treaty, and the committee took no action.[143]

The result of The HSUS's efforts was to drastically reduce the overall kill. There was no kill in 1985, and in 1986 only 1,348 seals were killed, all for subsistence—none for commercially valuable products. In two years, Grandy estimated, the campaigns had saved more than 38,000 seals from destruction. To accomplish this, The HSUS had mailed out millions of pieces of mail, filed a suit in the U.S. District Court, and placed newspaper advertisements across the country.[144]

In 1988 the Canadian government announced that it would ban the commercial slaughter of harp seal pups, the culmination of a long struggle in which The HSUS had done its part. Boycott pressure and a resulting decline in image removed all incentives for continuing the slaughter.[145]

Advertisements such as this one, which appeared in the New York Times in August 2003, called upon Americans to persuade Canada to end its seal hunt.

At the end of the twentieth century, the numbers of seals clubbed in the Pribilofs declined to approximately a thousand per year, and with the passing of those generations of Aleuts who pursued it extensively, seal clubbing promises to dwindle away there in the future. As late as 1992, The HSUS attempted to limit the permissible killing of Pribilof fur seals on the basis of subsistence claims, but it has not attempted any similar action of late. During the course of The HSUS's activism on this issue, the seal kill in the Pribilofs fell from its historic highs of 120,000, to 40,000, to its current low estimates.[146]

Sealing was by no means gone from The HSUS's agenda as the organization neared its fiftieth anniversary, however. In 2002 the world witnessed the largest slaughter of marine mammals in Canada since 1967, with a reported kill of more than 307,000. This number exceeded the Canadian government's own quota by more than 32,000 animals. Even more disturbing, Canada announced quotas for seal kills for the following three years—some 350,000 seal pups would be slaughtered each year, a total in excess of one million. In 2003 The HSUS launched a marine mammal protection campaign that rivaled the one it had waged in the early 1980s. The campaign included advertisements in *Business Week* and the *New York*

Times that called upon Americans to use their economic influence to persuade Canada to end the hunt. The HSUS also commissioned a public opinion survey that found that most Americans opposed the seal kill as a needless slaughter. Some 67 percent of those polled thought it important enough that they would be willing to change their plans rather than vacation in Canada so long as the killing continued.

Conclusion

During the late 1970s, Yale School of Forestry researcher Stephen R. Kellert, Ph.D., working under grants from the U.S. Fish and Wildlife Service, conducted exhaustive survey research on public attitudes, knowledge, and behavior concerning wildlife. HSUS staff members served on the project's external advisory board, along with representatives of the Environmental Defense Fund, the National Wildlife Federation, the League of Women Voters, the NAACP, and the AFL-CIO.[147]

Kellert interviewed Americans about their knowledge of animals, their participation in animal-related activities, and their beliefs concerning specific wildlife issues, including endangered species, predator control, hunting, habitat protection, population management, and trapping. The surveys also tested Kellert's typology of attitudes toward animals, the most common of which were the humanistic, moralistic, utilitarian, and negativistic/neutralistic. Together, and in active contention with one another, Kellert reported, these attitudes provided "the dynamic basis for the conflict and misunderstanding existing today over various issues involving people and animals."[148]

The mere participation of nonhunting constituencies in the development and execution of the Kellert surveys generated a firestorm of protest. Political pressure from members of the U.S. Senate forced the creation of advisory committee slots for representatives of the National Rifle Association and the American Farm Bureau and limited the impact of the committee, which met just once and did not strongly influence Kellert's project.[149]

Political pressure did not influence the survey outcomes, however, which provided the humane movement with encouraging signs of a shift in the direction of humanistic and moralistic attitudes against the traditional utilitarian outlook that underpinned American wildlife policy at virtually all levels. Only 18 percent of the survey population found nothing wrong with the use of steel-jawed leghold traps to capture animals, and 65 percent of those surveyed indicated that they were willing to pay more for tuna fish rather than see the industry continue to kill dolphins and porpoises in its nets. Only 35 percent of the informed public favored shooting and trapping coyotes, and just 8 percent favored the use of poisons to destroy them.[150]

The Kellert studies revealed a significant shift in public attitudes that was crucial to the rise of concern for wild animal and marine mammal populations. Yet, it was not a coincidence that The HSUS thrived as a wildlife and marine mammal advocacy organization from the 1970s on, especially after 1980. It was the result of a determined commitment to advance wildlife concerns in an ever-improving climate of public opinion. By 2004 the program work that had begun decades earlier with John Hoyt's hiring of Sue Pressman, Patricia Forkan, John Grandy, and others had become one of The HSUS's largest sections. Staff specialists within the Wildlife and Habitat Protection section helped to situate The HSUS as a significant player in the network of nongovernmental organizations devoted to wildlife and marine mammal concerns. Through the work of Natasha Atkins, John Hadidian, Sue Lieberman, Tony Povilitis, Naomi Rose, Allen Rutberg, and Teresa Telecky, and many others, The HSUS gained stakeholder status and assumed responsibilities in an array of working coalitions devoted to North American and international wildlife and marine mammal concerns. It sponsored its own research program in wildlife contraception and an array of initiatives devoted to nonviolent resolution in perceived arenas of conflict between human and animal interests. The HSUS was not just any voice for wildlife; it was a strong one.

The Broad Work of Humane Education

he HSUS was formed by advocates who were anxious to make a practical and immediate difference for animals, and their decision to pursue campaigns that produced prompt and discernible relief of animal suffering reflected such determination. At the same time, The HSUS's early initiatives were guided by the conviction that Fred Myers and other founders held in common—that the flow of animal misery in the world could best be halted by educational initiatives directed at the young. Like many animal protectionists, past and present, the founders of The HSUS appreciated the crucial importance of encouraging sensitivity to animals in future generations.

Once The HSUS had established itself and achieved the stability necessary for long-range planning, the humane education of children became a stronger organizational priority. With the support of early board members and HSUS branch officials like James T. Mehorter, a psychology professor, and Rear Admiral James C. Shaw, President Oliver Evans made humane education an organizational priority, seeking professional expertise and authorizing the preparation of age-appropriate education materials. Evans also encouraged staff members' interests in the development of a robust youth education program, a project that Dale Hylton and others nurtured during the late 1960s.

After he assumed the HSUS presidency in 1970, John Hoyt furthered these commitments by creating an academic center for the study of humane education, supporting evaluation studies, recruiting additional professional staff to work in this arena, and, finally, developing the property at East Haddam, Connecticut, that would become the heart of The HSUS's humane education outreach programs.

In subsequent years, with its youth education division thriving, The HSUS began to develop additional educational programs geared toward higher education, social work and law enforcement audiences, and the animal care and control community. With this broadened emphasis, The HSUS sought to promote concern for animals within a wide range of institutions and organizations.

The Humane Education of Children

The education of young people in the principles of kindness has been a priority of organized animal protection in the United States from the earliest years of anticruelty work. From the late eighteenth century on, growing appreciation for the value of the kindness-to-animals ethic to character formation in children led theorists and authors to emphasize it in domestic education and children's literature. In fact, this interest in the humane didactic predated the formal origins of animal protection.

After the first anticruelty societies formed in the mid-1860s, they quickly turned their attention to humane education as a long-term response to the spread of cruelty. Rather than prosecute adults for cruel conduct, why not place priority on the socialization of young people in the values of kindness? This approach also promised to create a future constituency for organized animal protection. By 1890 efforts to promote kindness clubs within the schools had coalesced in the "Band of Mercy" movement, launched by the Reverend Thomas Timmins and George Thorndike Angell of the American Humane Education Society (AHES), sister organization of the MSPCA. Major humane organizations assisted the formation of such groups through the production of literature, textbooks, and other materials. By the early 1900s, a national campaign for compulsory humane education had begun to gather momentum, and by 1920 such laws were in place in about twenty states.[1]

The presence of these laws, however, did not ensure the growth of humane education. It did not gain a foothold within teacher-training institutions, nor did it become a subject of scholarly inquiry. It did not even become more central to the work of SPCAs during the mid-

The HSUS's "Personalities and Pets," booth was one of the most popular stopping places for the one hundred thousand visitors to the New York Pet Show in 1965.

dle decades of the twentieth century. By the era of the Great Depression, the practical and financial burdens of shelter and hospital work, animal control responsibilities, and law enforcement consumed most of the resources and attention of local and regional organizations. Very few of them carried on extensive or well-financed outreach programs in the schools in their vicinity.[2]

The diminution of humane education was not solely the result of such constraints upon the animal protection movement, however. Many negative influences found their way into the educational system, and these were sometimes hard to displace. Nature-based education, for example, was frequently sponsored by organizations whose finances came from the manufacturers of sporting arms and ammunition.[3] Local or regional sensitivity about such issues as raising animals for food, or hunting, and the controversial nature of some topics, like animal experimentation, as a subject for classroom discussion also prevented humane societies from addressing certain forms of animal abuse in too direct a manner.

Undoubtedly, the animal protection movement's attention to humane education outreach did help to normalize the view that compassionate attitudes toward animals were crucial elements in a well-adjusted personality. Largely on the basis of anecdotal evidence, the view that animal abuse could lead to serious interpersonal violence gained some prominence during the middle decades of the twentieth century. At the same time, cruelty and kindness to animals were integrated into personality tests measuring individual adjustment, like the Minnesota Multiphasic Personality Inventory.[4]

When it first formed in the 1950s, The HSUS was less focused on promoting humane education than on extinguishing the misuse of animals in elementary and secondary schools and science fairs. This was an area of egregious misuse of animals, and youthful experimentation sometimes reached alarming depths. In 1958, for example, The HSUS campaigned against the use of living animals in rocket experiments by teenagers. It was a practice that threatened to spread in the wake of the Soviet Union's successful launching of *Sputnik*, with Americans focused on both education and space exploration.[5]

At the dawn of a new decade, with the Humane Slaughter Act passed and The HSUS stabilized and solvent, the real push for humane education of youth began. Board member Edith Goode persuaded Dorothy Thompson to write a piece in favor of humane education for the *Ladies' Home Journal*, and it appeared in February 1960. Thompson's piece, which drew heavily upon materials provided by HSUS director James Mehorter, attracted massive media attention to humane education and the problem of cruel experimental use in schools and led to thousands of inquiries. Two years later HSUS director Jacques Sichel organized a well-attended conference on humane education. At that event Fred Myers sounded the note that would guide The HSUS's approach to humane education advocacy in the future. "We are not exclusively societies for the protection of animals," he told his colleagues. "Indeed, I think that the much higher and more important concept is that we are societies for the betterment of people. The problems on which we work are those which determine whether the inner man and the inner child will be balanced, sane, happy, creative, all of the things that we want the people of the next generation to be."[6]

During the presidency of Oliver Evans (1963–1967), The HSUS laid a stronger foundation for its long-term humane education goals by establishing a relevant research agenda and a program for the development of appropriate literature. In the mid-1960s, staff members began to collaborate with Stuart Westerlund, Ph.D., in the Department of Education at the George Washington University on a project to explore the impact of humane education on early childhood development and to test various methods and techniques of humane education in a group of Washington, D.C., metropolitan area schools. HSUS officials hoped that a convincing pilot study concerning the value of humane education for character education would persuade a large national foundation to provide a major grant for adding it to the curriculum of the nation's schools.[7]

Westerlund's study concluded that students liked humane education, educators appreciated it and wanted to do it, and administrators were in favor of it. As Evans noted, however, efforts to institute programs "were frustrated because of the lack of teaching materials and the total unfamiliarity with the subject on the part of the teachers and school administrators." Most serious of all, the movement had utterly failed to win recognition for humane education from universities working in the field of education. Despite good intentions for many years, the humane movement had increasingly isolated itself from the educational process.[8]

Organizational deliberations about the way forward were guided as well by the recognition that the resurrection of compulsory humane education campaigns, popular between 1900 and 1925, was not the best approach. Rather, as one consultant told an HSUS gathering, "it has to be built into the attitudes of the educators." In 1965, for the first time ever, The HSUS staffed a booth at the annual convention of the National Education Association, offering services and materials to educators. This outreach would continue for many years.[9]

The success of humane education outreach did not depend solely upon professional educators, however, as Aida Flemming, wife of a member of the Canadian Parliament, demonstrated in 1959. Reinvigorating an older initiative, the nineteenth-century Band of Mercy, Flemming launched the Kindness Club, to harness the group-forming spirit of children and cultivate their interest in the study and protection of animals. Albert Schweitzer accepted the honorary presidency of the club with the observation, "True goodness requires us to respect the lives of all living creatures." In time The HSUS assumed much of the responsibility for promoting the spread of Kindness Clubs and helped to develop suitable material for distribution to young people. In 1964 The HSUS honored Flemming with its Humanitarian of the Year award (later renamed for Joseph Wood Krutch), the society's highest honor.[10]

In 1967, Flemming appealed to The HSUS to assume administration of her Kindness Club program to ensure its continuation beyond her lifetime. The HSUS cautiously agreed to take on a five-state pilot project to determine what materials and approaches would work best. In keeping with plans to make The HSUS's National Humane Education Center at Waterford, Vir-

In 1969 board chairman Mel Morse presented Kindness Club founder and president Aida Flemming with the National Humane Education Center's certificate of appreciation for her humane work with children.

ginia, the headquarters of a program for humane education, the pilot program was launched from there. Dale Hylton, who had long wanted to make education a stronger priority, was soon given the opportunity to evaluate the pilot project and make recommendations on the production of materials and the expansion of the program nationally in the most effective manner.[11]

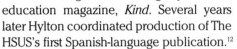

Soon after assuming direction of the (rechristened) KIND (Kids in Nature's Defense) program, Hylton initiated a monthly newsletter, produced on a mimeograph machine and folded and stapled in the evenings at home. In September 1974 the program introduced its first teacher's guide, and soon after, the newsletter grew into the organization's flagship humane education magazine, *Kind*. Several years later Hylton coordinated production of The HSUS's first Spanish-language publication.[12]

An early HSUS pamphlet had as its subject animals and schoolchildren.

During these years The HSUS cooperated with several individual pioneers of humane education. Author, illustrator, and naturalist Hope Sawyer Buyukmihci worked with staff members to develop literature for the program. So did Jean McClure Kelty, an Ohio English professor active with the HSUS-affiliated Animal Charity League of Youngstown. She authored a lesson manual, *If You Have a Duck*, which aimed to promote kindness to animals and people through a series of entertaining exercises and activities.[13]

Sandy Rowland (left) and Dale Hylton were involved in NAAHE's humane education program for a number of years.

Charlotte Baker Montgomery, author and illustrator of many children's books, wrote several of The HSUS's most important early humane education publications, including *Meeting Animal Friends* and *A Visit to the Animal Shelter*. Montgomery was also responsible for the launch of the Humane Education Workshop, a summer seminar at Stephen F. Austin State University in which a number of HSUS staff members participated. The HSUS recognized her steadfast support of its humane education programs and the broad impact of her work by honoring her with the 1983 Joseph Wood Krutch Medal.[14]

My Kindness Coloring Book was the work of Charlotte Baker Montgomery and Hope Sawyer Buyukmihci.

In the late 1960s, participants at The HSUS's annual conferences considered several resolutions pertaining to humane education. The first, in 1968, called for development of a suitable curriculum and its promotion in primary and secondary schools, with special emphasis on the elimination of animal experimentation in science education. The second resolution, adopted in 1969, called upon humane societies to seek endorsements for a program to implement humane education programs from leading universities and colleges.[15]

John Hoyt's 1972 hiring of John Dommers, a Connecticut science teacher with an interest in developing audiovisual materials to promote concern for animals and the natural environment, further strengthened The HSUS's capacities in humane education work. Operating first as education director under James C. Shaw of The HSUS's Connecticut branch, Dommers kept the same position when the branch was reincorporated as the New England Regional Office (NERO). Dommers made many contributions to The HSUS's catalogue of educational materials.[16]

In 1973 Hoyt hired Charles Herrmann III, Dommers's sometime collaborator as an editor of children's publications for Xerox Education Publications, as director of educational publications for The HSUS. Herrmann worked out of the National Humane Education Center in Waterford, helping Hylton to manage the KIND program and assisting HSUS staff members with the production of audiovisual material for individuals and the classroom.[17]

The HSUS's growing professionalization brought forward in-house initiatives that also advanced its humane education programs. In 1974 Guy Hodge wrote a unique book on careers in animal conservation and welfare, explaining the educational background and experience necessary for specific professions and providing helpful information for young people interested in the pursuit of such careers. *Careers: Working with Animals* went beyond the presentation of dry information, offering a discussion of the attitudes, emotions, and personal philosophies that students needed to consider before making a career choice. By late 1977 The HSUS had sold 20,000 copies, on its own and through a commercial publisher, and produced a filmstrip to introduce youngsters to veterinarians, veterinary technicians, groomers, kennel workers, animal control officers, park naturalists, animal behavior specialists, and others who work with animals.[18]

In 1976 the Youth Activities Department led one of the KIND program's most successful projects ever, the Bicentennial Animal Contest: seventy-five thousand children cast their ballots for fourteen animal candidates in an election that highlighted the contributions made by animals to American history. Whole schools participated, and newspapers around the country reprinted the ballot. The horse won, with the bald eagle coming in a close second.[19]

HSUS humane education specialists tried to design literature and material for children with the organization's overall program activities in mind. There was a strong emphasis on pet overpopulation and the promotion of spay-neuter as well as on companion animal issues like licensing and collaring of dogs. However, Michael Fox and other staff colleagues provided a steady stream of ideas for articles, features, and educational products to help children develop imaginative sympathy with animals in difficult situations, and the organization's youth-focused publications provided age-appropriate information concerning such topics: The HSUS's seal campaigns, its efforts to close down puppy mills, and HSUS consultant Dick Randall's work to reform predator control programs were all featured in NAAHE publications. Fox's *Wild Dogs Three*, a children's book that told the story of abandoned animals trying to survive in a rundown section of St. Louis, also appeared in NAAHE materials.[20]

The National Association for the Advancement of Humane Education

Charles F. Herrmann III (left) and John Dommers were active in education in the early 1970s.

In June 1972 John Hoyt signed a formal agreement with the University of Tulsa, Stuart Westerlund's current institution, to support the Humane Education Development and Evaluation Project (HEDEP). Westerlund received a grant from The HSUS to develop strategies for advancing humane education in the nation's schools. In 1974 this project formally incorporated as the National Association for the Advancement of Humane Education (NAAHE), with its basic purpose the development, evaluation, and distribution of integrated humane education materials for elementary and secondary schools. For a time the organization functioned from the University of Oklahoma under Westerlund's direction. A number of his graduate students conducted humane education evaluation studies, some of which became doctoral dissertations.[21]

At about the same time, The HSUS was concluding negotiations for the consolidation and assimilation of its Connecticut branch. An important part of the incorporation involved the 1973 donation of a property in East Haddam, Connecticut, which, along with James C. Shaw, who served as the first HSUS New England regional director, comprised the outstanding legacy of the now-extinguished Connecticut branch of The HSUS. The HSUS decided to centralize its humane education programs on the property, naming it the Norma Terris Humane Education and Nature Center in honor of its donor, Norma Terris (d. 1989). Terris was

The Norma Terris Center in East Haddam, Connecticut.

the stage and screen actress who created the role of Magnolia in the original Ziegfeld production of *Showboat* and a close friend of Shaw and his wife, Bettsy. At the center's dedication, John Hoyt reminded listeners of the organization's broader purpose of improving humankind. It was not simply a preoccupation with animal welfare that should motivate such a project, he advised, "but the promotion of a quality of humaneness of which kindness to animals is but one by-product." [22]

In 1977, in an effort to better meet the needs of humane society educators and individual teachers, The HSUS decided to end the Tulsa-based NAAHE/HEDEP project, while retaining Westerlund as an advisor. From then on The HSUS's educational outreach efforts would be centered at the Norma Terris Center and would consist of teacher training, program development, and community education initiatives (many of which were coordinated by John Dommers and Kathy Savesky), and Washington, D.C., where staff members Hylton, Herrmann, and Marcia Glaser helped to manage the program. One of the earliest results of the new arrangement was *Humane Education*, a journal edited by Herrmann. The quarterly contained articles on methods of teaching, the philosophy of humane education, a resources and materials evaluation section, a column devoted to news from local educators, and ready-to-use master sheets to support humane education activities. [23]

From then on an increasing portion of The HSUS's humane education outreach activity emanated from the NAAHE headquarters. Staff members supplied teaching kits, audiovisual aids, and other materials to teachers. The organization also developed programs to identify and honor appropriate films, books, and teaching materials. In time it began to offer recognition awards to outstanding educators in the field and to local organizations that demonstrated extraordinary commitment to the work. NAAHE's Teacher of the Year Award, highlighting exemplary teaching practices, honors board member Jacques Sichel, a diligent supporter of humane education within The HSUS between 1960 and 1980, and a scholarship fund established in James Shaw's memory supports students pursuing careers that help animals.

Throughout the 1970s and 1980s, NAAHE sought to establish itself as a hub of research and program assessment work collaborating with a network of interested educators. The organization sponsored, evaluated, or reported on research concerning the value of animals in the classroom, the influence of television programming, children's fears of animals, gender differences in attitudes, the expansion of humane attitudes toward animals to humane attitudes toward people, the impact of animals in the domestic environment, and the advantages of storytelling and other methods of pedagogy. NAAHE also provided annotated bibliographies of current and past research on humane education issues and sought to forge connections with teacher-training institutions where research and attention to humane education could be encouraged.

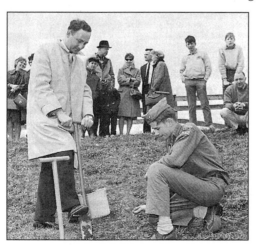

Kenneth Rollins, mayor of Leesburg, Virginia, planted a seedling on the grounds of The National Humane Education Center in March 1965.

The growing cadre of education professionals within The HSUS made it possible for the organization to evaluate the proliferating number of children's works devoted to animals. For many years The HSUS distributed a list of several hundred books that promoted humane values. From time to time, staff members also issued guidelines for parents and educators to help them evaluate the suitability of books they might be considering for purchase. [24] NAAHE provided another important service to the movement by monitoring children's publications for messages and material that reinforced ambivalent or harmful attitudes toward animals. Staff members chided children's publications when they sent the wrong message, celebrating rodeos, trapping, hunting, and other pursuits that caused harm and suffering to animals.

This capacity for reaction to the circulation of material that undercut the humane ideal became a very serious priority in the mid-1980s, especially after the release of Project WILD, a wildlife-focused educational package heavily promoted by fish and game agencies, among others. NAAHE staff joined members of the HSUS Wildlife section in pointing out the implicit biases of Project WILD and in stressing the need for conscientious efforts by instructors to balance the material they presented. Together, NAAHE and Wildlife sought to equip teachers with the necessary knowledge to recognize and remedy Project WILD's misleading and superficial treatment of concepts that were crucial to an assessment of its strong proconsumptive use philosophy.

In a similar process, NAAHE staff members collaborated with animal research division specialists to criticize a poster series issued by the U.S. Department of Health and Human Services (HHS) in 1993. The cartoon-style poster, "Let's Visit a Research Laboratory," took advantage of children's natural affection for animals to persuade them that laboratories were idyllic settings for animals and specifically dismissed the concerns expressed by humane advocates as "extremist" in character. HSUS staff members took particular umbrage at the federally funded poster set because NAAHE had a long-established policy of steering clear of animal research issues because of their controversial nature.[25]

The Development of *People and Animals* and *KIND News*

Nineteen eighty-one proved to be a benchmark year for NAAHE, with the production of a field-tested edition of *People and Animals: A Humane Education Curriculum Guide* developed for use in preschool through sixth grade. It was a major undertaking, the product of two years' work and a four-day conference in 1979 that brought together twenty-three leading humane educators. Organized around thirty-six concepts that fell under the four general headings of human/animal relationships, companion animals, wild animals, and farm animals, each concept was blended with a basic skill or traditional content area to produce activities in language arts, social studies, math, and health and science. Appropriate background material for teachers was included.[26]

NAHEE Director Kathy Savesky (right) demonstrates the feltboard game "Sharing Sam."

People and Animals emerged from the collaboration of NAAHE Director Kathy Savesky, John Dommers, and Charles F. Herrmann, all of whom brought relevant professional background in education and curriculum development. The Geraldine R. Dodge Foundation provided critical funding for production and distribution. Materials development was a costly and complex process, requiring knowledge of age-appropriate language, technical assistance from staff members and outside consultants, and other coordinating challenges.

Savesky's experience as education director of the Indianapolis Humane Society and director of AHES was crucial to the project, and major responsibility for *People and Animals* fell to her. Its production marked a new era in approaches to humane education. "We're trying to help kids develop a set of values for what is and isn't appropriate behavior toward animals," Savesky told a reporter. She pointed out, however, that lessons that simply dictate "kindness rules" for children to absorb do not provide the facts and understanding upon which compassionate conduct is based, and they "fall short of helping young people form lasting and workable systems for making ethical decisions."[27]

People and Animals represented an important step toward standardization and unification of what was a very fragmented humane education effort in which hundreds of local and national groups and advocates participated. Among other features, *People and Animals* identified specific areas in which educators from humane societies could be of assistance to classroom teachers. Simultaneously, NAAHE attempted to meet teachers' needs by encouraging local humane societies to establish resource centers and lending libraries where relevant materials could be procured easily.[28]

People and Animals also demonstrated that humane instructional material could become quite controversial. The Utah Farm Bureau forced the guide's withdrawal (in a state where important field testing was underway) because of its attempts to address "production farming."[29] At about the same time, the American Farm Bureau Federation issued a critique disparaging the guide on the grounds that "(1) those who have prepared the guide have little, if any knowledge about American agriculture, (2) vegetarianism pervades the guide, (3) animals are equated directly with humans, and (4) a restructuring of U.S. agriculture is implied."[30]

In 1983 NAAHE officials decided to replace its youth magazine, *Kind*, with *KIND News*, a four-page newspaper published on two levels, for grades one through three and grades four through six. While the old publication had gone to individual subscribers, the new one was inexpensive and better suited for teachers to order in bulk for classroom use, making it possible to serve children whose families did not necessarily provide them with any humane-oriented reading material. The new format also made it possible for educators affiliated with local humane societies to order mass quantities for distribution to schoolchildren.[31]

When elementary school reading specialist Patty Finch succeeded Kathy Savesky at NAAHE in 1985, she shifted the organization's emphasis from the *People and Animals* curriculum guide to *KIND News*. Significant organizational resources went toward improving the quality and increasing the circulation of *KIND News* and its companion publication, *Humane Education*, which became *Children and Animals* in 1985 and *KIND Teacher* in 1989.

According to Bill DeRosa, who joined the organization in 1983, NAAHE felt "that *KIND News* would provide a more consistent humane education intervention." "It was difficult to know if or to what extent—or for how long—*People and Animals* would be used once it reached a teacher's hands," DeRosa explained. Although he acknowledged that more time and effort could have been devoted to promoting the curriculum guide and further evaluating its impact, it was thought that *KIND News* was the more marketable resource, in part because it did not require as much teacher time or preparation and could simply be distributed to children for independent reading or to take home. Its use did not really depend so heavily upon a teacher's willingness to set aside class time for humane education. As it turned out, *KIND News* did prove itself to be teacher-friendly.[32]

"Right from the start," DeRosa explained, "The idea was to make *KIND News* an educational supplement that was fun and easy to read; if kids liked it, so would teachers. And it took off." The promotion/distribution vehicle for *KIND News* was the Adopt-a-Classroom program, initiated in 1986. At first NAAHE published *KIND News* four times per year, but by 1990 the publishing schedule included nine issues a year. In 1993 NAAHE began to offer the publication in three editions, for primary (grades kindergarten through two), junior (grades three and four), and senior (grades five and six) levels. Sent at first to just one thousand classrooms, *KIND News* was being read in some thirty-five thousand by 2003, reaching approximately 1.2 million children every year. It had, by DeRosa's reckoning, reached more children than any single humane education classroom publication in history.[33]

Kind magazine (above) was succeeded by KIND News.

Science Fairs, Dissection, and Youth Socialization

In addition to its efforts to promote and institutionalize humane education in the United States, The HSUS attempted to curb the excesses of youthful experimentation at science fairs. This was a growing problem in the mid-1950s and drew the attention of The HSUS's national office as well as its branches. In 1956 director Myra Babcock, M.D., directed a survey to determine whether there would be support among opinion leaders throughout the country for a prohibition on classroom experiments in which animals were slowly starved, inoculated with

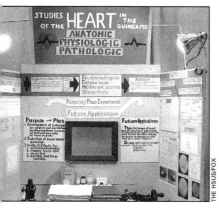

cancer, or denied the benefit of essential nutrients. In 1958 The HSUS went to court to enjoin teenage rocket club experimenters from shooting live animals into the air in homemade missiles. In 1960 Fred Myers and Pearl Twyne of the Virginia Federation of Humane Societies visited the superintendent of the Fairfax (Virginia) County school system to express their concerns about a science fair experiment in which a boy won acclaim for major surgery he had performed on rabbits in his bedroom "laboratory."[34]

In 1964, in an egregious case involving cancer experiments on chickens that dragged on for a number of years, the New Jersey branch brought charges against the school board of East Orange. This action ended all such experiments pending outcome of the trial, which took place in April 1966. The case became a flash point for confrontation between humane advocates and rep-

The late 1960s marked the beginning of The HSUS's intensive campaign to end the use of animals in classroom and science fair experiments.

resentatives of the National Society for Medical Research (NSMR), which obtained permission to enter the case, along with the New Jersey Science Teachers Association, as co-defendants. The NSMR brought in prominent scientists to suggest that the case challenged the right of companies and institutions of higher education to conduct such experiments in the state. In his testimony HSUS director James Mehorter emphasized humane concerns over students' lack of maturity and experience and the harmful effects such ill use of animals could have on developing personalities. A biology professor from the University of New Hampshire also testified against the practice. Notwithstanding, the judge ruled that it was legally permissible for high school students to conduct experiments on live animals for "educational purposes."[35]

In early 1967, with the verdict on appeal, The HSUS launched a campaign to halt harmful uses of animals in classroom and science fair experiments. Oliver Evans called upon HSUS branches, members, and affiliated societies to press parent-teacher organizations, school boards, and school administrators as part of a major effort to end objectionable practices. Service Department Director Patrick Parkes launched a comprehensive survey of science fair projects in Maryland as part of an effort to build a case for reform. The HSUS drafted a model law for distribution, and the publicity generated led the Connecticut education commissioner to launch "spot check" inspections in the state's school system to ensure compliance with humane principles.[36]

Unfortunately, a subsequent New Jersey Supreme Court verdict in the cancer experiment case ruled that high school students could legally experiment on live animals for educational purposes. As The HSUS would learn, moreover, the problem could reach still more terrible extremes, as it did in 1968, when The HSUS discovered young people performing heart transplants in the course of their studies.[37]

For a time the International Science and Engineering Fair (ISEF), which encompassed the final stage of competition for about 90 percent of the state and local science fairs, attempted to improve the treatment of animals in projects accepted for consideration. The

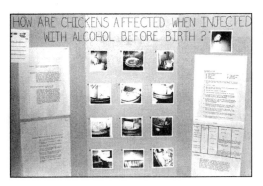

A high school science fair project from the 1970s.

campaign for reform gained some momentum in 1970, when California became one of the first states to prohibit the use of live animals in school experiments.[38]

In 1973 HSUS consultant Barbara Orlans drafted a set of guidelines for the use of animals in elementary and secondary school experiments, for distribution to the nine thousand members of the National Association of Biology Teachers (NABT). The guidelines discouraged experiments on warm-blooded animals, surgery on any living vertebrates, and experiments that might cause disease or other injurious reaction in vertebrate animals.[39] This was another issue on which The HSUS diverged from guidelines being circulated widely to humane societies by AHA.[40]

During the mid-1970s the science fair issue required more or less steady surveillance, as observers continued to encounter projects in which adolescents caused serious harm and suffering to cats, rats, mice, and guinea pigs.[41] Along with Orlans, Guy Hodge, Michael Fox, and other HSUS personnel put in time on the issue, traveling to fairs to document abuses and promote reforms. In 1976 the newly hired Fox found animal-based experiments at the ISEF "technique-oriented, repetitious, inhumane, and unimaginative." He judged that lack of competent supervision had resulted in severe abuse and suffering of animals in a number of projects, and The HSUS committed itself to extraordinary efforts to promote "rational, objective, ethical, and humane appraisal" of every science project undertaken by students at the secondary level. That same year The HSUS provided substantial financial support for Orlans's *Animal Care: From Protozoa to Small Mammals*, an important contribution to reform efforts.[42] Several years later, however, HSUS investigators found disturbing examples of overuse and misuse of animals at the ISEF. HSUS staff member Andrea Ward noted that mice, birds, rabbits, and dogs were all among the animals who lost their lives in dubious student experiments performed under inadequate adult supervision.[43]

In 1980 The HSUS published *Animals in Education: The Use of Animals in High School Biology Classrooms and Science Fairs*, by Heather McGiffin and Nancie Brownlee, to buttress its work on the topic. The next year NAAHE and other groups celebrated when the board of directors of the National Science Teacher's Association (NSTA) approved a code of practice for classroom and science fair use of animals. The code prohibited surgery on vertebrate animals, experimental procedures that caused vertebrates pain or discomfort, and the killing of animals in the presence of students. Unfortunately, in 1986 the NSTA relaxed its standard, permitting animal surgery under adult supervision and prohibiting only those experimental procedures that caused "unnecessary pain or discomfort." The new code also permitted the killing of animals for educational purposes.[44]

Although dissection had long been a subject of ambivalence for young people as well as for animal advocates, only in the 1980s did organized animal protection begin to devote time to challenging it on ethical or pedagogical grounds. At that time, The HSUS began to advance its view that dissection of preserved animals was inappropriate and unnecessary in the elementary and secondary school classroom. The costs of dissection, animal protectionists believed, went beyond animal suffering and death to the fostering of ambivalent attitudes toward animals on the part of the young. Biology studies, NAAHE and HSUS staff members argued, ought to focus on animals as living beings, emphasizing their behavior and relationship to the natural environment.[45]

As more and more young people developed coherent convictions about animals' inherent value, it became increasingly possible to frame their concerns about participation in dissection as a matter of conscientious objection. At the same time, the technology that emerged in the era of the personal computer introduced new and sophisticated programs, some of which offered perceived advantages over dissection. NAAHE staff members attended NABT and NSTA conventions and kept an eye on the literature comparing traditional instruction with dissection. In 1985 NAAHE produced two brochures on the question, "Does the Idea of Dissecting or Experimenting on Animals in Biology Class Disturb You?" and "The Living Science: A Humane Approach to the Study of Animals in Elementary and Secondary School Biology." In 1988 staff members provided suggestions for a major revision of the Holt, Rinehart and Winston laboratory manual *Modern Biology*, which subsequently incorporated information concerning alternatives to dissection and the possible rationales for abstention.[46]

While humane education specialists continued to send out materials on dissection to interested students, responsibility for this issue was increasingly assumed by the Animal Research Issues section of The HSUS. The section's specialists counseled hundreds of students, teachers, administrators, and others in regard to appropriate alternatives and supported a select few in their claims for conscientious objection. In 1987 the Jenifer Graham case brought the debate over dissection to a national audience. The HSUS took a leading role in the case after the Graham family approached NAAHE for advice. HSUS legal counsel Roger Kindler and director O.J. Ramsey met with school officials to express their support for Graham's refusal to dissect, and Ramsey served as her attorney. The HSUS stood by Graham until the satisfactory conclusion of her case.[47]

As an increasing number of students nationwide began to assert their principled objection to participation in dissection, and The HSUS became more aware of the continuing animal welfare problems associated with animals' capture, their treatment by biological supply companies, and their classroom use, the need for a comprehensive publication dealing with the subject became apparent. In 1999 Jonathan Balcombe, Ph.D., associate director of the Animal Research Issues section, wrote *The Use of Animals in Higher Education: Problems, Alternatives, and Recommendations*. Balcombe's work, published in 2000 by Humane Society Press, The HSUS's new publishing imprint, reviewed relevant scholarship, discussed available options for those who wished to avoid objectionable uses of animals, and synthesized relevant arguments concerning the pedagogical value of animal use.[48]

(Left) A frog model, an alternative to frog dissection, is an example of teaching resources promoted by The HSUS.

A New Name and a Broader Vision

For many years NAAHE had been incorporating environmental principles into its humane education curriculum and program materials. Not only was environmental education a natural fit; for years, it had also been a strong interest of staff members like John Dommers. In 1989 The HSUS's general effort to align its work with the growing global environmental movement resulted in a new name for NAAHE, the National Association for Humane and Environmental Education (NAHEE). The new designation better reflected its commitment to the goals of instilling good character through the promotion of kindness to people, animals, and the environment and to improve the organization's ability to serve and to interact with organizations and individuals working in the field of environmental education.

In succeeding years NAHEE moved well beyond its early efforts to provide humane education curriculum guides, materials, and services to educators and local schools. Through its professional development workshops, it sought to assist humane educators with experience in sheltering or animal welfare to acquire the knowledge of humane education trends, concepts, and strategies fundamental to their work. It also worked to create mechanisms whereby humane educators who lack formal educational credentials can gain the course work and experience that will make them more effective in the field. The establishment of Humane Society University (HSU) in 2001 led to heightened emphasis on this goal and created a new avenue for its realization. After the creation of HSU, NAHEE staff members collaborated with headquarters staff and outside consultants to develop a new on-line Master of Teaching program, one that situated humane education within a multidisciplinary context.

Such developments made it possible for animal care and control professionals, humane society volunteers, and others with an interest in the field to develop their understanding of key concepts, trends, and opportunities in humane education. Most humane education outreach remained within the province of animal care and control agencies that sponsored classroom visits and shelter tours and served as the principal source of literature and other materials for use by teachers. Not surprising, either, most humane education programs focused on companion animal issues to the exclusion of others, as a result of social, cultural, or political considerations or as a matter of declared or perceived primary mission.

During the last several decades of the twentieth century, NAHEE was in the forefront of efforts to create and test new approaches to humane education and to consolidate the results of studies that measure the effectiveness of humane education programs in building children's knowledge and improving their attitudes and behavior toward animals. While there was a relative lack of solid research supporting humane education's usefulness, the organization's efforts to promote evaluation studies did bear fruit. NAHEE was a key player in the attempt to investigate and validate the impact of values-based education aimed at changing children's attitudes toward animals and the environment.[49]

At the same time, as a new century dawned, the organization rekindled its earlier efforts to make a priority of preservice humane education training within university teacher-training programs. NAHEE initiated a campaign to persuade local humane societies to devote more of their resources to humane education work. In the era of the Internet, it was possible for NAHEE to enhance its outreach efforts through the development of websites serving children, teenagers, parents, advocates, educators, and others.

In 2001 NAHEE officials moved to develop a broader array of humane educational materials to supplement *KIND News*. By summer 2003 NAHEE had produced a new materials catalog, including coloring books, workbooks, lesson plans designed for integration into contemporary character education programs, and an assortment of Spanish-language materials.[50]

Training Initiatives, Law Enforcement, Public Policy, and Antiviolence Community Outreach

For decades humane society leaders at all levels lamented the absence of adequate training programs for their staff members. There were few proper and accredited sources of training for many occupations within the field of animal care and control. Beginning in the early 1960s, The HSUS tried to address this deficit through conferences, workshops, and accreditation visits, and HSUS programs played a crucial role in bringing a degree of professionalism to animal care and control. In addition, The HSUS fulfilled a vital service to the cause by providing professional training and counsel to officials in law enforcement, disaster response, social work, and other realms.

During the late 1970s and 1980s, much of this work took place under the auspices of The HSUS's Animal Control Academy in Alabama. There, HSUS staff and other instructors trained thousands of humane society and animal control personnel in the methods and techniques needed for dealing with cruelty investigation, shelter management, euthanasia, emergency and disaster relief, and illegal animal fighting.

Cruelty to Animals and Interpersonal Violence was published by Purdue University Press.

In more recent decades, partnerships with local animal care and control institutions made it possible to stage training workshops around the country. In 2002 The HSUS joined forces with the Law Enforcement Training Institute at the University of Missouri, Columbia, to train animal control and law enforcement professionals in the techniques of evidence gathering, interrogation, search and seizure, and testifying.

One of the most important areas of outreach to community-level agencies and organizations focused on the links between cruelty to animals and domestic abuse and other forms of social violence. Humane advocates have been attentive to these connections for years, and The HSUS has emphasized them since its inception. As early as 1963, academic investigators associated with the California branch of The HSUS helped to research a documentary that explored the relationship between cruelty to animals and juvenile delinquency.[51]

Randall Lockwood became the humane movement's key authority on cruelty to animals and other human violence in the mid-1980s.

The association between the mistreatment of animals and serious interpersonal violence did not become commonplace without effort, however. It reached broader public consciousness through the exertions of a diverse coalition of interests, at the heart of which stood The HSUS. From the mid-1980s on, it pushed for ways to measure and evaluate antisocial, aggressive, and destructive behaviors; advocated enhanced systems of reporting that take animal abuse into account; and sought to promote recognition of animal abuse as an important element in detection and intervention in social problems, social pathology, and psychopathology. At the same time, it tried to promote greater awareness of the degree to which animals were the targets of direct and threatened violence both within and outside of the domestic sphere.

During the same period, heightened concern for violence and its ramifications increased the opportunities for outreach on this crucial topic, and The HSUS's Randall Lockwood became the humane movement's key authority. Lockwood participated in countless training workshops aimed at law enforcement and social work professionals, forged links with FBI profilers and others who viewed cruelty to animals as an indicator of the potential to commit harsh acts of violence against humans, and provided expert testimony in a number of court cases.

In 1997 The HSUS's determination to increase public awareness of the connection between other forms of cruelty to animals and human violence coalesced as the First Strike™ initiative. A comprehensive effort to reach so-called frontline workers, legislators, animal control officers, law enforcement, judiciary, and domestic violence professionals, First Strike™ sought to persuade them of the significant overlap between forms of aggression like spousal, child, and animal abuse. Through First Strike™ The HSUS worked diligently to create and sustain interagency coalitions to better coordinate antiviolence initiatives, prosecute and punish the perpetrators of violent acts, and prevent future violence through early identification, intervention, and treatment of potential offenders and appropriate response to serious cases of animal abuse.

The HSUS First Strike™ kit contains materials for agencies, intervenors, victims of violence, and the general public.

First Strike™ also provided much-needed evidence and expertise in support of efforts by The HSUS's Government Affairs department to persuade state legislatures to pass legislation that classifies animal cruelty as a felony offense. Such groundwork has been essential to the broader campaign to incorporate animals within the scope of social work and law enforcement agencies' efforts to protect the potential victims of violence.

Lockwood's efforts to legitimize research in this area included the publication of Cruelty to Animals and Interpersonal Violence (1998), a volume co-edited with Frank Ascione of Utah State University. The work brought together classic articles from anthropology, developmental psychology, psychiatry, criminology, social work, biochemistry, sociology, and other disciplines in a single readily available source. It also helped to establish The HSUS as a source of credible psychological and social science literature on this crucial topic.

The HSUS and Higher Education

As animal issues began to receive greater attention in the 1970s and 1980s, the necessity for programs that targeted institutions of higher learning, social service agencies, and other organizations became increasingly obvious. As program objectives and the resources necessary to support them materialized, it became possible for The HSUS to undertake strong outreach efforts toward a variety of institutions and agencies. Here, too, as in the case of the traditional program areas, the addition of qualified personnel with good ideas and appropriate qualifications for advancing the organization's goals was a crucial element in The HSUS's success.

The most obvious channel for the extension of HSUS's educational programs was to colleges, universities, and graduate institutions. Focusing on humane education at the K–12 level, NAAHE had limited its contact mainly to colleges of education and to technical specialists who could help with curriculum development and related matters. With animal issues being discussed on university and college campuses, in philosophy, biology, psychology, and other fields, and campus activism on the rise, The HSUS moved to respond to the many new opportunities opening up in an era of increased concern for animals.

Before 1980 academic courses focusing on animals and society were rare. The HSUS provided crucial impetus for the inclusion of animal welfare courses in veterinary and animal science programs and, later, in the social sciences and humanities. The penetration of ethics discussions into the training of veterinarians, scientists, and psychologists was particularly notable, since consideration of moral and value issues had traditionally played only a small part in their training.

In 1985 The HSUS created a department of higher education programs. As Randall Lockwood described it, this new program area represented the natural necessary extension of traditional humane education programming, which had focused primarily on the elementary and secondary grades. "While childhood is the most sensitive period for shaping basic attitudes toward animals," he explained, "it is becoming clear that we cannot stop there." [52]

As Lockwood and other staff members recognized, the college years presented additional opportunities for humane outreach. The campus was a place where young people encountered new philosophies, ideas, and lifestyles and formed new affinities. Campus life also presented them with serious dilemmas, including ethically problematic uses of animals in undergraduate and graduate instruction, the mistreatment of domestic animals, and the prevalence of spectacles like rodeos and races that use animals in harmful or exploitive ways.

The new department incorporated and extended organizational efforts to raise the general awareness of humane issues on college campuses, serve as a reliable source of information for concerned students and faculty, initiate specific changes in curricula, investigate the treatment of animals at academic institutions, and provide guidance to students seeking to act upon their ethical concern for the welfare of animals. The HSUS would "always be available to college students," Lockwood assured, "to help them develop and preserve a humane ethic as they go through this challenging period of their lives."

In 1997 The HSUS created an annual contest and financial award to encourage the growth and refinement of courses dealing with the human-animal relationship. Submissions came from scholars in ethology, veterinary science, agricultural science, psychology, sociology, literature, history, law, philosophy, environmental ethics, and performance studies. By 2000 the number of courses offered nationwide exceeded one hundred, and approximately four thousand to five thousand students participated in such courses annually.

In the ensuing years, HSUS staff members strengthened the organization's links to institutions of higher learning by serving as instructors in animal studies programs, like the master's program in Animals and Public Policy at the Tufts University School of Veterinary Medicine, through adjunct teaching, and by regular visits to university and college campuses as lecturers, presenters, and conference participants. Staff members also collaborated with university-based scholars to produce monographs, articles, and other materials. In 2001 such collaborations found a ready forum in a new biennial public policy series, *The State of the Animals*.

The HSUS had launched HSU as an expansion of its efforts to advance understanding of animal-related concerns and to further establish the value of HSUS-sponsored training in the pursuit and development of animal-related careers. Through HSU, staff members from many local humane societies were able to take courses on-line and in person, studying practical management, social marketing, and other matters relevant to shelter operation. HSU began to coordinate many of The HSUS's efforts to disseminate its organizational knowledge, expertise, and support to professionals in law enforcement, disaster preparedness and response, and human social service. HSU also took preliminary steps toward the development of instructional programs with broad general appeal to those interested in the human-animal relationship.

Conclusion

While humane education had been a significant early priority of humane workers from the nineteenth century on, formal efforts to promote humane education had waned by 1954. The HSUS, a fledgling organization trying to establish itself, did very little to redress this situation in its early years. Beginning in the late 1960s, however, strong commitments from a succession of HSUS presidents, steady board support, staff enthusiasm, and the timely development of staff and physical facilities made The HSUS an acknowledged leader in the field of humane education. Through NAHEE and other divisions, it strove to cultivate young people's interest in animals and their care and to support them in their desire to embody the ideals of respect and compassion for all life. At the same time, NAHEE worked to assist teachers who wanted to introduce humane education into their classrooms and to provide shelter-based humane education specialists with materials, insights, and support in the execution of their programs for public and school outreach.

As The HSUS prepared to mark its fiftieth anniversary, it was an acknowledged leader in thought and action in the field of humane education, a major sponsor of research and evaluation initiatives, and a preeminent source of educational materials. Its educational division, NAHEE, had gained that stature by providing useful web resources, an expanding range of training workshops, improved marketing strategies for *KIND News* and other products, and sponsorship and analysis of research. At the same time, the organization was diligent in pushing for the integration of humane education into college-level teacher training curricula, in part through efforts to correlate its materials with the heightened interest in character education that took hold in the last years of the twentieth century.

The HSUS was also leading the way in the development of relevant adult education training programs. All of its divisions handled some aspects of higher education outreach, but staff members associated with HSU were engaged in a full agenda of reaching out to professionals in the fields of animal care and control, law enforcement, and social work. Through these and other activities, The HSUS made a crucial contribution to laying the foundations of a serious program of public and humane education in the postwar period.

CHAPTER 7

The HSUS in Action:
Field Services, Investigations, Regional Work, Disaster Relief, and International Assistance

he HSUS's original strategy for lifting the sights and the prospects of the animal protection movement's myriad local organizations rested upon the production and distribution of better educational materials, efforts to reach beyond the shelter doors to educate the broader public about humane concerns and conduct, and a determined focus on national solutions to national cruelties. But it also included a strong action-oriented program agenda, based on field work, investigations, relief services, and the projection of the organization's influence to a nationwide audience through the development of branches and affiliates. The HSUS's contemporary sections devoted to regional services, investigations, and disaster relief are the developed manifestations of Fred Myers's plan for an organization to help the humane movement meet its needs for technical and practical information and expertise, provide direct relief services in emergency situations, and confront cruelty by bringing out the facts about it to buttress reform efforts at the local, state, and federal levels.

In 1971, under John Hoyt, The HSUS established a stable system of regional offices to serve as the eyes and ears of the organization, informing the central office of trends and opportunities, representing its interests in regional affairs, and extending The HSUS's knowledge, experience, and organizational expertise to a broad range of constituencies. In addition to supporting ongoing work in The HSUS's traditional areas of concern—companion animals, laboratory animals, wildlife, and animals in agriculture, regional staff members handled cases, problems, events, contests, and miscellaneous issues that fell outside delineated programs.

Field services and investigations steadily expanded in the Hoyt era, each gaining separate section status. The HSUS's Field Services section (ceding its original duties to program staff members involved with animal sheltering, research and data services, and other areas) became responsible for a growing network of regional offices. For its part, the Investigations section pursued in-depth investigations with the goal of providing evidence to support reform initiatives. The two sections frequently combined their personnel and resources in campaigns designed to advance The HSUS's work.

During the 1970s and 1980s, disaster relief, which The HSUS pursued on an ad hoc basis, beginning in the mid-1960s, became the subject of a formal program to enhance the organization's capacity to serve. In the 1990s disaster relief assistance became a signature element in The HSUS's national and international identity. The organization that had begun modestly, pursuing relief work opportunistically and as feasible, had become a major partner in disaster relief services for animals.

The 1990s also witnessed the emergence of a robust international arm of The HSUS, Humane Society International, which was charged with extending humane work into areas of the world where needs were great and available assistance limited. HSI was an important element in The HSUS's determination to support humane work on a global basis.

As The HSUS marked its fiftieth anniversary, there was no humane organization in the world that could match its regional programs, investigating capacities, disaster relief work, and international assistance efforts. These action-oriented components of The HSUS's work made it a powerful force for animals' good.

Field Services and Investigations in the 1950s and 1960s

As might be expected in the case of a start-up organization, lack of funds limited the number of staff and programs to which The HSUS could make a commitment in the 1950s. Field services and investigative staff were among the first hires Myers made for The HSUS. Field service was an important early priority, and Larry Andrews, who had coordinated such activities at AHA, undertook similar work for The HSUS as director of field services. For several years, Andrews and his wife lived on the road, helping The HSUS to establish good relations with humane organizations and individuals across the country.

For the first decade of The HSUS's existence, field service operations included support and assistance to local societies and animal control agencies, the promotion of national issues, legislation at both the state and local levels, and the investigation of cruelty. Field workers covered a lot of territory and had many responsibilities. During the first three months of 1962, for example, HSUS staff traveled more than thirty-four thousand miles, visited forty-six local societies from Oregon to Puerto Rico, and handled inquiries from an additional thirty-seven animal care and control operations.[1]

In an era when many local societies lacked the resources to hire their own investigators or to develop strong collaboration with law enforcement authorities, HSUS field representatives provided much-needed energy and expertise in the identification, investigation, and prosecution of cruelty.[2]

As Field Services began to expand its staff in the early 1960s, it conducted The HSUS's early education and training initiatives, organized seminars for animal control officers, helped to inspect and correct conditions at local pounds, consulted with humane societies on building renovation, and assisted police with raids on animal suppliers.[3]

Fred Myers and Robert Chenoweth check blueprints at the Utah branch construction site.

Field Services comprised an essential part of The HSUS's program for improving the general field of humane work by promoting greater movement unity. In 1959 and 1960, John Miles Zucker successfully mobilized discordant factions within Puerto Rico's animal-protection community for a campaign to strengthen local animal cruelty laws. In 1960 Belton Mouras did something similar in Utah, bringing together three separate local organizations to form the Utah state branch of The HSUS. The following year Mouras repeated his success in the Dallas-Fort Worth area, uniting local leaders around a proposed animal shelter that opened later that year.[4]

Field service in the early years was closely associated with investigative work. The founding board and staff members of The HSUS not only considered investigations to be essential to the exposure of the era's "national cruelties," they also saw it as a defining element in the organization's identity. Myers, Andrews, Helen Jones, and Marcia Glaser all went into the field to gather evidence of cruelty. By 1956 The HSUS had hired its first investigators, and since then it has never been without such personnel.

The first investigators The HSUS recruited went to work in laboratories to observe and record conditions that might provide evidence of the need for national legislation to regulate animal use. One investigator worked in Tulane University laboratories. In 1958 his work there

Frank McMahon and the Pennsylvania SPCA's William Haines checked the physical condition of a boxer in a New Jersey city pound in the early 1960s.

produced evidence that animals were kept for years in inadequate caging, were subjected to unsupervised and frivolous operations and procedures by undergraduate students, and were denied post-operative care.[5]

The same year, investigator Thomas O. Hammond, an experienced animal caretaker and laboratory assistant, went to work as a laboratory technician at a medical institution in California. Hammond's revelations sparked litigation and provided early momentum to The HSUS's campaigns for laws that encompassed laboratory use of animals, including Representative Morgan Moulder's H.R. 3556, one of the first bills on the subject in the post-World War II era (see chapter 3).

Fred Myers personally participated in field work and investigations, visiting horse shows, public pounds, rodeos, slaughterhouses, and other sites of possible cruelty. His active efforts against cockfighting made him a much-vilified figure in underground publications like *Grit and Steel*.[6]

In 1962 in civil rights-era Mississippi, Myers and Director of Affiliates Philip T. Colwell, a former policeman, infiltrated a gang of dogfight enthusiasts. Colwell helped to organize a police raid on an all-day dogfighting extravaganza near Meridian. Myers followed up by pushing the FBI and the IRS to investigate whether the promoter-bookie behind the fights had been reporting his net income properly.[7]

The HSUS's determination to pursue investigative work was perpetuated under the presidency of Oliver Evans. "The outstanding quality of our Society is aggressiveness," he wrote to one potential donor. "We ask people to join and support the Society only so we can fight cruelty."[8] By the times Evans made this appeal in 1967, Frank McMahon, with six years of investigations for The HSUS under his belt, was a legendary figure within humane work. (McMahon, a Massachusetts native, had begun working with local humane groups while still in his teens. He served in the U.S. Navy between 1945 and 1949 and then came to Washington. He worked in real estate before joining The HSUS.)

During his thirteen-year career, McMahon scrutinized dozens of animal dealers; inspected hundreds of pounds and shelters; monitored zoos, circuses, and other captive wildlife enterprises; and attended more than three hundred rodeo events. His work turned up evidence that made possible the passage and subsequent revisions of the Laboratory Animal Welfare Act as well as local, state, and federal legislation concerning pound seizure, rodeos, wild horse roundups, and the soring of horses. McMahon even extended the reach of the Investigations department into the arena of marine mammal issues when he launched The HSUS's investigation of the Pribilof Islands seal harvest in the late 1960s.[9]

The basic guidelines for running an investigation were set during McMahon's tenure. Before 1970, in particular, the scope and intensity of investigations were limited by organizational finances. Budget constraints made it hard to undertake all of the work staff members considered to be important. At times, too, as in the case of animal theft and the supply of animals to laboratories (see chapter 4), issues of emerging importance and urgency claimed time and resources that might otherwise have been available for other investigations.[10]

In those years McMahon typically proposed the investigations he wanted to undertake, sometimes after reported incidents of cruelty from local societies or individuals, and discussion with administrators and fellow staff members ensued. He was sensitive to the desire of local organizations and HSUS branches to be involved in work that took place in their vicinity and, where appropriate, took steps to include them. While McMahon focused on how to plan and execute the investigation, develop information, secure photographic evidence, generate publicity, and pursue remedial action like the filing of charges, administrators concentrated on meeting the expenses involved, striking a balance between the needs of the investigation and those of other HSUS programs, and anticipating and addressing its possible legal ramifications.[11]

HSUS investigator Marc Paulhus (left) and Tennessee humane officials examined pig carcasses during a 1978 investigation that resulted in two persons being convicted of cruelty to animals.

Investigations and Field Services in the 1970s

In 1974 Frank McMahon died at age forty-eight, after a series of strokes. He was buried, as Fred Myers had been, at The HSUS's Waterford, Virginia, property, home of the National Humane Education Center. McMahon's passing marked the end of an era, but it did not end The HSUS's commitment to investigative work. Soon after the regional office structure emerged in the early 1970s, these offices began to employ their own investigators and to conduct their own investigations, many of which required steady collaboration between field representatives and Washington headquarters staff. By the mid-1970s, The HSUS had assembled an outstanding cohort of competent and experienced investigators. Frantz Dantzler, Ann Gonnerman, Marc Paulhus, Sue Pressman, Eric Sakach, Margaret Scott, Philip Steward, Bernie Weller, and Phyllis Wright were all capable of excellent investigative work, and The HSUS relied on their efforts to obtain documentation and evidence concerning dogfighting, cockfighting, greyhound racing, puppy mills, zoos, rodeos, the treatment of animals in entertainment, soring of Tennessee Walking Horses, and other issues.[12]

Celebrations of the 1976 Bicentennial Year produced a number of situations requiring the attention and energy of HSUS investigators. John Dommers of the New England Regional Office campaigned against the organizers of a greased pig contest at Old Saybrook, Connecticut, citing a law that forbade the harassment of animals for mere amusement. Investigators confiscated a number of unhealthy horses from wagons heading across the country to Valley Forge as part of the Bicentennial Wagon Train Pilgrimage to Pennsylvania. The HSUS harshly criticized organizers of the Wagon Train when they sold animals to slaughtering interests at the end of their long ride, and the society helped to purchase, and pension out, some of the animals so badly served by the escapade.[13]

The most conspicuous spectacle of animal misery to emerge during the Bicentennial was The Great American Horse Race, and here, too, HSUS investigators played a crucial role. The HSUS had sought to put an end to the race as soon as it was announced, but it was not possible to make a legal case. Owners of 150 horses, vying for a $25,000 prize, traveled from New York to California on modern-day blacktop roads. The HSUS asked local animal welfare organizations to monitor the race at all junctures, and Phil Steward attended the race's Memorial Day launch in Frankfort, New York. Even as the enterprise's organizers went bankrupt, and riders, veterinarians, and other personnel abandoned the race, The HSUS did its best to provide relief and assistance to the animals en route.[14]

Investigative, regional, and program staff members collaborated in many initiatives during the decade. In 1977 Dantzler and Jamie Cohen of ISAP teamed up with Union Pacific Railroad to develop an on-board system of transport that allowed hogs to receive "proper food, water, space, and opportunity to rest," making it possible to avoid the burdens and pitfalls of unloading trains en route to slaughtering facilities. The HSUS's harsh evaluation of earlier systems of transportation led to innovations in the design of Union Pacific's hog cars.[15]

The same year, Phil Steward and Southwest Regional Investigator Bernie Weller responded to a student's complaints about neglect and mistreatment of animals at North Texas State University. For almost two years, Steward and Weller kept the case moving, corresponding with university officials, USDA, the complainant, and local authorities. Finally The HSUS's photographic evidence of substandard conditions in the university laboratories put an end to complacency on the part of administrators, USDA inspectors, and the Denton County district attorney and resulted in positive changes within the facility.[16]

As their predecessors in the 1960s had done, 1970s-era field staff provided practical assistance and expertise to help local shelters improve their operations, negotiate with government, and troubleshoot their programs. Some investigations led to the closing of substandard kennels, or the renovation of inadequate pound facilities. The HSUS's work in this area sometimes hit the front pages of major newspapers. Weller got a pound manager fired in Pensacola, Florida, in 1975. In a case involving the Baltimore pound in 1976, The HSUS found Baltimore mayor William Donald Schaeffer receptive to its offers of assistance and counsel. Schaeffer placed a trusted aide on the case and ultimately assigned the city's public health veterinarian to full-time responsibilities at the pound.[17]

Regional staff members took on some investigations of prominent impact, too. In 1978 Sandy Rowland of the Great Lakes office signed a complaint against an Ohio man whose businesses included a pet shop, a grooming salon, a boarding kennel, and a pet cemetery. The shop was a substandard operation, and further investigation revealed that the man killed puppies he judged would not sell, hitting them on the heads with a hammer or wrench.[18]

The HSUS continued to investigate the animal trade in the 1970s, providing damaging evidence of overcrowded conditions; inadequate food, water, and shelter; and other improprieties at animal auctions and trade day sales in one Mississippi community. On one occasion Frantz Dantzler found twenty dogs crammed into a makeshift cage fitted onto a pickup truck. His colleague Marc Paulhus found fighting cocks for sale, even though cockfighting was illegal in the state. In January 1977 The HSUS threatened to sue the city of Ripley, Mississippi, in an effort to halt its monthly animal sale, an especially egregious occasion for neglect and mistreatment of animals. Some years later The HSUS used its knowledge of the Ripley flea market to force the University of Mississippi Medical School, then the subject of The HSUS's administrative complaint for violations of the AWA, to abandon its practice of purchasing at Ripley trade days.[19]

Budgetary constraints played a role in determining investigations strategy and forced investigations staff to develop criteria for the selection of cases to pursue. Investigators took into consideration the national or regional import of an investigation, the number of animals involved, and the prospects for local cooperation. But no single criterion was determinative, and The HSUS tried to stay true to its founding vision of providing principled and competent assistance to those seeking to help animals in need, whatever their circumstances and wherever they might be.[20]

The selection and development of investigative personnel has been one of The HSUS's most challenging burdens. Some have proved to be fearless in their dealings with animal abusers but lacked the finesse needed to interact with law enforcement officials and animal control agencies. Provoked by official indifference or outright neglect in the face of terrible cruelty, investigators sometimes found it difficult to contain their outrage. In the interests of achieving immediate relief or humane improvements, however, in-

A dog peers from a crowded, makeshift pen on the back of a truck during a Ripley, Mississippi, animal auction.

vestigators moderated their tone and approach where necessary, negotiating with responsible officials, advancing logical arguments and proposals, offering practical or technical assistance, and pursuing extended dialogue. In other cases, investigators chose to remind author-

Frantz Dantzler, a former aerospace electronics technician, was interviewed by a television crew against a backdrop of corralled wild horses in Idaho Falls, Idaho, in 1974.

ities in diplomatic tenor of the negative press coverage that would ensue in the event that corrective measures were not taken. On the rare occasion, too, The HSUS weighed in more fully with a threat of legal action. Handling these options in a range of situations where animals' lives were literally at stake demanded tact, discretion, sensitivity, and determination, and The HSUS employed many individuals so endowed throughout its history.[21]

HSUS investigators came from a variety of professional backgrounds. Bob Baker (with The HSUS from 1980 to 1993) was a stockbroker. Gail Eisnitz was a photographer. Lisa Landres was an elephant trainer. Eric Sakach was an illustrator. Frantz Dantzler began his working life as an aerospace electronics technician.

Former law enforcement personnel also served The HSUS very well. Phil Colwell, Bernie Weller, and Bob Reder were all ex-policemen who performed effectively as investigators. Although there were and always would be important exceptions, it frequently proved easier to socialize law enforcement professionals with the values and approaches of the humane movement than to provide knowledgeable humane advocates with the skills, background, and insights that could only be gained through direct experience with law enforcement. In this way The HSUS brought experienced, seasoned investigators into its ranks. Such precedents set the stage for the hiring of Rick Swain, a former Montgomery County, Maryland, police captain (who as a detective sergeant had been assigned to the Silver Spring monkeys case in 1981) as head of investigations for The HSUS in 1996.[22]

HSUS Gulf States investigator Bernie Weller was a former police officer.

In some instances investigators brought with them a serious interest in a particular issue, which then made its way onto the investigations agenda of The HSUS. In 1980, for example, Bob Baker, a former horse owner who had authored a book on the misuse of drugs in racing, drew The HSUS into investigations of the drugging of racehorses to numb or mask the pain of their injuries. Investigators interviewed jockeys, racetrack veterinarians, horse owners, track operators, trainers, and others. Staff members testified before state racing commissions in six states, and their work resulted in a restriction of drug use in most of these instances. The HSUS also worked with the American Horse Protection Association (AHPA) for legislation in Congress to prohibit the use of drugs in horseracing and helped to draft model legislation to curb abuses. While no bills were passed, Senate hearings were held, and furor over the issue produced a number of reforms within the industry.[23]

As The HSUS developed and enhanced its program staff, its investigators were increasingly able to take advantage of the skills and knowledge within the organization. Frequently, however, investigators developed their expertise on a particular topic through their work and later were able to provide expert support not only for future investigations but for program work as well. Marc Paulhus, who made himself an expert on equine issues, eventually moved from investigations and regional office management to vice president of The HSUS's Companion Animals section. Paulhus and Eric Sakach of the West Coast Regional Office exemplified the successful path of service that led from an investigator's position to the position of regional director.[24]

A number of significant national campaigns waged by The HSUS first arose from the work of regional investigators. The puppy mills campaign that took off as a national effort in the early 1990s came out of investigations carried out in the Midwest. For years the New Jersey regional office waged a struggle against a deer hunt held in the Great Swamp National Wildlife Refuge. This effort presaged The HSUS's broad commitment to reform in the nation's wildlife refuge management policies.[25]

At least one campaign that emerged from regional work reached the U.S. Supreme Court, after Southeast Regional Director Paulhus began to investigate Santeria animal sacrifice in the Miami vicinity. Paulhus's work led to the enactment of a legislative ban on animal sacrifice in the community of Hialeah, Florida, in June 1987. When the constitutionality of the law was challenged, both Paulhus and Michael Fox appeared as expert witnesses, Paulhus on the species and methods used and Fox on animals' pain. After the law was upheld in this trial and affirmed by the appellate court in Atlanta, it went to the U.S. Supreme Court, which reversed the decision—ruling that the law was too specifically directed toward a single religious organization—and declared the ban unconstitutional.[26]

Dispelling fears that this decision might encourage the proliferation of animal sacrifice as a protected religious practice, the Supreme Court held that governments could enforce more broadly based regulation or prohibition of animal sacrifice, including an extant anticruelty statute. HSUS Southeast Regional staff member Ken Johnson was paying attention. In June 1993, after the U.S. Supreme Court decision, Rigoberto Zamora, a Miami Santeria practitioner, publicly performed a Santeria ritual in which he killed three goats and one sheep by slitting their throats. Johnson videotaped the incident, in which one goat continued to bleat after being cut.[27]

In July 1995 Zamora was charged with four counts of animal cruelty (for the manner in which the animals were handled) under Florida's anticruelty statute, and his motion to have them dismissed on the grounds of religious freedom was rejected. The HSUS's Michael Fox and Melanie Adcock, both veterinarians, assisted the prosecution. The next year Zamora pled no contest: he received two years' probation and four hundred hours of community service. This conviction was upheld in 1997.[28]

HSUS investigations could become very elaborate, involving regional staff and national investigators in a collaborative effort to procure the evidence needed to attack cruelties on a national level. In the 1980s Bob Baker, Frantz Dantzler, Paul Miller, and Sandy Rowland participated in a complex operation that targeted a notorious high-volume animal dealer known to carry dogs across state lines without the required vaccination certificates on his way to deliver animals to major laboratories in his home state. The plan was to follow his tractor trailer (a triple-decker hog transport) from a dog auction in Routledge, Missouri, one of his many stops, all the way to Pennsylvania, where humane investigators in that state would use a prearranged warrant to stop the truck. Unfortunately, someone in the law enforcement chain tipped off the regional USDA representative on what was afoot, and the dealer paid a veterinarian to issue false certificates for the three hundred animals he was carrying.[29]

While investigating an animal-hoarding case in 1962, HSUS Director of Affiliates Philip T. Colwell found a puppy, only a few days old, in a cardboard box in a New Jersey dump. With the help of local humane agents, Colwell caught and removed almost fifty additional dogs and cats from the vicinity.

Despite this disappointment, Baker and Dantzler procured some excellent footage of sick and crowded animals in the dealer's transport vehicle. Later, their video and photographic evidence were crucial to the designation of dog theft as a felony in Michigan, Missouri, Pennsylvania, and Tennessee.[30]

Because so many practices in which animals were used and harmed continued to flourish despite the best efforts of the nation's humane community, the investigations staff frequently found it necessary to revisit areas in which The HSUS had already invested substantial effort. In the late 1990s the Investigations section conducted investigations of puppy mills, rodeo practices, and the Tennessee Walking Horse industry, all long-standing concerns that several generations of HSUS investigators had targeted in their work. However, the section also incorporated investigations focused on emerging concerns, like the slaughter of Canada geese by municipal authorities, the launching of an intensive egg-production facility by a shady entrepreneur, and the evolving trade in frogs for dissection.

Throughout its history the section perpetuated The HSUS's long commitment to positive collaboration with prosecutors and other law enforcement personnel in relevant cases. The HSUS provided investigative support and evidence, clarified the meaning and implications of anticruelty statutes, helped to identify targets for scrutiny, and sent its investigators out into the field with representatives of local societies and law enforcement agencies.

In the years following Rick Swain's appointment, The HSUS centralized its investigative functions, provided the section with its own budget, and gave it autonomy to strike a balance among its own priorities, the opportunities for new areas of investigation that randomly arose, and the expressed needs of program staff for reliable information and evidence about ongoing or emerging forms of cruelty. In this way the investigative capabilities of The HSUS were integrated as components of a larger strategy.[31]

At the same time, The HSUS took all reasonable steps to enhance its investigations team, adding skilled staff members with appropriate backgrounds in law enforcement, fraud investigation, and journalism, among other fields. In a world where laboratory animal suppliers, circus moguls, furriers, and agricultural interests spent a fortune on research, investigation, and other measures designed to discredit animal advocates, The HSUS responded by developing an Investigations section whose sophistication and professionalism had few equals in the nonprofit sector.

For fifty years, from its early efforts to publicize the highly visible cruelties of rodeos and soring, to its international investigations of the fur trade's darkest secrets, there was almost no arena of The HSUS's work that investigators did not influence through their activities. Their crucial contributions provided the facts and evidence needed to support the organization's program work, legislative agenda, and ongoing efforts to reach the public with the facts about cruelty to animals.

The Classic Investigations and Campaigns

Rodeo
With the exception of The HSUS's outstanding investigations of animal dealers, leading up to passage of the AWA (see chapter 3), few of its investigative activities before 1975 garnered more publicity than its persistent campaigning against rodeos and "bloodless bullfights." In these efforts The HSUS demonstrated that it would go anywhere to challenge the cruelties of these events and use legal methods to suppress them.

Its efforts against rodeos dated back to the organization's earliest years. The HSUS helped to organize the Wyoming Humane Society in 1958 and supported that organization's efforts to compel reforms in rodeos held in the state. In the late 1950s and early 1960s, Myers, Helen Jones, and other HSUS staff members regularly protested rodeos scheduled in Washington, D.C., and other communities.[32]

In 1961 The HSUS petitioned the Federal Communications Commission (FCC) to deny licenses to any stations that offer cruelty as entertainment, advancing the legal theory that this violated the requirement that such stations be operated "in the public interest." Later The HSUS filed suit in federal court in Washington, D.C., to block NBC-TV from televising rodeos in any state where its practices may violate the anticruelty statutes. "The essence of our request for an injunction," said Fred Myers, "is that the NBC method of telecasting rodeo cruelties is inimical to the public interest and is therefore a violation of the conditions under which television stations are granted licenses to use the publicly-owned radio frequencies." In the end, both the FCC and the court declined to act upon The HSUS's entreaties.[33]

Several years later, after NBC broadcast a ninety-minute show on Spanish bullfights, complete with an announcer who repeatedly called the events "beautiful" and praised the human participants for their courage, The HSUS continued to protest to the FCC. "The nation's most eminent and authoritative psychologists and psychiatrists are virtually unanimous in the opinion that such programs are adverse to the public interest—that they are psychologically harmful to children as well as adults," The HSUS's letter of protest read.[34]

In 1965 HSUS investigators made a strong push to expose rodeo's cruelties. Field representative Dale Hylton joined local societies in Nevada to protest the staging of bloodless bullfights in Las Vegas. Hylton publicized the events and their violation of Nevada's anticruelty laws. Frank McMahon testified on behalf of a bill to prohibit rodeos in Ohio. Traveling to West Virginia, both men denounced a rodeo event in White Sulphur Springs and signed a complaint charging one contestant with cruelty after a calf's leg was broken in a roping contest. "Cowboys seem to be very brave when it comes to jerking an animal around on the end of a rope, but not when it comes to facing a magistrate," Hylton observed.[35]

Dale Hylton presenting evidence of cruelty to rodeo animals to a special committee of the West Virginia legislature in 1966.

The HSUS appealed to the nation's most prominent Texan, President Lyndon Johnson, and to state and local officials to intervene when a series of "bloodless" bullfights was scheduled at the Houston Astrodome in February 1966. At "bloodless" bullfights, bulls were tormented, precisely as in the more commonly known form of these spectacles, by horsemen and matadors in capes. Many animals were injured during these events, even though the bull was not actually killed. In his letter The HSUS's Oliver Evans suggested that the events undercut the president's anticrime initiative, not only through their sheer violence and degradation but also through their flouting of extant anticruelty laws in the state of Texas. The president declined to intervene, but the Texas state's attorney filed an unsuccessful petition to stop the fights.[36]

The HSUS targeted the Houston event because its sponsor was planning events of the same kind at arenas around the country. As part of The HSUS's exploration of legal and other channels for the suppression of such events, Frank McMahon went to Houston with the aim of filing charges if any instances of demonstrable cruelty occurred. His presence was also part of The HSUS's attempt to develop evidence that the bullfights did result in animals' injury and the flow of blood. After witnessing banderillas pierce the Styrofoam protection guards covering the bulls' shoulders and penetrate their flesh, McMahon went looking for a local judge to issue a warrant charging participants in the contest with cruelty, but he could find none.[37]

In April 1966 McMahon's efforts to thwart the staging of another bullfight, this one in Cherry Hill, New Jersey, touched off a major confrontation. McMahon and Kay Clausing of Camden's Animal Welfare Association, an HSUS affiliate, generated sufficient publicity to drive the promoters across the river to Philadelphia. In a chaotic series of decisions, the promoters were first denied and then granted a permit from municipal authorities. The Pennsylvania SPCA and the Women's SPCA sought to stop the exhibitions through a restraining order. The judge first denied this request but retained jurisdiction over the case. After attending the first night's event to see for himself, he issued a next-day injunction barring "bloodless" bullfights as a "violation of law and a common public nuisance."[38]

Some time later staff members Patrick Parkes and Dale Hylton thwarted the effort to bring the bullfights to Washington, D.C., by meeting with the District of Columbia corporation counsel. After they showed him the film taken at the February event in Houston, the corporation counsel agreed that laws would be broken if the spectacles were staged in the nation's capital.[39]

A similar battle by members of the Animal Protective League resulted in a favorable ruling in Milwaukee, Wisconsin. However, promoters of the "bloodless" bullfight then attempted to switch the event to Waukesha County, thirty miles from the city. They also sued Wisconsin officials and the Animal Protective League of Milwaukee to prevent them from seeking an injunction against the rescheduled fights. The HSUS sent Frank McMahon, who testified in the circuit court and stipulated that The HSUS would become a named party in the suit.[40]

Unfortunately, the judge ruled in favor of the bullfight promoters in the Wisconsin case and denied rights of inspection to The HSUS and the Animal Protective League. As McMahon entered the arena, the announcer denounced The HSUS and its efforts to stop the event. McMahon was assigned a police escort and was followed everywhere he went.[41]

The poorly attended event was another setback for promoters, but the fight was not over. "Unquestionably," McMahon observed, "we are going to have to face many more attempts to schedule these spectacles….We can guarantee these promoters that there will be a 'fight to the death.' It will be a fight by The HSUS and its friends to eliminate all forms of bullfighting from our country."[42]

The HSUS had greater success in its efforts to ensure that bullfights would not be broadcast on television. In late 1966 the National Association of Broadcasters announced that arena bullfight events violated the Television Code to which approximately 65 percent of stations adhered.[43]

At the same time, half a dozen state legislatures were considering bills to prohibit the use of bucking straps, electric prods, and pain-producing devices in rodeos. In December 1966 Virginia campaigner Pearl Twyne described some of rodeo's most blatant cruelties on the CBS-TV's *Evening News* with Walter Cronkite.[44]

In 1967 the battle against both rodeos and "bloodless" bullfights heated up in half a dozen states. Humane advocates defeated rodeo and bullfight promoters in hearing rooms, legislative halls, and in the court of public opinion, registering decisive victories. Ohio's legislature was a crucial battleground, and HSUS staff members provided powerful testimony to refute the claims of veterinarians appearing on behalf of the Rodeo Cowboys Association and other interests. Humane advocates succeeded in defeating the rodeo interests' attempt to amend the Ohio law outlawing bucking straps and other pain-producing devices.[45]

Another round of the "bloodless" bullfight battle took place in Seattle, Washington, where a temporary restraining order put the fate of one such exhibition on hold until tried in a court of law. The HSUS's Texas film footage strongly influenced the judge in the case. This time, promoters of the fight responded by suing advocates Gertrude Peck and former HSUS director Arthur Redman for $200,000 in damages.[46]

One of the most serious obstacles to success emerged when rodeo promoters began to cite the support their events received from AHA. Branding The HSUS as the most radical antirodeo group in the country, a representative of the Rodeo Cowboys Association stated that AHA "works with us in the spirit of full cooperation" and that if all organizations were like AHA, "we'd have no problems." HSUS President Oliver Evans responded by condemning AHA's

Ohio humane activists and The HSUS's Frank McMahon (right) demonstrated placement of a bucking strap to state Senator Charles Carney, member of the Ohio Senate's Agriculture and State Agency Committee in 1967.

practice of "playing footsie" with rodeo interests, and Frank McMahon, commenting on an incident in Baltimore, observed, "strangely, our men seem to be able to see things that escape AHA agents, and the rodeo promoters seem scared that we see too much." [47]

In 1969 and 1970, The HSUS continued to push for legislation in several state legislatures.[48] Working with the affiliated Youngstown, Ohio, Animal Charity League, The HSUS brought a successful court action against rodeo promoters who permitted illegal use of the bucking strap in their events.[49]

The HSUS struck a great blow against rodeos with its formal petition to the FCC to prohibit the televised broadcast of rodeo on the grounds that the animals appear to be wild only as a result of an arsenal of devices used to inflict pain upon them. The contest, portrayed to the viewer as one between a lone and skillful cowboy and a wild and dangerous animal, "is a mere sham," The HSUS's petition stated.[50]

ROCKY MOUNTAIN NEWS

The cinching of a bucking strap on a horse coming out of the bucking chute made the rodeo industry's claim that horses buck "for the fun of it" a lot harder to believe when this photo appeared in the HSUS "Buck Rodeo" campaign.

Because weak anticruelty laws made it difficult to mount challenges to the events in some states, McMahon and others ultimately concluded that a federal prohibition of "bloodless" bullfights was the right solution.[51] In 1971 Representative William F. Ryan (D-NY) introduced a bill to prohibit interstate shipment of any animal for use in steer busting, calf roping, or steer wrestling at public events. The bill also proposed a ban on the buying, selling, and shipment of bucking straps, electric prods, steer bells, and other devices designed to make animals appear wild." [52]

By this time investigator Bernie Weller and field representative Guy Hodge were also monitoring the rodeo circuit. Hodge was surprised to discover that announcers at one Virginia rodeo told the audience that the horses used in bucking events were not wild. Weller (a onetime rodeo cowboy and livestock handler) attended the Klamath Falls, Oregon, rodeo, ill-famed in humane circles because sponsors rounded up wild horses by airplane for the rodeo and then sold them at auction afterward. Weller's partner in the investigation was Elizabeth Sakach of the Animal Welfare League of Reno, Nevada, whose son, Eric, would forge a long career as an investigator and regional director for The HSUS.[53]

In 1976, some five years after The HSUS's 1971 petition was filed, the FCC denied it on the grounds of violation of the First Amendment and doubts about whether rodeos were cruel.[54] At the same time, The HSUS continued to challenge both rodeos and bloodless bullfights in intermittent skirmishes, usually through its field offices. In 1985 the organization fought rodeo promoters in courtrooms and the Ohio legislature in a failing effort to defend the statute prohibiting rodeo cruelties, two decades after helping to secure its passage. The following year the Gulf States Regional Office assisted Texas officials trying to put a stop to the Huntsville prison rodeo.[55]

In the mid-1980s, HSUS investigators also went to the Omak Stampede Rodeo in Washington State, whose signature event, the Suicide Race, featured twenty horses and their riders rushing down a steep incline at a heart-stopping pace. Investigators Kurt Lapham and Eric Sakach believed their presence as observers made a difference, and negative publicity about the continuing deaths of equine participants resulted in a wholesale flight from sponsorship by major corporations once tied to the stampede.[56]

By the 1990s The HSUS was less active on the rodeo and bullfighting fronts. This was, in large measure, a result of the organization's program and policy review work, which assigned a lower priority to these issues than to other program areas. However, regional offices continued to work on the issue. Staff members observed many problems at Cheyenne, Wyoming's Frontier Days Rodeo, the so-called Daddy of 'em all.[57]

Soring

The "soring" of horses provides another classic example of The HSUS's early efforts to combine investigative work with hard-hitting public awareness campaigns and legislative redress. The focus of its efforts was the Tennessee Walking Horse, a breed descended from the southern plantation horse. A hidden cruelty lay behind the spectacle of the walking horse performing in a ring, with forelegs thrown high. Many owners and trainers produced the walker's award-winning gait not through training but by blistering the horse's legs, fetlocks, or feet through the use of chains, oil of mustard, oxide of mercury, nails, and other methods. Soring had proven to be impossible to stem through local or state anticruelty statutes.

The HSUS first began to report on its attempts to address horse show cruelties in 1960, policing events in Virginia, Maryland, and Pennsylvania, usually in cooperation with Pearl Twyne of the Virginia Federation of Humane Societies. In Virginia, where the anticruelty statute prohibited animals from being "over-ridden and ill-treated," The HSUS was able to file charges of cruelty against a nationally recognized horse trainer and one socially prominent exhibitor. The conviction of a Lynchburg horseman for exhibiting a horse with sored feet gained nationwide publicity.[58]

In late 1960 the Nashville Humane Association filed a complaint against three horse trainers for mistreating animals in their care. Believing that the case had national importance, The HSUS launched the first serious national campaign against cruelty to horses in show rings.

From that time on, The HSUS was a leader in the effort to investigate and expose the cruel methods involved in the showing and/or sale of horses whose gait was altered through painful procedures.[59]

After the Nashville case, Fred Myers, Patrick Parkes, and John Miles Zucker spent many weekends in Maryland, Pennsylvania, and Virginia monitoring the shows for cruelty. HSUS staff members corresponded and met with various horse show officials and were able to discourage some of the worst soring methods, like barbed wire in the feet. However, lack of funds and recognition that the number of animals involved was small in comparison to other cruelties limited The HSUS's pursuit of the campaign after 1964.[60]

By this time, however, Pearl Twyne and Joan Blue (d. 1986) of the AHPA were also very active on the issue, and The HSUS worked closely with them. In 1966 a bill to prohibit cruelty to Tennessee Walking Horses surfaced in the U.S. Congress.[61] In 1968 the Virginia legislature banned the infliction of pain or injury to the front hooves

An investigator for the Nashville Humane Association examines "soring" chains.

or legs of horses for the purpose of competition.[62] Twyne joined Blue in the effort to ensure successful enactment of Public Law 91-540 in 1970, treating the movement of "sored" horses as a matter of interstate commerce, to ban the use of blistering agents, burns, cuts, lacerations, or other cruel or inhumane methods or devices for modifying a horse's gait through pain.[63]

The Horse Protection Act of 1970 prohibited interstate shipment of sored horses, and it included a prohibition on the use of blistering agents, tacks, chains, and other instruments as well as a provision to make owners, trainers, and horse show promoters liable for any sored horses under their responsibility. The new regulations created considerable tumult and controversy at horse shows, as The HSUS cooperated with government officials, local organizations, and other national societies in an effort to see the law strictly enforced. Enforcement fell to USDA, in part because the passage of the Horse Protection Act happened to coincide with the approval of amendments to the AWA that same year.[64]

In the years that followed, Frank McMahon teamed up with Joan Blue to observe walking horse contests, and they continued to uncover evidence of animals with raw and oozing sores in the shows. They found USDA's enforcement efforts wholly inadequate. Of one show, McMahon reported, "The USDA has the right to pull pads and shoes from the horses, but this was not done, even in cases where horses were so sored that they limped or fell out of the show arena."[65]

At an oversight hearing in May 1973, McMahon told members of the Environment Sub-committee of the Senate Commerce Committee that The HSUS was receiving regular complaints about flagrant soring of Tennessee Walking Horses, despite regulations that had been in effect for over a year. McMahon, who harshly criticized USDA inspection procedures in his testimony,[66] was pleased to note that enforcement actions under the Horse Protection Act of 1970 rose after his appearance before the committee.[67]

Unfortunately, this diligence in enforcement practices did not last long, and the situation got worse in one respect. "Back in the 'sixties, it wasn't uncommon to see horses that were bleeding profusely right in the show ring," Patrick Parkes, HSUS vice president for field services, recalled in 1988. "The abuses were much more apparent than they are today. You couldn't attend a show without seeing scarred legs and bloody, open wounds." By the time Parkes made this observation, the industry had introduced a greater sophistication, making use of corrosive chemicals like diesel fuel and mustard oil, shoeing the animals tightly, trimming hooves down to their sensitive tissue, and concealing sharp objects like glass and nails between a horse's hoof and padded shoe.[68]

In 1984 AHPA filed suit against USDA, charging apathetic enforcement of the law first passed in 1970 and then strengthened in 1976. Four years later a federal court ruled in AHPA's favor, and USDA issued emergency regulations banning some of the objectionable practices. The Walking Horse industry—a $150 million concern that accounted for 4,500 jobs in Tennessee—quickly mobilized to fight.[69]

In 2000 The HSUS was still fighting the cruelty of soring, as Tennessee Walking Horse enthusiasts made use of more subtle chemicals and anesthetics to mask the impact of their misconduct. Political lobbying—to render USDA oversight ineffectual—and deceptive tactics within and outside of the show ring were the industry's stock in trade.[70]

Wild Horses

The HSUS's involvement with wild horse concerns dates back to the late 1950s, when it first placed its support behind Velma "Wild Horse Annie" Johnston's crusade to save the wild horses and burros of the West from mustangers, who brutally captured them to sell to pet food manufacturers and rendering plants and ranchers who sought to crowd the animals off land they preferred to use for cattle grazing. Before Johnston began her crusade, the number of wild horses and burros fell from an estimated two million at the turn of the century to just tens of thousands. The HSUS supported Johnston's 1959 campaign for a law to prohibit planes and trucks from rounding up wild equines.[71]

In August 1968 The HSUS filed suit against the Department of the Interior to stop the pending Bureau of Land Management (BLM) roundup and slaughter for dog food of a mustang herd in the Pryor Mountain region of Montana and Wyoming. Ultimately, Secretary of the Interior Morris Udall designated the Pryor Mountain area as a wild horse refuge, added acreage, and established a BLM committee (with Velma Johnston and Pearl Twyne as members) to determine the number of animals that the area could realistically support.[72]

In 1969 The HSUS again came to the rescue of wild horse populations when heavy snows trapped three hundred mustangs in central and northern Nevada. Nel-

The HSUS organized a hay drop for three hundred starving mustangs trapped by heavy snows in Nevada and later provided food and relief for animal victims of Hurricane Camille on the Gulf Coast in 1969.

Velma "Wild Horse Annie" Johnston received the 1972 Krutch Medal from HSUS President John Hoyt.

THE PHOTOMAKER

lis Air Force Base officials donated a C-54 aircraft and volunteers to load and fly a planeload of hay to the starving animals. The HSUS's Frank McMahon was on the scene, using a "spotter" plane to locate the trapped herds.[73]

With the passage of the Wild, Free-roaming Horse and Burro Act of 1971, the terms of battle for wild horse protection changed dramatically. Now, the nation's wild horses were to be "managed and protected" by the federal government. If thinning out herds was necessary, it was to be done with care, and a program was to be set up to provide suitable homes for them.[74]

In 1972 The HSUS honored Johnston with its highest honor, the Joseph Wood Krutch Medal. However, as all parties knew, the passage of the 1971 Act did not ensure the horses' protection from the assaults of ranching interests. Threats to the wild horse population continued to surface, as ranchers exploited every opportunity to reduce the horse population.[75]

In 1973 regional staff member Frantz Dantzler and wildlife representative Hal Perry saved twenty-nine horses from slaughter at a dog food cannery after investigating an incident in which seven wild horses had been driven off a cliff in Idaho. Johnston drew them into the case after getting a tip from an informant who had participated in an illegal roundup and slaughter of horses with a helicopter. Another twenty-five horses had died as a consequence of shock and injury en route to a canning company in Nebraska, to which HSUS investigators traced their shipment. In Washington, D.C., Frank McMahon pressed this issue with officials of the BLM, as The HSUS tried to penetrate the lies that enveloped the story of how the horses had died. HSUS investigators provided shocking evidence of cruelty, lack of compliance with federal regulations, and illegal conduct in the episode, whose specific details were far more grisly than they felt comfortable reporting on for *HSUS News*. Fifteen months after the incident, the federal government had taken no action, and The HSUS and AHPA brought suit against USDA and the Department of the Interior to gain access to their documented investigations of the BLM's failure to enforce the Wild, Free-roaming Horse and Burro Act. John Hoyt publicly criticized the government's inaction in a statement before the Wild Horse and Burro Advisory Board, stating that its lack of initiative in the matter "has resulted in a cruel hoax being perpetrated on the public by leading them to believe the law is now being effectively enforced."[76]

Dantzler condemned the peculiar brand of "Idaho justice" that led the state's brand inspector to declare that the surviving horses were owned by the very ranchers responsible for the grisly roundup. The horses bore no brand marks, and the ranchers had failed to observe procedures required by the Wild, Free-roaming Horse and Burro Act. In a public reaction to the ruling, Dantzler reviewed the details of the roundup, declaring The HSUS's dismay "that the horses may be returned to the same people who clamped hog rings in their noses, slit the throats and cut off the legs of horses whose hooves got caught among rocks, and drove uncooperative horses off a cliff."[77]

In late 1974 a federal judge ruled for the government in the suit filed by The HSUS and AHPA, even as western ranchers sought to have the Act declared unconstitutional. Dantzler's increasing knowledge of the roundup program, and his experience with government officials' obfuscation, led him to charge that the BLM was "a slave to cattle raisers' vested interests."[78] In 1976 The HSUS and AHPA teamed up to secure a permanent injunction to stop the BLM-authorized roundup in Challis, Idaho.[79]

In 1977, Dantzler, then HSUS director of field services, testified before the Senate Subcommittee on Public Lands and Resources in efforts to protect the gains embodied in the Act. The following year, Dantzler and Marc Paulhus testified before a similar House committee to fight off attempts to weaken humane safeguards previously incorporated into the BLM's Adopt-a-Horse Program. The HSUS investigators presented graphic evidence of the horrors and the practical deficiencies of the BLM program, especially the wholesale adoption of horses by individuals who later sold them to slaughterhouses, rendering plants, and rodeos for profit.[80]

Dantzler showed the House committee evidence of serious deficiencies in the BLM's own Palomino Valley Holding Area near Reno, Nevada. In one year the BLM had buried three hundred of two thousand horses near the site, and it was not hard to discover why. It was no place to keep horses. The corrals were packed with mud, and the animals had no protection from the cold and rain. The pens lacked drainage, and the lower sections were flooded. The animals had to eat their hay off of the muddy ground. Many horses showed signs of disease, but there was no veterinary treatment provided and no effort made to separate the healthy from the sick animals.[81]

Eventually, The HSUS joined with AHPA in a lawsuit against the Department of the Interior, charging that the BLM had mismanaged its wild horse program with terrible conse-

HSUS President John Hoyt, AHPA President Joan Blue, AHPA spokesman Lorne Green (of TV's Bonanza), author Hope Ryden, and HSUS Assistant General Counsel Roger Kindler celebrate the permanent injunction against the Challis, Idaho, wild horse roundup.

quences for the animals it rounded up. The suit asked that the BLM be forced to conduct an environmental impact study before every roundup and that it be enjoined from conducting any further roundups until its own holding area was managed humanely, in accordance with the law. The suit also sought to halt the abuse of wild horses under the adoption program.[82]

In January 1979 Dantzler provided information to ABC-TV's *20/20* for a feature segment on the BLM's mismanagement of the Adopt-a-Horse Program. Collaboration with AHPA remained very strong. In 1980 The HSUS and AHPA filed suit to stop eradication of the burros in the Grand Canyon.[83]

By the mid-1980s, the wild horse issue had become a program concern of The HSUS's Wildlife section and was also the subject of legislative initiatives at the federal level. In August 1984 the campaign for wild horses hit rock bottom, as the Ninety-eighth Congress tacked on nearly $17 million to a Department of the Interior appropriations bill for the purpose of rounding up more than seventeen thousand horses and burros—more than 35 percent of the estimated number on the nation's public lands. Western senators, led by Senator James McClure (R-ID), advanced dubious claims about the impact of wild horses and burros on the public lands in support of a new strategy that made use of the appropriations process rather than seek expanded authority for the BLM to sell the horses it did round up.[84]

After the BLM went through the $16.7 million windfall that resulted from McClure's gambit, a terrible glut of unadopted animals ensued. The capacity of adoption programs to deal with this population was limited, and the excess numbers set the stage for additional legislation granting the BLM the authority to sell the horses to anyone it chose—including rodeo and slaughterhouse interests.[85] Representative Bill Green (D-NY) had introduced provisions in the House appropriations bill to delete support for roundup and sale authority, but his move was blocked on procedural grounds.[86]

In 1990, almost two decades after the passage of legislation designed to halt American ranchers' war against wild horses, it was still going on, under the hapless auspices of the BLM. The HSUS continued to highlight the injustice of the agency's decimation of a population of just tens of thousands of horses while some 4.5 million domestic livestock roamed the lands. Against this onslaught The HSUS advocated a balanced approach that included recognition of the place of wild horses and burros on public lands.[87]

Chincoteague

As the history of its rodeo investigations suggested, The HSUS never let the argument of tradition prevent it from taking action against cruelty. But this commitment was also put to the test in other instances, like that of the Chincoteague, Virginia, horses, purportedly descended from those who survived the shipwreck of a Spanish galleon carrying wild mustangs to the New World in the sixteenth century, but more likely the descendants of animals turned loose by early settlers. Pony penning had its origins in livestock owners' need to claim, brand, break, and harness animals. By the early eighteenth century, penning had become an annual ritual event, festive and time honored.

The swim across the Assateague Channel (which separates the thirty-seven-mile-long sandbar off the Maryland-Virginia coast from the community of Chincoteague on the Delmarva Peninsula) dates from 1925. It developed from the decision to stage a fund-raising carnival for the Chincoteague Volunteer Fire Company in conjunction with the pony penning event. Attending crowds swelled by the late 1930s, and in 1947 the fire company began to add animals to the herd through purchases. The horses were permitted to graze on the recently established Chincoteague National Wildlife Refuge. Marguerite Henry's children's classic *Misty of Chincoteague* (1947) brought international attention to the pony penning event.

By the late 1960s, the auction sponsored by the fire department was the occasion of many disturbing practices. It was particularly brutal in 1971, the year Frank McMahon, Phyllis Wright, and Donna Truslow saw fights break out among stallions defending their bands, day-old foals separated from their mothers and sold, horses denied proper food and water, successful bidders carrying away their ponies without supervision, and not a single veterinarian on hand. Buyers jammed foals into trunks and backseats of cars, attendants beat animals with bullwhips and wooden boards, and firemen subjected the horses to harsh branding. The crowd gained further entertainment from the staging of "wild pony rides."[88]

In the early 1970s, The HSUS received permission from the Department of the Interior to supervise the roundup on Assateague. Subsequent negotiations led to other modifications, including the prohibition of sales of foals without teeth, the end of hot branding of adult horses, the segregation of stallions on Assateague Island, and the requirement that buyers provide adequate means of transporting their new horses from the site. Phil Steward continued to monitor the event during the mid-1970s and judged that organizers were doing a better job of complying with humane standards.[89]

When HSUS investigator Mark Paulhus went to Chincoteague in 1981, however, he discovered many of the agreed upon rules being flouted by the firemen. Foals as young as two

Mares, newly separated from their foals, were mounts in Chincoteague "wild pony rides."

or three weeks old were being auctioned off, and they were still being carted off in vans, box trucks, and other ill-equipped vehicles. Mares were forced into rodeo-type chutes, where those who wanted to test their "riding skills" mounted them as they were let into the corral." [90]

In the late 1980s, HSUS investigator Gail Eisnitz monitored the pony penning at Chincoteague. By then, The HSUS had added the charge that the fire company failed to provide the ponies with appropriate year-round care to its bill of indictments. The fire com-

THE HSUS/ROVNER

Compelling photographic evidence of cruelty, such as this photo of greyhounds pursuing a live domestic rabbit being used as a lure at a training track in Florida, was a major contribution by HSUS investigators, including Gail Eisnitz.

pany had also failed to ensure the presence of a veterinarian for a few years running, and several mares collapsed and died during the pony penning without receiving any veterinary care.[91]

Sadly, the problems at Chincoteague still existed in the early twenty-first century, as the event's boosters annually demonstrated their inability to supervise it. Volunteer firemen resorted to harsh and stressful handling practices, and impulse buyers continued to carry animals away in their vehicles under terms that HSUS attorneys believed were in violation of Virginia law. Field Service and Video department personnel videotaped the recurrent problems and sent the tapes to the U.S. Fish and Wild Service (FWS) in an effort to have the Chincoteague Volunteer Fire Company's permit rescinded for grazing ponies on the Chincoteague National Wildlife Refuge during the year. The HSUS's vigilance at the Chincoteague event had itself become a tradition.[92]

Dog Racing

In 1954 the principal companion animal issues addressed by The HSUS were the need for spay-neuter in keeping the companion animal population in check, the campaign to end the handing over of pound and shelter animals to medical and scientific institutions, and the establishment of the animal shelter in the United States as a professional, well-managed enterprise. By the late 1960s, the organization was becoming involved with burgeoning threats to animals—like animal fighting and dog racing—exploitive and harmful practices and industries that not only harmed companion animals but exacerbated the problem of animal overpopulation.

Greyhound racing found its way onto The HSUS's agenda in the early 1970s. While racing was legal in only nine states, promoters were planning an aggressive program to see it legalized in eleven others. For many years the training methods used included the chasing and tearing apart of live rabbits as lures. After five or six "coursings" in which the dogs were allowed to chase and kill a live rabbit in an enclosed field, they advanced to the track, where a live rabbit was hung by the back legs to a mechanical lure.[93]

In 1975 investigator Bernie Weller gave *HSUS News* readers a "behind-the-scenes" look at the training of racing greyhounds, describing his undercover experience at a Texas track where dogs trained for racing in other states. It was a grim account of terrible animal suffering. In 1977 other HSUS investigators went into the field to gather definitive evidence of the use of live rabbits for "coursing" greyhounds. Coursing had its own fan base, as spectators watched and wagered while dogs chased down jackrabbits and killed them, and these so-called training events also provided a convenient venue for selling, trading, and leasing racing dogs.[94]

The deaths of dogs who consistently fell behind the pack was another intolerable consequence of greyhound racing. Observers estimated that some 50 percent of the dogs bred for racing died before they reached the track because they failed to demonstrate the characteristics necessary for success. Their lack of socialization sometimes made them unsuitable for adoption, and humane officials suspected that dog breeders and trainers killed the animals they no longer valued to avoid the veterinary fees for euthanasia.[95]

Focusing on the National Greyhound Association meet in Abilene, Kansas, The HSUS asked the state's attorney general to halt the dog versus rabbit events by invoking Kansas's anticruelty statute. When he refused HSUS investigators asked USDA to declare coursing an "animal fighting venture," specifically prohibited by the AWA. USDA turned the matter over to the Department of Justice, and another year went by.[96]

In 1978 investigator Frantz Dantzler went back to Kansas with an ABC camera crew and reporter Geraldo Rivera in tow. After *20/20* showed footage of the event, the National Greyhound Association (NGA) outlawed the use of live rabbits in its coursing events. Although it did not pass, proposed federal legislation generated contemporaneous pressure that drove the NGA's decision, even as The HSUS remained critical of proposals that did not prohibit "coursing" in private. Throughout the decade The HSUS led the fight to stop the introduction of greyhound racing or its augmentation through wagering in California and several other states where it was under consideration.[97]

For a short while, dog racing even threatened to enter the District of Columbia as part of a gambling initiative proposed in 1979. The HSUS fought this proposal, just as it had opposed a 1973 campaign to bring the activity to Robert F. Kennedy Stadium as a means of reducing the stadium's construction debt.[98]

The HSUS continued its efforts to push reforms in the world of greyhound racing in the 1980s. In 1982 and 1983, John Hoyt and other staff members met with industry representatives to press for the adoption of artificial lures instead of live rabbits and other animals in training. In those years, too, the mass breeding and ultimate destruction of greyhounds moved to the forefront of humane concerns. Breeding exacerbated the general problem of animal overpopulation in the country, and industry operators relied on a supply of bullets to eliminate unwanted animals from their inventory.[99]

ABC's Geraldo Rivera interviews HSUS Chief Investigator Frantz Dantzler about the fate of rabbits used for coursing.

Throughout the 1980s HSUS staff members worked to thwart the goals of the industry. One of the emerging threats The HSUS sought to fend off was the legalization of dog racing on Native American reservations and trust lands. Regional investigators continued to monitor greyhound racing, cooperating with FWS agents to suppress the sale and interstate transportation of jackrabbits for "coursing," following up on complaints about greyhound breeders and kennels, and providing evidence that illegal training of greyhounds with live rabbits as lures was common at training tracks.[100]

By 1996 there were some signals that the racing industry had lost the popularity that had fueled its growth. The industry's own statistics indicated that attendance had declined and state gambling revenues tied to the racetrack had decreased by 25 percent and that it was losing its overall share of the American gambling market. Even so, the industry continued its efforts to extend operations, expand betting opportunities, and cash in on the use and suffering of animals.[101]

Dogfighting

There has never been a time when humane advocates did not treat the spectacle of animals fighting each other for humans' entertainment as a serious concern. In spite of the fact that dogfighting was usually considered to be illegal under state anticruelty statutes and was explicitly prohibited as a felony in a handful of states, it thrived in many locales. In fact, it was an extensive interstate activity in which dogs, spectators, equipment, and promotional literature crossed state lines with complete impunity. Animal fighting magazines and publications boldly made use of U.S. Postal Service second-class mailing privileges without repercussions. Indeed, The HSUS once presented congressional representatives with evidence that the most popular of dogfighting magazines, *Pit Dogs*, was being produced on a Department of Defense lithographic press, with paper taken from government supplies![102]

In the mid-1970s The HSUS's Frank McMahon likened dogfighting to an organized crime operation, one that required concerted cooperation on the part of law enforcement officials at all levels. State-by-state enforcement varied according to the disposition of police and judicial officials, and The HSUS uncovered some shocking examples of law enforcement agents shielding animal fighters from scrutiny and prosecution. In 1974 The HSUS concluded that a federal ban on dogfighting was the best way to proceed, and it found willing sponsors in Representative Thomas Foley (D-WA) and Senator Harrison Williams (D-NJ). Williams's bill, introduced in September, made dogfighting a federal offense by prohibiting the use of interstate commerce for transporting dogs trained or intended to be used to fight other dogs. Under the influence of The HSUS, Williams included provisions to prohibit activities preparatory to a fight (such as breeding, training, and sale of dogs for fighting), the manufacture and sale of training paraphernalia, the contribution of a site, and the use of the mails for promotional purposes.[103]

Then HSUS investigator Eric Sakach helped handle dogs in a dogfight raid in 1981.

While Williams's bill and related measures went nowhere, advocates also considered the option of extending the authority of the AWA to cover dogfighting. This occurred in 1976, as the AWA was amended to incorporate a ban on animal fighting ventures. However, for years no funds were budgeted for enforcement.[104]

In the meantime, however, HSUS investigators continued to assist law enforcement officials with the infiltration, raiding, exposure, and prosecution of dogfighters. In late 1979 Marc Paulhus and Eric Sakach infiltrated an Arkansas convention where state and federal law enforcement agencies subsequently arrested 250 animal fighting enthusiasts and seized an arsenal of weapons, a large cache of illicit drugs, and over half a million dollars in bets.[105]

The following year The HSUS brought suit against USDA and the Department of Justice for absolute failure to enforce AWA provisions designed to prohibit animal fighting. As part of its response to the government's motion for dismissal on the ground that The HSUS lacked standing to sue, The HSUS argued that it was a legally proper suit because "the Animal Welfare Act creates…legal rights for animals, i.e., the right not to be cruelly treated in fighting ventures, [however] the animals themselves have no 'forum' in which to assert the rights to protection and freedom from abuse that the Act was intended to afford." Unfortunately, in January 1981 a U.S. District Court judge dismissed the action, holding that the Court did not have the basic power "to oversee or second guess the allocation of prosecutorial resources."[106]

In the early 1980s, The HSUS focused its efforts on Ohio, which had passed an effective law making it a felony not only to promote or participate in dogfights but also to be a spectator at one, to own or train a fighting dog, or to accept money for admission to a dogfight. HSUS investigators worked hard in support of the bill, Great Lakes Regional Director Sandy Rowland testified on its behalf, and The HSUS cooperated with the Columbus Police Department's Organized Crime Unit to penetrate the state's dogfighting fraternity.[107]

Throughout the 1980s representatives of The HSUS joined law enforcement in many communities on raids and investigations. In 1981 Bob Baker, Rowland, and regional investigator Tim Greyhavens played principal roles in a major dogfighting bust in southern Illinois, one that involved the largest contingent of Illinois state troopers since the 1968 Democratic National Convention in Chicago. In 1983 Baker and investigator Paul Miller helped to bust Jack Kelly, editor of the dogfighting magazine *Sporting Dog Journal*. In 1988 Sakach helped Colorado authorities to bring to justice the self-described "Bad Bob," curtailing his career as an animal fighting entrepreneur. The same year Rowland and other HSUS personnel helped to bring the curtain down on a national underground fighting ring in southwestern Ohio. It was a significant raid in which the FBI played a large role, and law enforcement authorities seriously explored—for the first and only time—a prosecution of dogfighting under the AWA.[108]

Regional Director Sandy Rowland was a linchpin of The HSUS's efforts against dogfighting in the Great Lakes region in the 1980s and 1990s.

During the 1990s HSUS field personnel continued to assist law enforcement authorities with major raids on dogfights. Police and prosecutors, it appeared, were becoming more cognizant that the people who committed violent crimes against animals were frequently involved in violent activities directed at other human beings. Moreover, as Sakach suggested in 1993, "The police are learning that your local dogfight or cockfight is a likely place to meet up with lots of people with warrants outstanding for their arrest, as well as a likely site for drug dealing, gambling, illegal weapons, and other crimes."[109]

After a quarter-century of frustration at USDA's failure to focus on animal fighting cases (since 1976, the federal government had pursued just three dogfighting cases and no cockfighting cases at all), The HSUS launched a new legislative initiative against animal fighting. In May 2002, under the leadership of Senior Vice President for Communications and Government Affairs Wayne Pacelle, The HSUS secured legislation closing the loopholes on cockfighting and dogfighting in the AWA. In the new century, the battle shifted toward funding for AWA enforcement efforts.[110]

Cockfighting

HSUS investigators and lobbyists played an important role in the passage of 1976 legislation that barred interstate shipment of animals and birds for fighting and forbade use of the U.S. mail for promoting illegal animal competitions. The legislation secured fell short of the desired prohibition of cockfighting under the AWA. The law as passed contained a loophole on cockfighting, permitting the shipment of fighting cocks to Louisiana, New Mexico, and Oklahoma, where such events remained legal, as well as to U.S. territories and protectorates like Guam and Puerto Rico and to foreign countries, including Mexico and the Philippines.[111]

During the late 1970s and early 1980s, with cockfighting on the rise, both national and regional investigators participated in law enforcement raids. In 1987 HSUS staff members observed that cockfighting was illegal in forty-five states and a felony in fourteen of them, while thirty-two states made it unlawful to attend a cockfight. Even so, investigators noted, in Arizona, Missouri, New Mexico, Oklahoma, and Louisiana, cockfighting was not only practiced openly but was also a legal form of entertainment. The following year The HSUS launched an anticockfighting campaign to seek its prohibition in those states and to strengthen legislation in states like Kansas, Missouri, and Virginia, where extant statutes were ineffectual. A 1989 raid in Oregon, stemming from an informant's tip that The HSUS provided to law enforcement authorities, resulted in the arrests of more than three hundred people and a racketeering charge against one cockfighting derby impresario. A 1991 southeastern Ohio raid netted

Investigator Marc Paulhus helped secure birds seized in a cockfighting raid in the 1970s.

the membership list for the United Gamefowl Breeders Association.[112]

In the late 1990s, The HSUS launched a new round of efforts to suppress cockfighting, working on two 1998 state-level cockfighting initiatives that successfully outlawed the pursuit in Missouri and Arizona. At the federal level, The HSUS sought to close the loophole that enriched those who bred birds in states where the activity was prohibited and shipped them to states where animal fighting remained legal. In 1999 the Government Affairs department persuaded Wayne Allard (D-CO), the Senate's only veterinarian, to sponsor a bill to prohibit interstate shipments. The HSUS also secured the agreement of Representative Collin Peterson (D-MN), a frequent adversary in other arenas, to sponsor a companion bill. In a complex legislative battle, The HSUS and its congressional allies spared the anticockfighting provision from the fate of other animal-protection measures that opponents successfully "skinned" from the 2001 farm bill. HSUS investigators provided additional momentum for the cause by assisting law enforcement officials in a string of raids on larger cockfighting operations around the country.[113]

In 2002 The HSUS gained the support of Governor Frank Keating and wrestler Bill Goldberg, an Oklahoma native, for an initiative to outlaw cockfighting in the state. The two also helped The HSUS to defeat a countermeasure that proposed to double the number of voter signatures needed to place any animal-protection initiatives before the citizenry. "This measure creates two classes of citizenship in the initiative petition process," Keating declared. "It is unfair and undemocratic." The HSUS's initiative also survived a court challenge by the cockfighting lobby.[114] The HSUS waged the fight against cockfighting on another front, too, asking USDA to recognize and address the fact that cockfighting magazines like *The Gamecock*, *Grit and Steel*, and *The Feathered Warrior* were using the U.S. mail to promote cockfights, in violation of federal law. [115]

Dog and Cat Fur

In the late 1990s, the HSUS Investigations section successfully identified the widespread use of dog and cat fur in global garment, accessory, and trinket production and provided the American public with disturbing evidence of the callous practices that characterized the industry. In source countries such as China, the Philippines, and Thailand, HSUS investigators saw dogs and cats held in barren, unsanitary compounds and killed by horrific methods and followed the trail of blood, death, and fur to retail establishments in half a dozen countries—including the United States. Cagey fur industry marketers designated the products with misleading labels to obscure their origins.[116]

In December 1998, through coverage in the *Washington Post* and on the television newsmagazine *Dateline NBC*, the shocking details of the eighteen-month investigation caused an uproar that pushed at least one major retail outlet to immediate action. When Burlington Coat Factory learned that it was selling coats trimmed with dog fur, the company promptly responded by removing the offensive items from its racks.[117]

Working with Government Affairs and Companion Animals, HSUS investigators helped to publicize the terrible details of the industry, pressing the government to require labels that clearly identify products made from dog and cat fur. The HSUS also enlisted the support of television host Montel Williams and other celebrities in bringing the subject to national attention. In 2000 the U.S. Congress passed the Dog and Cat Protection Act, banning the sale of such products, as a direct result of The HSUS's campaign. Later, the effort to ban such products moved to Europe through the efforts of HSI.

HSUS Vice President, Investigations, Rick Swain oversaw the investigation into dog and cat fur garments in the 1990s.

Karakul

In December 2000 *Dateline NBC* made its viewers aware of The HSUS's year-long investigation of a fur industry secret—the slaughter of some four to five million newborn and unborn lambs for expensive garments made from their fur. With two animals, a mother and her baby, forced to die for each pelt, karakul (the common commercial designation of the lamb pelts) offered a disturbing twist on the question sometimes posed to those who wear fur: "How many animals had to die for that coat?" HSUS investigators traveled to the central Asian nation of Uzbekistan to demonstrate the falseness of industry claims about the production of karakul and to document the ruthlessness of its production in Uzbekistan, Afghanistan, Kazakhstan, Namibia, and South Africa, among other countries. The investigation yielded compelling videotape evidence of the grisly dimensions of the karakul trade, giving animal protectionists worldwide an opportunity to challenge designers, retailers, and the buying public with the evidence of what one HSUS investigator called "an obscenely frivolous waste of life."[118]

The Regional Office System

In the early years of The HSUS, Field Services encompassed virtually all of the organization's investigative functions, disaster relief activities, and direct assistance to local humane societies. After 1971, when The HSUS transformed its branch system into a network of regional offices, the Department of Field Services became responsible for their oversight, which included helping to implement The HSUS's national programs, responding to the needs of its constituents and partners around the country, and keeping the central office apprised of pertinent developments in the field. Over the years, the regional offices served, as Vice President for Field Services Melissa Seide Rubin put it in 2003, as "the eyes, ears, and voice of The HSUS."

The HSUS regional office system grew out of a state branch network that Fred Myers championed in the late 1950s. Through the branches, Myers hoped to find, enroll, and mobilize those who supported The HSUS's goals, wherever and however they were situated. Together, they would make The HSUS a dynamic vehicle for the abolition of animal suffering through the eradication of cruelty's causes. They would be particularly useful for advancing the work in communities where economic, geographic, or other reasons made the organization of a traditional humane society difficult. The result, Myers hoped, would be a greater unity of effort and a stronger humane movement.[119]

At the same time, in an era when The HSUS's total staff never numbered more than several dozen people, branch employees deepened the organization's capacities, frequently assisting their colleagues in other parts of the country. In 1965 New Jersey HSUS staff member Don Maxfield testified in support of successful humane slaughter legislation in Ohio and Indiana. Belton Mouras, whether working in Denver, Salt Lake City, or California, also traveled the country to testify for humane slaughter and other initiatives.[120]

The program suffered in part from the limited funds available to The HSUS in the 1960s. Even so, all of the branches had achieved a few victories for animals, and in some cases they had done much more. The New Jersey branch (1958), for example, with its energetic president, Jacques Sichel, did fulfill Fred Myers's vision of a branch that recruited members and

Norma Terris's bequest of property made possible the New England Regional Office and NAHEE headquarters building in Connecticut.

conducted program work. Sichel and his wife, Miriam, began in 1958 with a shoebox and 250 file cards as a membership base. Seven years later the New Jersey branch had almost five thousand members and a paid staff, the result of extraordinary personal involvement by Sichel and other branch directors.[121]

The branch waged a strong but unsuccessful decade-long struggle for the passage of humane slaughter legislation in the state and sued to stop the annual deer hunt at the Great Swamp National Wildlife Refuge. The branch worked hard in support of a state bill to prohibit the steel-jawed leghold trap, too, and filed a lawsuit challenging the makeup of the New Jersey State Fish and Game Council, arguing that the selection of members should not have been delegated to special interest groups with an interest in promoting hunting and fishing.[122]

The New Jersey branch also provided essential support for The HSUS's New York office, which operated intermittently between the 1950s and 1970s under the guidance of Helen Jones, Cleveland Amory, Charles Herrick, and others. One of the New York office's highest-profile actions was its display at the 1964 World's Fair. It was there that Nina Austenberg, who went on to many years of service in The HSUS's Mid-Atlantic Regional Office, first came into contact with the organization.[123]

While it was not recruiting many members into the national HSUS, the Utah branch (1960), under the leadership of Harold Gardiner, was operating an exemplary animal shelter facility in Salt Lake City, handling tens of thousands of animals every year, conducting investigations that resulted in cruelty charges and convictions, and undertaking some other humane work as well. In 1963 branch members defied a pound seizure law they deemed to be unconstitutional. After joining the HSUS board of directors in the 1970s, Gardiner served for over a quarter of a century. In addition, one longtime HSUS employee "went to school" at the Utah branch. Frantz Dantzler was its shelter manager from 1964 to 1972, gaining valuable experience that he would bring to the national headquarters and to field work a few years later.[124]

The Connecticut branch (1957), for its part, had waged a long struggle for humane slaughter legislation during the early 1960s. Later, branch members carried out extensive investigations of the abuse of live animals at science fairs and in the classroom. The branch also devoted its efforts toward the acquisition of a property for conducting educational work, an initiative that had extremely positive consequences for The HSUS in later years. James C. Shaw (d. 1988) and his wife, Bettsy, helped to lay the groundwork for the acquisition and development of property owned by their friend, Norma Terris. Ultimately, this property became the headquarters for both the New England Regional Office and NAAHE (see chapter 6). In addition to the Shaws and Terris, the Connecticut branch produced K. William Wiseman, who would go on to become chairman of the HSUS board in the 1990s; national HSUS board members Charlotte Griswold and Everett Smith; and Richard K. Morris of Trinity University, an early advisor on humane education and classroom use of animals who also helped to organize the 1976 benchmark conference, "On the Fifth Day."[125]

The California branch (1958) had also worked hard on humane slaughter legislation that passed in 1959. In the late 1960s, the branch protested the threatened burning of dogs as a protest against the Vietnam War and fought off a proposal to introduce dog racing to the state. Longtime HSUS investigator Bernie Weller and regional office director Charlene Drennon got their start as employees of the branch.[126]

Like the other state chapters, the Minnesota branch (1959) campaigned for a state humane slaughter law, securing the nation's second such statute in 1959. It was also responsible for an important revision of the Minnesota anticruelty statute that incorporated a requirement that humane shelter be provided for domestic animals in both winter and summer. The law relieved judges, prosecutors, and humane officers of the burden of having to determine just how much heat or cold an animal could tolerate, and the branch actively sought to see it enforced. However, by 1970 the branch was barely functional, with few members, virtually no assets, and little program activity, when Hoyt conducted an assessment study after taking office.[127]

Ultimately The HSUS's experience with building and sustaining branches was a mixed legacy. Hoyt quickly moved to end the branch system in favor of a regional office arrangement and set The HSUS on a course of identifying the best locations to situate them. In July 1971 The HSUS established a Great Lakes Regional Office in Fort Wayne, Indiana, and appointed John H. Inman to direct it. In July 1972 the Rocky Mountain Regional Office opened in Salt Lake City, serving Utah, Colorado, Wyoming, and Idaho. The Gulf States Regional Office in Corpus Christi came into existence in 1972 through the generosity of the Earl C. Sams Foundation, where trustees Gladys Sams Porter and Dodie Hawn committed to support a re-

Mid-Atlantic Regional Director Nina Austenberg joined the HSUS staff in the 1970s.

UTAH STATE BRANCH
HUMANE SOCIETY OF
THE UNITED STATES

HSUS
The Helping Hand

F. L. DANTZLER
SUPERVISOR

4613 SOUTH 4000 WEST
SALT LAKE CITY, UTAH
P.O. BOX 177
801 298-3548

An early business card of HSUS investigator Frantz Dantzler.

gional office for its first three years. In 1973 The HSUS opened a West Coast Regional Office in Sacramento, California, to serve California, Nevada, Oregon, and Washington. The HSUS also operated a New York City information office intermittently during the 1960s and early 1970s.[128]

Several other regional offices grew out of the discarded branch structure. The Connecticut branch became the New England Regional Office, the Utah branch was ultimately incorporated into the framework of the Rocky Mountain Regional Office (and later the North Central Regional Office), and the New Jersey branch ultimately became the Mid-Atlantic Regional Office. In many cases, branch staff members continued their work as members of the regional office system.

The new arrangement brought impressive early results. In 1973 regional staff members visited more than three hundred public pounds and humane society shelters, conducted nearly two hundred investigations, reached over 20 million people through publicity efforts, handled approximately eleven thousand letter and telephone inquiries, and spoke before 250 audiences.[129]

One important difference between the branch and regional office systems was that staffing decisions would now be made in Washington by executive staff, instead of by regional boards of directors, as under the old arrangements. Over the years, this gave John Hoyt, Patrick Parkes, Patricia Forkan, and other officials who did the hiring a chance to set general standards for the positions of regional director, regional investigator, and program coordinator, the most common openings available in the regions.

A few regional office staff members, like Nina Austenberg, Frantz Dantzler, Charlene Drennon, John Dommers, and Bernard Weller, came from the old HSUS branches. During the 1970s Hoyt, a minister himself, hired former clergymen, including Donald Cashen, Donald Coburn, John H. Inman, and Douglas Scott, who, he judged, brought a good combination of skills in administration, interpersonal relations, and communication to the regional office system.[130]

In time The HSUS would also recruit staff members for its regional offices, as it sometimes did for positions at its Washington headquarters, from the ranks of humane society personnel around the country. Dorothy Weller, for example, came to The HSUS from the Orlando Humane Society, where she had been executive director. She served in the regional offices in Corpus Christi, Texas, and the Great Lakes region before assuming a position at NAHEE, The HSUS's youth education division, in 1994. Ann Gonnerman, Wendell Maddox, and Phil Steward all came from local organizations where they had developed good reputations, as did Phil Snyder and Bill Meade, who had managed well-run humane society shelter operations in South Bend, Indiana, and Arlington, Virginia, respectively.[131]

Other national organizations provided a source of regional office staff members, too. Sandy Rowland worked as a field representative for The Fund for Animals, and Dennis White (1946–2001) was the longtime director of AHA's Animal Protection Division before becoming director of The HSUS's Southwest Regional Office.

In hiring regional directors, Patrick Parkes recalled, The HSUS looked for individuals who were "humane-minded, in tune with animal welfare concerns" but who would be equipped to handle cruelty situations rationally and professionally. Good communications skills were also deemed to be essential. Experience with humane society and shelter operations, as well as some administrative experience, became increasingly important after 1980. Where possible, The HSUS also looked to its regional representatives for "double duty," encouraging them to lend their expertise to HSUS initiatives beyond the realm of their geographic responsibilities.[132]

Regional personnel frequently served in a number of capacities and locations. Burton Parks, who once served in the Washington, D.C., headquarters as director of fund-raising, worked as The HSUS's southern area representative. Based in Pinehurst, North Carolina, Parks assisted local shelters and animal control programs with the expansion of their fundraising and community outreach efforts and tried to acquaint them with the technical assistance that The HSUS could provide. Bernard Weller (1932–1988) started at the HSUS California branch in 1968. As the organization expanded field operations in the 1970s, Weller helped to establish regional offices in Ft. Wayne, Indiana, Corpus Christi, Texas, and Orlando, Florida. Frantz Dantzler came up through the ranks, first working at the Boulder, Colorado, affiliate in 1962. After serving as shelter manager there, he became director of the Utah state branch. Eventually he served in the West Coast Regional Office as its director. In 1975 he came to Washington to help with the expansion of HSUS regional programs, investigations, and services.[133]

Periodic reassessments of the geographic coverage and impact of the regional offices resulted in changes over the years. A new regional office opened in Tallahassee, Florida, in 1983 to monitor activities in Florida, Georgia, North Carolina, and South Carolina. Led by Marc Paulhus, an investigator since 1977, the new office brought the total number of HSUS regional offices to seven. In 1984 Frantz Dantzler gave up his position as director of investiga-

tions to open The HSUS's new North Central Office in the Chicago area. The HSUS's eighth regional office served Illinois, Wisconsin, Iowa, Minnesota, and Missouri. In 1987 the Midwest Regional Office opened in Kansas City, Missouri, to serve Missouri, Kansas, Nebraska, and Iowa. In 1990 the South Central Regional Office opened in Knoxville, Tennessee. The HSUS added a Southwest Regional Office in 1995 and a Pacific Northwest Regional Office in 2001.[134]

Regional diversity has shaped the evolution of the offices, as directors focused their work in ways responsive to the communities

Frantz Dantzler (with AHPA's Joan Blue and Nebraska veterinarian William Burford, in Idaho in 1973) served in a number of regional capacities over a thirty-year career.

and states in which they had to operate. Working in an area in which wildlife rescue, rehabilitation, and relocation are in high demand, for example, Northern Rockies Regional Director Dave Pauli earned respect through his promotion of humane trapping techniques. With animal control officers for only three of fifty-four counties in Montana, the Northern Rockies Regional Office also provided critical assistance to sheriff's departments, municipal officials, and—where they existed—the region's animal shelters. "In a region where rodeo and hunting are primary lifestyles," Pauli told a reporter in 1996, "we take great pride in our having built a credible animal protection resource that is respected and used by most of our state government and law enforcement agencies."[135]

On several occasions, Field Services personnel confronted the challenges associated with working on tribal reservations, where state anticruelty laws do not apply and animal issues must be addressed through reservation-specific ordinances—if they are addressed at all. In such instances, The HSUS worked to ensure good diplomatic relations with the reservations, which are sovereign nations, recruited specialists to cover anticipated needs on-site, and con-

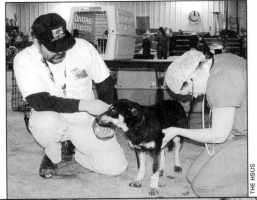

The HSUS's Dave Pauli tended a rescued dog in 1993; a spay/neuter clinic on a native American reservation helped to control pet overpopulation.

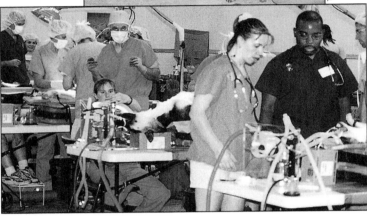

ducted preliminary assessments of law enforcement, community outreach, and social services bearing on the targeted concerns.[136]

The first recorded Native American project in which The HSUS participated was in its Navajo Nation initiative in 1991. Tribal leaders contacted The HSUS in late 1991, asking for help with an admitted proliferation of at-large strays. On just one day in July, animal control officers on the reservation—which covers sections of Arizona, New Mexico, and Utah approximately the size of West Virginia—captured more than 350 dogs. The HSUS sought to identify and strengthen local forces working to address animal care and control problems, initiate humane education programs within the Navajo Nation, and bolster tribal animal control services.[137]

Some years later HSUS animal care professionals traveled to the Fort Peck Indian reservation in Montana to conduct a brief but intensive assistance and education campaign. An inordinately high ratio of dog bites in an area plagued by rabies meant that human victims were forced to undergo expensive postbite treatment. In 1994 tribal officials at Fort Peck, a forty- by eighty-mile expanse home to more than ten thousand Sioux and Assiniboine, contacted The HSUS for assistance. The assistance team transformed the powwow grounds building into a temporary animal shelter, from which it launched aggressive attempts to capture loose-roaming dogs for treatment, identification, and rescue: more than five hundred dogs came through the shelter during The HSUS's time there. The HSUS also distributed leashes, collars, and literature to residents, issued spay-neuter certificates redeemable in Montana, and identified residents who had clearly contributed to the reservation's animal control problem for special visits and follow-up.[138]

In the late 1990s, the Native Nations spay-neuter and pet wellness programs were expanded under the auspices of the Remote Area Veterinary Services (RAVS) program, The HSUS's direct veterinary services arm, which began to provide spay-neuter and vaccination services for companion animals in poor, rural communities and on reservations. The RAVS team, frequently accompanied by regional office and HSI staff, also led veterinary assistance teams into some of the western hemisphere's neediest areas, including locations in Mexico, Guatemala, Paraguay, and Bolivia.

In 2001 the Southwest Regional Office opened a spay-neuter clinic and animal wellness center in Dallas, Texas, to provide lower-cost services for thousands of dogs and cats. It provided one more example of the degree to which The HSUS's regional offices were establishing their own identities and specialized programs.

As The HSUS's fiftieth anniversary approached, staff members at its regional offices anchored the organization's work in an ever-expanding range of ways. They sponsored a variety of training workshops. They provided advice to wildlife agencies and the general public as part of The HSUS's Living with Wildlife programs. They participated in numerous direct relief activities, promoting alternatives to goose roundups, preventing turtle and other wetland wildlife from finding their way onto busy highways, and helping to rescue and relocate stranded and endangered animals. They helped to coordinate response to high-profile cruelty cases, offering rewards for information leading to the arrest and conviction of perpetrators. They testified at and monitored trial proceedings. They were in the front lines of fights against greyhound racing, animal fighting, and other enthusiasms that harmed and killed animals.

The field offices also had important responsibilities for monitoring and advancing the status of state-level legislation. Such legislation covered a range of issues, but some common concerns in recent years have included the legal authority of shelters to directly acquire sodium pentobarbital for use in euthanasia; the promotion of lower-cost spay-neuter through license plate and other subsidy programs; higher standards of training for animal cruelty enforcement personnel; the safeguarding of caregivers' rights in senior citizen housing and other contexts; legislation to restrict the ownership of exotic animals; and the upgrading of dogfighting, cockfighting, and cruelty to animals from misdemeanor to felony status. The regional offices also played a role in the statewide ballot and referendum initiatives launched by The HSUS's Government Affairs department in the 1990s.[139]

A stranded horse headed toward a soft landing after a helicopter ride out of a canyon in Utah's mountains in 1991. The HSUS assisted in the rescue.

Disaster Relief

In its first fifteen years, The HSUS did very little disaster relief work. It was simply not possible to divert funds toward such activity. In 1969, however, staff members began to involve themselves in substantial rescue and relief work. Early in the year, Frank McMahon supervised an emergency feeding operation to save a herd of wild horses in Nevada. In the spring Mel Morse went to the site of the Santa Barbara, California, oil spill as part of a team to assess the harm done to sea lions, seals, and other animals. In the fall McMahon traveled to disaster areas in Mississippi and Louisiana after Hurricane Camille destroyed fifty-one miles of homes and businesses along the Gulf Coast. McMahon assisted local societies with their response to the plight of the hurricane's animal victims, addressing the urgent need for food and supplies, and helping the region's animal shelters to maintain twenty-four-hour schedules during the height of the crisis.[140]

In 1973, with demand for such services rising, Morse began to develop plans for a disaster relief program. Its goals included the establishment of an internal operation that would always be ready and able to respond to disaster situations, the initiation of overtures to coordinate relief services with the American Red Cross and other disaster preparedness agencies, and the organization of substantial efforts to influence decisions about how to care for animals in the case of disaster.

By 1976 Guy Hodge, then director of research and data services, had stepped in to coordinate The HSUS's newly created disaster relief program. In its first year, the program responded to more than a dozen disasters. Hodge's hobby of ornithology made him an ideal choice for leading bird rescue operations after oil spills, like those following the Chesapeake Bay spill of February 1976. Under his leadership The HSUS worked closely with officials of the U.S. Coast Guard, FWS, and EPA to coordinate relief efforts.[141]

*When the **Exxon Valdez** spilled oil off Alaska's coast in 1989, The HSUS sent staff to an otter-rescue center.*

When the Teton Dam in southeastern Idaho collapsed in 1976, Frantz Dantzler went to the Snake River Valley to support regional agencies in their efforts to safeguard animals.

Dantzler's experience underscored the value of such relief work in building goodwill with local communities. "The longer we stayed there, the more cooperation we experienced," he reported. "Once the citizens and authorities discovered we were serious people with a real role in the disaster, they began to work hand in hand with us."[142]

Hodge, Phil Steward, and others also went into action in December 1976 after an oil tanker leaked 133,000 gallons of oil into the waters near Wilmington, Delaware, affecting the shorelines of three states. The HSUS team treated almost three hundred birds, including ruddy ducks, Canada geese, whistling swans, herring gulls, mallards, and black ducks.[143]

HSUS investigator Hal Perry, a longtime campaigner against government predator control programs, took to the skies for rescue and surveillance work in the 1970s.

Just one year after its creation, the disaster relief program received a special recognition award from the state of New Jersey for its crucial intervention in feeding waterfowl confronted with a serious food shortage due to extremely cold temperatures along coastal marshes. Thousands of wintering waterfowl in this critical area survived because of The HSUS's contribution.[144]

In 1977 Phil Steward and Marc Paulhus brought emergency supplies, animal food, and first aid equipment to Johnstown, Pennsylvania, in the midst of the serious flood that jeopardized both human and animal lives. Steward and Paulhus joined the beleaguered staff of the six-month-old Humane Society of Cambria County, which had no power or running water. Individuals accepted at area relief centers found they were unable to keep their companion animals with them, and HSUS staffers began regular daily pickups with the promise that every animal would be returned once displaced citizens had reestablished their homes. While Steward and Paulhus were quick to credit the extraordinary dedication of shelter staff and local volunteers, who worked sixteen-hour days during the crisis, it was clear that The HSUS's development of a response mechanism had made a difference. "We were able to perform a real service in Johnstown, because of [The] HSUS's previous experiences with such catastrophes, and our knowledge of what must be done to help the animals in this unusual situation."[145]

During the 1980s, disaster response received less emphasis as The HSUS focused its attention on expanding other programs. Even so, regional and other staff members continued to respond to emergencies and to provide assistance when appropriate. Disaster relief services were channeled through The HSUS's regional offices, which coordinated the provision of equipment with local authorities. The HSUS was providing local societies, civil defense agencies, and other organizations with support and advice necessary for community response. In 1980 Frantz Dantzler and Eric Sakach went to Washington State after the eruption at Mount St. Helens occurred, wiping out all life within a twelve-mile blast area. The two worked with humane society personnel to rescue and shelter shocked and injured animals found at the limits of the devastated zone.[146]

In the 1990s Mel Morse's hope for a program that could act upon the goal of placing animals within the scope of every emergency operations plan again be-

Regional coordinator Joanne Bourbeau, a veteran of many East Coast disasters, lent a hand to a stranded animal in floods in the 1990s.

came a priority. The disaster preparedness plan of the Southeast Regional Office (SERO) of The HSUS, in place since 1992, proved to be fortuitous in August 1993 after Hurricane Andrew devastated a portion of South Florida. SERO Director Laura Bevan lived in the area for a month, coordinating the development of a temporary animal shelter and emergency veterinary services. HSUS staffers worked with local officials, the U.S. Army's 478th Civil Affairs Battalion, and others to distribute animal food, supplies, and water and to provide direct care and assistance. HSUS staff veterinarian Steve Kritsick, D.V.M., (1951–1994) and reservist Thelton McCorkle, D.V.M., toiled away in The HSUS's makeshift compound, administering care to a long line of animal patients rushed to the facility with injuries suffered during the chaos that followed the disaster.[147]

The capacities of the SERO would be tested again in 1998, when severe drought led to wildfires that threatened both human and animal populations. By that time, the SERO had developed Disaster Animal Response Teams in Florida, ready to assist in evacuating animals and setting up temporary animal shelters.[148]

The HSUS's disaster relief task force, comprised of staff members from a number of regional offices and The HSUS's Washington, D.C., headquarters, also went into action when the Mississippi River overflowed its banks during the Great Flood of 1993. Water spilled over from teeming rivers and spread over land encompassing four states. A similar team effort ensued in the wake of severe flooding in western states caused by a tropical storm system in 1997 and again in 1999 when Hurricane Floyd hit North Carolina. HSUS staff members also assisted local authorities in the crises that attended the Malibu fires and California floods of the late 1990s.[149]

HSUS workers gently clean the injuries of a rescued dog.

By 1995 The HSUS's relationship with the American Red Cross had coalesced, and the Red Cross sent out copies of the HSUS-produced disaster response video, *The Forgotten Victims*, to three hundred of its chapters. The following year the two organizations co-produced a brochure on how those with companion animals could prepare for disaster.[150]

In 1997 The HSUS enhanced its formal collaboration with the Federal Emergency Management Agency (FEMA), helping the agency to develop its study course on animals in disaster and exchanging website links. When The HSUS went into disaster areas to assist, as it did in tornado-devastated Oklahoma under Southwest Regional Director Dennis White in 1999, it often found communities relying on disaster management plans that did not include animals. The HSUS worked with local societies and volunteers to develop a system for recording information about missing and recovered animals. Such outstanding service culminated in a partnership agreement in 2000 between The HSUS and FEMA to promote and implement disaster plans encompassing the needs of animals and their caregivers. Under the name Project Impact, the program was a high-water mark in The HSUS's long history of disaster relief work.[151]

In 2003 Melissa Rubin and Anne Culver, HSUS director of disaster services, negotiated a Memorandum of Understanding with USDA's APHIS to coordinate disaster preparedness and response efforts for animals. The partnership posited exchange of information between The HSUS and USDA offices, jointly sponsored conferences, training exercises, and other collaborative efforts. The HSUS also agreed to provide technical advice and service in disaster situations. For its part, USDA agreed to ensure strong local and regional cooperation as well as assistance to HSUS teams seeking access to afflicted areas.[152]

By 2004 the Disaster Services department had developed unparalleled expertise and resources to respond to the needs of those who provide emergency relief and care to animals in the wake of disaster. The HSUS was involved in regular dialogue with federal, state, and local government agencies to ensure the inclusion of animals in disaster plans and continued to cultivate normal relations with veterinary associations and private relief groups. The HSUS hosted two national conferences on disaster planning and response for animals, drawing emergency managers and other employees of state and local government as well as members of the animal care and control communities. At the same time, the organization attempted to equip its regional offices with appropriate disaster equipment and planning capabilities for disaster response.

Humane Society International

The formation of an active international division in the early 1990s was a natural outgrowth of the expanding vision and capacities of The HSUS. The program coalesced under the leadership of longtime HSUS staffer Janet Frake and Neil Trent, an animal welfare professional with three decades of experience at the RSPCA and WSPA. By 1998, with Frake and Trent in place as administrative director and executive director, respectively, HSI was ready to make a proper reckoning of what it wanted to accomplish and where it wanted to project its influence.

HSI board and staff members began by identifying priority goals: (1) enhancing the international animal protection movement's capacity for action, (2) promoting the worldwide adoption of humane slaughtering practices, (3) addressing the surplus companion animal problem that affected virtually every nation in the world, and (4) developing a strong prowildlife program.[153]

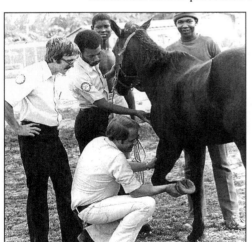

In 1978 HSUS investigator Phil Steward (holding horse's leg) inspected racehorses in the Bahamas with then RSPCA officer Neil Trent (standing, in glasses). In 1999 Trent became executive director of HSI.

The prospects for capacity building in the Internet era were considerable, as HSI staff members discovered when they launched *hsi-animalia@lists.hsus.org*, an open forum electronic list that encouraged the exchange of information concerning common challenges and practices. The value of the list quickly became evident as participants from a broad range of nations helped one another to address and resolve problems about which they might never have communicated otherwise. HSI moved quickly to augment this feature with a web-based library of pertinent literature and technical advice.[154]

Humane Society International Australia, a semiautonomous HSI affiliate, proved to embody the success of the goal of capacity building. Established with an eye to creating a strong local financial base for HSI's international programs, it became the most successful HSI affiliate. Under the direction of Michael Kennedy and Verna Simpson, Humane Society International Australia also developed a good working rapport with government officials, particularly in the wildlife protection arena, became an important part of HSUS/HSI international treaty initiatives, and by 2003 began to fund HSI programs in Asia and Africa.

HSI also moved to forge the kinds of links between The HSUS's domestic resources and the needs of international campaigners that Paul Irwin had intended to be a distinguishing element in HSI's work. Collaboration with the Companion Animals section resulted in a program that brought selected workers from animal care and control agencies from around the world to participate in training sessions at The HSUS's annual Animal Care Expo. At the same time, HSI staff arranged for international participants to spend a few days at North American shelters in advance of the conference to provide further exposure to the high stan-

HSUS/HSI's John A. Hoyt (left) and Paul G. Irwin prepare to release a young rehabilitated ocelot into the Costa Rican jungle.

dards of policy and practice that HSI hoped to encourage. The program quickly exceeded expectations, and by 2004 the HSI component at Animal Care Expo took up a full day of sessions.[155]

To meet its second priority, HSI built a partnership with the U.N. Food and Agriculture Organization (FAO) to promote both the techniques and the proper equipment for humane handling, transport, and slaughter of animals destined for the food supply. HSI produced a video (filmed in a South African facility representative of the conditions that might be typical elsewhere in the world) and developed a poster and training guide for global distribution. Like The HSUS's campaign for the Humane Slaughter Act in the United States more than four decades earlier, the initiative stressed the economic advantages of humane techniques. Together with the FAO, HSI conducted training sessions and workshops in Africa, Asia, and Central America.[156]

HSI sought to forge similar relationships with the World Health Organization (WHO), the Pan-American Health Organization (PAHO), and other agencies with an interest in promulgating better standards in animal care and control. By 2000 HSI was coordinating advanced training for WHO veterinarians in technical skills at a facility in Italy, providing travel and expense stipends for those who committed to stage training sessions once they returned to their own duty assignments.[157]

In tackling the worldwide crisis of dog and cat overpopulation, HSI tried to extend the "L.E.S." approach—legislation, education, and sterilization—that Phyllis Wright had made the centerpiece of The HSUS's 1970s-era offensive to curb the problem of surplus animals in the United States. At the insistence of HSUS Senior Vice President and Chief of Staff Andrew Rowan, however, HSI added a new component to such programs—the extensive study, documentation, and measurement of outcomes. HSI put its energies into pilot programs in the Bahamas (funded in part by the Pegasus Foundation) and Taiwan—where it helped to secure that nation's first animal-protection law in 1998.[158]

The wildlife component of HSI's work proved to be more difficult to sustain, as managers found it hard to secure proper funding. Still, there were notable successes. In 1994 HSI sent Guy Hodge to South Africa to support an oiled-bird rescue operation after a devastating oil spill caused by the sinking of the ore carrier, *Apollo Sea*. The next year, HSI sponsored an investigation of the bear parts trade in China. HSI also sustained an environmental education center in Costa Rica and launched a campaign to change attitudes about keeping wild animals as household pets. In 2000 HSI published the Spanish-language proceedings of the second HSI-sponsored Neotropical Conference on Wildlife Rescue held in San José, Costa Rica. Humane Society Australia also registered many successes in the wildlife protection arena, under the direction of Kennedy and Simpson.[159]

Without abandoning its readiness to support international wildlife protection work when the opportunity surfaced, HSI nevertheless adopted a fourth priority initiative aimed at improving the lot of the world's estimated 300 million working equines. This program sent staff members and consultants associated with The HSUS's RAVS to other nations, to provide basic instruction in domestic animal care to veterinary professionals and the lay public. Such initiatives helped animals and the people who relied upon them by encouraging better basic care, discouraging reliance on crude and harmful veterinary treatment, and, as Michael Fox had observed, by serving "to promote and strengthen compassionate attitudes by showing that something can be done."[160]

Conclusion

In an organization blessed with excellent program staff and known for the quality of its publications and technical expertise on hundreds of animal cruelty issues, it was sometimes easy to overlook the action-oriented components of The HSUS. Nevertheless, the determination to undertake prompt, principled, and effective action to identify and expose cruelty and suffering, wherever it occurred, was a fundamental premise of The HSUS's founding cohort and one upon which successive generations of staff members in field service, investigations, disaster relief, and international outreach continued to base their efforts.

In the current era, many organizations carry out investigations of cruelty. However, until the maturation of The HSUS's investigations strategy under Frank McMahon and his successors, the humane movement in the United States had accomplished very little on that front. Today many organizations have field offices and representatives. But during its first fifty years of existence, The HSUS's efforts to build and sustain such a network, first through its branch and affiliate structure and then through its regional office system, were unequaled by any animal-protection organization. While not necessarily the pioneering force in disaster relief or international work by humane campaigners, The HSUS began to make substantial commitments to these activities in the 1970s, and they became ever more important in its attempt to extend protection and relief to animals both nationally and, in the last decade of the twentieth century, internationally. These accomplishments comprised a legacy of action not to be overshadowed by The HSUS's program area work.

Moved by the Spirit of Compassion

"he great fault of all ethics hitherto," Albert Schweitzer wrote in *Out of My Life and Thought,*

has been that they believed themselves to have to deal only with the relations of man to man. In reality, however, the question is what is his attitude toward the world and all life that comes within his reach. A man is ethical only when life, as such, is sacred to him, that of plants and animals as that of his fellow men, and when he devotes himself helpfully to all life that is in need of help. Only the universal ethic of the feeling of responsibility in an ever-widening sphere for all that lives—only that ethic can be founded in thought. The ethic of the relation of man to man is not something apart by itself: it is only a particular relation which results from the universal one.[1]

More than eighty years later, Schweitzer's comment is, unfortunately, still applicable to most government, social, religious, educational, and philanthropic institutions as well as to many environmental organizations that purport to include animals within their purview. In the twenty-first century, the majority of these entities remain largely anthropocentric—unconcerned and unengaged with the many avoidable miseries that humankind inflicts upon animals and untroubled by the possibility that their indifference diminishes the good work they do accomplish.

This ethical deficit is what makes the contributions of The Humane Society of the United States and like organizations historically significant. The HSUS's history is, in large part, the history of the effort to realize Schweitzer's vision of a world in which no animal goes uncared for, no animal's pain or suffering goes without succor, and humanity has fully embraced the view that human goodness and compassion should extend toward all living beings. But it is also part of the history of efforts to encourage humankind to set its ethical sights higher, to demand more of itself, and to recognize the treatment of nonhuman life—at all times and in all places—as a crucial litmus test of our moral and spiritual evolution.

To its credit, The HSUS has sought to apply standards of ethical treatment to the condition of animals in an impressive diversity of situations—not just to the popular and charismatic dolphin but also to the wholly unprotected laboratory mouse, not just to the majestic bald eagle but also to the much disdained prairie dog, not just to the ecologically endangered primate but also to the harshly confined laying hen. This consistency in the face of cruelty—real or threatened—has been a hallmark of The HSUS's five decades of work.

It would have comforted Fred Myers—who confided to Mel Morse that he felt "pretty well worn down" by his own humane labors—that millions of Americans have embraced the same path of service in the ensuing years. The HSUS, the organization Myers founded, has not had to go it alone. Other groups have been formed, other strategies adopted, and other programs pursued. While animals have continued to suffer at human hands, it is also true that organized concern for animals has found ever broader and stronger expression.

Nor has animal protection work represented a distraction from more urgent and pressing concerns or, as harsher critics might charge, a form of misanthropy. It is in fact, a vineyard ripe with benefits to humankind. The call for peaceful coexistence with nonhuman animals and due concern for their interests assumes and seeks to create a world organized around principles of decency, justice, and sustainability that ensure the survival of both humans and nonhuman animals. The humane vision is all-embracing and deeply compatible with and, indeed, essential to, the finest aspirations of humankind for a better world. As The HSUS's founders hoped, an increasing number of people have come to appreciate that concern for nonhuman animals does not demean humankind but rather ennobles it, and that a serious regard for the interests of nonhuman animals is a matter of profound self-interest for human beings.

The exact number of animals whose lot has been directly or indirectly improved through the work of The HSUS over fifty years can never be known. While it is hard to quantify precisely the spread of the humane ethic, a few observations about The HSUS's role in promoting animal protection can be made. In a half-century of work, The HSUS has been the source of education, insight, and training for millions of people. At the same time, it has forged a reputation for reliable and responsible advocacy work. It has been one of the principal facilitators of information exchange in the humane field, providing some of the best literature available. It has fielded a cadre of professional and scientific experts without parallel in the world. While the fortunes of a handful of other organizations have waxed and waned, The HSUS has seen steady growth and the maturation of a durable and successful institutionalized framework for responding to the many challenges that threaten animals' well-being.

The campaign to fulfill Schweitzer's vision is, of course, unfinished, and it has not been a simple story of linear progress. Half a century into the modern struggle to promote and protect animals' well-being, and despite the achievements of The HSUS and other groups, some of the gains achieved in recent decades are in jeopardy. New threats, born of new technologies and objectives, have emerged. Cruelty and indifference toward animals still thrive in many quarters. Both wild and domestic animals in a broad range of situations within and outside the United States remain threatened.

Even so, there are reasons for hope, courage, and perseverance. Schweitzer's notion of reverence for life calls for dynamic and substantial action, both individual and collective. If there is any value in looking at organized animal protection's past, it is to reinforce the importance of principled and resolute activity. The fate of nonhuman life continues to depend on the goodwill and concerted effort of individuals moved by the spirit of compassion, to tireless, unselfish, and often unheralded labor. The reality is that few if any of the positive developments recorded in these pages would have occurred without the participation of determined advocates. The same will be true for those advances to come.

Foreword

[1]Undated document. Fred Myers. HSUS History and By-Laws, Filebox 3099-1245.

Chapter One

[1]Robert Chenoweth, "The Humane Movement," in HSUS, *New Frontiers of the American Humane Movement* (Washington, D.C.: HSUS, 1960), 73.

[2]Jacques Sichel, *The HSUS Handbook* (Washington, D.C.: HSUS, 1969), 2a.

[3]Sichel, *The HSUS Handbook*, 2.

[4]Mrs. George F. Milliken, "The Record of The HSUS In Its First Five Years," *HSUS News* (November 1959): 16; Jacques V. Sichel, "Fred Myers: Introduction and Homage," undated speech, HSUS History and By-Laws Filebox 3099–1245; and Christine Stevens, "Laboratory Animal Welfare," in Animal Welfare Institute, *Animals and Their Legal Rights*, 4th ed., (Washington, D.C.: AWI, 1990), 68.

[5]Milliken, "The Record of The HSUS In Its First Five Years": 16; Sichel, "Fred Myers: Introduction and Homage"; Christine Stevens, "Laboratory Animal Welfare," 68; Ed Myers, personal communication (14 April 2003); and Marianne Myers Atkinson, interview (24 May 2003).

[6]William A. Swallow, *The Quality of Mercy* (Boston: Mary Mitchell Humane Fund, 1963), 165; and Sichel, *The HSUS Handbook*, 50.

[7]"We Confess to Being Jealous," *HSUS News* (August 1957): 6; "Gandhi on Endowments," *HSUS News* (September 1958): 8; HSUS, *Annual Report of the President* (Washington, D.C.: HSUS, 1958), 12; "ASPCA Urges More Monkeys in Missiles," *HSUS News* (August 1959): 6; "President's Address," *HSUS News* (November 1959): 6; and Milliken, "The Record of The HSUS In Its First Five Years," 16.

[8]John A. Hoyt, interview by Kim Stallwood, Archive (Baltimore, Md.: Animal Rights Network, 29 March 2001).

[9]Fred Myers, undated (1955) memo, "To Members of the National Humane Society," HSUS History and By-Laws Filebox 3099–1245; "Ex-Newsman Declares He Was Never a Red," *New York Herald-Tribune* (16 March 1956); "Some Comments About Our Enemies," *HSUS News* (May 1957): 3; and Belton P. Mouras, *I Care About Animals: Moving from Emotion to Action* (New York: A.S. Barnes, 1977), 122–123.

[10]"AHA Asks Court to Change NHS Name," *National Humane Society News* (June 1956): 3; "Name of NHS Changed to The Humane Society of the United States," *National Humane Society News* (January 1957): 1; and Milliken, "The Record of The HSUS In Its First Five Years," 16.

[11]"Name of NHS Changed to The Humane Society of the United States," *National Humane Society News* (January 1957): 1; *HSUS News* editorial (April 1962): 10; *HSUS News* editorial (September 1964): 3; and "HSUS Protests Issuance of Code Seal to Columbia Movie," *HSUS News* (January 1966): 8.

[12]"Larry Andrews Resigns: Elected Director," *HSUS News* (September 1956): 5.

[13]"Behind the Scenes," *HSUS News* (March 1956): 5; "Campaign to Reduce Dog and Cat Breeding Pushed Nationally," *HSUS News* (June 1956): 2; and Helen Jones, "Autobiographical Notes," *Between the Species* 4, no. 1 (Winter 1988): 71.

[14]Sichel, *The HSUS Handbook*, vol. 2, 552; Patrick B. Parkes, personal communication (26 March 2003).

[15]"NCAWS Incorporated," *HSUS News* (March 1959): 2; NCAWS entry, Anna Belle Morris Fund Ledger, Filebox 3099–1930; Jones, "Autobiographical Notes": 71–74; and Patrick B. Parkes interview (13 March 2003).

[16]"Senate Committee Schedules April Slaughter Bill Hearing," *HSUS News* (April 1956): 1.

[17]Fred Myers, undated document, 10, 1963, in "Fred Myers," History and By-Laws, Filebox 3099–1245.

[18]Fred Myers, "Policing a Rodeo," *HSUS News* (August 1957): 2; "Dog Warden Arrested," *HSUS News* (June 1958): 8; and Ed Myers, personal communication (14 April 2003).

[19]Parkes, interview (13 March 2003); Patrick B. Parkes, personal communication to Ed Myers (17 April 2003).

[20]*HSUS News* (May 1957): 6.

[21]"NHS Inaugurates First Branch in Illinois," *National Humane Society News* (March 1956): 1; Milliken, "The Record of The HSUS In Its First Five Years": 16; Swallow, *The Quality of Mercy*, 165; and Patrick B. Parkes and Jacques V. Sichel, *Twenty-Five Years of Growth and Achievement: The Humane Society of the United States, 1954–1979* (Washington, D.C.: HSUS, 1979), 7. Dallas Pratt described the way in which the New York HSUS chapter's Virginia Milliken harnessed his interest in the work in "The Long Way Round to the Animals," *Between the Species* (Winter 1987): 48.

[22]Patrick B. Parkes, personal communication (23 March 2003).

[23]Ibid.

[24]Ibid.

[25]Ibid.

[26]Sichel, *The HSUS Handbook*, 70.

[27]"Alice Wagner, Former HSUS Director, Dies," *HSUS News* (Summer 1977): 27; "William Kerber," *HSUS News* (Summer 1990): 9; "Roger Caras Is Elected to HSUS National Board," *HSUS News* (March 1970): 2; and Sue Pressman, "Amanda Blake," *HSUS News* (Fall 1989): 5.

[28]"HSUS Director Jacques Sichel Dies," *HSUS News* (Winter 1981): 7.

[29]Lee Edwards Benning, *The Pet Profiteers: The Exploitation of Pet Owners—and Pets—in America* (New York: Quad-

rangle, 1976), 41–42; "National Humane Leader Dies," *HSUS News* (Spring 1978): 8; and Lois Stevenson, "Doc Thomsen Leaves a Legacy of Kindness," *Sunday Star-Ledger* (30 April 1978).

[30]"International Humane Slaughter Law Sought Through U.N.," *HSUS News* (January 1957): 4; "Lifetime of Humane Work Ends with Death of Miss Goode," *HSUS News* (March 1970): 3; and Lynda Birke, "Supporting the Underdog: Feminism, Animal Rights, and Citizenship in the Work of Alice Morgan Wright and Edith Goode," *Women's History Review* 9, no. 4 (2000): 693–719.

[31]Fred Myers, memo to all HSUS directors (18 March 1960), History and By-Laws, Filebox 3099–1245; Parkes and Sichel, *Twenty-Five Years*, 4; and Fred Myers, "Report of the Executive Director," in HSUS, *New Frontiers of the American Humane Movement*, 4–5.

[32]Parkes, interview (13 March 2003).

[33]Myers, memo to all HSUS directors (18 March 1960).

[34]Ibid.; Parkes and Sichel, *Twenty-Five Years*, 6.

[35]"Frank McMahon Loses Fight for Life," *HSUS News* (Summer 1975): 6.

[36]"President's Address," *HSUS News* (November 1959): 5; Sichel, *The HSUS Handbook*, Vol. 2, 380.

[37]"National Leadership Conference Lays Plans," *HSUS News* (November 1962): 1–2.

[38]Fred Myers to Mel Morse (9 August 1962); Fred Myers, undated memo (1963), 9, HSUS Filebox 3049–1245.

[39]Myers to Morse (9 August 1962); Edith Goode, memorandum to the Board of Directors (4 January 1965), HSUS Filebox 3049–1245; Parkes, interview (12 March 2003); and Marianne Myers Atkinson, interview (24 May 2003).

[40]"To All HSUS Members" (4 April 1963), HSUS Filebox 3049–1245; "HSUS Founder, Treasurer Dies," *HSUS News* (Winter 1975–1976): 3.

[41]"Humanitarians Cautioned on Rash of Weak Lab Legislation; Urged to Support HSUS Bills," *HSUS News* (November 1964): 3.

[42]Parkes and Sichel, *Twenty-Five Years*, 20; Ben Hayes, interview (2 April 2003); Parkes, personal communication (26 April 2003).

[43]Dale Hylton, personal communication (29 May 2003).

[44]Ibid.

[45]"Board Resolution Wins Ballot, Amends By-Laws," *HSUS News* (May 1966): 1.

[46]Myers to Morse (9 August 1962); "In Memoriam," *HSUS News* (Summer 1988): 2.

[47]Sichel, "Fred Myers: Introduction and Homage," 2; "John A. Hoyt Elected President of Humane Society of the United States," *HSUS News* (March 1970): 2; and Hoyt, interview (29 March 2001).

[48]Parkes and Sichel, *Twenty-Five Years*, 26–27; Hoyt, interview (29 March 2001).

[49]Hoyt, interview (29 March 2001); Parkes, interview (13 March 2003).

[50]Hoyt, interview (29 March 2001); and John A. Hoyt, interview by Kim Stallwood, Archive (Baltimore, Md.: Animal Rights Network, 31 May 2001).

[51]See, for example, *Report of the President* for 1976 and 1992, HSUS History and By-Laws, Filebox 3099–1245.

[52]"Board Appoints New Committee to Study Long Range Problems," *HSUS News* (October 1970): 2; Hoyt, interview (31 May 2001).

[53]"The World's Greatest Humane Problem," *Report to Humanitarians* 5 (September 1968): 1; *President's Report*, 1978; Hoyt, interview (31 2001).

[54]Hoyt, interview (29 March 2001).

[55]Fred Myers, personal communication to Oliver Evans (19 August 1963), HSUS History and By-Laws, Filebox 3099–1245; "Announcement," *HSUS News* (May–June 1968): 1; Mouras, *I Care About Animals*, 120; and Hoyt, interview (29 March 2001).

[56]John A. Hoyt, "Reflecting on Progress," *HSUS News* (Winter 1973): 4.

[57]*Washington Star* (7 May 1971); John A. Hoyt, "New Occasions Teach New Duties," *HSUS News* (July 1971): 5.

[58]John Hoyt, "Living Legacies," *HSUS News* (Summer 1981).

[59]Hoyt, interview (29 March 2001); John C. MacFarlane, personal communication to John A. Hoyt (13 August 1973), Filebox 3099–315.

[60]Sichel, *The HSUS Handbook*, 4.

[61]Roderick Frazier Nash, *The Rights of Nature: A History of Environmental Ethics* (Madison, Wis.: University of Wisconsin Press, 1989), 60.

[62]*http://www.nobel.se/peace/laureates/1952/schweitzer-lecture.html*. Accessed June 2003.

[63]"Humanitarian of Year to Mrs. Flemming for Work with Children," *HSUS News* (November 1964): 3.

[64]Sichel, *The HSUS Handbook*, 930.

[65]Nash, *The Rights of Nature*, 74–76.

[66]Joseph Wood Krutch, *The Great Chain of Life* (Boston: Houghton Mifflin, 1957), 165; "Two Books You Should Read," *HSUS News* (May 1957): 4; *HSUS News* (March 1959): 1; and *HSUS News* (May 1959): 1.

[67]Joseph Wood Krutch, "What Does Violence Say About Man?" *Saturday Review* (27 March 1965).

[68]John A. Hoyt, memo to Board of Directors (12 February 1971, 1970–1974), Filebox 3099-1949; Richard Morris and Michael Fox, eds., *On the Fifth Day* (Washington, D.C.: Acropolis Books, 1978), 137.

[69]Oliver M. Evans, "A New Moral Imperative," *HSUS News* (Winter 1976–77): 4–5; Patrick B. Parkes, "A Review," *HSUS News* (Fall 1977): 1.

[70]Patrick Parkes, personal communication (7 April 2003).

[71]Sichel, *The HSUS Handbook*, 4a.

[72]John A. Hoyt, "A Policy Statement Regarding Various Animal Utilization Projects and Procedures" (14 April 1978), 2.

[73]"Education on TV," *HSUS News* (November 1962): 1.

[74]"Laboratory Animals," *Report to Humanitarians* 18 (December 1971): 3.

[75]"Delegates Elect Five Perpetual Members at HSUS Annual Meeting," *HSUS News* (November–December 1969): 2; Parkes, personal communication (26 April 2003).

[76]Hoyt, interview (29 March 2001).

[77]"Wildlife Expert Named to Staff," *HSUS News* (May 1971): 1.

[78]"Vet Joins Staff," *HSUS News* (November 1972): 1; "Name Veterinarians to Advisory Group," *HSUS News* (October 1973): 7; and "Reflecting on Progress," *HSUS News* (Winter 1973): 4.

[79]*Report of the President*, 1976; "Annual Report 1977," insert, *HSUS News* (Spring 1978); "Forkan Appointed Vice President," *HSUS News* (Fall 1978): 14.

[80]*Report of the President*, 1976.

[81]Paul G. Irwin, "Formulating a Development/Fund Raising Plan" (9 April 1976), Filebox 3099–390.

[82]James Smart, "Dogs Get Their Own Psychologist," *Philadelphia Bulletin* (4 February 1972); Michael W. Fox, *Understanding Your Dog* (New York: Coward, McCann and Geoghegan, 1972); "Dr. Michael Fox Joins HSUS," *HSUS News* (Summer/Fall 1976): 15; Kathy Hacker, "Animal Rights: For Billion of Animals, Progress Means Suffering," *Philadelphia Bulletin* (28 September 1980); and Michael W. Fox, "Autobiographical Notes," *Between the Species* 3, no. 2 (Spring 1987): 98–101.

[83]"Animal Societies in Court Fight Over $6 Million," *Philadelphia Bulletin* (6 January 1970); Documents in HSUS-ISAP 1974, Folder Filebox 3099–707.

[84]Hoyt, interview (29 March 2001).

[85]Ibid.

[86]"Dr. Andrew Rowan to Join ISAP Staff," *HSUS News* (Spring 1978): 14.

[87]*Report of the President*, 1977.

[88]"HSUS's Frantz Dantzler: A Big Man Doing a Big Job," *HSUS News* (Spring 1977): 9.

[89]Michael Fox, interview by Kim Stallwood, Archive (Baltimore, Md.: Animal Rights Network, 19 April 2001); Ben Hayes, interview (2 April 2003); Charles F. Herrmann, III, interview (17 April 2003); and Patricia Forkan, interview (29 April 2003).

[90]*Report of the President*, 1978.

[91]Charles F. Herrmann, III, interview (17 April 2003); Deborah Salem, interview (21 April 2003).

[92]Ibid.

[93]*Report of the President, 1977*; *Report of the President*, 1978; and Parkes and Sichel, *Twenty-Five Years*, 31.

[94]"Common Goals: HSUS and the RSPCA Share Ideas on Animal Welfare," *HSUS News* (Winter 1981): 11.

[95]"AWA Enforcement Axed?" *HSUS News* (Spring 1985): 30; "The Budget's Bad News," *HSUS News* (Spring 1987): 27.

[96]Forkan, interview (29 April 2003).

[97]*Report of the President*, 1983; Forkan, interview (29 April 2003).

[98]*Report of the President*, 1981.

[99]Ibid.; John A. Hoyt, "Making Earth Our Home," *HSUS News* (Spring 1990).

[100]*Report of the President*, 1981.

[101]*Report of the President*, 1984.

[102]Ibid.

[103]*Report of the President*, 1982, 1983, 1984, 1985, 1986.

[104]*Report of the President*, 1984; *Report of the President*, 1985; and John A. Hoyt, "The Benefits and Consequences of Animal Rights," *HSUS News* (Summer 1986).

[105]John A. Hoyt, "A Sense of Where You Are," *HSUS News* (Winter 1989): 12–14.

[106]*Report of the President*, 1985.

[107]Michael W. Fox, "Animal Rights and the Law of Ecology," *HSUS News* (Fall 1977): 20–21; "Animal Rights—An Ethical Examination," *Washington Star* (28 April 1978).

[108]"Farm Animal Progress," *HSUS News* (Summer 1984): 28.

[109]John A. Hoyt, "Building the World's Bridges," *HSUS News* (Fall 1978): 32.

[110]Fox, interview (19 April 2001).

[111]John A. Hoyt, "The Consequences of the Means," *HSUS News* (Spring 1981); John A. Hoyt, "Joint Resolutions for the 1990s," *HSUS News* (Spring 1991): 24–25.

[112]John W. Grandy, interview (14 March 2003); Fox, interview (19 April 2001); Michael Fox and John Hoyt, interview by Kim Stallwood, Archive (Baltimore, Md.: Animal Rights Network, 8 November 2001); and Courtney L. Dillard, Ph.D., interview (31 May 2003).

[113]*Report of the President*, 1980, 1984; Forkan, interview (29 April 2003); and Forkan, interview (30 May 2003).

[114]Andrew N. Rowan, "Cruelty and Abuse to Animals: A Typology," in Frank R. Ascione and Phil Arkow, eds., *Child Abuse, Domestic Violence, and Animal Abuse* (West Lafayette, Ind.: Purdue University Press, 1999), 328.

[115]"Problems After Cruelty Trials," *HSUS News* (Summer 1989): 36; Randall Lockwood, Ph.D., "Untangling the Web," *HSUS News* (Spring 1993): 33–35.

[116]Roger Kindler, "A Legal Defeat for Animals," *HSUS News* (Fall 1993): 10–11.

[117]Randall Lockwood, Ph.D., and Ann Church, "Deadly Serious: An FBI Perspective on Animal Cruelty," *HSUS News* (Fall 1996): 27–30; "Our First Strike against Violence," *Animal Update* (Summer 1999): 1.

[118]*Report of the President*, 1981; Forkan, interview (23 April 2003).

[119]Susan S. Lieberman, "Here Today, Gone Tomorrow," *HSUS News* (Fall 1987): 16–19.

[120]John A. Hoyt, "Enlarging Our Outreach," *HSUS News* (Winter 1990).

[121]Hoyt, interview (31 May 2001)

[122]Debra Firmani, personal communication (22 April 2003).

[123]Angela O. Harkavy, "Earth Charter Moves Forward," *HSUS News* (Fall 1995): 12; John A. Hoyt, "Encoding Respect for Animals as Individuals," *HSUS News* (Summer 1997).

[124]John A. Hoyt, "A New President at the Helm," *HSUS News* (Spring 1992); Paul G. Irwin, "An Inspiration and a Guiding Force," *HSUS News* (Winter 1997).

[125]David O. Wiebers, "Healing Society's Relationship with Animals: A Physician's Views," *HSUS News* (Fall 1991): 26–27; David O. Wiebers, "Animals in Medical Research: Vision of a New Era," *HSUS News* (Winter 1992): 9–11.

[126]Andrew Rowan, personal communication (28 April 2003).

[127]Richard H. Farinato and David L. Kuemmerle, "The Ratite Craze," *HSUS News* (Fall 1996): 14–17.

[128]Paul G. Irwin, "Ballots Over Bullets," *HSUS News* (Winter 1995); Salem, interview (23 April 2003); Wayne Pacelle,

interview (17 May 2003); Forkan, interview (30 May 2003).

[129]Irwin, "Ballots Over Bullets"; Wayne Pacelle, "Landslide Year for Wildlife," *HSUS News* (Spring 1997): 6–8.

[130]Pacelle, "Landslide Year for Wildlife."

[131]Wayne Pacelle, "The Persecution of the Lion," *HSUS News* (Winter 1996): 16–18.

[132]Wayne Pacelle, "Ballot Measures on Animal Protection Since 1990," undated personal communication.

[133]Pacelle, interview (17 May 2003).

[134]Pacelle, "Ballot Measures on Animal Protection Since 1990."

[135]Wayne Pacelle, "2002 Farm Bill," undated personal communication.

[136]Peter Singer, "Animal Liberation at 30," *New York Review of Books* (15 May 2003): 26.

[137]Betsy Dribben, "International Strategies," *HSUS News* (Spring 1996): 21–22.

[138]John A. Hoyt, "Enlarging Our Vision, Extending Our Outreach," *HSUS News* (Winter 1992).

[139]Hoyt, interview (31 May 2001).

[140]Andrew Rowan, personal communication (31 May 2003).

[141]Patricia Forkan, "Good Laws Doomed," *HSUS News* (Fall 1995): 32–34; Betsy Dribben, "International Strategies," *HSUS News* (Spring 1996): 21–22.

[142]Dribben, "International Strategies."

[143]Paul Irwin, "A Tale of Two Agendas," *HSUS News* (Spring 1998).

Chapter Two

[1]Christian P. Norgord, "Brutal Butchering Demands New Humane Legislation," *National Humane Review* (July 1952): 4–5; "Painless Slaughter," *National Humane Review* (January 1953): 21; and "Humane Slaughter in Denmark," *National Humane Review* (December 1953): 17.

[2]Fred Myers, "Lessons Taught by Humane Slaughter Victory," *HSUS News* (September 1958): 6–7.

[3]"Chances Good for Humane Slaughter Law This Winter," *National Humane Society News* (September 1955): 1; "Humane Slaughter Drive Is Sweeping Country," *National Humane Society News* (March 1956): 1; and Mrs. George F. Milliken, "The Record of The HSUS in Its First Five Years," *HSUS News* (November 1959): 16.

[4]"H.R. 8540 Is Best Bill," "Humane Slaughter Drive Is Sweeping Country," *National Humane Society News* (March 1956): 3; "How 5,000,000 Women Were Lined Up Behind Slaughter Reform Drive," *HSUS News* (June 1956): 2; "Churches Rally Behind Drive for Federal Humane Slaughter Law," *HSUS News* (June 1958): 3; Myers, "Lessons," 7; and Patrick B. Parkes and Jacques V. Sichel, *Twenty-Five Years of Growth and Achievement: The Humane Society of the United States, 1954–1979*, (Washington, D.C.: HSUS, 1979) 4–5. Martha Griffiths (1912–2003) went on to become the strongest congressional champion of the inclusion of women in the Civil Rights Act of 1964.

[5]"Senate Committee Hears Slaughter Reform Demands," *HSUS News* (June 1956): 4; "What Happened in the Last Congress," *HSUS News* (September 1956): 3.

[6]"Congressmen Continue Probe of Packers Despite Politics," *HSUS News* (September 1956): 1; Myers, "Lessons," 7; and Emily Stewart Leavitt, "Humane Slaughter Laws," in Animal Welfare Institute (AWI), *Animals and Their Legal Rights*, 4th ed. (Washington, D.C.: AWI, 1990), 53.

[7]"Humane Slaughter Drive Enters Home Stretch," *HSUS News* (March 1957), 1.

[8]"Humane Slaughter Bills Near Test," *HSUS News* (May 1957): 2.

[9]Paul W. Kearney and Richard Dempewolff, "Let Us Have Mercy on These Dumb Animals," *Reader's Digest* (January 1961): 47; Jacques V. Sichel, "Humane Slaughter Legislation," in HSUS, *New Frontiers of the American Humane Movement* (Washington, D.C.: HSUS, 1960), 20–22; and Mel Morse, *Ordeal of the Animals* (Englewood Cliffs, N.J.: Prentice-Hall, 1968), 73–80.

[10]"Humane Slaughter Bill Moves Toward Victory," *HSUS News* (August 1957): 1.

[11]Ibid., 6; "Favorable Action on Humane Slaughter Probable," *HSUS News* (December 1957): 1.

[12]"Slaughter Bill Going to Floor Fight," *HSUS News* (June 1958): 1; Leavitt, "Humane Slaughter Laws," *Animals and Their Legal Rights*, 54.

[13]"Humane Slaughter Bill Signed by President Eisenhower," *HSUS News* (September 1958): 1; "Senator Humphrey Lauds HSUS in Analysis of Victory," *HSUS News* (November 1958): 4.

[14]Fred Myers, personal communication to Wilbur M. Brucker (13 June 1960); Fred Myers, personal communication to Congressman W.R. Poage (13 June 1960), Slaughter–File, Filebox 3099–601; and AWI, *Animals and Their Legal Rights*, 54–55.

[15]Sichel, "Humane Slaughter Legislation," 19; Morse, *Ordeal*, 68, 72.

[16]Fred Myers, personal communication to B.C. Preacher (19 August 1960), Slaughter–Correspondence, Filebox 3099–601; "HSUS Urges Benson to Stiffen Enforcement of Humane Slaughter Law," *HSUS News* (November 1960): 1.

[17]Fred Myers, "Lessons Taught by Humane Slaughter Victory," *HSUS News* (September 1958): 7–8.

[18]*HSUS News* editorial (February 1962): 1.

[19]Myers, "Lessons Taught by Humane Slaughter Victory," 8; "Convention Report," *HSUS News* (November 1958): 8.

[20]Fred Myers, "Executive Director's Annual Report," *HSUS News* (November 1959): 8.

[21]*Bulletin to Florida Humane Societies* (29 December 1960), Slaughter–Florida, Filebox 3099–606; Kearney and Dempewolff, "Let Us Have Mercy on These Dumb Animals," 45.

[22]"To All HSUS Directors" (18 March 1960), History and By-Laws, Filebox 3099–1245; "Work Continues for Humane Slaughter Laws," *HSUS News* (July–August 1961): 2; and "Humane Slaughter Laws Now Cover More than 1,200 Packing Plants," *HSUS News* (November 1961): 3.

[23][Fred Myers], undated testimony (1960), 4, Slaughter Legislation, Filebox 3099–601; Kearney and Dempewolff, "Let Us Have Mercy on These Dumb Animals," 46.

[24][Fred Myers], undated testimony (1960), 4–5, Slaughter Legislation, Filebox 3099–601; "Humane Society Backs Senate Bill," *Troy News* (31 March 1965).

[25]Kearney and Dempewolff, "Let Us Have Mercy on These Dumb Animals," 47; Belton Mouras, personal correspon-

dence to Fred Myers (18 May 1961), Slaughter–Oklahoma, Filebox 3099–601; and Don Kendall, "New Slaughter Method Wins Societies' Approval," *Hutchinson News* (23 January 1961).

[26] Mouras, personal communication to Myers (18 May 1961), Slaughter–Oklahoma, Filebox 3099–601; Helen Jones, personal communication to Belton Mouras (7 August 1961), Slaughter–Pennsylvania, Filebox 3099–601; and Jacques V. Sichel, Testimony on Behalf of New Jersey Humane Slaughter Legislation, undated, Slaughter–New Jersey, Filebox 3099–601.

[27] "The Humane Society and Anti-Schechita," *Jewish Press* (17 December 1965).

[28] "Canada's Humane Law and Regulations," *National Provisioner* (9 January 1960); Sichel, Testimony on Behalf of New Jersey Humane Slaughter Legislation; Sichel, "Humane Slaughter Legislation," 22; Kearney and Dempewolff, "Let Us Have Mercy on These Dumb Animals,"47–48; and Patrick B. Parkes, personal communication (2 April 2003).

[29] Sichel, Testimony on Behalf of New Jersey Humane Slaughter Legislation.

[30] Helen Jones, letter to the editor, *Jewish Press* (15 September 1961); Sichel, Testimony on Behalf of New Jersey Humane Slaughter Legislation; and Patrick B. Parkes, personal communication (4 April 2003).

[31] "Kosher Slaughtering with Humane Slaughtering Device," Food Handling Machine Corporation advertisement, with article and HSUS statement, in Slaughter, Jewish Ritual Filebox 3099–601; Belton Mouras, personal communication to Thomas Gilmartin (2 February 1961), Slaughter–Ohio; Belton Mouras, personal communication to Mendel Small (21 March 1961), Slaughter–Missouri; Lewis Timberlake, personal communication to Elaine G. Watford (9 March 1962), Slaughter–Michigan, Filebox 3099–601; and Fred Myers memo (24 May 1961), Slaughter–Connecticut, Filebox 3099–601.

[32] Sichel, "Humane Slaughter Legislation," 21; "Rabbis Testify for Amendment," *Cleveland Press* (23 March 1961); "On Humane Slaughter," *Jewish Newsletter* (18 September 1961): 3; "Humane Slaughter Laws Won," *HSUS News* (April 1962): 9; "Campaigns for Humane Slaughter Laws Started in Eight States," *HSUS News* (February 1963): 2; "Humane Slaughter Campaigns Being Pushed in Three States," *HSUS News* (March 1964): 1; "Assembly Defeats Animal Killing Plan," *Philadelphia Bulletin* (19 May 1964); "Humane Slaughter Bill Is Enacted in Ohio," *Philadelphia Bulletin* (27 May 1965); "Painless Slaughtering Decreed by New Law," *Philadelphia Bulletin* (15 September 1965); "Slaughter Law Passed in Indiana; Defeat Predicted in Other States Despite Vigorous State Campaigns," *HSUS News* (March–April 1967): 7; and "Humane Slaughter Laws Are Enacted in Illinois, Iowa," *HSUS News* (July–August 1967): 8.

[33] "ASPCA Patents Pave Way for State Humane Slaughter Legislation," *HSUS News* (July 1964): 2; *Bulletin from The Humane Society of the United States* (19 February 1965), in Slaughter–Ohio, Filebox 3099–601; and Sichel, Testimony on Behalf of New Jersey Humane Slaughter Legislation.

[34] "Humane Society Head Praises Pennsylvania Laws to Protect Animals," *Philadelphia Inquirer* (27 December 1965); "Humane Slaughter Law Stirs Bitter Battle," *HSUS News* (January 1966): 8; and Robert D. Fleming, personal communication to Oliver Evans (30 December 1965), Slaughter–Pennsylvania, Filebox 3099–601.

[35] "Slaughter Bill Nears Passage in Missouri; Indiana Stops Threat," *HSUS News* (March–April 1969): 8.

[36] Seymour Krim, "Kosher Slaughter—Friends of Animals Stir up Anti-Semitic Fear," *New York Herald-Tribune* (13 March 1966); "Rabbis Suing Times On Kosher-Bill Ad," *New York Times* (16 March 1966); Morse, *Ordeal*, 72; and John C. Macfarlane, personal communication to Mrs. George Milliken (6 June 1972), Filebox 3099–315.

[37] Fred Myers, personal communication to Raymond Starr (2 September 1960); Frederic L. Thomsen, personal communication to Belton P. Mouras (20 October 1962); Fred Myers, personal communication to Belton Mouras (30 October 1962), Slaughter, Stunning Equipment–Correspondence, Filebox 3099–601; Fred Myers, personal communication to Ray Cuff (17 April 1961), Slaughter–Missouri Livestock Loss Prevention, Filebox 3099–601; Fred Myers, personal communication to American Meat Institute (18 May 1960); and Fred Myers, personal communication to J. Wismer Pedersen (18 May 1960), in Slaughter, Humane Slaughter Techniques, Correspondence 1960–1964.

[38] "Federal and State Humane Slaughter Laws," *Report to Humanitarians* 15 (March 1971): 1.

[39] "Kosher Slaughter," *Report to Humanitarians* 16 (June 1971): 3; David Bird, "Connecticut Researchers Study Humane Slaughter," *New York Times* (8 December 1974).

[40] "Man's Greatest Cruelty to Animals," *Report to Humanitarians* 15 (March 1971): 1–2.

[41] Ibid.

[42] John C. Macfarlane, 18 May Speech to New York State Humane Convention, Filebox 3099–315; John A. Hoyt, "Working Toward Humane Slaughter," *HSUS News* (June 1972), 4.

[43] John C. Macfarlane, 18 May Speech to New York State Humane Convention, Filebox 3099–315; "Toward Humane Slaughter of All Food Animals in the U.S.," *Report to Humanitarians* 21 (September 1972); and David Bird, "Connecticut Researchers Study Humane Slaughter," *New York Times* (8 December 1974).

[44] *New York Times* (4 January 1972); Policy and Program Committee Minutes (6–7 January 1972), Meetings Program and Policy, Filebox 3099–390; and John C. Macfarlane, personal communication to Rabbi Sheldon C. Freedman (25 July 1972), Filebox 3099–315.

[45] "Man's Greatest Cruelty to Animals," *Report to Humanitarians* 15 (March 1971): 2; "Kosher Slaughter," *Report to Humanitarians* 16 (June 1971): 3; and Temple Grandin, "Humane Livestock Handling," *HSUS News* (Winter 1979): 2.

[46] "Researchers Optimistic on Funds," *Hartford Courant* (27 January 1974); Bird, "Connecticut Researchers Study Humane Slaughter"; and Edwin J. Harragan, memo (20 January 1975), Filebox 3099–315.

[47] Encil E. Rains, personal communication to Malcolm P. Ripley (12 September 1973), Filebox 3099–315; John C. McFarlane, personal communication to John A. Hoyt (1 November 1973), Filebox 3099–315; John C. Macfarlane, personal communication to Ralph P. Prince (9 January 1975), Filebox 3099–315; and Temple Grandin, "Progress in Livestock Handling and Slaughter Techniques in the United States, 1970–2000," in Deborah J. Salem and Andrew N. Rowan, eds., *The State of the Animals: 2001* (Washington, D.C.: Humane Society Press; 2001), 103.

[48] Fowler C. West, personal communication to John C. Macfarlane (23 May 1973); John A. Hoyt, personal communication to Susan Warner (10 September 1973), Filebox 3099–315.

[49] Grandin, "Humane Livestock Handling," 1–3; Temple Grandin, "Problems with Kosher Slaughter," *International Journal for the Study of Animal Problems* 1, no. 6 (1980): 375–90.

[50] Joel Ollander, personal communication to John A. Hoyt (15 December 1978), in *HSUS News* (Winter 1979); 1978 Resolutions, *HSUS News* (Winter 1979): 24; and "In Memoriam: Max Schnapp," *HSUS News* (Spring 1995): 4.

[51]Temple Grandin, "Improving Kosher Slaughter," *HSUS News* (Spring 1989): 9–10; Grandin, "Progress in Livestock Handling and Slaughter Techniques," 103.

[52]Peter Singer, *Ethics Into Action: Henry Spira and the Animal Rights Movement* (Lanham, Md.: Rowman and Little-field,1998), 156–160.

[53]"Survey Shows Packers Obeying Federal Slaughter Law," *HSUS News* (January–February 1967): 1, 6.

[54]"Bill Would Reduce Cruelties of Slaughter for U.S. Meat Imports," *Report to Humanitarians* 16 (June 1971): 1.

[55]Macfarlane, 18 May Speech to New York State Humane Convention; "Essential Facts About the Gunter Humane Slaughter Bill, H.R. 8055," *Report to Humanitarians* 25 (September 1973): 2–3.

[56]George E. Brown, "Humane Treatment of Animals—Another Piece of the Puzzle," *HSUS News* (Spring 1977): 4.

[57]Brown, "Humane Treatment of Animals," 4; Peggy Morrison, memo (2 June 1977), ISAP–Humane Slaughter, Filebox 3099–707.

[58]Patricia Forkan, personal communication to Robert F. Welborn (18 May 1978), Slaughter Legislation, Filebox 3099–601; "HSUS Testifies on Humane Slaughter," *HSUS News* (Summer 1978): 17; "Humane Slaughter," *HSUS News* (Summer 1978): 22; "Humane Slaughter Act Becomes Law," *HSUS News* (Winter 1979): 30; and Patricia Forkan, interview (29 April 2003).

[59]Forkan, personal communication to Welborn (18 May 1978), Slaughter Legislation, Filebox 3099–601; and "HSUS Testifies on Humane Slaughter," 17.

[60]Brown, "Humane Treatment of Animals," 4; "Humane Slaughter Act," *HSUS News* (Fall 1978): 24; Phil Gailey, "Humaneness Before Slaughter," *Washington Star* (21 July 1978); "Humane Slaughter Act Becomes Law," 30; and Leavitt, "Humane Slaughter Laws," 56–57.

[61]"The World's Greatest Humane Problem," *Report to Humanitarians* 5 (September 1968): 1–12; "The Real Ripoff in the Humane Movement," *Report to Humanitarians* 35 (March 1976): 4.

[62]"Factory Farming: And Now the Good News," *HSUS News* (Winter 1981): 2; "Livestock Lib: Protest Grows on Way Many Farmers Confine Pigs, Hens, Veal Calves," *Wall Street Journal* (18 December 1981).

[63]Michael W. Fox, interview by Kim Stallwood, Archive (Baltimore, Md.: Animal Rights Network, 19 April 2001); Michael Fox, "Suffering: The Hidden Cost of Factory Farming," *HSUS News* (Winter 1978): 15–20; and David Nevins, "Scientist Helps Stir New Movement for 'Animal Rights' that Works for More Humane Conditions on Farms and in Labs," *Smithsonian Magazine* 11 (April 1980): 47–58.

[64]"Factory Farming Win," *HSUS News* (Fall 1981): 30.

[65]"'Factory' Farming Update: Humane Alternatives Pay," *HSUS News* (Summer 1981): 4–6; Deborah Salem, Linda Mickley, and Michael W. Fox, "Farm Animal Welfare: New Directions and Developments," *HSUS News* (Winter 1984): 4.

[66]Salem, Mickley, and Fox, "Farm Animal Welfare," 8; "New Scrutiny Given Farming," *HSUS News* (Winter 1984): 31.

[67]"How Can You Keep Them Down on the Farm After They've Seen NAAHE?" *Utah Holiday* (February 1983): 11–12.

[68]"Animal Rights and the Producer," *Farm Supplier* (October 1984), in Misc. Media Articles, Filebox 3099–18; "Animal Welfare Advocate Reports Results of Scientist, Vet Survey," *Feedstuffs* 17 (November 1980): 35.

[69]"Persuading the Private Sector to Act Humanely," *HSUS News* (Spring 1983): 14–17; "Paté Resolution Lives," *HSUS News* (Spring 1985): 2; Diana S. Greene, "The Paté de Fois Gras Case," *HSUS News* (Summer 1985): 4–5.

[70]Greene, "The Paté de Fois Gras Case," 4–5.

[71]"Humane Alternatives Pay," 4–6.

[72]"No Veal This Meal," *HSUS News* (Winter 1982): 2; "No Veal This Meal," *HSUS News* (Spring 1982): 5–7; *Report of the President*, 1982; and Salem, Mickley, and Fox, "Farm Animal Welfare," 8.

[73]Michael W. Fox, "USDA 'Launders' Study Showing Calves Suffer on Factory Farms," *HSUS News* (Fall 1984): 16–17.

[74]"Bennett Boon for Calves!" *HSUS News* (Fall 1987): 29; "HSUS Speaks on Veal Bill," *HSUS News* (Fall 1989): 32; "House Stalls on Veal Bill," *HSUS News* (Winter 1990): 30; and Melanie Adcock and Mary Finelli, "The Dairy Cow: America's 'Foster Mother,'" *HSUS News* (Winter 1995): 20–24.

[75]"'Breakfast of Cruelty' Boycotts Prompt Action by Egg, Pork Producers," *HSUS News* (Summer 1987): 25.

[76]Michael W. Fox, "The Dairy Cow Debacle: The Government Mandates Face Branding," *HSUS News* (Summer 1986): 3–9; "Hot-Iron Branding Decision Noteworthy," *HSUS News* (Summer 1986): 36.

[77]Michael W. Fox and Linda Mickley, "Genetic Engineering: Cornucopia or Pandora's Box," *HSUS News* (Spring 1984): 14–18; Michael W. Fox, "The HSUS Tries Legal Remedies to Combat Genetic Engineering Experiments," *HSUS News* (Winter 1985): 13; "The Animal-Patenting Decision: Should People Own New Forms of Life?" *HSUS News* (Summer 1987): 6–7; and Fox, interview, 24 May 2001.

[78]"Buying Valuable Time," *HSUS News* (Fall 1987): 26; "Animal-Patenting Update," *HSUS News* (Spring 1988): 22; "Animal Patent Granted," *HSUS News* (Summer 1988): 34; "Reviewing Animal Patents," *HSUS News* (Winter 1990): 29; "Patenting Bills Introduced," *HSUS News* (Summer 1992): 34.

[79]Michael W. Fox, "Moving Nature Off Its Course," *HSUS News* (Spring 1986): 12–13; "BGH Causes National Brouha-ha," *HSUS News* (Spring 1994): 5–6.

[80]Michael Fox, "The Cloning Controversy," *HSUS News* (Summer 1997): 11–14.

[81]Michael Fox, "The Cattle Threat: Our Taste for Beef Damages the Environment," *HSUS News* (Earth Day 1990): 24–27; Michael Fox, "Humane Sustainable Agriculture," *HSUS News* (Winter 1992): 26.

[82]"Making a More Humane Choice," *HSUS News* (Summer 1988): 6–8.

[83]"Spreading the Good Word," *HSUS News* (Winter 1989): 5–6.

[84]Melanie Adcock, "The Truth Behind a Hen's Life," *HSUS News* (Spring 1993): 11–13; "HSUS Food Campaign Gaining Speed," *HSUS News* (Summer 1993): 3; and "More Good News for Hens," *HSUS News* (Winter 1995): 3.

[85]"Chickens Are Not Egg-Laying Machines," *Animal Update* (September/October 2001): 2.

[86]Paul Irwin, "'The Eating with Conscience' Fire Storm," *HSUS News* (Spring 1994).

[87]John Hoyt, foreword, in *Farm Animal Welfare and the Human Diet* (Washington, D.C.: HSUS, 1983); "Spreading the Good Word," *HSUS News* (Winter 1989): 5.

[88]"Calling It Organic," *HSUS News* (Summer 1991): 33; Fox, "Humane Sustainable Agriculture."

[89]*HSUS News* (Summer 1998): 3.

[90]"Organic or Not," *Humane Activist* (September/October 2002): 3.

[91]"Humane Society to Press for Law Protecting Dogs," *Washington Star* (6 October 1956); "Transportation Reform Program Launched," *HSUS News* (March 1964): 1; and "Transportation by Rail," *Report to Humanitarians* 5 (September 1968): 8.
[92]"Livestock Trucking Bill," *Report to Humanitarians* 17 (September 1971): 3; "Dangers to Livestock in Trucks Described," *HSUS News* (Autumn 1974): 9.
[93]"Livestock Transportation: Too Much Cruelty, Too Little Industry Concern," *HSUS News* (Fall 1984): 8–13; *HSUS Close-Up Report: HSUS Exposes Livestock Transportation Cruelty* (9/84).
[94]"Downers Plight Described," *HSUS News* (Spring 1992): 29; "Long Journey to Slaughter," *HSUS News* (Summer 1992: 7.
[95]"A New Tactic to Help Downers," *Humane Activist* (January/February 1999): 5.
[96]Wayne Pacelle, interview (26 May 2003).
[97]"No to Feed Drugs," *HSUS News* (Spring 1985): 30.
[98]Paul G. Irwin, "Informed Consumers, Industry Backlash," *HSUS News* (Summer 1998).
[99]"Antibiotic Backlash," *Humane Activist* (May/June 2002): 1.
[100]Adcock, "The Truth Behind a Hen's Life," 11–13; Adcock and Finelli, "The Dairy Cow: America's 'Foster Mother,'" 20–24.
[101]Melanie Adcock and Mary Finelli, "Against Nature: The Sensitive Pig Versus the Hostile Environment of the Modern Pig Farm," *HSUS News* (Spring 1996): 34–38; "NFAAW," *HSUS News* (Winter 1998): 2.
[102]Paul G. Irwin, "Overview: The State of the Animals in 2001," in Salem and Rowan, 12.
[103]Peter Singer, "Animal Liberation at 30," *New York Review of Books* (15 May 2003): 26.
[104]Michael Appleby, interview (8 May 2003).
[105]"An Impassioned Plea for Animals," *Humane Activist* (September/October 2001): 3; "Agriculture Appropriations Update," *Humane Activist* (September/October 2002): 2; and "Federal Appropriations Bill Includes Money to Hire Humane Slaughter Inspectors, Advance Animal Welfare," press release (26 February 2003), *http://www.hsus.org/ace/18475.*
[106]*www.halthogfactories.com.*

Chapter Three

[1]"HSUS Discovers Illegal Cruelty to Animals in Big Laboratories," *HSUS News* (June 1958): 2; "Convention Report: HSUS Laboratory Study," *HSUS News* (November 1958): 8.
[2]Fred Myers, personal communication to Dr. Spencer M. Free, Jr. (4 May 1961), History and By-Laws, Filebox 3099–1245; William Russell and Rex Burch, *Principles of Humane Experimental Technique* (London: Methuen, 1959); and "The Real Facts About Tissue Cultures, Mathematical Models and Computers, and the Gas Chromatograph, as Substitutes for Live Animals in Laboratories," *Report to Humanitarians* 10 (December 1969): 2.
[3]Christine Stevens, "Laboratory Animal Welfare," in AWI, *Animals and Their Legal Rights* (Washington, D.C.: AWI, 1990), 67.
[4]"Humane Workers Win Louisiana Victory," *HSUS News* (May 1959): 1–2; Stevens, "Laboratory Animal Welfare," 67–68; and Andrew N. Rowan, *Of Mice, Models, and Men: A Critical Evaluation of Animal Research* (Albany: State University of New York, 1984), 51–54.
[5]"Convention Resolutions," *National Humane Review* (November 1953): 13; Stevens, "Laboratory Animal Welfare," 69.
[6]Stevens, "Laboratory Animal Welfare," 69; "Seizure Law Beat in Miami But Another Enacted in New Orleans," *HSUS News* (September 1958): 2.
[7]"NHS Staff Members Inspect Laboratory Animal Quarters," *HSUS News* (January 1957): 4; "Humane Societies Fight to Protect Lab Monkeys," *HSUS News* (April 1955): 1; "NHS Board Acts Again to Help Lab Monkeys," *HSUS News* (September 1955): 1; "Prosecution of Monkey Shipper Planned," *HSUS News* (March 1956): 1; "Continued Cruelty to Monkeys Shows Need for International Organizations," *HSUS News* (May 1957): 4; "Indian Government Asks HSUS About Monkeys," *HSUS News* (February 1958): 5; "New Protection Won for Monkeys," *HSUS News* (June 1958): 4; "Housing of Beagles Used for Tests by Food and Drug Administration," *Animal Welfare Institute Information Report* (January–February 1960): 1; and "FDA Plan Stirs Beagle Battle," *Philadelphia Bulletin* (21 February 1960).
[8]"HSUS Charges Medical School with Illegal Cruelty to Animals," *HSUS News* (November 1959): 1–2; "HSUS Files Cruelty Charge Against Stanford University Laboratory," *HSUS News* (March 1960): 1; "California Health Board Whitewashes Lab," *HSUS News* (May 1960): 1; "HSUS Carries Fight Against Laboratory Cruelties to California Superior Court," *HSUS News* (June 1960): 1; "Three Research Doctors Sue California Branch for $240,000; CME Case to State Supreme Court," *HSUS News* (August 1960): 2; "HSUS Lawyers Begin Questioning of Med School Researchers in L.A.," *HSUS News* (November 1960): 2; "California HSUS Appeals Lab Case," *HSUS News* (March–April 1961): 8; Jacques Sichel, personal communication to Senator Harrison A. Williams, Jr. (3 December 1960), Slaughter–New Jersey, Filebox 3099–601; Fred Myers, "Report of the Executive Director," *New Frontiers in Humane Work* (Washington, D.C.: HSUS, 1960), 6; *Animals in a Research Laboratory* (Washington, D.C.: HSUS, 1961); and Patrick B. Parkes and Jacques V. Sichel, *Twenty-Five Years of Growth and Achievement: The Humane Society of the United States, 1954–1979* (Washington, D.C.: HSUS, 1979), 10.
[9]"HSUS Gets $10,000 Foundation Grant," *HSUS News* (March–April 1961): 4; "Duke Foundation Helps HSUS Statistical Study of Animal Experiments," *HSUS News* (April 1962): 1; and "More Hope for Laboratory Animals," *Report to Humanitarians* 18 (December 1971): 2–3.
[10]"Special Committee Polls Opinion Leaders on Attitude to Animals," *HSUS News* (November 1962): 2.
[11]"Seizure Law Beat in Miami But Another Enacted in New Orleans," *HSUS News* (September 1958): 2; "Tulane Lab Study Exposes Cruelty," *HSUS News* (September 1958): 4.
[12]"Senator Cooper Introduces Laboratory Animals Bill," *Animal Welfare Institute Information Report* (March–April 1960): 1.
[13]Sichel, personal communication to Williams (3 December 1960), Slaughter–New Jersey, Filebox 3099–601; "HSUS Pushes Fight to Rescue Government Lab Dogs" and editorial, *HSUS News* (May–June 1961): 6.
[14]Robert Chenoweth, "Statement by the Board," *HSUS News* (June 1960): 9.

[15]"The Moulder Bill—An Editorial," *HSUS News* (November 1961): 7; Fred Myers, "Report of the Executive Director," 7; Parkes and Sichel, *Twenty-Five Years*, 8; "Support for Protection of Laboratory Animals Grows in Congress," *HSUS News* (February 1963): 1; and "Public Opinion Is Chief Fear of Laboratory Animal Research Men," *HSUS News* (July 1964): 4.

[16]"The Moulder Bill," 7; "Washington Post Calls for Hearing on Laboratory Animals Bill," *Animal Welfare Institute Information Report* (May–June 1962): 1; and "Mail for Moulder Bill Piles up in Congress; Hearing May Be Near," *HSUS News* (February 1962): 1.

[17]"Animals Are Cruelly Abused in U.S. Labs, Congress Told," *Philadelphia Bulletin* (28 September 1962).

[18]"Support for Protection of Laboratory Animals Grows in Congress," *HSUS News* (February 1963): 1; "Laboratory Law Moves to Congress Action," *HSUS News* (May 1963): 1; "Representative Claude Pepper Boosts Campaign for Laboratory Law with New Bill in House," *HSUS News* (September 1963): 1; "Policies, Principles, and Programs," *HSUS News* (January 1964): 5; and "Humanitarians Cautioned on Rash of Weak Lab Legislation; Urged to Support HSUS Bills," *HSUS News* (November 1964): 7.

[19]"Laboratory Law Moves to Congress Action," *HSUS News* (May 1963): 1; Cleveland Amory, *Saturday Evening Post* (1 June, 3 August 1963); Edith Goode, *Memorandum to the Board of Directors and Staff of The HSUS* (14 January 1966), 7, Filebox 3099–1245; and Parkes and Sichel, *Twenty-Five Years*, 10.

[20]Claude Pepper, "The Strategy of Laboratory Animal Legislation," *The First Ten Years*, 20–2; Fred Myers, undated memo (1963), 11, 16, Filebox 3099–1245.

[21]"Continuing HSUS Investigations Confirm Charges of Lab Cruelty," *HSUS News* (March 1964): 4.

[22]"British Report Exposes Weakness of Lab Act; Findings Confirm HSUS Stand for Strong U.S. Law," *HSUS News* (May 1965): 1.

[23]Frank McMahon, Statement to U.S. House of Representatives Livestock Subcommittee: (2 September 1965), HSUS Filebox 3099–490.

[24]"Humane Society Raiders Discover Sick, Starved, Injured Laboratory Dogs Hidden on New York State Farm," *HSUS News* (November 1963): 1.

[25]"Humane Chief Urges Probe of Cruelty in 'Medical Lab Zoos,'" *Philadelphia Bulletin*, 21 December 1964; "Seven State Animal Traffic Exposed by Decisive HSUS Action Against Pennsylvania Laboratory Supplier," *HSUS News* (January 1965), 1; "Dierolf Arrested Again," *HSUS News* (May 1965), 8; "Dog Farm Owner Claims Immunity from Prosecution," *Philadelphia Bulletin*, 27 November 1965; and "Dog Farmer is Held Again in West Chester," *Philadelphia Bulletin*, 1 December 1965. Dierolf pled guilty to cruelty in two cases, once was convicted after a plea of not guilty, and saw a fourth charge dismissed on a technicality. On the disposition of these cases, see Frank McMahon, Statement to U.S. House of Representatives Livestock Subcommittee, 2 September 1965, HSUS Filebox 3099-490.

[26]"Animal Society Calls State 'Clearing House for Cruelty,'" *Philadelphia Bulletin* (22 December 1964); "Cruelty to Animals Is Charged," *Philadelphia Bulletin* (27 December 1964); "Humane Society Bill Introduced," *Philadelphia Bulletin* (17 March 1965); "Legislature Stalls Bill on Animal Cruelty," *Philadelphia Bulletin* (27 August 1965); "Humane Society Head Praises Pennsylvania Laws to Protect Animals," *Philadelphia Bulletin* (27 December 1965); "Humane Society Official Hails State's New Dog Law," *Philadelphia Bulletin* (26 January 1966); and "Campaign Pushed for Federal Action Against Theft of Pets for Laboratories," *Philadelphia Bulletin* (31 January 1966).

[27]"Setter from Pennsylvania Kennel Is Center of Capital Tizzy," *Philadelphia Bulletin* (2 December 1965); "Lab Dog Rescued from Research; Case Proves that Stolen Pets Are Sold to Experimental Labs," *HSUS News* (January 1966): 2.

[28]"U.S. Humane Society Says Cruelty to Dogs Is Continuing in State," *Philadelphia Inquirer* (20 July 1966); "Pennsylvanian Given Highest Humane Award," *HSUS News* (September 1966): 6.

[29]"Campaign for Laboratory Law Progresses with New Bill in House of Representatives," "Laboratory Bills—An Editorial," *HSUS News* (July 1965): 1–2; "Support for Rogers Bill Grows; Senate Bill Introduced," *HSUS News* (November 1965): 2; Letter # 37-A, Rogers-Pepper Form Letter, Rogers Bill, Pepper Bill 1965, Filebox 3099–490; and "Not Partial to HSUS," *Report to Humanitarians* 27 (March 1974): 7.

[30]*HSUS News* editorial (January 1966): 7.

[31]"Congress Holds Hearing on Pet Theft Bills; HSUS Testimony Exposes Nationwide Traffic," *HSUS News* (September 1965): 1; "Campaign Pushed for Federal Action Against Theft of Pets for Laboratories," *Philadelphia Bulletin* (31 January 1966); and Stevens, "Laboratory Animal Welfare," 73.

[32]"Bill Signed to Curb Theft of Pets for Research and to Insure Humane Use," *Philadelphia Bulletin* (25 August 1966); Stevens, "Laboratory Animal Welfare," 73–74.

[33]Frank McMahon, Statement to U.S. House of Representatives Livestock Subcommittee (2 September 1965), and Oliver Evans, Statement to U.S. House of Representatives Livestock Subcommittee (2 September 1965), HSUS Filebox 3099–490; "Congress Holds Hearing on Pet Theft Bills; HSUS Testimony Exposes Nationwide Traffic," *HSUS News* (September 1965): 1.

[34]"Confessed Dog Thief Tells House There Ought to Be a Law," *HSUS News* (September 1965): 2.

[35]"Rep. Poage Sponsors New Bill, Schedules Hearing as Dealer Legislation Moves Toward Victory," *HSUS News* (March 1966): 2; *Life*, "Concentration Camp for Dogs" (4 February 1966): 22–29; "HSUS Raiders Hit Two Maryland Dog Dealers, Rescue Sick, Injured Dogs Bound for Medical Research," *HSUS News* (March 1966): 1; and "Doctors Tell Senate of Need for More Dogs in Research," *Philadelphia Bulletin* (28 March 1966).

[36]"Secret HSUS Agent Investigates Lab Animal Dealers, Gathers Proof of Wholesale Cruelty," *HSUS News* (March 1966): 3.

[37]Ibid.; Dale Hylton, personal communication (29 May 2003).

[38]"U.S. House Passes Amended Poage Bill; Strong Senate Bill Sought," *HSUS News* (May 1966): 2.

[39]Stevens, "Laboratory Animal Welfare," 75–76.

[40]Oliver Evans, "Humane Choice," *Washington Post* (6 June 1966); Legislative Report, to HSUS Branches, Affiliates, and Other Societies (9 June 1966), Filebox 3099–490; "Senate-House Conference Committee Continues Sessions on Dealer Bill; Passage of Senate Version Likely," *HSUS News* (July 1966): 1; and Stevens, "Laboratory Animal Welfare," 86.

[41]"LBJ Signs Poage-Magnuson Act," *HSUS News* (September 1966): 1–2.

[42]"HSUS Agent Investigating Lab Animal Traffic Found Guilty, Fined on Dog Dealer's Charges," *HSUS News* (Septem-

ber 1966): 4; "USDA Proposes Poage-Magnuson Regulations; and HSUS Recommends Some Strengthening Provisions," *HSUS News* (January–February 1967): 6.

43"Johnson Signs Pets' Charter," *Boston Traveler* (24 August 1966); "Bill to Protect Animals by President," *Miami Herald* (25 August 1966); "125 Charges of Cruelty to Dogs Are Filed," *Philadelphia Bulletin* (30 August 1966); "Unlawful Release of Animals to Research Laboratories Bared in HSUS Probe of Ohio Dog Pound," *HSUS News* (September–October 1968): 2; "HSUS and Local Society Rescue Starving Dogs, Maryland Dealer Found Guilty of Animal Cruelty," *HSUS News* (May–June 1968): 2; and "HSUS Sued by Animal Dealer After Raid Which Rescued Hundreds of Sick, Ailing Animals and Birds," *HSUS News* (March–April 1967): 4.

44"Implementation of Poage-Magnuson Act Threatened: Appropriations Battle Won as Congress Adjourns," *HSUS News* (November 1966): 1; "Struggle for Laboratory Animal Law Narrows to Choice of Bill; Rogers Bill Still the Strongest," *HSUS News* (November 1966): 2; and "Poage-Magnuson Act, New Congress May Affect Laboratory Campaign; Decisive Year Predicted by HSUS," *HSUS News* (January–February 1967): 7.

45"Ex-Police Chief Pleads Guilty; Charges Arose from HSUS Findings," *HSUS News* (January–February 1967): 11; "Testimony of Dog Law Agents Helps Animal Supplier to Win Case," *HSUS News* (March–April 1967): 8.

46"Raids on USDA Licensed Dog Dealers in Two States Show Futility of Self-Regulation," *HSUS News* (July–August 1967): 9.

47"The Care of Animals," *New York Times* (17 October 1967); "Support for Rogers-Javits Bill Continues to Mount, Reaches New High for Lab Animal Legislation," *HSUS News* (November–December 1967): 5; and "Suicidal Split Over Enforcement Agency Poses Serious Threat to Protection of Research Animals," *HSUS News* (January–February 1968): 1.

48"Answers to Your Questions About the Rogers Bill," *Report to Humanitarians* 2 (December 1967): 5.

49Aldo Beckman, "Two Wives Block Lab Animal Bill," *Chicago Tribune* (1 July 1968); "Laboratory Animal Legislation–Where Do We Go from Here?" *Report to Humanitarians* 6 (December 1968): 1–11.

50"Laboratory Animal Legislation," 1–11.

51"Amended Rogers-Javits Lab Bill Due for Introduction; Enactment This Year Is Considered Likely," *HSUS News* (May–June 1969): 1; "The Rogers-Javits Bill–Will It Work?" *HSUS News* (Special Issue June 1969): 3; and "USDA Vet Testimony in Cruelty Lab Favors Laboratory Animal Dealers," *HSUS News* (September–October 1969): 2.

52"Public Law 89-544–Is It Really Working?" *HSUS News* (Special Issue June 1969): 2; "HSUS Demands USDA Take Action Against Two Lab Animal Dealers," *HSUS News* (July–August 1969): 3.

53*Report of the President*, 1970; R.M. Wooten, "Lab Animals," *The Virginian-Pilot* (25 July 1970), Legislation Folder, Filebox 3099–490; and "Passage of Animal Welfare Act Is Significant Step Forward in Struggle for Animal Protection," *HSUS News* (February 1971): 4.

54*Report of the President*, 1970; "Passage of Animal Welfare Act Is Significant Step Forward," 4.

55Ibid.; "The Animal Welfare Act of 1970," *Report to Humanitarians* 16 (June 1971): 3.

56Wooten, "Lab Animals."

57"Congressional Committee Hears Laboratory Reform Demands," *HSUS News* (October 1970): 1.

58"Army Ignores Federal Law at Animal Research Facility," *HSUS News* (Summer 1975): 4–5.

59John A. Hoyt, "The Defense Department on Beagles," *HSUS News* (March 1974): 6.

60Constance Holden, "Beagles: Army Under Attack for Research at Edgewood," *Science* 185 (1974): 131–32; "Replacements Sought for Pentagon Beagles," *Philadelphia Bulletin* (6 January 1974); "Animal Lovers Seek Test Ban," *Philadelphia Bulletin* (23 June 1974); *Report of the President*, 1974; "Army Ignores Federal Law at Animal Research Facility," *HSUS News* (Summer 1975): 4–5; Michael Satchell, "Man's Assault on Animal Kingdom in the Name of Science," *Washington Star* (6 August 1975); and "USDA Scores Army on Laboratory Cages," *HSUS News* (Autumn 1975): 13.

61"Scientific Community Examines Use of Animals in Research," *HSUS News* (Winter 1975–1976): 8–10.

62Satchell, "Man's Assault on Animal Kingdom."

63*Report of the President*, 1972; "Scientific Community Examines Use of Animals in Research," *HSUS News* (Winter 1975–1976): 8–10.

64Michael Fox, interview by Kim Stallwood, Archive (Baltimore, Md.: Animal Rights Network, 24 May 2001).

65Program and Policy Committee Meeting, 26–27 April 1979, 4, in Meetings Program and Policy, Filebox 3099–390; "The Easing of Creaturely Pain," *New York Times* (1 March 1981).

66Minutes, meeting of ISAP, July 11 and 13, 1978, ISAP 1977–78, Filebox 3099–77; "Animal Experimentation Report Released," *HSUS News* (Spring 1979): 15.

67Andrew N. Rowan, "Twenty Years of Effort—and Failure—at America's Regional Primate Centers," *HSUS News* (Fall 1982): 22–25; "One Voice Raised," *HSUS News* (Summer 1983): 30; *Report of the President*, 1984; and Andrew Rowan, personal communication (29 May 2003).

68Franklin M. Loew, editorial, *International Journal for the Study of Animal Problems* 1, no. 1 (January–February 1980): 8.

69Pat Clagett, "Draize Update," *HSUS News* (Spring 1981): 12–13; Andrew Rowan, "Beauty and the Beasts," *HSUS News* (Spring 1979): 4–6; and Rowan, personal communication (29 May 2003).

70Peter Singer, *Ethics into Action: Henry Spira and the Animal Rights Movement* (Lanham, Md.: Rowman and Littlefield, 1998).

71Andrew Rowan, undated memo (October 1982), Folder Filebox 3099–321; Rowan, personal communication (29 May 2003).

72"Alternatives Study Begins," *HSUS News* (Spring 1984): 29; "Alternatives First," *HSUS News* (Summer 1986): 30.

73*Report of the President*, 1985.

74Deborah L. Reed, "Choosing to Care," *HSUS News* (Winter 1991): 4–6.

75Andrew N. Rowan, "Laboratory Animals and Alternatives in the 80's," *International Journal for the Study of Animal Problems* 1, no. 3 (May/June 1980): 162–169; "Federal Report," *HSUS News* (Winter 1981): 31; and "HSUS Suit Dismissed," *HSUS News* (Summer 1982): 36.

76 "Federal Report," *HSUS News* (Winter 1981): 31; "HSUS Voices Heard on Hill," *HSUS News* (Winter 1982): 9.

77"HSUS Voices Heard on Hill," 9; "The Second 'Great Monkey Trial': Science Defends Its Treatment of Laboratory Primates," "HSUS Gives Pre-Trial Aid," *HSUS News* (Winter 1982): 25–26, 32; "HSUS Suit Dismissed," *HSUS News* (Summer 1982): 36; and "The HSUS Files Suit Against USDA," *HSUS News* (Winter 1982): 27.

[78]"Lab Raided in Florida," *HSUS News* (Spring 1984): 36.

[79]"Try, Try Again," *HSUS News* (Summer 1985): 30; "NIH Animal-Protection Provisions Hurdle Veto, Become Law," *HSUS News* (Winter 1986): 30.

[80]"Vetoed: Lab Animal Protection," *HSUS News* (Winter 1985): 29–30.

[81]"Lab Animal Flash," *HSUS News* (Summer 1985): 29; "'Farm Bill' Would Help Lab Animals," *HSUS News* (Winter 1986): 31; and "Two Laws, Good News," *HSUS News* (Spring 1986): 28.

[82]"'Farm Bill' Would Help Lab Animals," 31.

[83]On the two cases, and the ensuring furor over the neglect and mistreatment of animals in laboratories, see Deborah Blum, *The Monkey Wars* (New York: Oxford University Press, 1994), 105–52; and Lawrence and Susan Finsen, *The Animal Rights Movement in America: From Compassion to Respect* (New York: Twayne Publishers, 1994), 62–71.

[84]"NIH Chimpanzee-Breeding Program: Bad News for Primates," *HSUS News* (Spring 1987): 22–3.

[85]"USDA Standards Not Good Enough," *HSUS News* (Fall 1990): 32; "AWA Comments Sent to USDA," *HSUS News* (Winter 1991): 23.

[86]"Wanted: Better USDA Reporting," *HSUS News* (Spring 1993): 9.

[87]"More Protection?" *HSUS News* (Summer 1986): 28.

[88]"Animal Use in Military Testing," *HSUS News* (Summer 1992): 34; "Spotlight," *HSUS News* (Summer 1994): 4; and "A New Federal Bill," *HSUS News* (Winter 1995): 6.

[89]Martin L. Stephens, "Clarifying Our Position," *HSUS News* (Spring 1991): 21–3.

[90]"USDA to Protect Farm Animals," *HSUS News* (Summer 1990): 35; Martin L. Stephens, "Smallest Among Us," *HSUS News* (Spring 1995): 32.

[91]"Closing a Lethal Loophole," *HSUS News* (Winter 1990): 11–12.

[92]"USDA to Protect Farm Animals," *HSUS News* (Summer 1990): 35; "The HSUS, ALDF Sue USDA," *HSUS News* (Fall 1990): 36; and "Key Decisions on Lab Animals," *HSUS News* (Summer 1991): 33.

[93]"No Exclusions," "Standing Addressed," *HSUS News* (Spring 1992): 9–10, 36.

[94]Stephens, "Smallest Among Us," 35.

[95]"Coverage of Birds, Mice, and Rats Under the Animal Welfare Act," *Pain and Distress Report* 1, no. 2 (2000): 1; "Passage of Farm Bill Denies Protection to Birds, Rats, and Mice," *http://www.hsus.org/ace/14121*.

[96]"The Layman's Guide to Alternatives," *HSUS News* (Spring 1986): 14–19; "Senate Hearings on LD-50 Test," "Tsongas on Alternatives," *HSUS News* (Winter 1990): 29; and "Alternatives to Animal Testing," *HSUS News* (Fall 1990): 34–5.

[97]"The Fourth Wave," *HSUS News* (Spring 1998): 11–13; "Russell and Burch Award," *http://www.hsus.org/ace/12630*.

[98]John Hoyt, "Enlarging Our Effectiveness," *HSUS News* (Fall 1991); David O. Wiebers, Jennifer Leaning, and Roger D. White, "Animal Protection and Medical Science," Lancet 343 (9 April 1994): 902–4; and "Animal Protection and the Medical Community," *HSUS News* (Fall 1995): 23–25.

[99]"'Alternatives': A Good Year," *HSUS News* (Spring 1996): 8–10.

[100]Ibid., 10; "The Fourth Wave," *HSUS News* (Spring 1998): 11–13.

[101]"Open Letter to Dan Glickman," *Humane Activist* (July/August 2000): 3; "USDA Receives More Than 2,500 Comments on Pain and Distress," *Pain and Distress Report* 1, no. 2 (2000): 1.

[102]"The HSUS Comments on Statements Made by Americans for Medical Progress," *Pain and Distress Report* (July 2002): 4.

[103]"Time to Address Pain and Distress," *Humane Activist* (July/August 2002): 2.

[104]Ibid.

[105]Rowan, personal communication (29 May 2003).

Chapter Four

[1]"Spaying Fees," *National Humane Review* (October 1953): 3; Frederick L. Thomsen, "Some Personal Reflections about Fred Myers," *Report to Humanitarians* 44 (June 1978): 3–4; J.D. Ratliff, "Vivisection: An Explosive Issue Again," *Reader's Digest* (March 1961): 60; and Jean McClure Kelty, "The Unsheltered Society," address before National Leadership Conference of The HSUS, September 15–18, 1966.

[2]Boris M. Levinson, "Psychology of Pet Ownership," in *Proceedings of the National Conference on the Ecology of the Surplus Dog and Cat Population*, May 21–23, 1974, 19–21; Evan McLeod Wylie, "Needed: Birth Control for Cats and Dogs," *Reader's Digest* (March 1974): 217–219.

[3]"Drive Against Breeding Gets New HSUS Push," *HSUS News* (June 1958): 8; "Peanuts," *HSUS News* (September 1958): 3.

[4]"'Sexually Frustrated Dogs,'" *National Humane Society News* (March 1956): 3; "Further Moves to Reform ASPCA," *HSUS News* (January 1964): 8.

[5]"HSUS Retains Lawyer to Help Missouri Society," *HSUS News* (March 1959): 3; "Mo. Vets Attack," *HSUS News* (May 1959): 7; and *HSUS News* (August 1959): 2.

[6]"HSUS Helps Cities Meet Animal Problems Humanely, Efficiently," *HSUS News* (August 1959): 7; "Group Endorses Humane Society Center Here," *Washington Star* (8 November 1962).

[7]"HSUS Managing Illinois Society in Emergency After Leader's Death," *HSUS News* (July 1962): 6; "HSUS Managing N.J. City Pound," *HSUS News* (February 1963): 1; "Ex-Police Chief Pleads Guilty; Charges Arose from HSUS Findings," *HSUS News* (January–February 1967): 11; and Frank McMahon, Statement to U.S. House of Representatives Livestock Subcommittee, 2 September 1965, HSUS Filebox 3099–490.

[8]"Dog Warden Arrested," *HSUS News* (June 1958): 8; "Euthanasia Improved," *HSUS News* (March 1959): 2; and "HSUS Wins Injunction Against Public Dog Shooting in Ohio," *HSUS News* (June 1960): 10.

[9]John Miles Zucker, personal communication to Alan Braun (23 February 1961), Slaughter Correspondence, Filebox 3099–601; Lewis Timberlake, personal communication to Oscar Schmidt (10 June 1963), in Slaughter, Stunning

Equipment–Correspondence, Filebox 3099–601; "HSUS Euthanasia Committee Makes Interim Report; Testing of Methods Begins," *HSUS News* (July–August 1961): 8; and Murdaugh Madden, memo, ISAP, HSUS-ISAP, 1974, Filebox 3099–707. On the fate of the Electrothanator, subsequently abandoned as ambiguous in its humaneness, see "Alternatives to the Decompression Chamber," *Report to Humanitarians* 32 (June 1975).

[10]*HSUS News* (February 1962): 7; Patrick B. Parkes, personal communication (23 April 2003); and Frantz Dantzler, interview (23 April 2003).

[11]Dantzler, interview (23 April 2003).

[12]"Fort Worth Society Sponsors Animal Control Seminar," *HSUS News* (September 1964): 2; "Five-State Field Trip Brings Help for Local Humane Societies Facing Variety of Pressing Problems," *HSUS News* (July–August 1967): 3.

[13]"Two Societies Join HSUS Affiliates," *HSUS News* (March–April 1961): 5; "West Virginia Affiliate Takes Over Inhumane Shelter," "Dog Dealer Hit With Seventeen Violations in Surprise Act," *HSUS News* (September 1964): 4, 6.

[14]"Economy Shelter," *HSUS News* (July–August 1961): 6; "New Pueblo Shelter," *HSUS News* (February 1963): 6.

[15]Fred Myers, personal communication to Oliver Evans (19 August 1963), History and By-Laws, Filebox 3099–1245; "Color Motion Picture Released by HSUS," *HSUS News* (May 1964): 4; *HSUS News* (July 1965): 1; and "New Film Slated for Release in September," *HSUS News* (July–August 1967): 3.

[16]"HSUS Building National Humane Education Center to Serve Entire U.S. Movement," *HSUS News* (November 1963): 2; "Animal Refuge Center Slated Near Waterford," *Washington Star* (28 November 1964); Edith Goode, memorandum to the Board of Directors (4 January 1965), John A. Hoyt, personal communication to Philip A. Bolen (25 April 1973, 27 July 1973), Filebox 3049–1245; and Dale Hylton, personal communication (28 May 2003).

[17]Goode, memorandum to the Board of Directors (4 January 1965), Hoyt, personal communication to Bolen; "Center's Spay Clinic Competes with the Euthanasia Room," *HSUS News* (July 1971): 4; and "HSUS Units Spay 2,000 in 1972," *HSUS News* (Winter 1973): 3.

[18]Dale Hylton, personal communication (29 May 2003).

[19]Ibid.

[20]Ibid.

[21]Ibid.

[22]John A. Hoyt, "A Case for Spay/Neuter Clinics," in *Conference on the Ecology of the Surplus Dog and Cat Population*, 1974: 62; John A. Hoyt, personal communication to Catherine Briggs (12 March 1974); John A. Hoyt, memo to Board of Directors (4 December 1972), NHEC Folder, Filebox 3099–1245; and Patrick B. Parkes, personal communication (22 April 2003). In 1971 and 1972, the HSUS subsidy of the NHEC animal control program was between $15,000 and $20,000.

[23]Ann Cottrell Free, "Animals Won Her Heart Early," *Washington Star* (14 March 1966); "Key NHEC Post Goes to Maryland Leader," *HSUS News* (January–February 1969): 3; *Report of the President*, 1971; Paul G. Irwin, "Farewell, Phyllis Wright," *HSUS News* (Winter 1993); and John A. Hoyt, interview, by Kim Stallwood, Archive (Baltimore, Md.: Animal Rights Network, 29 March 2001).

[24]"HSUS's Phyllis Wright Explains the Right Way," *HSUS News* (Summer/Fall 1976): 12–13.

[25]Charles F. Herrmann and Phyllis Wright, "How Humane Is Your Society?" *HSUS News* (Winter 1978): 1–3; Deborah L. Reed, "Solving Animal Problems in Your Community," *HSUS News* (Summer 1985): 15.

[26]"Affluence Is Fueling Pet Industry Growth," *New York Times* (21 September 1969); Michael Satchell, "The Pet Bomb," *Washington Star* (16 April 1972).

[27]"Humane Society's Viewpoint on Animal Control," *Nation's Cities* (February 1974): 31.

[28]"Spaying Promoted on TV," *HSUS News* (November 1972): 8.

[29]Calvin Zon, "Dog Packs," *Washington Star* (19 October 1973); Alan Beck, "Ecology of Uncontrolled and Unwanted Pets," in *Ecology of Surplus Dog and Cat Populations*, 31–39; "The Reign of Dogs and Cats," *HSUS News* (Spring 1977): 10; and Geoffrey Handy, personal communication (10 April 2003).

[30]"Permits for Pet Animal Owners versus Licenses for Individual Animals," *Report to Humanitarians* 35 (March 1976): 5; Andrew N. Rowan and Jeff Williams, "Success of Companion Animal Management Programs: A Review," *Anthrozoös* 1, no. 2 (Fall 1987): 110–121.

[31]"Humane Society's Viewpoint on Animal Control," 31.

[32]Deirdre Carmody, "Critics Assert ASPCA Here Is Guilty of Cruelty to Animals," *New York Times* (21 June 1971); "Coalition Acting on the ASPCA," *New York Times* (23 July 1971); "County Seeks Inquiry Into Alleged Abuses at Animal Shelter," *Washington Star* (16 November 1979); "The HSUS Accreditation Program," *HSUS News* (Autumn 1974): 5; John A. Hoyt, "HSUS Accreditation Program: What's It All About?" *HSUS News* (Summer 1977): 33; "Animal Lover Sees Need for People Control," *Washington Star* (9 November 1977); "Accreditation Update," *HSUS News* (Winter 1981): 6; and Martha Armstrong, interview (28 May 2003).

[33]"'77 is Banner Year for HSUS Workshop Program," *HSUS News* (Fall 1977): 18; Parkes, personal communication (22 April 2003).

[34]Deborah L. Reed, "Solving Animal Problems in Your Community," *HSUS News* (Summer 1985): 14–16.

[35]Susan Bury Stauffer, "It Takes a Gentle Hand," *HSUS News* (Spring 1981): 16–17; "Two Weeks at The HSUS's Animal Control Academy," *HSUS News* (Spring 1983): 20–23.

[36]*Report of the President*, 1983.

[37]"Animal-Control Accord Signals New Era of Cooperation," *HSUS News* (Fall 1985): 24–25.

[38]"Accreditation Becomes Our PETS Program," *HSUS News* (Fall 1985); Armstrong, interview (28 May 2003).

[39]"Accreditation Becomes Our PETS Program"; Deborah L. Reed, "PETS: A New Program Emphasizes the People Who Make Animal Control Work," *HSUS News* (Fall 1985): 9–10.

[40]Kim Antino, interview (5 June 2003); John Snyder, interview (5 June 2003); and Kate Pullen, personal communication (5 June 2003).

[41]Geoffrey Handy, "Fifth Expo Works Its Charm," *HSUS News* (Summer 1996): 4–5.

[42]HSUS, *Annual Report*, 2002, 67; Armstrong, interview (28 May 2003); and Stephanie Shain, interview (2 June 2003).

[43]"Center's Spay Clinic Competes with the Euthanasia Room," *HSUS News* (July 1971): 4; Andrew Rowan, personal communication (2 June 2003).

44Guy Hodge, "Veterinarians and Birth Control for Pets," *HSUS News* (October 1973): 8; "Pet Sterilization Bill Vetoed," *Washington Star* (16 July 1974); "Federal Legislation," *HSUS News* (Summer 1977): 24; Alan Beck, preface, in Iris Nowell, *The Dog Crisis* (New York: St. Martin's Press, 1978), xvii; "Virginia Supreme Court Rules in Vets' Favor," *HSUS News* (Spring 1986): 36; and Martha C. Armstrong, Susan Tomasello, and Christyna Hunter, "From Pets to Companion Animals," in Deborah J. Salem and Andrew N. Rowan, eds., *The State of the Animals: 2001* (Washington, D.C.: Humane Society Press, 2001), 74.

45Correspondence in Spaying–ISAP, Filebox 3099–707.

46"IRS Clears Michigan Societies' Full-Service and Spay/Neuter Clinics," *HSUS News* (Winter 1985): 36; Murdaugh Stuart Madden and Roger Kindler, "Huron Valley Spay/Neuter Clinic Ruling," *HSUS News* (Spring 1985): 36; and Murdaugh Stuart Madden and Roger Kindler, "Veterinarians Seek Statute to Suppress Society-sponsored Clinics," *HSUS News* (Summer 1985): 36.

47"Aiding Charitable Hospitals," *HSUS News* (Fall 1987): 27; Armstrong et al., "From Pets to Companion Animals," 74–75.

48"New Drug Promises Help in Breeding Control," *HSUS News* (March 1959): 5; "Quick, Chemical 'Vasectomy' to Be Tested," *Washington Star* (20 April 1973); "'The Pill' Is Urged for Pets," *Washington Post* (24 April 1973): A6; and "FDA Approves Canine Birth Control Pill," *HSUS News* (Spring 1975): 14.

49"The Pill," *Report to Humanitarians* 12 (June 1970): 2; HSUS Grant Application, Trustees Under Will of George Whittell, staff meetings, ISAP, Filebox 3099–321.

50Geoffrey Handy, interview (9 April 2003); Armstrong, interview (28 May 2003); and Rowan, personal communication (2 June 2003).

51Madden memo, ISAP, HSUS–ISAP (1974), ISAP update (September 1976–March 1977), ISAP 1977–78, Filebox 3099–707.

52Wylie, "Needed: More Birth Control for Cats and Dogs," 217–222; Program and Policy Committee Minutes (19 July 1978), 2 in Meetings Program and Policy, Filebox 3099–390; Hoyt and Fox interview (8 November 2001); John Snyder, personal communication (14 March 2003); Rowan, personal communication (2 June 2003); and Stephanie Shain, personal communication (2 June 2003).

53*Draft of HSUS/HSI Report on Companion Animal Chemical Sterilization* (Washington, D.C.: HSI, 1995), in possession of Martha Armstrong (28 May 2003); Handy, interview (9 April 2003).

54Robert C. Bay, personal communication to Sue Pressman (12 June 1972), HSUS Euthanasia, Filebox 3099–707.

55"Officials Cooperate in HSUS Investigation of Brownsville City Pound," *HSUS News* (January–February 1967): 5.

56Hylton, personal communication (29 May 2003).

57"HSUS Sues City of San Antonio to Control Animals Humanely," *HSUS News* (Summer 1972): 6.

58"Free Plans Offered," *HSUS News* (March 1956): 3; "Air Force Says 'Altitude' Chamber Is Humane," *HSUS News* (January 1957): 3; "Rapid Decompression in High Altitude Chambers—Humane or Cruel," *Report to Humanitarians* (June 1972); "Some Frank Talk about the Decompression Chamber," *Report to Humanitarians* 31 (March 1975); "Alternatives to the Decompression Chamber," *Report to Humanitarians* 32 (June 1975); and T. Carding, *Euthanasia of Dogs and Cats, Special Report, World Federation for the Protection of Animals* (April 1977): 4–9.

59"Rapid Decompression in High Altitude Chambers: Humane or Cruel," *Report to Humanitarians* 20 (June 1972): 1, 3.

60John A. Hoyt, personal communication to Encil E. Rains (18 May 1973), HSUS-Euthanasia, ISAP, Madden memo, ISAP, HSUS–ISAP (1974), in Filebox 3099–707.

61"Rapid Decompression in High Altitude Chambers: Humane or Cruel," 1; "The Decompression Chamber," *Report to Humanitarians* 45 (September 1975): 1, 4.

62"Animal Lovers Kidnap Machine," *Washington Daily News* (5 November 1971); "Dallas Bans High Altitude Decompression Chamber," *HSUS News* (Spring 1975): 3; "Concerned Citizens Unite for Humane Euthanasia," *HSUS News* (Summer 1977): 19; "State Legislation," *HSUS News* (Summer 1977): 24; "ASPCA Adopts Barbiturate for Euthanasia," *HSUS News* (Spring 1978): 8; and Christine Stevens, "Dogs," in *Animals and Their Legal Rights*, 4th ed. (Washington, D.C.: AWI, 1990), 119.

63"Is T-61 a Humane Substitute for Sodium Pentobarbitol?" *Report to Humanitarians* 43 (March 1978): 5.

64"Cruel Killer Drug," *Report to Humanitarians* 15 (March 1971): 4; ISAP Update (September 1976–March 1977), ISAP 1977–78, Filebox 3099–707; and J.R. Eppley, personal communication to John A. Hoyt (11 February 1977), ISAP–Fort Dodge, Filebox 3099–707.

65Susan Bury Stauffer, "It Takes a Gentle Hand," 16–17; "Two Weeks at the HSUS's Animal Control Academy," 20–23; and Armstrong et al., "From Pets to Companion Animals," 78.

66"District of Columbia Studies Regulations to Control Pet Shops," *HSUS News* (January–February 1967): 12.

67"HSUS Sued by Animal Dealer After Raid Which Rescued Hundreds of Sick, Ailing Animals and Birds," *HSUS News* (March–April 1967): 4.

68"Retail Sale of Pets Becomes Legislative Issue in Illinois," *HSUS News* (May–June 1967): 7; Parkes, personal communication (10 April 2003).

69"California Branch Protest Wins State Action for Baby Animal Bill," *HSUS News* (January 1965): 1; and "Salmonella Infection Linked to Cruel Easter Chick Trade," *HSUS News* (March 1966): 1.

70"HSUS Requests Results in Turtle Sale Ban," *HSUS News* (Summer 1975): 11; "Ban Is Urged on Turtle Sales," *Washington Star* (4 May 1975); and "Turtle Sales Continue Despite Ban," *HSUS News* (Winter 1981): 32.

71"Dealer Arrested, Pleads Guilty in Interstate Puppy Mill Case," *HSUS News* (November 1965): 7.

72Memo (31 May 1974), ISAP–Meeting with Pet Industry, Filebox 3099–707; "Puppy Mill Misery," *HSUS News* (Fall 1981): 6.

73"Close-Up Report: Puppy Mills, An American Disgrace," *HSUS News* (Winter 1976–1977): 18–19; Shain, personal communication (2 June 2003).

74"Puppy Mills," 18–19.

75"Puppy Mill Misery," *HSUS News* (Fall 1981): 5.

76Ibid.

77"HSUS Shows at AKC Contest," *HSUS News* (Winter 1985): 2; "Federal Support for the AWA," *HSUS News* (March

1991): 33.

[78]"Puppy-Mill Media Blitz," *HSUS News* (Summer 1990): 7; "Puppy Mills Raided," "Boycott Stirs Up Breeders," *HSUS News* (Fall 1990): 30; and "New Pet-Store Law," *HSUS News* (Spring 1991): 29.

[79]"Puppy Protection Act Introduced," *HSUS News* (Winter 1992): 29.

[80]Rachel A. Lamb, "A Congressional Howl," *HSUS News* (Fall 1995): 10–11.

[81]Armstrong et al., "From Pets to Companion Animals," 83; Armstrong, interview (28 May 2003).

[82]"Puppy Mill Misery," 9.

[83]"Committee Probing Puppy Shipments," *Corpus Christi Caller* (26 August 1973).

[84]Mordecai Siegel, "Animal Air Travel: A Life and Death Gamble," *Dogs* (September 1974): 20.

[85]Ibid.

[86]"Pet Air Travel," *News and Observer* (June 11, 1973); Michael W. Fox, personal communication to Ann Gonnerman (6 July 1978), Shipment of Animals–Airlines, Filebox 3099–601.

[87]Lowell Weicker, "A Senator Reports: Animal Welfare Act Amended," *HSUS News* (Summer/Fall 1976): 1.

[88]John A. Hoyt, personal communication to Patti A. Hylands (January 4, 1974), Shipment of Animals–Airlines, Filebox 3099–601.

[89]"Animals as Air Cargo," *HSUS News* (Autumn 1974): 3; "Animals in Transit Now Protected," *HSUS News* (Fall 1977): 8–9. The HSUS successfully fought off Amtrak's effort to gain an exemption from its scope; see "Animal Transportation," *HSUS News* (Spring 1978): 17.

[90]"USDA Weakens Transport Standard for Animals," *HSUS News* (Summer 1978): 8; "Transport Temperatures," *HSUS News* (Winter 1979): 32.

[91]Deborah Dasch, "Is Air Transport Safe for Companion Animals?" *HSUS News* (Fall 1985): 22–23.

[92]"Improving Air Transport for Companion Animals," *HSUS News* (Summer 1987): 24.

[93]Joseph W. Barnes, "Friend of Every Friendless Beast," *Rochester History* 25, no. 4 (October 1973): 21.

[94]*HSUS News*, editorial (May 1963): 2; "Humane Society Raiders Discover Sick, Starved, Injured Laboratory Dogs Hidden on New York State Farm," *HSUS News* (November 1963): 1; Dallas Pratt, *Painful Experiments on Animals* (New York: Argus Archives, 1976), 147–48; and AWI, *Animals and Their Legal Rights* (Washington: AWI, 1990), 69.

[95]"Seizure Law Beat in Miami But Another Enacted in New Orleans," *HSUS News* (June 1958): 2; "Myers Calls Connecticut Pound Seizure Bills Misleading, Economically Unsound; Urges Defeat of Proposal," *HSUS News* (March–April 1961): 2; and "Humane Societies Win One, Lose Two in Seizure War," *HSUS News* (May–June 1961): 1.

[96]"Utah Branch Defies New Seizure Law as Unconstitutional," *HSUS News* (July 1963): 1.

[97]"HSUS Field Agent Prosecutes Dog Dealer," *HSUS News* (May 1963): 6; "Fast Action by HSUS Field Men Convicts Dog Dealer in Bribery Attempt on Shelter Operator," *HSUS News* (November 1964): 2; "New Jersey Branch Champions Society Shelters vs. Commercial Pounds," *HSUS News* (January 1965): 4; "Raids on Dog Dealers Continue; Tennessee Dealer Fined," *HSUS News* (September 1965): 6; and "HSUS Agent Charges Pennsylvania Animal Dealer with Cruelty," *HSUS News* (November 1965): 1.

[98]"Law Curbs Use of Stolen Pets by Scientists," *Miami News* (25 August 1966).

[99]"California Branch Fights Pound Seizure Law, Seeks Support of Humanitarians Throughout State," *HSUS News* (November 1966): 4; "Pound Seizure Forces Beaten in California; Washington Becomes New Target in Shifting Struggle," *HSUS News* (January–February 1967): 10; "San Diego Board Votes Sale of Stray Animals to Medical Research," *HSUS News* (July–August 1967): 8; "Bill Introduced in New Jersey as Pound Seizure War Spreads Rapidly," *HSUS News* (March–April 1967): 6; "Pound Seizure Threat Defeated in N.J." *HSUS News* (May–June 1967): 3; and "Takeover of Wisconsin Society Fails; Members Oust Research Forces," *HSUS News* (January–February 1968): 5.

[100]*Animal Welfare Act 1966–1996: Historical Perspectives and Future Directions* (Washington, D.C.: WARDS, 1998), 13; Armstrong, interview (28 May 2003).

[101]John Hoyt, "Preempting the Possible," *HSUS News* (Winter 1985); Michael A. Giannelli, "Dogs and Cats by the Pound," *HSUS News* (Summer 1985): 22–23.

[102]"National Pound Seizure Ban Introduced in the House of Representatives," *HSUS News* (Summer 1986): 26–28; "Pound Seizure Bill Battered," *HSUS News* (Fall 1986): 25.

[103]"All Hail S. 1457," *HSUS News* (Fall 1987): 26.

[104]"1988 Legislative Year in Review," *HSUS News* (Winter 1989): 35; Armstrong, interview (28 May 2003).

[105]Armstrong et al., "From Pets to Companion Animals," 73.

[106]"The HSUS Urges Everyone to 'Be a P.A.L.'" *HSUS News* (Fall 1987): 10–11; "Be a P.A.L.—and Get an Award," "Our Congressional 'P.A.L.s'" *HSUS News* (Winter 1988): 4, 31; and "'Be a P.A.L.' Winners Named," *HSUS News* (Spring 1989): 5–8.

[107]John A. Hoyt, "Until There Are None, Adopt One," *HSUS News* (Summer 1991): 23–25; "HSUS Urges Breeding Moratorium," *HSUS News* (Summer 1993): 4–7; and "Moving Toward a New Ethic," *HSUS News* (Winter 1994): 11–13.

[108]"Moving Toward a New Ethic," 11.

[109]Kenneth White, "HSUS Issues a Challenge," *HSUS News* (Spring 1994): 9–10.

[110]Parkes, personal communication (10 April 2003).

[111]Randall Lockwood, interview (9 April 2003).

[112]Randall Lockwood and Guy Hodge, "The Tangled Web of Animal Abuse: The Link Between Cruelty to Animals and Human Violence," *HSUS News* (Summer 1986): 10–15.

[113]Randall Lockwood and Ann Church, "Deadly Serious: An FBI Perspective on Animal Cruelty," *HSUS News* (Fall 1996): 27–30.

[114]*HSUS Annual Report*, 1999, 12; Wayne Pacelle, interview (17 May 2003); Armstrong, interview (28 May 2003).

[115]Randall Lockwood, "Dangerous Dogs Revisited," *HSUS News* (Fall 1992): 20–22.

[116]Ibid.

[117]Randall Lockwood and Kate Rindy, "Are 'Pit Bulls' Different? An Analysis of the Pit Bull Terrier Controversy," *Anthrozoös* 1, no. 1 (Summer 1987): 2–8; Randall Lockwood, "Vicious Dogs," *HSUS News* (Winter 1986): 22–24; and Lockwood, "Dangerous Dogs Revisited," 20–22; and *HSUS News* (Spring 1996): 2.

[118]Julie Miller Dowling and Cynthia Stitely, "Unwanted Burden: Animal Shelters Debate the Role of Euthanasia," *HSUS*

News (Winter 1998): 22–8.

[119]Ibid., 24.

[120]Jacques V. Sichel, *The HSUS Handbook*, Vol. 2 (Washington, D.C.: HSUS, 1969); 650a, 650d.

[121]Ibid., 650b.

[122]Dowling and Stitely, "Unwanted Burden," 28.

[123]"Humane Society to Press for Laws Protecting Dogs," *Washington Star* (6 October 1956); Fred Myers, "Report of the Executive Director," *New Frontiers of the American Humane Movement* (Washington, D.C.: HSUS, 1960), 7; and Patrick B. Parkes, personal communication (8 May 2003).

[124]"Federal Law Labeled Ineffective; HSUS Begins State Campaigns," *HSUS News* (September 1965): 8.

[125]"Stamp Sought to Honor Bergh for One-Man War on Cruelty," *New York Herald-Tribune* (26 January 1941); "New Commemorative Stamp Honors Humane Movement," *HSUS News* (May 1966): 6.

[126]Iris Nowell, *The Dog Crisis* (New York: St. Martin's Press, 1978); Kathleen Szasz, *Petishism? Pets and Their People in the Western World* (New York: Holt, Rinehart, and Winston, 1968).

[127]*Report of the President*, 1976; "Pets in Housing," *Animal Activist Alert* (March 1985): 2; Shain, interview (2 June 2003).

[128]"Wishes of Deceased," *HSUS News* (Summer/Fall 1976): 22; Murdaugh Stuart Madden, "Arrangements for Pets in Your Will," *HSUS News* (Fall 1978): 27.

[129]*HSUS News* (Fall 1986): 26; "A Socks by Any Other Name," *HSUS News* (Summer 1993): 2; "Who Is the Best 'First'?" *HSUS News* (Winter 1997): 3; "Leader Becomes a Kindred Spirit," *Animal Update* (Fall 1999): 7; and John Hoyt, interview by Kim Stallwood, Archive (Baltimore, Md.: Animal Rights Network, 31 May 2001).

[130]Armstrong, interview (28 May 2003).

[131]Ibid.

[132]Leslie Sinclair and Randall Lockwood, *Forensic Investigation of Animal Cruelty* (in press); Patricia Forkan, interview (2 June 2003).

[133]"The Iditarod Revisited," *HSUS News* (Summer 1992): 5–6; Leslie Isom, "New Chapter in Iditarod Saga," *HSUS News* (Fall 1995): 17.

[134]Martha Armstrong, "To Stem the Tide of Dogs," *HSUS News* (Winter 1998): 30–33; Neil Trent, interview (29 May 2003).

Chapter Five

[1]Natasha Atkins, "The Endangered Species Act: Is It at the Brink of Extinction?" *HSUS News* (Winter 1982): 5.

[2]"Grandy Moves to Humane Society," *Defenders* (April 1982); John A. Hoyt, "A Commitment Reaffirmed," *HSUS News* (Winter 1982).

[3]Vicki McKinney Daitch, "From Sympathy to Synergy: Humane Activism in the Modern Environmental Movement," (Ph.D. diss., University of Illinois at Urbana-Champaign, 2000): 92–93, 99.

[4]"Neuberger Sponsors Humane Trap Bill," *HSUS News* (August 1957): 8; Daitch, "From Sympathy to Synergy," 109–114.

[5]"Humane Slaughter of Sea Animals Urged by UN," *HSUS News* (June 1958): 4.

[6]*National Humane Society News* (June 1956): 1; "1,400,000 Animals Killed July 4," *HSUS News* (July 1964): 8; "Final Survey of Animal Highway Deaths Planned," *HSUS News* (May 1966): 12; and "Research Aimed at Roadway Deaths," *HSUS News* (June 1974): 6–7.

[7]Oliver Evans, "New Horizons," *The First Decade 1954–1964* (Washington, D.C.: HSUS, 1964), 65 ; *HSUS News* (May 1957): 1; HSUS, *Annual Report*, 1958, 5, Filebox 3099–1949; "A New Look at Sportsmanship," *HSUS News* (July 1966): 6; Jonathan Fieldston [Fred Myers], "Lust to Kill"; and "Anti-Hunting Article Reprinted," *HSUS News* (November 1966): 1. "Lust to Kill" originally appeared in AHA's *National Humane Review* (December 1952): 4–5, 20–21.

[8]"Bow Hunting Cruelties Under Growing Attack by California Branch," *HSUS News* (July 1966): 6.

[9]"Predator Destruction Under Fire from HSUS and Federal Agency," *HSUS News* (July 1964): 2, 4; "HSUS Backs Dingell Bill," *HSUS News* (July 1965): 4; and "Protection Sought for Predatory Mammals Through Federal Law," *HSUS News* (May–June 1967): 8.

[10]"Big HSUS Conference Probes New Areas of Animal Protection, Lays Plans to Combat Major Cruelties," *HSUS News* (September 1966): 3.

[11]HSUS-ISAP, 3rd draft, Mel L. Morse, personal communication to William P. Murray, Jr. (26 July 1973), in Staff Meetings, Filebox 3099–321.

[12]"Wildlife Expert Named to Staff," *HSUS News* (May 1971): 1; "Regional Offices to Assist Locals," *HSUS News* (Summer 1972): 1.

[13]"HSUS Asks Federal Court to Stop Poison Program," *HSUS News* (May 1971): 1–2; John A. Hoyt, "Why Our Government Is Killing Our Wildlife," *HSUS News* (January 1972): 4; and "U.S. Ends Poisoning of Predators," *HSUS News* (March 1972): 1–2.

[14]"U.S. Ends Poisoning of Predators," 1; "Sheepmen Push to Use Poison," *HSUS News* (Winter 1973): 1.

[15]"Administration on Predators: Let States Kill," *HSUS News* (June 1972): 1–2; "Sheepmen Push to Use Poison," 1.

[16]"Coyote Poisoning Halted," *Washington Star* (5 March 1974); "Woolgrowers Win Round on Predator Control," *HSUS News* (Autumn 1975): 13; and "Uncle Sam's Anti-Coyote Crusade," *HSUS News* (Spring 1979): 20.

[17]Natasha Atkins, "Government Report on the 1080 Collar," *International Journal for the Study of Animal Problems* 2, no. 1 (1981): 10–12.

[18]"The HSUS Wins 1080 Fight," *HSUS News* (Summer 1983): 21; "A Poisonous Policy Reversal," *HSUS News* (Winter 1984): 28; "Reagan's Proposed Budget," *Animal Activist Alert* (March 1986): 1; "Dr. Grandy Joins NADCAC," *HSUS News* (Summer 1988): 2; and Susan Hagood, "ADC's Lethal Actions," *HSUS News* (Spring 1995): 7–8.

[19]"Careers: From Killer of Wildlife to Defender of Wildlife," *Kind* (May–June 1982): 26–28.

[20]Dick Randall, "Predator Control: Decades of Useless Slaughter," *HSUS News* (Spring 1991): 16–20.

[21]"ADC," *HSUS News* (Winter 1998): 2–3.

[22]"USDA Skirts Voter-Approved Law and Then Retreats," *Humane Activist* (January–February 2002): 3.

[23]"HSUS Fights to Save African Animals from Watery Grave," *HSUS News* (September 1966): 8; "Frank McMahon Loses Fight for Life," *HSUS News* (Summer 1975): 6.

[24]"HSUS Investigates 64 Zoos," *HSUS News* (July 1971): 1; Jack Anderson, "Some Zoos Called Dens of Horror," *Philadelphia Bulletin* (26 July 1971); "Most Large Zoos Obey Law, Philadelphia Spokesman Contends," *Philadelphia Bulletin* (26 July 1971); "Zoo Conflicts Cause Suffering for Animals," *HSUS News* (Spring 1975): 13; "HSUS Tells Pittsburgh Its Zoo Is Stagnating," *HSUS News* (Summer 1975): 12; "Trenton Zoo 'Barbaric,'" *Philadelphia Bulletin* (30 May 1980); and Hoyt, interview by Kim Stallwood, Archive (Baltimore, Md.: Animal Rights Network, 31 May 2001).

[25]"The Humanitarian as Irritant," *HSUS News* (Summer 1981): 2; Sue Pressman, "Ten Substandard Zoos," *HSUS News* (Summer 1983): 10–14; *Report of the President*, 1989; and John W. Grandy, "Zoos: A Critical Reevaluation," *HSUS News* (Summer 1992): 12.

[26]Grandy, "Zoos: A Critical Reevaluation," 12.

[27]"HSUS Releases Tuffy from Tank," *HSUS News* (November 1971): 1; "HSUS Saves Bear in Condemned Cage," *HSUS News* (Summer 1972): 1; "Ex-Bank Bear Gets New Lair," *Washington Star* (7 November 1974); and "It's Lonely at the Top," *HSUS News* (Spring 1981): 3.

[28]"Zoo Closes," *HSUS News* (Fall 1987): 31; Randall Lockwood, "Life After Slater Park," *HSUS News* (Fall 1993): 25–26.

[29]T.E.D. Klein, "They Kill Animals and Call It Art," *New York Times* (13 January 1974).

[30]"Cruelty to Animals in the Film Industry," *HSUS News* (Autumn 1975): 3–6.

[31]"Sue Pressman Means Business," *HSUS News* (Winter 1976-77): 10–11.

[32]"HSUS Alert: It's Circus Season," *HSUS News* (June 1974): 3; Jeanne Roush, "Animals Under the Big Top," *HSUS News* (Spring 1981): 18–21.

[33]"Oregon Ranch Raided," *HSUS News* (Winter 1985), 35; "Animal Welfare Organizations and Government Officials Try to Close Shoestring Operation," *HSUS News* (Fall 1985), 26–28; "Exotic Animal Auctions," *HSUS News* (Spring 1988), 7–9; Allen T. Rutberg, "Wildlife: Wanted Dead or Alive," *HSUS News* (Winter 1992), 23–25; and Eric Sakach, personal communication, 22 December 2003.

[34]"Spotlight," *HSUS News* (Summer 1996), 2; Dave Pauli, personal communicaton, 22 December 2003.

[35]Michael Winikoff, "Blowing the Lid off Canned Hunts," *HSUS News* (Summer 1994): 38–43.

[36]"Lust to Kill" *National Humane Review* (December 1952): 4–5, 20–21.

[37]Paul G. Irwin, "Overview: The State of Animals in 2001," in Deborah J. Salem and Andrew N. Rowan, eds., *The State of the Animals: 2001* (Washington, D.C.: Humane Society Press, 2001), 3.

[38]"Senate Will Consider Law to Stop Shooting Animals from Aircraft," *HSUS News* (February 1971): 1; "Loophole Discovered in Aerial Killing Ban," *HSUS News* (June 1972): 8.

[39]"HSUS Wins Court Battle to Stop Public Hunt in Wildlife Refuge," *HSUS News* (February 1971): 3.

[40]*Washington Star* (13 February 1973).

[41]"HSUS-New Jersey Protests Great Swamp Deer Hunt," *HSUS News* (Spring 1978): 23; Tom Porch, "Humane Society Protests Hunt," *Philadelphia Bulletin* (4 December 1979).

[42]"Deny HSUS Appeal on Refuge Hunting," *HSUS News* (Autumn 1974): 6.

[43]"Hoyt Addresses Game Managers," *HSUS News* (Summer 1972): 7; "Hunting Unjustified as Sport, Hoyt Says," *HSUS News* (April 1973): 4; "Game Managers Hear 'Respect for Life' Ethic," *HSUS News* (Summer 1975): 13; and John A. Hoyt, "Open Season on CBS," *HSUS News* (Autumn 1975): 2.

[44]"Who Pays the Bill for Hunting?" *HSUS News* (Spring 1981): 22–24.

[45]"Coalition Works to Modify Impact of 'Project WILD,'" *HSUS News* (Winter 1985): 19; "Project WILD Uproar in California," *HSUS News* (Summer 1985): 33.

[46]"Refuge Hunting Attacked," *HSUS News* (Spring 1985): 36.

[47]Ibid.; "Refuge Suit Setback," *HSUS News* (Fall 1986): 31.

[48]"Victory at Loxahatchee," *HSUS News* (Winter 1985): 31; "HSUS Sues to Protect Mountain Lions," *HSUS News* (Summer 1985): 36.

[49]"Arnett Resigns," *HSUS News* (Winter 1985): 30.

[50]"Refuge Progress," *HSUS News* (Fall 1987): 28; *Report of the President*, 1989.

[51]"Refuges—The Next Step," *HSUS News* (Spring 1988): 22; "Refuge Suit Victory," *HSUS News* (Spring 1988): 28.

[52]John Hoyt and Michael Fox, interview by Kim Stallwood, Archive (Baltimore, Md.: Animal Rights Network, 8 November 2001).

[53]John W. Grandy, personal communication (6 June 2003).

[54]Ibid.

[55]"Victories in the West," *HSUS News* (Winter 1995): 9–10; Wayne Pacelle, "Another State Ballot Victory," *HSUS News* (Summer 1996): 6–8.

[56]Pacelle, "Another State Ballot Victory," 6–8.

[57]Wayne Pacelle, "Landslide Year for Wildlife," *HSUS News* (Spring 1997): 7.

[58]Susan Hagood, "Hunters' Privilege: State Wildlife Agencies Cling to the Past," *HSUS News* (Fall 1996): 9–12.

[59]Pacelle, "Landslide Year for Wildlife," 9; Wayne Pacelle, interview (26 May 2003).

[60]Tony Povilitis, "Living with Deer," *HSUS News* (Fall 1989): 24–27.

[61]"Senate Hearing on Horses Held," *HSUS News* (Fall 1991): 28–29; Allen T. Rutberg, "New Day for Wild Horses," *HSUS News* (Spring 1993): 5–6; "Spotlight," *HSUS News* (Spring 1996): 2; and Jay F. Kirkpatrick, "Wildlife Contraception: A New Way of Looking at Wildlife Management," *HSUS News* (Fall 1991): 23.

[62]*Report of the President*, 1989; Kirkpatrick, "Wildlife Contraception," 22–25; Allen T. Rutberg, "New Day for Wild Horses," *HSUS News* (Spring 1993): 5–6; and Jay F. Kirkpatrick and Allen T. Rutberg, "Fertility Control in Animals," in Deborah J. Salem and Andrew N. Rowan, eds., *The State of the Animals: 2001* (Washington, D.C.: Humane Society Press, 2001), 186–187.

[63]"Kinder, Gentler Elephant Control," *HSUS News* (Winter 1997): 30–31; "Summer Success in South Africa," *HSUS News* (Fall 1998): 9.

[64]"For Benign Control," *HSUS News* (Fall 1996): 33–34.

[65]"Spotlight," *HSUS News* (Spring 1996): 3; "Darting Does," *Animal Update* (Summer 1999): 2–3.

[66]"Concern for Imperiled Wildlife Grows Popular," *HSUS News* (October 1970): 6.

[67]"HSUS Assists Nelson in Trapping Bill Draft," *HSUS News* (May 1971): 7; *Report of the President*, 1976; Program and Policy Committee (22–23 March 1976), Meetings Program and Policy, Filebox 3099–990; and "Society Completes Trapping Study," *HSUS News* (Winter 1976–77): 17.

[68]Margaret Morrison, "The Ohio Story," *HSUS News* (Winter 1978): 4–6; Harrison A. Williams, "Pain and Profit: The Story of the Steel Jaw Trap," *HSUS News* (Winter 1978): 14–15.

[69]Ann Church, "New Jersey Trapping Triumph Rewards Animal Welfarists," *HSUS News* (Spring 1984): 24; "Fall Actions Seek Trapping's Downfall," *HSUS News* (Winter 1986): 14; "Trap Ban Trial Ends," *HSUS News* (Fall 1986): 30; "New Jersey Trap-Ban Trial Ends in Victory," *HSUS News* (Winter 1987): 23; and John W. Grandy, "Suffolk County: Anatomy of a Victory," *HSUS News* (Spring 1987): 25.

[70]*Report of the President*, 1984; "Fall Actions Seek Trapping's Downfall," *HSUS News* (Winter 1986): 14; and "Trapping in the Nineties: Who Pays the Price?" *HSUS News* (Fall 1992): 9–11.

[71]"Victories in the West," *HSUS News* (Winter 1995): 9–10; Pacelle, "Another State Ballot Victory," 6–8; *Humane Activist* (January/February 1999): 4; and Pacelle, interview (26 May 2003).

[72]Patrick B. Parkes, personal communication (2 June 2003).

[73]"The HSUS Launches 'The Shame of Fur' Campaign," *HSUS News* (Fall 1988): 6; *Report of the President*, 1989; Patricia Ragan, "Fur on the Run" *HSUS News* (Winter 1990): 9–10; and "Bottom Drops Out of Fur Market," *HSUS News* (Summer 1990): 5.

[74]Wayne Pacelle, "House Cuts Mink Subsidy," *HSUS News* (Fall 1995): 9–10; Wayne Pacelle, "The Mink Subsidy: At an End?" *HSUS News* (Winter 1996): 7.

[75]"HSUS Launches Fur-Free 2000," Matthew Scully, "A Designer's Evolution," *HSUS News* (Fall 1998): 23; Danielle Bays, "Is Fur Really 'Back'?" *HSUS News* (Winter 1998): 11.

[76]"Going Undercover to Expose the Truth behind Persian Lamb Fur," *Animal Update* (Spring 2001): 2.

[77]"Blackbird Reprieve," *Washington Star* (20 November 1974); "Blackbird Killing Confirms HSUS Fears of Cruelty," *HSUS News* (Spring 1975): 5.

[78]John Hadidian, "Protection Close to Home," *HSUS News* (Spring 1996): 10–12.

[79]Margaret Baird, personal communication, 1 July 2003.

[80]John F. Kullberg, "Shelters Without Walls," *HSUS News* (Spring 1995): 37–39.

[81]"Wildlife Rehabilitation Training Center Opens," *HSUS News* (Fall 1995): 6.

[82]John W. Grandy and John Hadidian, "Making Peace With Canada Geese," *HSUS News* (Spring 1997): 33.

[83]"Disappearing Wildlife," *HSUS News* (June 1972): 9; "ESA Reauthorization," *HSUS News* (Spring 1985): 31; James A. Tober, *Wildlife and the Public Interest: Nonprofit Organizations and Federal Wildlife Policy* (New York: Praeger Publishers, 1989), 85–101; and *Report of the President*, 1989.

[84]John W. Grandy, "CITES: A Good Year," *HSUS News* (Summer 1985): 28–29.

[85]Teresa M. Telecky, "CITES: In the Interim," *HSUS News* (Winter 1993): 18.

[86]Susan S. Lieberman, "The Ivory Trade: Death Knell for Africa's Elephants," *HSUS News* (Spring 1988): 17–19; John W. Grandy, "Good News from CITES," *HSUS News* (Winter 1990): 5; and Teresa Telecky, "A Critical March," *HSUS News* (Winter 1992): 19–21.

[87]"A Question of Morality," *HSUS News* (Spring 1992): 16–20; "Ivory Trade Renewed Despite Lack of Safeguards," *Humane Activist* (May/June 1999): 1.

[88]"Interior Dilutes Importation Ban on Exotic Pets," *HSUS News* (Spring 1975): 8.

[89]Greta Nilsson, "The Cage Bird Trade," *HSUS News* (Winter 1978): 8–10.

[90]Ann Church, "The First Domino Falls in New York," *Animal Activist Alert* (March 1985): 1; Susan S. Lieberman, "Wildlife in Transit," *HSUS News* (Summer 1988): 22–25; and *Report of the President*, 1989.

[91]"Traffic in Misery," *HSUS News* (Fall 1991): 14–18; John A. Hoyt, *Animals in Peril: How Sustainable Use Is Wiping Out the World's Wildlife* (Garden City, N.Y.: Avery Publishing, 1994), 43.

[92]"U.N. Stockholm Meeting Deals with Animals Only as Crops," *HSUS News* (Summer 1972): 3.

[93]Teresa Telecky and Doris Lin, "Trophy of Death," *HSUS News* (Fall 1995): 27–29.

[94]Ibid., 29.

[95]Matthew Scully, "Hunting for Fun and 'Charity,'" *New York Times* (17 April 1999).

[96]"What Are They Thinking?" *Animal Update* (Spring 1999): 7; "Smithsonian at Center of Trophy Hunting Scandal," *Humane Activist* (March/April 1999): 2.

[97]Suzy Sanders, "Searching for Solutions," *HSUS News* (Summer 1996): 10; Wayne Pacelle, "2002 Farm Bill," undated personal communication.

[98]"International Humane Slaughter Law Sought through U.N.," *HSUS News* (January 1957): 4; "Humane Slaughter of Sea Animals Urged by UN," *HSUS News* (June 1958): 4; and "Lifetime of Humane Work Ends with Death of Miss Goode," *HSUS News* (March 1970): 3.

[99]Patricia Forkan, interview (29 April 2003).

[100]"Federal Report," *HSUS News* (Winter 1993): 35; Forkan, interview (29 April 2003).

[101]"The Whales' Year at Last," *HSUS News* (Fall 1981): 14; "Humane Victory Harpooned," *HSUS News* (Winter 1982): 3.

[102]"HSUS Votes to Join Whaling Boycott of Japan Products," *HSUS News* (Summer 1974): 1; Patricia Forkan, "Are We Saving the Whales?" *HSUS News* (Winter 1976–77): 3; idem., "The Fight Continues," *HSUS News* (Fall 1977): 2–4; and idem., "Whales at a Crisis Point," *HSUS News* (Fall 1991): 12.

[103]*Report of the President*, 1980, Filebox 3099–1949; "The Whales' Year at Last," 14; and "Humane Victory Harpooned," 3.

[104]"Moving Towards 1986," *HSUS News* (Fall 1983): 4–7; and Forkan, interview (29 April 2003).

[105]Patricia Forkan, "Japan Declares War on Whaling Moratorium," *HSUS News* (Winter 1985): 22–3; "Whales Win in Court, Protesters Target JAL," *HSUS News* (Spring 1985): 9; Campbell Plowden, "Whaling Moratorium: An Agonizing Step Away," *HSUS News* (Fall 1985): 12; and *Report of the President*, 1985.

[106]Plowden, "Whaling Moratorium: An Agonizing Step Away," 12; *Report of the President*, 1985.

[107]Campbell Plowden, "'Studying' Whales to Death," *HSUS News* (Fall 1986): 20–21; Campbell Plowden, "Research Loopholes Tighten for Whalers," *HSUS News* (Fall 1987): 8–9; "Iceland Defies Pleas to Halt Research Whaling," *Animal Activist Alert* (December 1987): 1; "Research Whaling Continues," *HSUS News* (Fall 1988): 7; and Forkan, "Whales at a Crisis Point," 12.

[108]"Pilot Whale Hunt Attacked," *HSUS News* (Fall 1985): 13.

[109]Hoyt, *Animals in Peril*, 51–54.

[110]"The Years of the Irish Proposal," *HSUS News* (Fall 1998): 10.

[111]Betsy Dribben, "A Victory for Whales at IWC," *HSUS News* (Fall 1996): 36–37; Forkan, interview (29 April 2003).

[112]"Whale Watch," *Humane Activist* (January/February 2001): 5.

[113]"Suing to Save the Right Whale," *Animal Update* (September/October 2001): 2.

[114]Paula Jewell, "Whales Die at Shedd Aquarium," *HSUS News* (Winter 1993): 5–6.

[115]Mike Winikoff, "Keiko: Halfway Home," *HSUS News* (Spring 1996): 4–6.

[116]"End Japan's Whale Killing Plans," *Humane Activist* (May/June 2002): 7; "Japan's Still Blubbering," *Humane Activist* (July/August 2002): 7.

[117]Humane Society International Opening Statement to the 52nd Meeting of the International Whaling Commission, Australia, July 2000.

[118]"The HSUS Dusts Off Tuna Boycott Buttons," *HSUS News* (Summer 1983): 15.

[119]"Zero Mortality," *HSUS News* (Summer 1977): 23; "HSUS Probes Humaneness of Porpoise Taking by Tuna Fisherman," *HSUS News* (Fall 1977): 27.

[120]"The HSUS Dusts Off Tuna Boycott Buttons," 15.

[121]"Dolphin Death," *Close-Up Report* (June 1988).

[122]Campbell Plowden, "Animal Groups Unite to Oppose Driftnet Permit," *HSUS News* (Fall 1987): 24–25.

[123]"Dolphin Death," *Close-Up Report* (June 1988); "A New Arena for Dolphins," *HSUS News* (Summer 1991): 35; and Forkan, interview (29 April 2003).

[124]"A New Arena for Dolphins," 35.

[125]Ibid.; "Dolphins' Fate Hinges on GATT," *HSUS News* (Fall 1991): 7; "A Deadly Decision," *HSUS News* (Winter 1992): 27.

[126]"Federal Report," *HSUS News* (Winter 1993): 35.

[127]Wayne Pacelle, "Selling Dolphins Down the River," *HSUS News* (Winter 1996): 5–6; "A Narrow Escape for Dolphins," *HSUS News* (Winter 1997): 9–10.

[128]"Drift Net Victory," *HSUS News* (Summer 1996): 34.

[129]"Dolphin Safe or Dolphin Deadly?" *Animal Update* (Fall 1999): 1.

[130]"Caught in the Middle?" *HSUS News* (Fall 1996): 18-21.

[131]Patrick B. Parkes and Jacques V. Sichel, *Twenty-Five Years of Growth and Achievement: The Humane Society of the United States, 1954–1979* (Washington, D.C.: HSUS, 1979), 6; "Humane Slaughter of Sea Animals Urged by UN," *HSUS News* (June 1958): 4; and "U.S. Asked to Help Save Seals from Hunt Cruelty," *HSUS News* (May–June 1961): 1.

[132]"HSUS Urges Canadian Authorities to Stop Cruelty in Seal Hunt," *HSUS News* (March–April 1967): 5; "HSUS Goes to Pribilofs," *HSUS News* (July–August 1968): 4.

[133]"Optimistic Report of Task Force Holds Hope of Stopping Clubbing," *HSUS News* (September/October 1968): 6.

[134]Ibid.

[135]"Seal Hunt Brutality Reaches New High," *HSUS News* (October 1970): 4.

[136]"HSUS Urges Ban on Seal Killing," *HSUS News* (March 1972): 5; "The Seal Slaughter Continues," *HSUS News* (Spring 1977): 5–6; and HSUS, *Interim Report on the Seal Hunts in North America* (February 1980), 75.

[137]"HSUS Presses U.S. to Uphold Ban on Importation of Sealskins," *HSUS News* (Autumn 1975): 8.

[138]"Court Bans Import of Baby Sealskins from South Africa," *HSUS News* (Fall 1977): 27; "Harp Seal Killing Pointless and Obscene," *HSUS News* (Spring 1978): 4–5; and HSUS, *Interim Report on the Seal Hunts in North America*, 75.

[139]"The 70% Solution: A Missed Opportunity to Protect the Pribilof Seals," *HSUS News* (Summer 1981): 24–25; Forkan, interview (29 April 2003).

[140]"Close Call for Seals," *HSUS News* (Fall 1981): 31.

[141]"Time Expires for Fur Seal Treaty, Grows Short for Seals," *HSUS News* (Winter 1985): 18; "Law Notes," *HSUS News* (Fall 1984): 35.

[142]John W. Grandy, "The Pribilof Seal Hunt: An Eyewitness Report," *HSUS News* (Fall 1984): 18.

[143]"The HSUS Seal Campaign," *HSUS News* (Spring 1985): 10–11; Stacy Wyman, "Forty-four Senators Commit Themselves to Oppose Fur Seal Treaty," *HSUS News* (Summer 1985): 12–13; and *Report of the President*, 1985.

[144]Grandy, "The Pribilof Seal War: Animal Welfare Wins a Battle," 18–20; Frantz Dantzler, "Monitoring the Pribilof Subsistence Seal Hunt," *HSUS News* (Fall 1986): 23; and *Report of the President*, 1986.

[145]"Increasing Protection for Marine Mammals," *HSUS News* (Spring 1988): 5.

[146]"1991 Annual Report," *HSUS News* (Summer 1992): 18; John W. Grandy, interview (14 March 2003).

[147]Tober, *Wildlife and the Public Interest*, 124.

[148]Stephen R. Kellert, "Perceptions of Animals in America," in R.J. Hoage, ed., *Perceptions of Animals in American Culture* (Washington, D.C.: Smithsonian Institution Press, 1989), 11–12.

[149]Tober, *Wildlife and the Public Interest*, 124–125.

[150]Ibid., 125; Dena Jones Holma, comp., *Attitudes Toward the Outdoors: An Annotated Bibliography of U.S. Survey and Poll Research Concerning the Environment, Wildlife, and Recreation* (Jefferson, N.C.: McFarland Publishing, 1994), 228.

Chapter Six

[1]Bernard Unti, "The Quality of Mercy: Organized Animal Protection in the United States before World War Two," (Ph.D. diss., American University, 2002).

[2]Bernard Unti and Bill DeRosa, "Humane Education: Past, Present, and Future," in Deborah J. Salem and Andrew N. Rowan, eds., *The State of the Animals II: 2003* (Washington, D.C: Humane Society Press, 2003), 31–50.

[3]HSUS, *The First Decade: 1954–1964* (Washington, D.C.: HSUS, 1964), 47.

[4]Ibid., 33.

[5]"Mousenik Firers, Facing Suit, Send Up Rubber Rodent," *Philadelphia Bulletin* (1 January 1958); "HSUS Board Acts Against Anti-Humane Education," *HSUS News* (May 1959): 1.

[6]Dorothy Thompson, "A Question of Value," repr. in HSUS, *Animals and Children in Elementary and Secondary Schools* (Washington, D.C.: HSUS, 1960); James T. Mehorter, "Animals and Children in Schools," *New Frontiers of the American Humane Movement* (Washington, D.C.: HSUS, 1960), 38; Patrick B. Parkes, personal communication (11 May 2003); and HSUS, *The First Decade*, 37.

[7]"HSUS and GW University Join in Humane Education Study Project," *HSUS News* (November 1964): 1; Oliver Evans, "New Horizons," *The First Decade*, 68.

[8]Concept paper, NAAHE/Westerlund, 1973–83, Filebox 3099–1181.

[9]HSUS, *The First Decade*, 44; "Top Educators Reached at NEA Convention with Humane Education," *HSUS News* (July 1965): 7.

[10]"Humanitarian of Year to Mrs. Flemming for Work with Children," *HSUS News* (November 1964): 3.

[11]"HSUS to Take Over Kindness Club; NHEC Will Administer Pilot Program in Five States," *HSUS News* (September 1966): 2; Dale Hylton, "Presentation," *NAAHE Journal* (Winter 1976): 26; and Dale Hylton, personal communication (29 May 2003).

[12]Hylton, "Presentation," 26.

[13]"NHEC Assumes Administration of Kindness Club in All Fifty States," *HSUS News* (May–June 1969): 6.

[14]"Charlotte Baker Montgomery," *Humane Education* (December 1983): 8.

[15]Parkes, personal communication (11 May 2003).

[16]"HSUS Opens Office for New England," *HSUS News* (Winter 1973): 3.

[17]"Herrmann to Aid KIND Publications," *HSUS News* (March 1974): 5.

[18]"HSUS Prints Book on Animal Careers," *HSUS News* (Autumn 1974): 11; Charles F. Herrmann, III, "Animal-Related Careers: A Humane Goal for Youth," *HSUS News* (Spring 1975): 9; and *Report of the President*, 1977, Filebox 3099–1949.

[19]*Report of the President*, 1976.

[20]Michael W. Fox, *Wild Dogs Three* (New York: Putnum, 1977).

[21]"NAAHE on the Move," *HSUS News* (Summer 1977): 25.

[22]"HSUS Opens National Center to Serve Humane Educators," *HSUS News* (January 1974): 3; Patrick B. Parkes, "Norma Terris: In Memoriam," *HSUS News* (Winter 1990): 12.

[23]John Dommers and Kathy Savesky, "Setting the Pace for Humane Education," *HSUS News* (Spring 1978): 9.

[24]Charles F. Herrmann, III, "Choosing 'Humane' Books for Children," *HSUS News* (Fall 1978): 22–23.

[25]Willow Ann Soltow, "What's Wrong with This Picture?" *HSUS News* (Spring 1993): 6–8.

[26]Kathy Savesky, "People and Animals: An Organized Approach to Humane Education," *HSUS News* (Summer 1981): 12–15.

[27]Doreen Adams Madden, "Humane Publications Produced in Salem Road Log Cabin," *Regional Shopper and Reporter* (27 January 1986).

[28]Kathy Savesky, "People and Animals," 12–15.

[29]Lance Gurwell, "Protests Cancel 'Humane Education' Curriculum," *Ogden Standard-Examiner* (5 September 1982).

[30]*Critique of People and Animals: A Humane Education Curriculum Guide*, Humane Education Curriculum Guide, Responses, Filebox 3099–1181.

[31]"Kind News Promises a Bright New Approach," *HSUS News* (Fall 1983): 14–15.

[32]Bill DeRosa, personal communication (8 May 2003).

[33]Ibid.

[34]"Special NHS Committee Studies School Animal Experiments," *HSUS News* (June 1956): 2; "HSUS Fights in Court and in National Publicity to Keep Animals Out of Rockets," *HSUS News* (February 1958): 1; and "HSUS and Other Societies Battle Cruelty in Schools," *HSUS News* (May 1960): 2.

[35]"HSUS Action Halts Animal Experiments in New Jersey High School Experiments," *HSUS News* (July 1964): 5; "Depositions Taken in Student Test Case," *HSUS News* (July 1965): 1; "Live Animal Experiments Ruled Legal in N.J. Schools; and Appeal, HSUS Countercampaign Planned," *HSUS News* (May 1966): 9.

[36]"Campaign under Way to End Classroom Cruelty," *HSUS News* (January–February 1967): 6; "HSUS Steps Up Investigation of Cruel Uses of Animals in Science Education, Seeks Remedial Laws," *HSUS News* (May–June 1967): 1.

[37]"State Supreme Court Upholds Verdict in N.J. 'Chicken Case,'" *HSUS News* (March–April 1967); "Heart Transplants on Animals Continued in Ohio School System," *HSUS News* (March–April 1968): 3.

[38]"Bill Bans Live Animal Lab in High School," *Los Angeles Herald-Examiner* (11 August 1970).

[39]"Animals in School Projects," *HSUS News* (Summer 1973): 6.

[40]F. Barbara Orlans, January 1974 memo to humane societies, CEO Individual Retired Files L–Randel, Filebox 3099–475.

[41]"Humane Progress Halts at Largest Science Fair," *HSUS News* (Summer 1975): 10.

[42]"Cruel Experiments at Science Fair," *HSUS News* (Summer/Fall 1976): 4–5.

[43]"Cruelty at Science Fairs Continues," *HSUS News* (Summer 1978): 31.

[44]"NSTA Loosens Restrictions on Use of Animals in Schools," *Animal Activist Alert* (March 1986): 2.

[45]"Rejecting Dissecting: A Humane Alternative," *Animal Activist Alert* (March 1985): 2.

[46]"Cutting Out Dissection," *HSUS News* (Winter 1991): 3; Jonathan Balcombe, "Toward Cruelty-Free Education," *HSUS News* (Fall 1993): 6–8.

[47]"Frogs Here," *HSUS News* (Summer 1987): 2; "Conscientious Student Sues," *HSUS News* (Winter 1988): 36; "Dissection Suit Advances," *HSUS News* (Spring 1988): 28; "Graham Case Resolved?" *HSUS News* (Fall 1988): 36; "An Interview with Jenifer Graham," *HSUS News* (Winter 1989): 27–29; and "Dissection Suit May Be Resolved," *HSUS*

News (Winter 1989): 36.

48 Jonathan Balcombe, "In the Name of Learning," *HSUS News* (Fall 1994): 5–11; Jonathan Balcombe, "Students' Concerns Triumph," *HSUS News* (Fall 1995): 8–9; and Martin L. Stephens, interview (April 2003).

49 Unti and DeRosa, "Humane Education: Past, Present, and Future," 31–50.

50 DeRosa, personal communication (8 May 2003).

51 "Cruelty-Crime Link Programmed for TV," *HSUS News* 8, no. 1 (February 1963): 5; Karen Peterson, "Children and Pet Abuse," *HSUS News* (Winter 1973): 6.

52 Randall Lockwood, "Taking Humane Concerns to College," *HSUS News* (Winter 1985): 24–25; "Research Focus: Children, Animals, and Education," NAAHE (January 1986).

Chapter Seven

1 "HSUS Field Workers Travel 34,000 Miles in First Quarter," *HSUS News* (April 1962): 12.

2 "HSUS Field Agent Prosecutes Dog Dealer," *HSUS News* (May 1963): 6.

3 "Fort Worth Society Sponsors Animal Control Seminar," *HSUS News* (September 1964): 2.

4 "Credit Where Credit Is Due," *HSUS News* (August 1960): 3; "Texas Area Societies Studying Unity Plans with HSUS Assistance," *HSUS News* (November 1961): 4; "New HSUS Branch Chartered for Thirty Northeast Texas Counties," *HSUS News* (April 1962): 4; and Patrick B. Parkes, personal communication (8 April 2003).

5 "Seizure Law Beat in Miami But Another Enacted in New Orleans," *HSUS News* (September 1958): 2; "Tulane Lab Study Exposes Cruelty," *HSUS News* (September 1958): 4.

6 Patrick B. Parkes, personal communication to Ed Myers (17 April 2003); Ed Myers, personal communication (14 April 2003); Tammy Field, telephone interview (15 April 2003); and Deborah Salem, personal communication (8 May 2003).

7 "HSUS Raiders Chase Armed Dog Fight Gang into Mississippi Swamp," *HSUS News* (July 1962): 1; Fred Myers to Internal Revenue Service (5 July 1962), in HSUS, Internal Revenue Service, 1958–1972, History and By-Laws Filebox 3099–1245.

8 Oliver Evans, personal communication to James Garner (3 April 1967), Fiftieth Anniversary Record Group, Box 1.

9 "Optimistic Report of Task Force Holds Hope of Stopping Clubbing," *HSUS News* (September–October 1968): 6.

10 Patrick B. Parkes, personal communication (29 April 2003).

11 Ibid.; Patrick B. Parkes, personal communication (22 May 2003).

12 *Report of the President*, 1974; Patrick B. Parkes, personal communication (2 May 2003).

13 "Animal Abuse Spoils Bicentennial," *HSUS News* (Summer/Fall 1976): 8–9; "Unofficially, It's Been a Real Trip," *Washington Star* (9 June 1976).

14 "Animal Abuse Spoils Bicentennial," 8–9.

15 "HSUS Works with Union Pacific Railroad to Improve Ride for Hogs," *HSUS News* (Fall 1977): 15.

16 "Animal Lab Cleans Up," *HSUS News* (Summer 1977): 20–21.

17 "Weller Assists Local Societies," *HSUS News* (Summer 1977): 15; "Another Kansas Puppy Mill Shut Down," "HSUS Helps Two Texas Towns Plan Improved Pounds," *HSUS News* (Fall 1977): 16; *Report of the President*, 1975; and "Baltimore Pound Gets Cleaned Up," *HSUS News* (Winter 1976–77): 1.

18 "Ohio Pet Store Owner Charged with Cruelty to Animals," *HSUS News* (Summer 1978): 12–13.

19 "HSUS Attacks Animal Slave Market," *HSUS News* (Spring 1978): 2–3; "Slave Traders Sidetracked," *HSUS News* (Fall 1985): 5.

20 "HSUS's Frantz Dantzler: A Big Man Doing a Big Job," *HSUS News* (Spring 1977): 8; Parkes, personal communication (22 May 2003).

21 Patrick B. Parkes, personal communication (26 March 2003); Parkes, personal communication (22 May 2003).

22 Randall Lockwood, interview (15 April 2003).

23 *International Journal for the Study of Animal Problems* 1, no. 1 (1980): 53–54; *Report of the President*, 1980, Filebox 3099–1949; and "Crisis: A Sport Swept by Scandal," *HSUS News* (Summer 1981): 8–10.

24 Andrew Rowan, personal communication (17 February 2003).

25 Nina Austenberg, Jennifer Lewis, and Ann Church, "Taking a Stand Against Wildlife Refuge Exploitation," *HSUS News* (Summer 1984): 4–5; Parkes, personal communication (2 May 2003).

26 Marc Paulhus, "Santeria on Trial," *HSUS News* (Winter 1990): 24–7; "HSUS Files Brief in Santeria Case," *HSUS News* (Fall 1990): 36; Roger Kindler, "A Legal Defeat for Animals," *HSUS News* (Fall 1993): 10–11; Parkes, personal communication (2 May 2003); and Randall Lockwood, personal communication (4 June 2003).

27 Aminda Marques Gonzalez, "Protesters, Church, Rap Unusual Public Santeria Sacrifices," *Miami Herald* (27 June 1993); Mirta Ojito, "Santeria Priest Faces Charges in Animal Slaughter," *Miami Herald* (12 July 1995); Manny Garcia, "Santeria Priest Claims Constitutional Right in Animal Killing," *Miami Herald* (9 August 1995); and Lockwood, personal communication (2 June 2003).

28 Armando Correa, "Trial of Santeria Priest to Begin Today," *Miami Herald* (30 July 1996); Cynthia Corzo, "Santeria Priest OKs Deal with Prosecutors," *Miami Herald* (31 July 1996); Santeria Priest Gets Deal," *Fort Lauderdale Sun-Sentinel* (1 August 1996); Armando Correa, "Order to Work for Church Upsets Santeria Priest," *Miami Herald* (21 August 1996); and Lockwood, personal communication (2 June 2003).

29 Patrick B. Parkes, personal communication (2 June 2003).

30 Ibid.

31 Rick Swain, interview (29 May 2003).

32 Fred Myers, "Policing a Maryland Rodeo Reveals Cruelty Behind Scenes," *HSUS News* (August 1957): 2; "TV Rodeo Sponsors Offer Weak Defense," *HSUS News* (May 1958): 1; "Seminary Rodeo Drive Set Despite Humane Drive," *Washington Star* (31 May 1962); and "Wyoming Society Sues State Officer to Stop Rodeo Cruelties," *HSUS News* (November 1962): 1.

33 "Rodeo Court Test Started by HSUS," *HSUS News* (March–April 1961): 1; "HSUS Anti-Rodeo Injunction Suit Moves

Ahead in Federal Court," *HSUS News* (May–June 1961): 7; and "NBC and ABC Plan New Glorification of Rodeo Cruelties," *HSUS News* (July 1962): 7.

[34]"NBC Reaches Telecast Low Level in 90 Minutes of Blood and Cruelty," *HSUS News* (February 1963): 8.

[35]"Unity Pays Off," *HSUS News* (July 1964): 1; "Bloodless Bullfights Provoke Bitter Battle in Las Vegas," *HSUS News* (March 1965): 8; "Victory in Sight for Ohio Rodeo Bill," *HSUS News* (May 1965): 4; and "Cruelty Charged at West Virginia Rodeo," *HSUS News* (July 1965): 8.

[36]"HSUS Asks President Johnson to Help Stop Bloodless Bullfights," *HSUS News* (January 1966): 1; "Weak Texas Statute Stymies Effort to Prevent Bullfights," *HSUS News* (March 1966): 7.

[37]"Weak Texas Statute Stymies Effort to Prevent Bullfights," 7.

[38]"HSUS Acts Against Bloodless Bullfights in Several Areas; Philadelphia Bans Spectacles," *HSUS News* (May 1966): 4.

[39]Ibid.

[40]Ibid.

[41]Ibid.

[42]"Legal and Economic Losses Hit Hard at Bullfighting Promoters," *HSUS News* (July 1966): 3.

[43]"Television Code Review Board Bans Bullfighting Programs," *HSUS News* (January–February 1967): 7.

[44]"Gains Mount in Rodeo Fight as More States Introduce Legislation," *HSUS News* (January–February 1967): 9.

[45]"Opposition to Drive Against Rodeo Cruelties Stiffens as Connecticut and Ohio Become Battlegrounds," "Humane Societies Fight Bullfight Promoters Across the Nation, Win Victories in Florida, New Mexico," *HSUS News* (March–April 1967): 1, 6; "Humane Forces Fight Hard to Keep Anti-Bucking Strap Law," *HSUS News* (July–August 1967): 6; and "Victory in Ohio; Bill to Amend Bucking Strap Law Dies in Senate," *HSUS News* (September–October 1967): 3.

[46]"Legal and Economic Losses Hit Hard at Bullfighting Promoters," *HSUS News* (July 1966): 3.

[47]"Rodeo Interests Brand HSUS as 'Radical'; Society's Campaign Brings Massive Counter Attack," *HSUS News* (May–June 1967): 2.

[48]"Rodeo Cruelties under Heavy Fire in HSUS Educational Campaign," *HSUS News* (March–April 1969): 3; "Animal Charity League Halts Use of Bucking Strap in Local Rodeo," *HSUS News* (September–October 1969): 8; and "Lesson to Be Learned from Tie-Up of Rodeo Bill in Pennsylvania," *HSUS News* (January–February 1970): 3.

[49]"Humane Societies Win Big Court Victory Against Rodeo Interests," *HSUS News* (October 1970): 3.

[50]"Rodeo Effort Gains Momentum," *HSUS News* (May 1971): 3.

[51]"Bloodless Bullfights Held in Texas Despite Strong HSUS Opposition; Solution Lies in Federal Law," *HSUS News* (November 1966): 7.

[52]"The Rodeo Controversy," *HSUS News* (July 1971): 3.

[53]Ibid.

[54]Program and Policy Committee Minutes (8–9 July 1976), Meetings, Program and Policy, Filebox 3099–1245; "Legal Roundup," *HSUS News* (Winter 1976–1977): 24.

[55]"California 'Bloodless Bullfight' Stopped," *HSUS News* (Fall 1977): 17; Murdaugh Stuart Madden and Roger Kindler, "Ohio Bucking Strap Law Upheld by Court of Appeals," *HSUS News* (Fall 1985): 36; and "Bucking Disappointment," *HSUS News* (Summer 1986): 34.

[56]"Death to the Horses," *HSUS News* (Fall 1987): 34.

[57]"Cruel Days at Frontier Days," *HSUS News* (Winter 1994): 30–31.

[58]"Walking Horse Cruelties Attacked by Law, Persuasion, Publicity," *HSUS News* (May 1960): 3; "Victories Won Over Horse Show Cruelties in Court and Show Ring," *HSUS News* (June 1960): 1.

[59]"Cruelty Charges Dismissed[,] Horse Trainers Go Free," *HSUS News* (January–February 1961): 4; "Three Walking Horse Owners Ousted," *HSUS News* (March–April 1961): 2; and Fred Myers, "Report of the Executive Director," *New Frontiers of the American Humane Movement* (Washington, D.C.: HSUS, 1960), 6.

[60]Patrick B. Parkes, personal communication (5 May 2003).

[61]"Bill Introduced in Senate to Stop Walking Horse Cruelties," *HSUS News* (May 1966): 10.

[62]Pearl Twyne, "Horses," in AWI, *Animals and Their Legal Rights*, 4th ed. (Washington, D.C.: AWI,1980), 133.

[63]"Bill Aimed at Cruel Soring Practices Is Now Before Congress," *HSUS News* (July–August 1969): 1; "Bill to Protect Tennessee Walking Horses Stalled in Committee," *HSUS News* (March 1970): 4; "Walking Horse Bill Passed by Congress," *HSUS News* February 1971): 7; and Marc Paulhus, "Joan R. Blue," *HSUS News* (Spring 1987): 13.

[64]"Investigators Find Sored Show Horses," *HSUS News* (November 1972): 1; *Animal Welfare Act 1966–1996: Historical Perspectives and Future Directions* (Washington, D.C.: WARDS,1998), 32.

[65]"USDA Fails to Stop Sored Show Horses," *HSUS News* (Summer 1972): 2; "Investigators Find Sored Show Horses," 1.

[66]"Soring Law Loopholes," *HSUS News* (Summer 1973): 5.

[67]"Five Trainers Fined for Soring Horses," *HSUS News* (January 1974): 9.

[68]"Dark Days in Shelbyville," *HSUS News* (Summer 1988): 20–21.

[69]Ibid.

[70]"The Politics of Sore Horses," *Humane Activist* (May/June 2000): 1.

[71]"Convention Resolutions," *HSUS News* (March 1960): 7; "HSUS Annual Conference Honors Wild Horse Annie," *HSUS News* (November 1972): 1; and "In Memoriam," *HSUS News* (Fall 1977): 12.

[72]"Wild Mustangs in Montana Face Threat of Extermination; BLM Attitude Considered Arbitrary," *HSUS News* (July–August 1968): 8; "Court Action Brings Agreement; Federal Agency to Halt Mustang Kill in Pryor Mountains Range," *HSUS News* (September–October 1968): 4; and Patrick B. Parkes, personal communication (6 May 2003).

[73]"HSUS Helps Save Trapped Nevada Mustangs," *HSUS News* (March–April 1969): 1.

[74]"Wild Horses Threatened by U.S. Government Bias," *HSUS News* (Autumn 1975): 14–15.

[75]"HSUS Annual Conference Honors Wild Horse Annie," *HSUS News* (November 1972): 1; "In Memoriam," 12.

[76]"HSUS Saves Wild Horses from Slaughter," *HSUS News* (April 1973): 1–2; "No Federal Action in Wild Horse Case," *HSUS News* (June 1974): 4; and Frantz Dantzler, interview (2 June 2003).

[77]"Wild Horses and Idaho Justice," *HSUS News* (Autumn 1974): 2.

[78]"HSUS Loses Wild Horse Case," *HSUS News* (Winter 1974): 2; "Wild Horse and Burro Law Declared Unconstitution-

al," *HSUS News* (Spring 1975): 3; and "Wild Horses Threatened by U.S. Government Bias," *HSUS News* (Autumn 1975): 14–15.

[79]"Legal Roundup," *HSUS News* (Winter 1976–1977): 23.

[80]"Federal Legislation," *HSUS News* (Fall 1977): 22; "Wild Horses," *HSUS News* (Spring 1978): 17.

[82]"HSUS Sues to Protect Wild Horses," *HSUS News* (Summer 1978): 2–3.

[83]"ABC Exposes Plight of Wild Horses," *HSUS News* (Spring 1979): 3; "Future of Burros in Grand Canyon Splits Ranks of Environmentalists," *Washington Star* (22 May 1980).

[84]"Wild Horses Lose a Big One," *Animal Activist Alert* (December 1984): 3; "Horse Roundups Begin," *HSUS News*, (Spring 1985):31; and "'Omnibus' Runs Over Wild Horses," *HSUS News* (Summer 1985): 30.

[85]"One Step from the Dogfood Can," *HSUS News* (Fall 1985): 30.

[86]Ibid.; "More Maneuverings for Wild Horses," *HSUS News* (Winter 1986): 31.

[87]Paula Jewell and John W. Grandy, Ph.D., "Horse Wrangling," *HSUS News* (Fall 1990), 11–13.

[88]"Chincoteague Ponies Suffer Abuse at Annual Roundup, Auction," *HSUS News* (November 1971); "The Chincoteague Swim," *HSUS News* (Fall 1981): 17–19.

[89]Robert Pear, "Pony Roundup Gentler, Humane Society Aides Say," *Washington Star* (26 July 1972); Robert Pear, "Chincoteague Ponies on the Auction Block," *Washington Star* (27 July 1972); "HSUS Forces Improvements in Chincoteague Pony Event," *HSUS News* (November 1972): 5; Corrie M. Anders, "Wild Ponies Swim Again," *Washington Star* (26 July 1973); "Famous Chincoteague Pony Roundup Improves Due to HSUS Efforts," *HSUS News* (Winter 1976–77): 19; and "The Chincoteague Swim," *HSUS News* (Fall 1981): 17–19.

[90]"The Chincoteague Swim," 17–19.

[91]"Behind the Scenes at Chincoteague," *HSUS News* (Fall 1989): 14–17; "Chincoteague 1990," *HSUS News* (Fall 1990): 7.

[92]Melissa Seide Rubin, personal communication (3 June 2003).

[93]"Society Cites Dog Racing Cruelties," *HSUS News* (Summer 1973): 1; "Promoters Step Up Efforts to Legalize Dog Racing," *HSUS News* (Spring 1975): 6.

[94]Bernard M. Weller, "The Scream of a Rabbit," *HSUS News* (Autumn 1975): 10–12; "Run Rabbit Run," *HSUS News* (Summer 1977): 12.

[95]"Promoters Step Up Efforts to Legalize Dog Racing," *HSUS News* (Spring 1975): 6.

[96]"Death Continues to Be Par for the Course in Coursing," *HSUS News* (Summer 1978): 14–16.

[97]"Let's Put Greyhound Racing Out of the Running," *HSUS News* (Spring 1977): 1–2; David Espo, "Cruelty to Animals Defies Legal Process," *Philadelphia Inquirer* (28 May 1978); "Death Continues to Be Par for the Course in Coursing," 16; and "Greyhound Racing Industry Wounded by HSUS Onslaught," *HSUS News* (Fall 1978): 9.

[98]"Society Cites Dog Racing Cruelties," *HSUS News* (Summer 1973): 1; Michael Davis, "Dog Racing, Part of Initiative, Held Cruel," *Washington Star* (29 April 1980).

[99]John Hoyt, "Why We Oppose Greyhound Racing," *HSUS News* (Winter 1985): 10–11.

[100]"Goodbye, Greyhounds," *HSUS News* (Fall 1985): 34; "Racing on Indian Lands," *HSUS News* (Spring 1986): 26; "Four More Years," *HSUS News* (Summer 1986): 30; and Laura Bevan, "Hounding Racing in Its Stronghold," *HSUS News* (Winter 1990): 6–8.

[101]Leslie Isom, "Approaching the Finish Line?" *HSUS News* (Winter 1996): 8; "Not Fit for a Dog," *Humane Activist* (July/August 2002): 3.

[102]"Humane Societies Hit America's Cruelest Sport," *HSUS News* (February 1962): 4–5.

[103]Harrison Williams, "The Solution: A Comprehensive Federal Law with Federal Enforcement," *HSUS News* (Winter 1975): 8–9; "Dog Fighting on the Increase, Poses Tough Law Enforcement Problems," *HSUS News* (Winter 1975): 8–9.

[104]"Dog Fighting on the Increase in Absence of U.S. Ban," *HSUS News* (Winter 1975–76): 14–15; "The Foley Bill," *Report to Humanitarians* 35 (March 1976): 8.

[105]Ed Remitz, "What Happens in 'The Pit' Shouldn't Happen to a Dog," *Sacramento Union* (24 February 1980); "Major Dogfight Raided," *HSUS Close-up Report* (January 1980); and Eric Sakach, personal communication (2 June 2003).

[106]"Animal Fighting Suit Continues," *HSUS News* (Winter 1981): 32; "Animal Fighting Suit Dismissed; Appeal Planned," *HSUS News* (Spring 1981): 32; and "Dogfight Brief Filed," *HSUS News* (Fall 1981): 32.

[107]Julie Rovner, "Crackdown on Dogfighting," *HSUS News* (Winter 1981): 26–7; Parkes, personal communication (2 June 2003).

[108]"Rocky Mountain Bust," *HSUS News* (Summer 1988): 13; Sandy Rowland, "A Rare Day in June," *HSUS News* (Fall 1988): 28–30; Patrick Parkes, personal communication (10 April 2003); and Randall Lockwood, interview (4 June 2003).

[109]Randall Lockwood, "Untangling the Web," *HSUS News* (Spring 1993): 33.

[110] "Agriculture Appropriations Update," *Humane Activist* (September/October 2002): 2.

[111]"Act Against Cockfighting Magazines," *Humane Activist* (January/February 2002): 2; Wayne Pacelle, personal communication (5 June 2003).

[112]"HSUS Investigation Leads to Fifty Arrests in Cockfight Raid," *HSUS Close-Up Report* (June 1978); "Cockfight Raids," "Cockfight Trial Averted," *HSUS News* (Winter 1985): 35; "Cockfight Crackdown Succeeds," *HSUS News* (Winter 1989): 8–9; "Cockfighters' Feathers' Ruffled," *Animal Activist Alert* (December 1987): 1–2; "Closing in on Cockfighting," *HSUS News* (Winter 1988): 7–11; "Oregon Promoter Found Guilty," *HSUS News* (Spring 1991): 29; "Raid Ended Years of Cockfight," *Columbus Dispatch* (13 May 1991); and Pacelle, personal communication (5 June 2003).

[113]"Act Against Cockfighting Magazines," 2; Wayne Pacelle, interview (26 May 2003); and Eric Sakach, personal communication (2 June 2003).

[114]"Ballot Measure Okayed," *Humane Activist* (January/February 2002): 3; "Heroes and Zeroes," *Humane Activist* (September/October 2002): 4.

[115]"Act Against Cockfighting Magazines," 2.

[116]"A Fur Frenzy," *Animal Update* (Spring 1999): 1; "Betrayal of Trust: The Global Trade in Dog and Cat Fur," *http://www.hsus.org/ace/12014*.

[117]"A Fur Frenzy," 1.

[118]"Mary Wore a Little Lamb," *Humane Activist* (January/February 2001): 1; "Going Undercover to Expose the Truth

behind Persian Lamb Fur," *Animal Update* (Spring 2001): 2.

[119]"HSUS Launches State Committee Plan with Unit in Connecticut," *HSUS News* (December 1957): 2; "Second HSUS State Unit Organized in New Jersey," *HSUS News* (February 1958): 2; and *Draft of Proposed Plan for HSUS Administrative and Fiscal Operation* (November 1971), Norma Terris Center History, Filebox 3099–1181.

[120]"Slaughter Victory in Colorado; Campaigns Sweep Other States," *HSUS News* (March 1965): 7; "Humane Slaughter Law Enacted by Ohio," *HSUS News* (May 1965): 8.

[121]Jacques V. Sichel, personal communication to John Hoyt (25 March 1974), in Jacques Sichel, Filebox 3099–225

[122]Mary E. Archibald, "Bill to Restrict Steel-Jawed Traps Gets Support from Humane Society," *Philadelphia Bulletin* (26 February 1970); "N.J. Branch Challenges Game Council Make-up," *HSUS News* (April 1973): 4.

[123]Nina Austenberg, personal communication (2 June 2003).

[124]"HSUS Utah Branch Seizes Abused Animals, Charges Kennel Owner," *HSUS News* (September–October 1969): 6; "Utah Branch Defies New Seizure Law as Unconstitutional," *HSUS News* (July 1963): 1; Minutes, Long-Range Strategy and Planning Committee Meeting, Filebox 3099–990; and Frantz Dantzler, interview (23 April 2003).

[125]"Kindness to Animals Adopted as Policy in Connecticut Schools," *HSUS News* (March–April 1968): 3; Parkes, personal communication (29 April 2003).

[126]"News of HSUS Branches," *HSUS News* (March 1959): 4; "California Branch Rescues Lab Dog," *HSUS News* (February 1962): 1; "Dog Burning Threats Provoke Anger," *HSUS News* (Jan.–Feb. 1969): 8; and "Humanitarians Defeat Bill to Legalize Dog Racing in the California," *HSUS News* (September–October 1969): 3.

[127]"News of HSUS Branches," *HSUS News* (May 1959): 8; "Branch Action Saves Freezing Horses," *HSUS News* (February 1962), 6; Minutes, Long-Range Strategy and Planning Committee Meeting, Filebox 3099–990.

[128]"Society Opens Office for Midwest Region," *HSUS News* (July 1971): 1; "Regional Offices to Assist Locals," *HSUS News* (Summer 1972): 1; Dodie Hawn-Earl Sams Foundation File, CEO Retired Individual Files R–Stevens, Charles (1988), Filebox 3099–476 ; "Regional Office Opens for Pacific States," *HSUS News* (October 1973): 12; "HSUS New York Office Opens at New Address," *HSUS News* (November–December 1967): 1; and "Information Office Opens in New York," *HSUS News* (Summer 1972): 12.

[129]*Report of the President*, 1973.

[130]John A. Hoyt, interview by Kim Stallwood, Archive (Baltimore, Md.: Animal Rights Network, 29 March 2001).

[131]Patrick B. Parkes, personal communication (12 May 2003).

[132]Ibid.

[133]"Southern Area Office Helps Solve Problems," *HSUS News* (Summer 1975): 12; "HSUS's Frantz Dantzler, A Big Man Doing a Big Job," 8–9.

[134]"Southeast Office Opens," *HSUS News* (Winter 1983): 35; "North Central Office Opens," *HSUS News* (Winter 1983): 34; "New Office Opened," *HSUS News* (Spring 1986): 31; "HSUS Opens New Office," *HSUS News* (Fall 1990): 31; and Arnold Baer, personal communication (2 June 2003).

[135]Michael Winikoff and Melissa Seide Rubin, "Protecting the Wild Frontier," *HSUS News* (Winter 1996): 12–13.

[136]Melissa Seide Rubin, "Many Hands Help Fort Peck," *HSUS News* (Winter 1997): 14–17.

[137]Martha C. Armstrong, "Navajo Nation Saga," *HSUS News* (Winter 1997): 16.

[138]Ibid.

[139]Parkes, personal communication (2 May 2003); Arnold Baer, interview (2 June 2003).

[140]"HSUS Helps Save Trapped Nevada Mustangs," *HSUS News* (March–April 1969): 1; "Oil-Soaked Sea Lions, Seals Seem Unharmed, Investigation Reveals," *HSUS News* (May–June 1969): 7; and "HSUS Goes to Relief of Animal Victims of Hurricane Camille," *HSUS News* (September–October 1969): 1.

[141]"'We Felt So Helpless': Thousands of Birds Die in Chesapeake Bay Oil Spill," *HSUS News* (Spring 1976): 6–7; "Disaster Relief Program Aids Oil-Soaked Birds," *HSUS News* (Spring 1977): 11–12.

[142]"HSUS Coordinates Animal Rescue," *HSUS News* (Summer/Fall 1976): 6–7.

[143]"Disaster Relief Program Aids Oil-Soaked Birds," 11–12.

[144]"HSUS Receives Award for Disaster Relief Work," *HSUS News* (Summer 1977): 14.

[145]"Flood," *HSUS News* (Fall 1977): 10–12.

[146]"Volcano Destruction Hurts Animals, Too," *HSUS News* (Fall 1980): 27.

[147]Laura Bevan, "Struggle and Triumph in Andrew's Wake," *HSUS News* (Winter 1993): 12–16.

[148]"HSUS in Action: Florida Wildfires," *HSUS News* (Fall 1998): 24–25.

[149]"Saving Animals from the Flood," *HSUS News* (Fall 1993): 21–23; "Help in High Waters," *HSUS News* (Spring 1997): 17–20; Laura Bevan, personal communication (2 June 2003); and Sakach, personal communication (2 June 2003).

[150]*HSUS News* (Summer 1996): 20, 30.

[151]Melissa Seide Rubin and Jorge Ortega, "No One Can Be 'Too Ready,'" *HSUS News* (Winter 1998): 13; Chris Champine, "Facing Nature's Fury," *Animal Update* (Fall 1999): 2–3; and Vicky George, "HSUS and FEMA Partner in Disaster Plans," *Animal Update* (Spring 2001): 3.

[152]Melissa Seide Rubin, personal communication (2 June 2003).

[153]Ibid.

[154]Ibid.

[155]Ibid.

[156]Ibid.

[157]Ibid.

[158]Ibid.

[159]"Penguins Rescued," *HSUS News* (Winter 1995): 25–26; "Prescription for Misery," *HSUS News* (Spring 1995): 19–22; Neil Trent, interview (29 May 2003); and Janet Frake, interview (5 June 2003).

[160]Michael Fox, "Progress in Nilgiri," *HSUS News* (Winter 1998): 35; Trent, interview (29 May 2003).

Conclusion

[1] Albert Schweitzer, *Out of My Life and Thought* (New York: Henry Holt and Company, 1990), 188.

A

F

G

1990s ballot initiatives, 35–37
airborne, 36
Joseph Wood Krutch's condemnation of, 17
of birds, 125–126
vs. contraception in wildlife, 127–128
Hylton, Dale, 12, 89–90, 148, 150
euthanasia efforts of, 97
on pound seizure, 105

I

Iditarod race, 112
If You Have a Duck, 148
Illinois
Champaign County Humane Society, 87
Immunocontraception in wildlife, 127–128
Improved Standards for Laboratory Animals Act, 79
Inman, John H., 183
Institute for Behavioral Research, 78
Institute for the Study of Animal Problems (ISAP), 53, 75
creation of, 21–22
euthanasia study by, 98
publications of, 22
sterilization study by, 96
wildlife protection review, 117
Institutional animal care and use committees (IACUCs), 80, 83
Interagency Coordinating Committee on the Validation of Alternative Methods (ICCVAM), 82
Interfaith Council for the Protection of Animals and Nature, 31
Internal Revenue Service (IRS)
ruling on animal control entities, 95
International City/County Management Association (ICMA), 92
International Commission for Northwest Atlantic Fisheries, 141
International Conference on Fertility Control for Wildlife Management, 128
International issues
1990s efforts, 34, 37–38
captive animals, 122–123
HSI efforts, 113
wildlife protection, 134–135
International Journal for the Study of Animal Problems, 22
International Kindness Club, 16
International Science and Engineering Fair (ISEF), 153–154
International Standards Organization (ISO) treaty, 38
International Whaling Commission (IWC), 37, 136–139
Investigations, 162–164
Iroquois Brands, Ltd., 54
Irradiated foods, 58
Irwin, Paul G., 20–21, 25, 40
becomes president, 32
on international efforts, 38
land protection efforts of, 31

J

K

and euthanasia methods, 98

L

M

N

R

U

W

Y

Z

PROTECTING ALL ANIMALS: A FIFTY-YEAR HISTORY OF THE HUMANE SOCIETY OF THE UNITED STATES